COLONIAL SURVEILLANCE

COLONIAL SURVEILLANCE

TECHNOLOGIES OF IDENTIFICATION AND CONTROL IN JAPAN'S EMPIRE

Midori Ogasawara

STANFORD UNIVERSITY PRESS
Stanford, California

Stanford University Press
Stanford, California

Library of Congress Cataloging-in-Publication Data

Names: Ogasawara, Midori, author.
Title: Colonial surveillance : technologies of identification and control in Japan's empire / Midori Ogasawara.
Description: Stanford, California : Stanford University Press, 2026. | Includes bibliographical references and index.
Identifiers: LCCN 2025027446 | ISBN 9781503644243 (cloth) | ISBN 9781503644717 (paperback) | ISBN 9781503644724 (ebook)
Subjects: LCSH: Mass surveillance—Japan—History—20th century. | Biometric identification—Japan—History—20th century. | Internal security—Japan—History—20th century. | Social control—Japan—History—20th century. | Manchuria (China)—History—1931-1945. | Japan—Colonies—History—20th century.
Classification: LCC DS888.25
LC record available at https://lccn.loc.gov/2025027446

Cover design: Lindy Kasler
Cover art: Labour Card issued by the Manchurian Labour Association in 1940, including extensive information on the bearer, such as address, ethnicity, occupation, employer, skills, bodily features, literacy, and religion. Fingerprint from a National Passbook issued by the Manchurian Empire Government. Courtesy of author.
Typeset by Newgen in 10/14.5 and Cardea OTCE

The authorized representative in the EU for product safety and compliance is: Mare Nostrum Group B.V. | Mauritskade 21D | 1091 GC Amsterdam | The Netherlands | Email address: gpsr@mare-nostrum.co.uk | KVK chamber of commerce number: 96249943

To tens of millions of bare lives whose voices were never listened to under the Japanese occupation in Northeast China

CONTENTS

PREFACE   ID Troubles   ix
           WHO DEFINES WHO YOU ARE

ACKNOWLEDGMENTS   xvii

INTRODUCTION   Colonial Surveillance and Violence   1

CHAPTER ONE   A Genealogy of Identification   22
                CLASSIFYING PEOPLE IN EMPIRES

CHAPTER TWO   Constructing "Japanese" and Internal Others   53
                THE KOSEKI SYSTEM AS SURVEILLANCE

CHAPTER THREE   Japan's Maximum Surveillant Assemblage   79
                SEPARATING "BANDITS" FROM "INNOCENTS"
                IN THE COLONIAL THRESHOLD OF "MANCHUKUO"

CHAPTER FOUR   Bodies as Risky Resources   118
                FINGERPRINTING FOR LABOR CONTROL

CHAPTER FIVE   Fatal Classification for Imperial Science   161
                UNIT 731 AND JAPAN'S SECRET BIOLOGICAL
                EXPERIMENTS

CONCLUSION   Troubles Continued   199
                IDENTIFICATION AND IDENTITY IN
                THE POST-COLONIAL ERA

CONTENTS

APPENDIX   Field Notes   217

NOTES   231

BIBLIOGRAPHY   263

INDEX   279

ID TROUBLES

Who Defines Who You Are

It was 2003 when I first experienced a biometric identification system. I was an investigative journalist working for Japan's national newspaper and, for my reporting, had tried out a pilot system for iris-scanning that had been jointly adopted by Japan Airlines and Japan's Ministry of Land, Infrastructure, and Transport. The "e-check in" system being tested at the Tokyo-Narita Airport had been created to potentially fast-track first- and business-class passengers who want to skip the onerous security screening processes at post-9/11 airports. The process began with a photo shoot of my face and iris, and the data were immediately stored in the airline's database. Then, I moved to security screening and looked up at a camera, which ran my iris data against the database.

The system failed me. To try again to get approval from the machine, I pulled my hair back tightly and opened my eyes as wide as possible in front of the camera. But the machine still did not recognize me, which made me nervous. I asked myself, "What's wrong with you?" It was an upside-down moment for my self-identity: The iris scanner had the authority to identify me, though I knew better than anyone else that I was truly me. The machine was more trusted to prove my identity than I was. More precisely, a tiny piece of my bodily information was being used to define who I was. Strangely, I felt that the failure of the biometrics to properly identify me was my fault: I didn't fit into the mathematical format, and, after all, the latest science should be accurate and objective. Perhaps, it was this first blow in my personal history of ID troubles that prompted me to question the relationship between identity and identification.

Border control systems changed drastically after September 11, 2001, and all foreign travelers were required to provide biometric identification like fingerprints and photographs at U.S. airports. Though I have always had a valid Japanese passport, the biometric data collections made me anxious. The new surveillance systems embodied suspicion toward all foreigners as potential terrorists. I have nothing to hide, but how can I know what to hide when I am uncertain what the authorities are looking for? When I first provided my fingerprints at the San Francisco International Airport in 2005, I asked the border control officer, "How do you use my data? How long are you going to keep it?" He replied, "I don't know." An officer who didn't know how his organization would use travelers' data had the power to deny or allow me entry at the border. What does my biometric data tell him about who I am? My question went deeper with this second blow in my personal history of ID troubles.

For several years, most of my American and Canadian friends were unaware of the drastic post-2001 changes in identification systems at U.S. borders. U.S. citizens are still not required to provide their fingerprints when leaving or reentering the country. Canadians were also exempt from the new post-9/11 requirements under a special agreement with the United States. Threat is predominantly seen as coming from outside rather than being created inside the country. In addition, the U.S. Enhanced Border Security and Visa Reform Act of 2002 required international travelers from countries under the U.S. Visa Waiver Program to be equipped with electronic passports. So those countries scrapped the old passport systems and built new ones to store personal data on microchips. Electronic passports were put into use at other international borders, and biometric identification rapidly proliferated under the so-called War on Terror led by the United States, the United Kingdom, Australia, Canada, and other countries. Use of biometrics for passport systems had been discussed in the International Civil Aviation

Organization before but never had been justified, mainly because of privacy concerns. The 9/11 tragedy gave governments and technology industries leverage to convince citizens to accept previously unacceptable measures for security purposes. Today, airport biometric screenings have been normalized at many borders and have expanded from foreign visitors to include citizens. The construction of biometric borders at this scale was unimaginable without the emergency and subsequent war that was used to justify suspending constitutional freedom and protection for citizens in the name of preventing terror.

Have biometric identification and electronic surveillance, then, made the world a safer place? More than a quarter century later, is there no more terror or fewer violent activities?

In 2013, Edward Snowden unveiled the secret facilities of the post-9/11 world that had been built with the electronic nuts and bolts of the War on Terror. A former contractor for the U.S. National Security Agency (NSA), Snowden disclosed extensive classified documents to show how the U.S. government had covertly sucked up personal data from digital networks. The NSA, historically rooted in World War II and officially founded at the advent of the so-called Cold War,[1] embedded mass surveillance systems within telecommunications infrastructures, through which it accessed and stored all kinds of communication data—emails, chat messages, cellphone conversations, social media posts, internet-browsing activities, and so on. The NSA's top-secret documents shocked the public and showed how these surveillance activities, secretly authorized by the Bush administration in the aftermath of 9/11 and expanded under the Obama administration, were thoroughly spying on U.S. citizens and other citizens alike.

This was surely one of the biggest ID troubles in my life, but it was no longer my personal issue. It was everybody's issue, as NSA surveillance was and is indiscriminate and worldwide.

I held a personal interview with Mr. Snowden via a video channel in 2016. He told me that the program called Special Source Operations played a central role in covert data acquisition in the early twenty-first century. Special Source Operations typically set up surveillance operations at the landing sites of international transoceanic cables, called "choke points" in NSA jargon.[2] The telecommunications companies, such as AT&T and Verizon, "willingly" helped the NSA establish secret rooms within their telecoms buildings and operationalize surveillance devices that copied all communications data going through the telecom's facilities.³ Snowden said, "The government calls this bulk collection, and everyone else calls it mass surveillance."⁴

Perhaps one of the most significant facts that Snowden unveiled, and that changed our long-term perspective on communication and surveillance, was the intimate collaboration between the intelligence agencies and Silicon Valley. Thanks to the global expansion of internet businesses, the NSA took advantage of partnering with Google, Microsoft, Facebook, Yahoo!, Apple, and other U.S. service providers under the program PRISM, to access their customer data.⁵ The NSA cannot practice that scale of mass surveillance without the assistance of powerful corporations. Because the communications vessels and repositories belonged to private companies, few imagined that the government could grab so much data so easily. It is worth remembering that until the 2013 Snowden revelations, people who said that tech companies were involved in state surveillance were usually called paranoid or conspiracy theorists.

Tech companies possess an enormous capacity to collect and use customers' data for their own profit, and they developed a leading business model: surveillance capitalism.⁶ Google spearheaded a business model of data analytics that identifies specific groups of potential buyers and effectively advertises products to those groups. Often without an internet user's consent, personal data are marketed toward people's constant consumption and other behavior modifications. Social media offers a major site for collecting, retaining, and using personal data because users are willing to disclose their lives there. And beyond online activities, cameras and microphones in mobile phones have extended aggressive tactics to see and hear users' offline activities, including conversations and emotions. Every aspect of life has become visible to tech companies and monetized for surveillance capitalism.

Personalization of information services can be useful for internet users, but is this a fair game? Users can't feel trouble lurking under the surface until they confront the final moment of unwanted classification, exclusion, elimination, rejection, disapproval, or other maltreatment. The watcher is more privileged than the watched in the dynamics of surveillance. That is why Mr. Snowden sent a crucial warning to democracy: The emergence of digital surveillance will amplify the power imbalance between the government and the people. While people's lives are made transparent to the government, people cannot see what the government sees. "The extraordinary powers of surveillance," Snowden told me, "will inevitably, in time, be used to limit dissent. And when we start limiting dissent, what we're truly doing is limiting progress. We're foreclosing on our own future."

Ten years after his courageous whistle-blowing, Snowden looked back at the NSA systems as "child's play" compared to the predatory technologies of surveillance that have proliferated in the 2020s, such as Pegasus spyware and facial recognition systems targeting journalists, activists, dissidents, and other members of civil societies as security threats.[7]

Everybody's rights to privacy and civil liberties are at stake under digital dragnets of mass surveillance. Yet the dragnets have caused more serious problems for *some* people who fall into specific social categories. Though the policies of mass surveillance were written in a universal tone, and ostensibly for the public good, Muslims and people with Arabic names tend to be disproportionately stopped at borders, sent to secondary inspections, and even put on "no-fly lists."[8]

In Canada, where I live, the Canadian citizen Maher Arar was suspected of being connected to Al-Qaeda—a claim that later proved baseless. In 2002, he was detained at JFK International Airport in New York on his way to Montreal from a family visit in Tunisia.[9] Without any official charges, Arar was sent to a prison in Syria via Jordan, where he was interrogated and tortured. His wife, Monia Mazigh, and their supporters' tireless campaign eventually succeeded in bringing him home a year later, but behind the scenes, there was international surveillance collaboration between Canada and the United States. The Royal Canadian Mounted Police had long placed Arar under surveillance and provided his data to the Federal Bureau of Investigation to facilitate his capture, so this was not a case of misidentification.[10] The case was shaped by the Royal Canadian Mounted Police's categorical suspicion of Muslim men. Post-9/11 security brought not safety to the innocent citizen, but life-threatening abduction.

What happened to Mr. Arar exemplifies the unequal impact of identification and surveillance. Muslim communities in Canada and other

Western countries are still disproportionately targeted by law enforcement and spy agencies. The arrest and extradition of Hassan Diab, a
Canadian sociology professor, is another case in point.[11] His Kafkaesque
story embodies the ongoing Islamophobia produced and reproduced by
the Western War on Terror.

When mass surveillance systems do not serve all members of societies equally, what are they used for? Scientific methods of identification
cannot save the vulnerable from the prejudiced eye. Furthermore, science and technology are not free from the cultures and value systems
that produce them. They are constructed within political climates and
arbitrary allocations of the resources of the time—namely, military
budgets. Crises always crank up surveillance technology to the next
level; the COVID-19 pandemic was no exception.[12] The War on Terror
was not the first or last case. Constant updates of identification systems
may be reinforcing internal boundaries of race/ethnicity, gender, class,
and other social categories.

The first two decades of the twenty-first century gave me enough
time to observe whether mass surveillance systems and biometric technologies have succeeded in securing the world. They have not. Then
why have enormous quantities of time, money, and energy been still
invested to identify each person through their biological elements, and
why are biometrics trusted as truth over other accounts of a person?
New technologies themselves did not give me the answer. I began to
explore where the impetus for identification came from historically and
how the means of identification ultimately focused on the bodies of individuals. I took a sociological journey back through a longer timeline,
parallel to my own ID troubles in the first quarter of the twenty-first
century. I found the imperial competitions over colonies in the late
nineteenth century to be the genesis of modern biometrics and decided
to delve into Japanese identification systems invented to build the nation-state and empire around the same period. This book is an invitation to you to connect your experiences of ID troubles with a bigger
picture of identification, surveillance technology, and colonial story.

What is often missing in today's surveillance and technology debates
is sociohistorical scope. Researchers pay a lot of attention to technological novelties and try to anticipate what new technology will unfold. But
power relations and cultural context are often overlooked in the single

lens of technological determinism. To speculate about outcomes, the media go to engineers and administrators who created and promoted the technology and rarely ask questions of historians or sociologists. As technology is the symbol of modern civilization and human progress, all kinds of positive prospects are advertised by corporations and governments. Yet no one can see the future, so the discussion tends to lack evidence or fall into wishful thinking. Uncertainty looms large. If we want more informed conversations, we need to look back to past human experiences of surveillance and technological advancement. As no technology is created in a political vacuum, past cases offer concrete social contexts and consequences of technology: who was affected, how, and by which new technology.

Walter Benjamin suggests that every human being has the potential to find the real meaning of the past, which otherwise flits by and is never recognized in the present.[13] The past, especially the marginalized past, is fragmented and forgotten unless someone pays attention. Although it is challenging to capture the true picture of the past, Benjamin famously stated: "The past carries with it a temporal index by which it is referred to redemption. There is a secret agreement between past generations and the present one."[14] Benjamin's philosophy of history serves to rescue confined meanings of the past, and, in turn, those emancipated meanings can form an alternative view of the present, how we understand our lives and contemporary social phenomena.[15]

It is a crucial time to understand identification, surveillance, and technology. Far beyond my personal ID troubles described earlier, systematic ID troubles can be automated by artificial intelligence technologies if they are overlooked. After joining the sociohistorical journey of ID troubles in this book, I hope that you will obtain a clearer view of our technological present and imagine alternative futures.

ACKNOWLEDGMENTS

This book is an expression of my twenty-year journey, which has been supported by many fellow travelers. None of the words in this book was written without their professional advice, generous friendships, and collective will to build a more caring and peaceful tomorrow. None of the dark facts told in this book was unpacked without their bright, transcultural community efforts toward a common humanity.

My journey began in the territory of the Haudenosaunee and Anishinaabek, or Kingston, Ontario, Canada, in 2005, where David Lyon welcomed me (and my yet-unknown but expected new family member in my belly) to the master's program in the Department of Sociology at Queen's University. Since then, I have been honored to spend time with David and Sue Lyon as my lifelong mentors and best friends. David's respectful pedagogy has given me wings to fly the intellectual world, and Sue has brought wisdom to my life outside sociology. The Surveillance Project, codirected by David, Elia Zureik, and Yolande Chan, became my academic home at Queen's, where I immediately found warm friendships with research associate Emily Smith and administrator Joan Sharpe. They helped my transition to grad school, sociology, and Canada all at once. The Surveillance Project was an intimate and free space where I could grow my ideas in conversation with other grad students—Jason Pridmore, Martin French, Daniel Trottier, and Çağatay Topal—or visiting scholars Elin Palm and Rosamunde Van Brakel.

In Queen's Sociology, Laureen Snider as the graduate adviser and Michelle Ellis as the graduate secretary understood the challenges I faced as a pregnant international student and gave me compassionate care. I will never forget my wonderful cohorts, including Patti Mayer and Wei Liu, who threw a baby shower for me and took turns bringing meals to my place after the baby was born. Because of their help, I was able to meet the creative artist Sharon Muilwyk, who babysat over the next few years. Other young Japanese parents (yes, we were!) in Kingston backed up my first-time parenting. All these spontaneous support networks allowed me time to focus and complete my MA thesis in 2008, the very first step to this book. This research was supported by the Government of Canada Award.

The previous year, I had the extreme luck to get to know Kit Miller, my English coach in the John S. Knight Professional Journalism Fellowships at Stanford University. Kit has provided comprehensive editing of my English-language articles, and the culmination of her incredible generosity is this book. Her sharp sense of justice fully grasps what I mean in the text and elevates my communication to better expression. Now as a creative quilt activist, Kit represents the best of the American people to me.

When I came back to Queen's Sociology for this project in 2013, to further explore identification technologies and their colonial roots, the Surveillance Project had grown into the Surveillance Studies Centre. The center included me in a more intellectually diverse circle of graduate students—Sachil Singh, Özgün Topak, Özge Girgin, Rui Hou, Delano Aragao Vaz, Debra Mackinnon, Alana Saulnier, and Ciara Bracken-Roche—postdoctoral fellows Scott Thompson and sava saheli singh, and visiting scholars Marta M. Kanashiro, Rafael Evangelista, and Asako Takano. Every interaction with them pushed me to think critically about the global map of techno-politics. My dear friends Derya Güngör, Gaye Onurer, Atm Shaifullah Mehedi, Elham Yousefinejad, and Robyn Saaltink in the Department of Sociology completed my ideal multicultural community in Kingston; together we went through every academic milestone and life challenge, from exams and teaching assistantships to day-to-day survival as single parents. I am deeply grateful to my kind Japanese-mom community in Kingston, too, including Saori, Tomoko, Keiko, Nanae, Naomi, and Kayo, for unconditionally supporting me in family emergencies and sharing their colorful motherhood.

My fieldwork in China in 2016 was almost mission impossible. So, special thanks go to history professor Emily Hill, the Chinese liaison officer Zhiyao Zhang, and associate vice-principal (international) Kathy O'Brien at Queen's University (this story is unfolded in the appendix). Their commitment made my ethnography possible, and this research would not stand without those narratives. Upon our arrival at Jilin University in China, Professor Li Shuyuan helped my family and me to settle in on campus and to access the Jilin University Library archives. I am particularly grateful to Pan Sijie at the Jilin City Workers Memorial Museum for putting me in contact with Mr. Lü Guiwen, who testified about fingerprinting identification at the Fengman Dam in 1941-42. To fully understand his and other colonial survivors' stories, I hired two gifted graduate students at Jilin University, Liu Jiahui and Yu Chi, as interpreters. I am thankful to them for devoting their time to transcribing all in-depth interviews during my limited stay in Donbei.

In Heilongjiang Province, Director Jin Chengmin at the Unit 731 War Crime Evidence Exhibition Hall and Professor Yang Yanjun at the International Center for Unit 731 Research at Harbin Academy of Social Science offered me access to relevant historical materials and assisted me in arranging interviews with family members of Unit 731 victims. In a tour to eastern Heilongjiang, the journalist Liu Jingyan helped me build trust with the family members of Unit 731, and Tan Tian's snappy translation sparked the lively conversations.

Before I embarked on this field trip, Japan's civil society educated me on the independent investigations on Japan's occupation of China. At the Unit 731 Biological War Research Center, the lawyer Keiichiro Ichinose, the civil historian Shigeo Nasu, and Yukiko Yamabe, who participated in the 1949 Chinese Revolution, suggested Chinese experts I should reach out to. Professor Masataka Mori at Shizuoka University gave me the most helpful advice for intercultural communication: to clearly and passionately vocalize what I'm looking for, even if it sounds like "too much" in Japanese culture. That approach proved accepted when we shared a common purpose of historical justice across national borders.

Back in Canada, my project was funded by the Vanier Canada Graduate Scholarship, Mitacs Globalink Research Award, and Senior Scholar

Exchange Scholarship by the Canada Learning Initiative in China, but I experienced economic crises toward the end of this project. The Ban Righ Centre, a refuge for mature female students on Queen's campus, consistently helped precarious me with emergency relief, tuition bursary, and professional development funds. The Ban Righ staff's emotional support was exceptional during that tough time. My big circle of professional advisers—John Torpey, Emily Hill, David Murakami Wood, Rob Beamish, Annette Burfoot, and David Lyon—had heated discussions on my research outcomes in 2018. I took all your points and brought in new narratives, details, and visuals to this book, overhauled the text, and strengthened my arguments. This work may still be controversial, but your time and my time were not wasted.

An early summary of this research was published as "Bodies as Risky Resources: Japan's Colonial Identification Systems in Northeast China" in Robert Heynen and Emily van der Meulen's edited volume *Making Surveillance States: Transnational Histories* (University of Toronto Press, 2019). But my steps in this book project were suspended by my Banting Postdoctoral Fellowships research with another gracious mentor Valerie Steeves at the University of Ottawa, the COVID-19 pandemic, and my move west to take a professorship at the University of Victoria, which sits on the Ləkʷəŋən (Songhees and Xʷsepsəm/Esquimalt) Peoples' territory. After two very busy years teaching, the Centre for Asia-Pacific Initiatives at UVic offered me Visiting Researcher Fellowships, which finally allowed me to refocus on the book project in the fall of 2023. I am sincerely grateful to the center's director Victor V. Ramraj, associate director Helen Lansdowne, and acting director Pooja Parmar for supporting an anxious new member in this way, and to my colleague Sujin Lee for sharing her own book-making experience in each stage, including how to create time for research under the pretenure pressure! I also thank my amazing colleagues and passionate students in the Department of Sociology for consistently aiding my transition, acting out thoughtful solidarity, and sharing joys and sorrows in work and life. My smart research assistant Sahr Malalla helped me put together the proposal and format the references.

It was my fantasy that my book come out of the same house that published Agamben's *Homo Sacer*. My editor, Dylan Kyung-lim White of Stanford University Press, has patiently and effectively guided my way from proposal to submission. His steadfast suggestions were invaluable, as well as the editorial assistant Justine Sargent's timely support. Many thanks to two anonymous reviewers for their careful reading, constructive criticism, and firm validation of my work. Bridgette Werner of Through Line Editing contributed to my final revision process by adding clarity to the discussions and smoothing out the text. Erin Ivy of Newgen walked through the copyediting process with me by offering flexibility and accountability.

I am forever indebted to my life partner, Ken Mizokoshi, and our child, Yuma Libera Mizokoshi Ogasawara, for this project. We managed to travel China together and tackle the same objectives together. Ken's linguistic ability in communicating in Chinese enabled me to imagine this project as our dream, and his professional skills in photography brought extra life to this book. Then-ten-year-old Yuma's presence turned out to be an icebreaker when visiting Chinese households, where he learned lavish hospitalities. Thanks to my fellow travelers, I was able to overcome many obstacles, and I look back on our adventures with a smile. I am also thankful to my parents, Mieko and Hirokazu, for giving me life, freedom, and guts.

In the end, I am most grateful to the participants in my fieldwork, the survivors of Japanese settler colonialism and war crimes, and their families, for sharing their ever-disheartening family stories with me. "I want you to work harder"—Mr. Wang Xuancai's words have stuck in my mind, as do Ms. Sang Guifang's tears and Ms. Li Fengqin's agony. Mr. Yuan Wenqing's difficult life after losing his father and Mr. Li Gang's generous attitude toward Japanese people equally oblige me to share their words with the public. The warmth of Mr. Lü Guiwen's touch never leaves my hand. Listening to the previously unheard voices of their intergenerational bare lives, I feel an immense responsibility to continue this quest.

COLONIAL SURVEILLANCE

INTRODUCTION

COLONIAL SURVEILLANCE
AND VIOLENCE

[When I arrived in the mine,] the first fingerprints I gave were both index fingers. To receive salaries, the left index finger. The color [of the ink] was black. Not only coalminers, but also all farmers were required to have fingerprinting on their ID card. Laborers for laborer's card, teachers for teacher's card, and merchants for merchant's card. Everyone older than sixteen years old needed fingerprinting. The mining company gathered and held our individual labor cards to prevent us from escaping the mine. We could not go anywhere without the ID card.
 —*(Zhang Jiren, former miner in Fushun Mine)*[1]

Jixi City (鶏西市) is located approximately four hundred kilometers to the east of Harbin, the capital city of Heilongjiang Province, China. Harbin is known for its Western-style architecture, such as the Russian Orthodox churches and synagogues built by czarist Russia along the route of Trans-Siberian Railroad. While tourists flood this northern city to see the historical buildings and monuments, few extend their trip to Jixi, another site that offers rich sources of China's modern history. I was one of those tourists who had no idea of Japan's involvement in the city before my fieldwork trip to northeast China in the fall of 2016. Chinese historians there helped me organize a brief excursion to

MAP 1.1. The location of "Manchukuo" and Japan's other colonies in northeastern Asia in the late 1930s. Provinces and cities were marked in the present names.

eastern Heilongjiang, and my little research team—consisting of a local journalist, interpreter, driver, myself, and my family—arrived in Jixi City, home to 900,000 people then.[2]

Early the morning after we arrived, I left the hotel and saw our driver walking ahead of me on the street and entering a small shop. A cloud of white steam floated out of the shop into the crisp outside air, along with the hum of voices. These were good indications of a locally endorsed breakfast place offering delicious steamed buns. So I followed him, walked into the shop, and ordered a couple of pickled veggies and pork buns with a bowl of millet congee over the counter, in the same manner as other customers in the crowded shop. By the time I found a seat at a table, the driver had noticed me, and as soon as I sat, he shouted to the crowds: "No worries! She is a *good* Japanese. She is a university researcher, came to investigate how badly Japanese hurt us here, and let others know about it."

Of course, I had general knowledge of Japan's invasion, colonization, and war crimes in China when I embarked on this research, and that was why I had chosen Northeast China as the site of my field research on identification and surveillance technologies. Northeast China is the area, among other parts of China, where Japan most deeply colonized and even declared the establishment of a new nation, "Manchukuo" (1932–1945), placing it under the total control of Japan's troops Kwantung Army. But I had no idea that Japanese industries had operated many coal mines in Jixi, or that tens of thousands of miners had been forced to work, punished, injured, or killed under Japanese occupation. Around the mines were mass graves of unknown workers, called *wanrenkeng* (万人坑) or "pits of ten thousand corpses," where the dead or dying workers were thrown and buried. This meant that many city residents had a relative or knew someone among their family, friends, or acquaintances who had been abused by Japanese companies—that any of the people enjoying a quick breakfast in the cozy shop may have lost a loved one at the hands of colonizers, and that my presence may have broken their morning peace. It was a very different way of experiencing colonial history from learning it in books. I suddenly found myself in the midst of unforgotten horrors and pain that people in Jixi had been experiencing since the Japanese colonization of the 1930s.[3] I had not even thought of the memories alive in the air when I stepped into the warm shop, filled with local working-class men. But their wounds were still fresh and personal to the extent that our kind driver needed to declare that this Japanese woman would not cause any harm to them, at least not intentionally. It threw me into the rough waters of their lived experiences and collective memories at the local, familial, and individual level of Japan's wrongdoings. And I sincerely thanked the driver for talking to the other customers and preemptively protecting me from possible and reasonable rage against Japanese descendants.

That was also the day that I saw for the first time real artifacts of the ID cards Japan issued to the local population during the occupation. Finding colonial ID cards that had been created under Japan's Manchukuo puppet regime in Northeast China and examining them was the whole purpose of my trip. I had come all the way from eastern Canada, where I lived, following a long battle with the Kafkaesque bureaucracy to obtain a research visa to allow me to stay in China for three months. I had been unable to find Japan-issued ID cards at museums or archives in big cities, such as Harbin or Changchun, and had no luck in Japan either, but finally I found them in a small glass case in the Jixi City Museum.

FIGURE 0.1. Various kinds of identification cards issued by the Japanese colonial agencies in Northeast China in the period 1920s–1945. Public exhibition in Jixi City Museum, Heilongjiang Province, 2016. Photo by Ken Mizokoshi.

Exhibited there were twelve ID cards issued by the Japanese labor management organizations, the Manchukuo government, and its police branches. Interestingly, there was also an ID card issued by the Republic of China after the downfall of Manchukuo in 1945 and before the establishment of the People's Republic of China in 1949. Many of them attached a photograph of the bearer and a fingerprint—the latest identification technologies of the time. The text on the cards noted that it was mandatory to carry the ID cards. Workers were required to register and bear fingerprinted ID cards to enter Manchukuo from other parts of China; recruiters for migrant workers carried a certificate allowing them to enter and leave Manchukuo borders; workers needed to carry an Occupational Skill Card that listed their job skills and histories of public services for Manchukuo; residents were required to carry a Resident Card to prove their status to live in their towns and villages; and finally, the National Passbook became mandatory for all Manchukuo "nationals" to carry as the ultimate means of identification. It was more than twenty pages long and listed the bearer's residential address,

FIGURE 0.2. A National Passbook, issued by the government of Manchukuo. The bearer's name, date of birth, occupation (coal miner), race (Han) are stated, along with his photo and the right index fingerprint. The passbook has more than twenty pages to record personal information. Public exhibition in Jixi City Museum, Heilongjiang Province, 2016. Photo by Ken Mizokoshi.

family members, ethnicity, religion, job, education, vaccine record, and so on. As Manchukuo was a unilateral mirage of Japan's imperial desire, so had the National Passbook been to me—until that moment.

Why did Japan collect personal data from workers and residents on such a detailed level and in wide ranges? How effective was the use of fingerprint technology, the forerunner of biometrics? Why did Japan develop such intricate nets of identification and surveillance systems in Manchukuo? These were the initial questions I pursued in my research, but after the breakfast incident that morning, I needed to tackle another one: How did the identification and surveillance systems involve Japan's industrial occupation and military operations? In other words, how can I make sense of the relationship between the colonizers' ostensibly nonviolent, administrative work of identification and local people's overwhelmingly violent experiences of Japanese occupation in Northeast China?

HISTORICAL SCOPE OF CONTEMPORARY INQUIRIES

In the twenty-first century, we are increasingly using, and perhaps used by, technologies of identification and surveillance on a daily basis. In the early twenty-first century, as more people have enjoyed wider access to information and faster communication enabled by digital technologies, most public views on technology have been optimistic, if not euphemistic. The internet convinced many users that interactive communication would set the world free and promote democracy, mutual understanding, and peace. However, in the 2010s, Edward Snowden pivoted popular discourse by disclosing that the U.S. National Security Agency had utilized the digital communication infrastructure as a site of mass surveillance. The Facebook-Cambridge Analytica scandal in 2018 particularly shocked Western media, as they realized that behavior modification induced by data analytics had occurred not only in marketing and consumption but also in elections and political choice. The tone of public debate became ominous or nihilistic in the 2020s, and accordingly, more people are concerned about the danger of convenient technologies in the age of artificial intelligence.

Surveillance studies, an interdisciplinary area of study in which I have been researching, emerged from this turbulent current of public discourse. Yet the growing discussion around digital technology and big data has mainly chased the novelty of technology. Digital technologies are new, and digital innovation keeps happening. We are amazed and scared by the next level of automation, speed, interoperability, or invisibility of technology. As Shoshana Zuboff repeats in her influential book *The Age of Surveillance Capitalism*, the technological capacities of mass surveillance are indeed "unprecedented."[4]

Yet identification and surveillance have been practiced for thousands of years of human history.[5] The Bible describes how Jesus's expectant parents went to Bethlehem for national registration under the Roman empire. China's Tang dynasty implemented household registration systems in the seventh century. For taxation, conscription, and other governmental operations, as well as for religious entities, people registered their names, addresses, and family members with authorities, which constituted identification systems. The transatlantic slave trade, for instance, would have been impossible without the surveillance of enslaved people. Simone Browne dissects the different stages of slavery, from chaining Black men and women to slave ships to searching for runaway slaves, to show how much surveillance was involved in slavery and, in turn, how slavery shaped modern surveillance techniques and technologies.[6]

To historically ground the conversation about our technological future, we must open our eyes to the past, especially the marginalized past.[7] We ought to know who confronted the negative outcomes of new technology and how the memories of negative outcomes have been forgotten or hidden from public discourse on new technology. The unknown past offers a rich repository of knowledge about our technological future because we live in a future of the past. We can evaluate from the present what new technologies promised in the past. For example, did technology mitigate poverty as was advertised? Did it help set people free as we believed it would? Did it make the world safer as expected? History may not exactly repeat, but there are tendencies and patterns from which we can learn how not to repeat the same mistakes and how to understand the future implications of contemporary processes.

My journey into the marginalized past begins in late nineteenth century Japan and is guided by sociological methodology and situated in a transnational perspective. I explore the emergence of national identification systems in modern Japan and the transformation of identification techniques in its colonies and occupied areas, along with Japan's imperial expansion in East Asia. The term *national identification systems* refers to those systems by which the state registers and identifies a population and assigns individuals a centralized ID number. Normally, national ID systems collect individuals' personal data, link different kinds of personal data to ID numbers, and use the data for multiple purposes. Population registration can be traced in historical records back to ancient times. However, the extensive documentation of people's personal details emerged through the rationalization of bureaucracies in the modern Western state,[8] and it evolved from covering only a part of the population to covering the entire population.[9] Conscription, crime control, and colonial management have been the major spheres of this early development of modern ID systems.[10] Earlier surveillance studies on this subject include the rise of the information state in England,[11] the history of passports in Europe,[12] the invention of fingerprinting in colonized India,[13] the American origins of ID systems during slavery,[14] the colonial development of IDs for policing in the Philippines,[15] and the "biometric state" of South Africa.[16] The ID system has been a common phenomenon throughout civilization, and it continues to be a hallmark of modernity, from early modern to post- or late-modern times.

As mentioned already, early identification techniques entered a new phase due to the emergence of information and communication technologies (ICTs) in the late twentieth century, the capacities of which enormously increased the amount of data collected across time and space. In fact, national ID systems were proposed in the early stages of the War on Terror,[17] as seen in the United States, United Kingdom, or Canada, which had previously opposed developing such systems in a liberal or libertarian tradition. With the parallel proliferation of electronic devices and networked databases, the national ID number came to play a more powerful role in connecting a wide range of data beyond government use, and became incorporated into private marketing strategies. Once-discrete flows of data now converge in the surveillant assemblage,[18] and they grow like a rhizome in our everyday lives, with the distinction between public and private blurred. People's personal data are used by governments and corporations to classify individuals into "desirable" and "undesirable" categories. This has resulted in *social sorting*, affecting individuals' opportunities and life choices, as David Lyon suggests.[19] While surveillance increases the efficiency of existing political and economic systems, it also reproduces existing inequalities, generates new ones, and produces "rational discrimination" when social sorting is embedded in data flows, thus creating a form of "cumulative disadvantage" among marginalized groups.[20]

The post-9/11 securitization of identity and identification also broke down previously respected privacy protections and proliferated biometric technologies, whether in government or the private sector. *Biometrics* can be defined as "measurable physiological or behavioral characteristics that can be used to identify an individual," according to Canada's privacy commissioner. For example, "fingerprints, iris patterns, facial features, DNA, voice signatures, and even physical movements" are all biometric markers.[21] Many ID systems have employed biometrics as the ultimate identifier of the individual, because biometrics cannot be forgotten like passwords, and they are supposedly difficult to counterfeit, unlike a passport, for example. In this mathematical understanding of a human being, the body is seen as the final evidence of self and the original source of data in today's global techno-political complex.[22] In fact, close attention to the body goes far beyond the physical domain, reaching into the mental state of a person. Surveillance capitalism activates cameras and microphones in smartphones, then collects and uses the data for calculations to predict and modify individuals' future actions for shopping or voting. Identification and identity increasingly become a starting point for these data analytics, which call on both historical and present-day inquiries.

JAPAN'S MARGINALIZED PAST

Given the above sociopolitical landscape, this book investigates how and why the modern Japanese government created a system to register and identify subjects of the nation while simultaneously expanding as an empire. Why Japan? Because Japan disseminated modern technologies of identification card systems and biometrics in East Asia. This case provides the opportunity to simultaneously study a nation-state *and* empire that constructed extensive identification systems to manage diverse populations. In a transnational context, Japan mimicked Western identification technologies, particularly the British empire's schemes, while also establishing its own characteristics. In transwar and postcolonial perspectives, Japanese imperialism left a model of a mandatory identification card system—including biometrics—in East Asia after its collapse in 1945. The identification technologies Japan brought to the region survived and thrived as part of an administrative foundation and authoritarian surveillance, shaped by the newly independent governments of the former colonies.

After the 1867 Meiji Restoration, Japan first developed a national registration and identification system as the very basis of its modern institutions under a new constitutional monarchy. It is a family-based registration system—rather than individual, like Western-style systems—called the *koseki* (戸籍) system. It is the foundation of all kinds of administrative services including taxation, voting, education, welfare, and so on, to this day. Everyone who is born Japanese is required to register their birth, marriage, divorce, and death in *koseki*, and *koseki* is cross-referenced with all significant changes in family members' lives. The private sector, such as employers, also requests a copy of *koseki* to validate a subject's family members. Despite a democratic change in Japan's legal system after its defeat in World War II, including the abolition of the official patriarchy, the Koseki Act underwent only minor revisions. Its all-encompassing mission continues to be that the state record and update the life courses of individuals through the framework of family.

In its colonies and occupied areas, Japan developed various types of national ID systems to accompany its wars of aggression and expansion of the Great Empire of Japan in East Asia. Colonial ID systems paid particular attention to tracking the movements of individuals. Here, I observe a transition of ID techniques from collective to individualistic, where ID cards and biometrics were used to identify individuals on the basis of their bodily features and to track the movements of individual bodies. The transition occurred in colonies because *koseki* came up short when it came to identifying individuals in motion. Thus, I hypothesize that today's mass surveillance schemes targeting individual bodies are rooted in and were developed within colonial relations. In the Japanese context, ID techniques focusing on individual bodies began in

Manchuria or Northeast China after the 1920s,[23] when Japan obtained a lease for the region through the Russo-Japanese War (1904-5) and later occupied the area with armed forces (1931), declaring it the state of Manchukuo (1932). Japanese companies and troops issued a compulsory ID card to residents and migrant workers and employed fingerprinting as a scientific means of identification and a symbol of modern governance. To this day, Japan has no compulsory national ID card or biometrics for its own citizens. Though fingerprint identification had been introduced to the Japanese prison and criminal justice systems in 1908,[24] biometrics for civil population were widely tested on the colonial soil and applied mainly to the colonial Others.

The various kinds of ID cards I saw in the Jixi City Museum evidenced the unique identification policies that Japan implemented in Manchukuo. No parallel schemes of biometric identification have been practiced in Japan. As the epigraph to this chapter testifies, the local people were coerced into dipping their fingertips in black ink, placing them on ID cards and documents, and presenting the ID card to authorities on a daily basis. Otherwise, they were unable to find a job, move to other cities, receive salaries, or come home. Japanese administrative documents and propaganda magazines of the time show that biometric ID cards were introduced for two primary purposes: to find security threats and to mobilize labor power for production. Colonial ID cards helped Japanese colonizers classify the local population either as potential security threats—such as "bandits" or "communists"—or as labor power available to colonial industries. Rigorous biometrics were implemented to carefully check, restrain, and control the mobility of individuals in the occupied land.

It was often fatal to be identified and categorized as "bandit," "communist," or "spy" in Manchuria, whether the charge was true or false. As Pierre Bourdieu put it, "The fate of the group is bound up with the words that designate them."[25] As a case in point, thousands of Chinese were categorized as security threats and sent to a secret military project called Unit 731 in the Kwantung Army. Unit 731 was a facility for biological and poison gas warfare; prisoners there were used as live subjects to test plague, bacillary dysentery, frostbite, and other diseases, or they were dissected by Japanese medical experts for anatomical experiments.[26] The cruel processes of classification are documented in the

Kwantung Gendarmerie's "Special Transfer" files. Using the policing networks linked with biometric identification systems, Japan collected personal data on those who potentially resisted the occupation and rationalized their slaying using the data in the documents, whether the data were accurate or not.

To be clear, the Manchurian ID systems were not created for the purpose of human slaughter. But colonial techniques of population management covertly merged with the arbitrary selection of "threats" or "others" to advance war technologies and scientific discoveries. It was not accidental killing, but the systematic operation of counterinsurgencies and counterintelligence, deeply involving and facilitated by identification and classification. Through sociological investigation, this book uncovers the path from managerial identification to sovereign violence.

DUAL BLIND SPOTS OF PATRIARCHY AND COLONIALISM

The negative consequences of Japan's national ID systems have received very little attention to this day. Those consequences have fallen into two blind spots in the public eye: The *koseki* system has been taken for granted, and the colonial past has been obscured.

First, the family-based *koseki* system has been normalized as the basis of administrative relations between the state and individuals in Japan, and few academics have critically examined *koseki* and other national ID systems with regard to their relationship to state surveillance. Accordingly, *koseki* has been socially naturalized to the extent that many Japanese people, if not most, believe that all governments in the world have the same, all-encompassing registration system, and they would be puzzled as to how other governments govern their nations without *koseki*.

Against such a social mindset, the civil researcher Bunmei Satō pioneered a critical analysis of *koseki* and scrutinized its exclusionary characteristics in relation to Japanese citizenship and a patriarchal family order.[27] *Koseki* requires classification to name a head of the family, normally the husband, and to define the rest of the family members, wife and children, in relation to the head. It structures the family on the basis of the patriarchal ranking, accepts only members of the same surname in one *koseki*, and excludes children who are born out of wedlock.

As *koseki* is the foundation of all administrative services, the male-centered value of *koseki* is instilled in every public relationship. Hiroshi Tanaka is another early scholar who looked for the historical roots of Japan's modern identification system, particularly the use of fingerprinting for the postwar Alien Registration System.[28] I owe much to their insights on questioning the normalized ID systems as tools of patriarchal and colonial surveillance.

Second, a considerable portion of Japan's colonial wrongdoings has not been openly debated in postwar Japan or, needless to say, during wartime under the conditions of government censorship. Most Japanese soldiers who came back from the battlefields of China and other parts of Asia kept silent publicly about their cruel deeds against the local people during the war, and some even boasted about acts of killing, raping, and torturing to show off how brave and mighty they were as soldiers, but only within their intimate circles. Japanese history textbooks clearly state the surrender of the Great Empire of Japan to the Allied Forces, more precisely, the United States, but they remain ambiguous about Japan's defeat in relation to China and other Asian countries.[29] Japanese war leaders had rarely treated neighboring countries as sovereign states, and they promulgated the view that the Japanese military had attempted to liberate its Asian brothers from European powers and construct the Greater East Asia Co-Prosperity Sphere (Daitōa-Kyōeiken, 大東亜共栄圏). As a result, the former colonies and other Asian regions occupied by Japan tend to fall outside of public recognition of the unconditional surrender. The lack of recognition, and the ambiguity surrounding it, helped the Japanese government maintain a colonial myth that it was the leader of Asia, even after the fall of the empire.

Accordingly, any speaking out on war crimes, especially Nanjing Massacre (1937), the military's Comfort Women sex-slavery system, and Unit 731, continue to evoke emotional controversy in Japan to this day. Historical revisionists, including leading politicians, business executives, and professors, have repeatedly attacked and denied the Korean and Chinese narratives of Japan's war crimes. Japanese war discourse is centered on the victim's side of the experience, such as the atomic bombing of Hiroshima and Nagasaki and the carpet-bombing and strafing of major cities by the United States, and the perpetrator's side of the experience is marginalized in public education. Furthermore, critical reflections on colonialism before the Pacific War have been pushed out of public sight in the postwar construction of Japan's collective memories.

In fact, how to remember Manchukuo is also controversial in terms of whether or not it should be seen as a nation. Manchukuo is an English translation of 満洲国, or 満州国 in Japanese, meaning the "state of Manchuria." However, it is usually written 偽満洲国 or 偽満 in Chinese, meaning the pseudo-state of Manchuria, emphasizing that it was fake, manufactured by the Japanese Army. The Japanese academic texts that take a critical approach toward Manchukuo often use quotation marks around the term, "Manchukuo," to remind readers of this manufactured aspect. In this book, I do not use scare quotes every time this term appears, but I acknowledge the gap that the two languages show on the same artifact and have no intention to naturalize Manchukuo as a nation. Quite to the contrary, even the geographical term *Manchuria* (満洲 or 満州), referring to the northeastern region of China, is not really neutral in my sense. While Japanese often uses this term, connoting the independence from the rest of China, Chinese more often uses the term *Northeast* (東北).

Denialism and revisionism of Japan's colonial crimes have raised diplomatic tensions in East Asia on occasion, but especially over the past decades amid the surge of right-wing online discourse.[30] Korean and Chinese accounts of Japanese colonialism have been labeled "anti-Japanese," to be politically undermined and ignored. By exposing an alternative narrative, my research counters this tendency, with the conviction that the colonial influence and impacts of Japan's national ID systems in East Asia should be disclosed to and acknowledged by the Japanese public and beyond. This is important not only for the reconciliation of the past but also for better political choices in the future. The past and future are crucially guiding each other, now more than ever.

Doubly blinded by the normalization of the patriarchal *koseki* system and the taboo regarding Japan's colonial past, only a few scholarly works have addressed the Manchurian ID systems.[31] It is my contribution to make visible the patriarchal and racializing aspects of Japan's ID systems and to explore the connection between identification and colonial violence. Given the current expansion of digital surveillance, my goal is to contribute to bringing ethical considerations for individual liberty and dignity to ID systems, to seek a role for meaningful democratic participation in regulating surveillance technology, and to construct more respectful and peaceful relationships among global communities.

METHODS TO PROBE SURVEILLANCE AND VIOLENCE

To carefully probe connections between identification systems and sovereign violence, I combine sociological methods for this study: a genealogical approach, institutional ethnography, and field research. Genealogy is a methodology of historical research that seeks to unearth the genesis, formation, and transformation of a system and ideology, Michel Foucault suggested, drawing on Friedrich Nietzsche's *On the Genealogy of Morals*.[32] Taking a genealogical approach, Foucault investigated the fields that had been neglected or forgotten in previous analyses, such as punishment, madness, and sexuality. Thus, genealogy does not construct a linear history but rather redeems fragmented elements of the past and revives the meaning of past events that were previously hidden or masked with other, normalized meanings.

In his own genealogical work, Foucault focused on the practices of system and ideology: how things are given form in the ways they are. This gave rise to numerous studies of techniques and technologies that enable system and ideology to produce and reproduce subjects in particular ways. Such a focus is relevant to my research, too, to discover how the techniques and technologies of Japanese colonial ID systems were practiced and what kinds of ideologies were behind the ID systems in creating various actors of imperial Japan. Because the details of these systems are mostly unknown, it is important to investigate the systematic means and processes of identification in practice, along with probing peoples' experiences with the systems. Through a genealogical approach, I bind one point to another in the past, draw its connection to the present, and illuminate the colonial origin of today's surveillance techniques and technologies.

Dorothy Smith's methodological concept of institutional ethnography gives an important shape to my genealogical investigation on colonial experiences of identification systems, with special reference to the researcher's positionality.[33] Smith proposes institutional ethnography as "a method of inquiry that works from the actualities of people's everyday lives and experience to discover the social as it extends beyond experience."[34] Coming from feminist sociology, she criticizes the positivist approach of mainstream sociology and attempts to create an alternative to the objectified subject of knowledge of established social scientific discourse. For Smith, mainstream sociology tends to conceal positions of power embedded in daily settings. So, mainstream researchers do not problematize, but rather support, institutionalized power, organizing public and private interactions in their most ordinary appearance. Those are the ruling relations Smith aims to unpack through institutional ethnography, an "internally coordinated complex of administrative, managerial, professional, and discursive organization that regulates, organizes, governs, and otherwise controls our societies."[35]

To make ruling relations visible, the researcher starts with the actualities of people's lives and problems at the bottom of society, rather than from an organizational point of view from the top, and indicates the sites of problems in institutional relations. Thus, the main strength of institutional ethnography is to have marginalized voices heard and to hold institutionalized power accountable for social problems. This approach leads my investigation straight to the marginalized experiences of Japanese colonial ID systems, unravels negative consequences of ID systems at the bottom of society, and holds today's ID systems accountable for similar discriminatory effects. Smith's methodologies are intended to achieve social justice.

Fieldwork was necessary to weave narratives and lay out ruling relations from the bottom of colonial society, though it was never easy. The Japanese Army destroyed documents related to colonial management, especially about Unit 731, at the point of surrender to the Allies. The generation of Chinese people who lived through Japanese occupation is disappearing. Nevertheless, in my field research, Chinese scholars and journalists helped me find the colonial ID cards in Jixi City, as well as administrative documents compiled by the Kwantung Army. I was able to interview a ninety-six-year-old survivor who was forced to work at a dam construction site during the occupation and had all ten fingerprints taken by the colonizers. I met five descendants of Unit 731 victims in their homes and listened to their family histories and hardships. As my research visa was for only three months, my allotted time for discovery in China was limited. I tried repeatedly to extend the visa throughout my stay in China, but the bureaucracy defeated me. (See my field notes in the appendix.) But this field research taught me how crucial it is to physically go beyond national borders to learn people's experiences, even in the age of the internet. The world is not so connected as internet companies advertise. Japan and China have sat beside to each other since time immemorial, but they maintain completely different narratives and understandings of the same colonialism.

GROUNDING THE LIVED EXPERIENCES

Colonial survivors' narratives modified the course of my investigation to lay out ruling relations in the occupied Northeast China, after all methodological considerations above. One of my first challenges in the fieldwork was that the colonial survivors I interviewed did not see the importance of Japan's ID systems, because their colonial experiences were overwhelmingly violent. Their fathers and uncles were captured by the Kwantung Gendarmerie, and their families didn't know what happened to them until the late 1980s. The families suffered profoundly for the rest of their lives because of the disappearance of their loved ones, who were often the breadwinners in their households. In many cases, younger family members later died of starvation or lack of medical care. The ID card or fingerprinting was just a tiny piece of insignificant memory. This made me realize what colonialism meant for them: Just as when I faced the ongoing pain in the breakfast shop in Jixi, colonialism obliged me to relate the stories that are significant to the narrator. Otherwise, my work would lack contact with the lived experiences of colonial surveillance. The ID system is important, but it's only part of the big picture of colonial surveillance, and my interviewees' experiences with colonial surveillance were, more than anything else, exposed as sovereign violence.

This gap of knowledge struck me again at the library at Jilin University when I was looking for descriptions of colonial surveillance and violent outcomes in Japanese publications from the 1930s and 1940s. There were none. The available Japanese-written articles did not describe any violent implications of colonial surveillance. If any mentioned ID cards and fingerprints, those were described as benevolent and advanced technologies for "security." The connection between surveillance and violence was completely erased from the beginning of the Japanese-written history of Manchuria.

As such, disturbing facts of colonial surveillance have been unrecorded, unacknowledged, or underestimated on the side of colonizers. I shudder to think that today's surveillance-violence nexus could also be obliterated at the very site of production of surveillance technologies. The obliteration can block or narrow the public view of the negative consequences of surveillance technologies.

Thus, this book grounds the lived experiences of Chinese survivors of Japanese imperialism as the defining feature of my study, but it extends beyond their experiences as institutional ethnography. Despite the generally hidden or ambiguous consequences of surveillance, my research indicates that identification systems played a significant role in colonial rule. Japanese colonizers increasingly relied on ID schemes to maintain the Manchurian occupation over time. For the colonizers who settled in the contested territory, almost the entire population was potentially "bandits," or supporting "bandits," on the one hand. On the other hand, the colonizers needed "innocents" for labor power. Thus, I argue that the biometric ID card systems handled dual tasks: sorting the population into "desirable" and "undesirable" and exploiting it as a resource.

The ID cards and biometrics were the special means, among other Manchurian security operations, of exhaustively classifying individuals for the two demands above. They were subtle but powerful as coercive systems. For the colonized, the more they were identified and tracked, the less chance they had to resist the colonizers. The surveillance systems rendered the entire population visible and vulnerable to sovereign violence; as a result, if they were deemed dissenters, they were captured, tortured, or killed systematically. Colonial atrocities cannot be understood merely through analyzing the final moments of massacres. They must be contextualized in the preceding institutional processes that led to that final exertion of force, in which surveillance is a preparatory step to sovereign violence.

THE ROAD MAP

In summary, this book unpacks the relationship between national identification systems and empire building and analyzes how surveillance
techniques assisted in the perpetration of colonial violence. I invite
readers to delve into the little-known genealogy of modern-day identification systems, and the colonial roots of the surveillance technologies
that saturate our digital lives in the twenty-first century. Interestingly,
imperial powers in the late nineteenth to early twentieth centuries
share with today's neoliberalism political economic interests in surveillance technologies applied to human bodies: biometrics.

What is little known and will be investigated in this book are the
detailed consequences of Japan's colonial surveillance, and the connection between the ID systems and sovereign violence in Manchuria. The
unilateral exertion of brutality was the overall experience that the local
population commonly expressed and remembered about the Japanese occupation. To fill the epistemological gap between Japan's administrative
systems of identification and Chinese experiences of colonial violence,
I sociologically trace a historical thread from two different ends. One
is the development of national identification systems in modern Japan
and its colonies, and the other is the institutions of forced labor and war
crimes. I examine war crimes committed by Unit 731 as one of the most
nefarious cases of sovereign violence because the Japanese military rationalized and justified the scientific massacre perpetrated in the facility using the systems of identification, surveillance, and classification.

Here is a road map to our sociohistorical journey.

The next chapter offers a transnational genealogy of identification
systems against the backdrop of the modern development of the information state, bureaucracy, war, and imperial competition. Technologies
of identification emerged across the history of modern civilization. To
analyze the identification technologies, Michel Foucault's concepts of
disciplinary power, biopower, and population control, the key concepts
of surveillance studies, are introduced. But I point out the intrinsic limitation of these Foucauldian theories, as my critique and theoretical contribution to surveillance studies, and bring in Giorgio Agamben's bare
life and Achille Mbembe's necropolitics to my analytical framework

on the exclusionary effects of colonial identification. In this way, I set the stage for my sociological account of Japan's colonial identification system in occupied Northeast China.

Chapter 2 takes up an in-depth analysis of the *koseki* system as surveillance. I provide a brief prehistory of *koseki* and the registration systems prior to the Westernization of Japan. I discuss the significance of *koseki* as a modern invention that classified individuals within a patriarchal family framework and led them to pledge supreme loyalty to the emperor. In Taiwan and Korea, *koseki* branded racial marks onto the local populations and strictly prohibited them from merging with the Japanese. People in the colonies were circumscribed in a state of exception to judicial rules, where their personal data were directly used for policing and assimilation. The colonial *koseki* was not as constructive as the Japanese one with regard to producing a national identity and adapting to a new empire. It classified Koreans, Taiwanese, and other ethnic groups as second-class subjects and legitimated the segregation of internal Others.

Chapter 3 turns to Japan's colonization of Northeast China and maps out Japan's surveillant assemblage in which multiple governmental and private actors participated, from the Kwantung Gendarmerie in the Japanese Army to the Mantetsu research section. Manchukuo was a uniquely paradoxical zone among Japan's colonies, what I call the *colonial threshold*—an ambiguous sphere in which law and sovereign violence become synonymous: Manchukuo supposedly had its sovereignty but was a de facto colony of Japan in an undeclared war. Japan was unable to implement *koseki* or enact nationality law due to this fabricated sovereignty on the one hand, and, on the other hand, it invented more aggressive forms of identification without parliamentary or judicial restraints. Security laws and decrees were rapidly compiled in the name of civilization. The ad hoc murder of Chinese people was legalized as "severe punishment." A colonial survivor shares his family history in this chapter and describes how his family experienced Japan's extensive surveillance networks involving new tactics, to cut off flows of materials and information between armed "bandits" and "innocent" villagers. All these tactics of a security state created situations in which ID cards were used.

Against the backdrop of surveillant assemblage, the biometric identification card is closely analyzed as a powerful means of population control in chapter 4. This chapter details how the fingerprinted ID systems took up the dual tasks of preempting potential rebellion and simultaneously mobilizing the local Chinese people as cheap labor power, depending on changing political agendas over time. The transformation of the political agenda is divided into three phases of the fourteen-year life of Manchukuo. In the first period (1932-36), ID cards were used to restrict the numbers of migrants and restrain their movements. But this policy was modified in the second period (1937-40), because of a labor shortage in the outbreak of the Chinese-Japanese War (1937). The Labor Card System and the Fingerprint Management Bureau were officially founded as part of Manchurian government in this phase. Then, in the final period (1941-45), the discrete systems of fingerprint identification converged in 1944 in the National Passbook System, to mobilize the whole population for total war. This chapter includes the narrative of a Chinese man who experienced fingerprint identification in a labor camp, where each worker's body was treated as a risk and as a resource for imperial greed.

Chapter 5 focuses on Kwantung Army Unit 731, the secret biological war facility and a devastating consequence of Japan's colonial surveillance. The Kwantung Gendarmerie systematically selected and sent Chinese dissidents to Unit 731 for human experiments. The Kwantung Gendarmerie's "Special Transfer" files testify to how Chinese dissidents and soldiers were classified and turned into expendable resources through identification and surveillance. Valuable narratives from family members of Unit 731 victims are vital to this chapter. Their stories must be told to illuminate the asymmetrical effects of surveillance between watchers and the watched.

To end the journey of colonial surveillance, the book's conclusion briefly narrates what happened to the identification technologies established in Northeast China after the fall of the Japanese empire. Despite the radical dismantling of imperial institutions, similar biometric methods followed the former colonial populations of Koreans and Taiwanese who resided in postwar Japan. The compulsory fingerprinting of former colonial subjects was finally abolished in 2000, but it soon made a comeback for all foreign travelers visiting Japan, as a new security measure during the War on Terror. This completes a full circle of institutional ID troubles in the past hundred years, starting from this chapter.

CHAPTER ONE

A GENEALOGY OF IDENTIFICATION

Classifying People in Empires

SMALL MAN The noblest part of a human being is one's passport. And creating a passport is more complicated than creating a human. A human can come into existence anywhere, by accident or without good reasons. But not a passport. That's why it's accepted if it's good, but a man can be as good as he wants but no one will accept him.

BIG MAN So you could say, the human is just a kind of mechanical device for carrying the passport. A man placing his passport in his shirt pocket is like a vault storing a bunch of stocks, which itself doesn't have any value, but carries value within.
—(Bertolt Brecht, Flüchtlingsgespräche/ Conversations in Exile)[1]

Bertolt Brecht (1898–1956), the prominent German playwright known for *The Threepenny Opera* and *Mother Courage and Her Children*, was exiled from Nazi Germany from 1933 to 1948. He wrote the above text during his brief residence in Finland from 1940 to 1941, after his time in Denmark and Sweden, and before he went to the United States via Moscow. The Nazis revoked Brecht's German citizenship, the U.S. government placed him under Federal Bureau of Investigation (FBI) surveillance, and postwar McCarthyism eventually sent him back to Europe.[2] Throughout his exile, the words of the epigraph to this chapter must have summed up his feelings about ID troubles: His identification documents represented him more than any other aspect of his identity. *Conversations in Exile* sharply articulates an upside-down relationship between identity and the identification system.

Today, you don't have to be a refugee or an exile to put yourself in Brecht's shoes when crossing international borders. Border authorities will never accept you, however wonderful you may be, without a genuine passport or errorless ID document. Undocumented people are sent back as illegal or detained as unlawful under this permit system. Brecht's line, "the human is just a kind of mechanical device for carrying the passport," is not just sarcasm. The ID system revokes a determinant of personal identity from the subject. In so doing, it exercises more power to define individual identity than the individual does.

The social process of identification plays a crucial role in shaping identity. Although identity indicates an ontological manifestation about the self to be respected and recognized, the term is derived from *idem*, "the same," or *identidem*, "time and again," in Latin. It denotes "not uniqueness, but the features that the various elements of a group had in common."[3] Thus, self-identity develops over time through adopting, rejecting, or negotiating the social categories a person may represent, such as "women" or "men," "Korean" or "Japanese," "Christian" or "Buddhist," and "working class" or "middle class." One cannot identify oneself without the social categories existing prior to the being, so individuals acquire their personal definition of self by interacting with categories. An individual's self-identity is more likely to rely on, rather than be independent from, how others recursively define them through categories. Or a struggle may arise between what an individual thinks about themself and what others think about them, in the event that they do not match. This two-way, push-pull, possibly contradictory character of identity is shown in the dual meanings of the term "identify": distinguishing one from another and belonging to a similar collective. Personal identity is thus a social identity, whether it agrees with, or is opposed to, the dominant categories.[4]

Brecht did not overlook the dialectic relation of identity and identification. He goes on:

SMALL MAN But anyway, a human is necessary to the passport. Of course, the passport is the main thing to be respected, but it's not perfect

without the human belonging to it. It's in the same way that a surgeon
needs a patient to operate on. . .and the same way in a modern country.
The main thing is the Fuhrer or the Duce: but they need people to lead.
They're great men, but someone has to be a little man, otherwise it
doesn't work.[5]

Brecht indicates not only the subordinate role of the human subject to
the identification system but also the discursive role of the passport
system in making national subjects. The "great men"—implying Hitler,
Mussolini, or political leaders in general—need "little men" as followers who believe and support their authority. Using the example of the
passport system, his script epitomizes how social institutions are internalized in individuals and create the subjects who support those institutions. This leads Brecht's readers to the next question: How does
power make people believe and support its systems? Using the carrot
or the stick? While it is generally believed that ID documents benefit
the bearer by guaranteeing their rights and entitlements, Brecht implies that the absence of ID information would be a nightmare for those
in power. Big Man says, "Imagine if you and I were running around
without papers saying who we are, why, they wouldn't be able to find us
when our turn came to be deported."[6]

It could be true. But it has become increasingly difficult to imagine
the absence of personal information in the twenty-first century. Border
security or law enforcement can unlock one's cellphone or laptop, track
one's movements, and interpret the data as they wish. Far beyond the
passport system, multiple identification systems are constantly up and
running in the digital era, generating mass surveillance systems and
creating people's identities as "little men."

In this chapter, I explore the genealogy of modern identification systems and set the global stage for subsequent chapters' analysis of Japan's
colonial ID systems. I first explain why I consider the use of ID systems
to be a form of population surveillance and how surveillance studies has
helped me grapple with the interactive processes of identification and
identity. I introduce four key concepts of surveillance studies: social
sorting, population control, categorization, and construction of the subject. These are articulated with Michel Foucault's concept of biopower
and its regulatory characteristics.[7] If readers are already familiar with
those concepts, they can skip these theory sections and move on to the

history sections, but these social theories are essential constituents of my sociological vantage point in discussing colonial surveillance and addressing my theoretical contribution.

Then, I draw a historical trajectory of identification techniques and technologies, from the rise of the information state in sixteenth-century Europe to the establishment of the passport system in the twentieth century, and from the development of anthropometry in criminal investigations to the invention of fingerprinting for colonial management in the nineteenth century. By juxtaposing the scientific interest in human bodies that emerged among European nation-states, their colonies, and the transatlantic slave trade, I deliberately unveil the marginalized past of surveillance and pursue hidden connections among discrete technologies from a transnational perspective.

Last, by drawing out the violent consequences of colonial surveillance, I argue that the popular notion of biopower demonstrates an intrinsic limit to address human experiences of colonial surveillance. I discuss what kinds of theoretical interventions are needed to go beyond Foucauldian approaches.

ID SYSTEMS AS SURVEILLANCE

My work focuses on the surveillance aspect of a national identification system, among other characteristics, and discusses surveillance over a population as a central role of regulatory systems in both internal nation building and external colonization. Identification systems do not merely verify who a person claims to be nor certify who they are. There is an extended dynamism beyond verification. Because identification needs to specify who a person is and who a person is *not*, it entails classification.[8] The question "Who is this person?" constantly begs the question "What kind of person is this?"[9] A specification of similarities and differences comes into play to define who an individual is, depending on the social context, and this is usually achieved through categorizing kinds of people. The institutions that build ID systems can freely impose collective categories to classify people and determine who they are through groupings based on ideas of race/ethnicity, age, gender, income, occupation, education, and so on. Being included in or excluded from a category is crucial, because ID systems use these categories to afford different treatment to different kinds of people, such as providing or denying access to basic rights or privileges.[10] Thus, identification necessarily interweaves assessment, categorization, and inclusion or exclusion.[11]

For these reasons, David Lyon states that "identification is the starting point of surveillance."[12] Identification creates the basis for surveillance that has a concrete impact on the individuals subjected to it. In fact, the process of identification itself is surveillance: specifically the filing and checking of personal details reflecting particular categories. Lyon, a leading sociologist who established the multidisciplinary field of surveillance studies, defines surveillance as "the focused, systematic and routine attention to personal details for purposes of influence, management, protection or direction."[13] Surveillance systems can be built for a variety of purposes, from the increasingly dominant reason of "security" to the vast sphere of entertainment. For good or ill, surveillance is never neutral. Whether they are citizens, workers, or consumers, people are sorted as either eligible or ineligible for rights and resources through the classification of their personal data. Lyon calls this effect of today's data processing *social sorting* and draws attention to its negative consequences on already-marginalized groups of people.[14]

National ID systems or ID cards existed long before surveillance studies emerged in the late 1990s, along with the development of information and communication technologies. But through a theoretical lens, the ambiguous characteristics of ID systems in a modern nation-state, the tensions between care and control, conformity and coercion, and the naturalized practice of bureaucracy and exclusionary categorization of subjects are all clarified more fully in relation to today's formation of power. The rapid expansion of surveillance systems in public and private domains in the past decades clearly indicates that surveillance is central to analyzing how today's power operates through accessing more data on different aspects of people's lives. The identification system is one arena in which surveillant power can be increased.

Because today's data processing often takes place far from the subjects of the data, behind electronic screens or in networked databases, it is not easy for subjects to feel or sense the consequences of their own personal data, given intentionally or unintentionally. Thus, the concept of social sorting unveils this intangible process of personal data collection that classifies people advantageously and disadvantageously. As a result of social sorting, data processes more often reproduce, rather than counter or mitigate, existing social orders. Although extensive data collection is a phenomenon of the digital age, accompanied by much initial optimism for the internet's democratizing influence,[15] technology's novel and powerful capacity has been quickly folded into the dominant practices of political economic actors, states, and corporations. In this sense, social sorting can be understood as a function that reproduces and reinforces the existing social order, and as an analytical tool, it can be applied to historical contexts, including those that preceded the electronic age, as the authors Scott Thompson and Simone Browne have demonstrated conclusively.[16]

When I applied social sorting to my study of the Manchurian biometric identification systems, I found that Japanese colonizers sorted the people of occupied Northeast China into "desirable" and "undesirable" categories. National ID systems in general can serve different purposes, from taxation to conscription, from educating to rationing, depending on the motives of the nation-state. Such systems are a technique for population control. The national ID system sorts the population into groups that deserve rights and groups that do not. It can establish a hierarchical order among the groups and mobilize them for different purposes. From the first, a mechanism of inclusion and exclusion is incorporated into identification systems. Is there an all-inclusive ID system? If rights and resources were guaranteed equally to everyone in a society, there would perhaps be no need to identify individuals. Passports, driver's licenses, student cards, and voting identification—these all guarantee registered people legitimate access to certain rights and resources while simultaneously excluding others. Crucially, those excluded others are often rendered invisible in ID systems. In other words, the ID system can be used as a covert technique to limit or ban certain people from accessing certain rights and resources while also proclaiming the democratic principle of rights and resources for everyone.

MAKING UP PEOPLE

While social sorting exposes the classifying effects of ID systems, the concept of population control infers who has been historically targeted by ID systems and for what purpose. Applied to colonial ID systems, social sorting reveals the sovereign power's desire to classify the colonial population in different standards from the metropolitan ones and structure discriminatory treatment. The colonial sorting also reveals that verification is not the primary imperative of the ID system; rather, categorization is.[17] In fact, the ID system does not necessarily stabilize one's personal identity; instead, it can destabilize and transform personal identities through ceaseless categorization.

The categorization of people, or construction of the subject as the effect of categorization, has long attracted social scientists' attention.[18] They have examined the construction of the subject through socialization processes. Peter Berger and Thomas Luckmann, in their classic work on the sociology of knowledge, describe knowledge as a person's internalization of social institutions.[19] In this view, identification and identity are two different poles of knowledge on the person shaped by the institution and themselves, corresponding with each other. Anthony Giddens supports this view with his concept of duality of structure.[20] Social structure, as a recursively organized set of rules and resources, is not external to human agents but is internal to their activities. This duality of structure, in social systems and in human agency, explains that the system is both the medium and the outcome of human actions, and so it simultaneously constrains and enables those actions.[21] Thus, categorical structure is inscribed within agency, reflexively monitoring one's own actions.

More actively, Ian Hacking suggests that categories "make up people": New slots are created to shape and enumerate people, and people in turn adhere to those categories.[22] Although every configuration of a category has its own background, the category and the "kind" of people come into being hand in hand. "The systematic collection of data about people has affected not only the ways in which we conceive of a society, but also the ways in which we describe our neighbor. It has profoundly transformed what we choose to do, what we try to be, and what we think of ourselves," states Hacking.[23]

Thus, categorization can function as a certain type of frame to construct a certain type of subject who sees the world through institutional categories. In other words, the ID system is a site where power constructs the subjects of institutions by giving them categorical roles. This function is illuminated with regard to the *koseki* system in chapter

2. The *koseki* significantly contributed to framing family as a patriarchal unit, giving hierarchical roles to the family members, and making up people who were loyal subjects of the emperor, the supreme leader of the new nation-state.

THE FEMINIST QUESTION OF IDENTITY

Not everybody adheres to roles molded by new categories, and categories cannot always make up people. Categorization also exposes the contradictions and resistance among individuals during the process of making up people. For example, feminist studies questioned the collective category of "women" and revealed the arbitrary process of categorization. When the complete categorization of women failed, through the consciousness of contradiction, feminist scholars discovered gender roles, which are socially and culturally constructed and separate from biological sex. In postwar America, the expectation that all women—because of their biology—would fulfill prescribed gender roles caused a national phenomenon of malaise and depression among middle-class women that came to be known as the "problem with no name."[24] These identity crises and struggles led many women to realize that the "personal is political."[25]

Judith Butler pushes the boundaries of gender beyond biological sex, the allegedly absolute difference between men and women.[26] Butler argues that biological difference has also been socially discovered, emphasized, and defined in male-dominated societies. Reversing Simone de Beauvoir's inquiry in *The Second Sex*[27]—"one is not born, but rather becomes, a woman"—she posits the impossibility of *becoming* "a woman," a binary category of gender, because this secondary category was imaginarily constructed and imperatively imposed. In other words, there is no original *being* in the category of woman. The category is only arbitrarily identified, incorporated, and assigned to individuals as a category dependent to that of "man," which is the primary category in heterosexual normative institutions. Identification fails or at least causes a conflict within individuals, because it is not possible for a person to finally become a category collectively and compulsorily constructed.[28] Thus, for Butler, "[g]ender is the repeated stylization of the body, a set of repeated acts within a highly rigid regulatory frame that congeal over time to produce the appearance of substance, of a natural sort of being."[29] As housekeepers or caregivers, women have strived to perform gender roles within prescribed categories, which have materialized and naturalized feminine constructs, including their biological bodies. But these women could never purely and completely identify with subordinate categories that are discursively created.

This is analogous to Japan's national ID systems, constructed during its nation building and colonial expansion. This imaginary aspect of arbitrary categories is clearly displayed in the contrast between the *koseki* systems implemented in Japan and in Taiwan and Korea (chapter 2). *Koseki* succeeded in building a collective identity of loyal subjects among the Japanese to serve imperial Japan. The Taiwanese and Korean people were forced to adopt the identity of loyal subjects of Japan, but the effect of "making up people" was inherently limited, and instead, the ruling ideology tended to reaffirm impossibility of turning them the perfect subject. However much the Taiwanese and Korean people assimilated themselves to Japanese culture and worshipped the emperor, they were marked as second-class subjects, and their loyalty was never trusted.

For resistance, this may be good news. If coercive categories are reproduced through performance, one can also resist them by ceasing to perform or pretending to perform. In the colonies, anti-imperial battles and protests kept erupting during the Japanese occupation (chapters 3-5).

FROM DISCIPLINARY TO CONTROLLING SURVEILLANCE?

These key concepts in surveillance studies—social sorting, population control, categorization, and construction of the subject—are associated with Michel Foucault's understanding of modern surveillance in one way or another. And his concepts of disciplinary power and biopower are most widely applied in surveillance studies.

In *Discipline and Punish*,[30] Foucault revived the idea of the panopticon, which was Jeremy Bentham originally proposed as an architectural design for low-cost supervision, framing it as the model of the carceral network of modern institutions such as prisons, military facilities, factories, hospitals, and schools. The panoptic design allows for a guard in a central tower to watch over inmates who are isolated in each cell; but the inmates are never able to see the guard through the shaded windows of the tower. They are constantly exposed to visibility, but supervision is exercised through invisibility. This asymmetrical relationship of visibility-invisibility induces in the inmates a state of consciousness that assures the "automatic functioning of power." The individual internalizes the gaze of the supervisor and begins internal self-monitoring.[31] The panopticon represents a disciplinary power that constructs docile bodies through soul training. This model demonstrates how social institutions inscribe the rules within the self, that is, the construction of a subject who practices self-monitoring.

After theorizing disciplinary power, Foucault suggested the more overarching concept of biopower as the regulatory mechanism of modern sovereignty over a population in *The History of Sexuality, Vol. 1.*[32] There, he observed that the West had undergone a fundamental transformation of the mechanisms of power, from the "right to kill" to the right to "foster life."[33] Destroying life, like a king in an absolute monarchy executing his people in a public spectacle of the death penalty, has become merely one element among several mechanisms of a sovereign state "working to incite, reinforce, control, monitor, optimize and organize the forces" to govern the population. This shift is characterized as a replacement of the ancient right to take life or let live, with a more modern concept: the power to foster life or disallow it to the point of death.[34] Here the population emerges as a new object of modern power, and interventions no longer always have destructive effects on people. Rather, they apparently serve to increase the population's biological well-being.

Foucault asserts that both the disciplinary and the biopolitical characters of modern power developed necessarily along with the formation of capitalism. Disciplinary power has repeatedly trained the human body on an individual basis—"'got rid of the peasant' and given him 'the air of a soldier'"[35]—for productivity in modern institutions such as military, factory, and school. Through subjecting individuals to this technique, disciplinary power molded the individual's mechanical body and soul to external and internal perfection, whether as an industrial worker or a loyal citizen.[36] Biopower, in contrast, works for the administration of bodies and calculated management of life on a mass basis.[37] To reinforce the docility and availability of labor power, capitalism requires the "methods of power capable of optimizing forces, aptitudes, and life in general without at the same time making them more difficult to govern."[38] Thus, not only institutions such as factories and schools but also numerous, diverse, and continuous techniques for achieving the subjugation of bodies and the control of populations have been invented to give the population extra life and to strengthen the sovereign power to its fullest.[39]

But because of the emphasis on the centralized structure of surveillance, the panopticon has also attracted several criticisms. In one compelling critique, Kevin Haggerty and Richard Ericson suggest that surveillance systems are increasingly decentralized, their networks converged into "the surveillant assemblage" of discrete systems, beyond a panoptic enclosure of space.[40] Inspired by Gilles Deleuze and Félix Guattari,[41] they employ a metaphor of "rhizomatic" practices for a surveillant assemblage, in which "a rhizome may be broken, shattered at a given spot, but it will start up again on one of its old lines, or on new lines."[42] In fact, Deleuze points to a transformation of Foucault's disciplinary society into what he calls "societies of control." Deleuze famously suggests that in a disciplinary society "power both amasses and individuates, that is, it fashions those over whom it's exerted into a body of people and molds the individuality of each member of the body. . . . [In control societies, we are] no longer dealing with a duality of mass and individual. Individuals become 'dividuals,' and masses become samples, data, markets, or 'banks.'"[43] This "dividuality" of the body and the self indeed represent the main features of today's discrete flows of personal data in networked databases. These ever-dividing-but-growing characteristics also capture liquidity or flexibility of late modernity or postmodernity.[44] In addition, today's surveillance is not operated only by the state. Corporate actors are actually the drivers operating electronic systems, as the collection of personal data has become a fundamental business model in the twenty-first century.[45] There are numerous towers with numerous guards who expect not disciplinary results, but consumption.

Disciplinary or controlling societies? The debates in surveillance studies have sometimes been divided between these two influential models. However, it would be misleading to say that disciplinary power is disappearing in the digital age. Edward Snowden and others blew the whistle to inform the public that the U.S. National Security Agency (NSA) had equipped digital technologies to collect personal data for disciplinary purposes. The NSA partnered with multiple private actors in the form of a surveillant assemblage, but states still hold legitimate power in shaping, organizing, regulating, and peeping at personal data in discrete systems, both within and outside of juridical procedures.[46] In this sense, disciplinary power and controlling power are supplementary to each other. The relation between the two is neither binary nor exclusive. As Lyon suggests, "The two seem to coincide and often mutually support each other. Indeed, there may be disciplinary practices *within* control mechanisms, and vice-versa."[47] In my view, they increasingly create a spiral of surveillance in which the use of one calls for the use of the other. In this book, I critically apply both models to Japan's national ID systems and connect the managerial effect of identification to the disciplinary outcomes of sovereign violence.

INTERNAL PACIFICATION OR IMPERIAL CRISIS

The modern origins of state surveillance activities, including national identification systems, are often traced back to the establishment of nation-states and bureaucracy in Europe. The registration of people and their belongings with local authorities was promoted as a utopian idea during the sixteenth century and had been established as the foundation of identification by the seventeenth century.[48] Identification requires two steps: registration and verification. It operates on the basis of the officially registered information in the records and verifies that information against an individual's details. In France during the sixteenth and seventeenth centuries, for example, all royal subjects were required to register their name, status, and place of residence, to "detect the wolves among the sheep."[49]

Population became both the subject and the object of governing nation-states, and surveillance was mobilized to collect information about the people in a given territory. In his book *The Nation-State and Violence*, Anthony Giddens finds that "information storage is central to the role of 'authoritative resources' in the structuring of social systems spanning larger ranges of space and time than tribal cultures. Surveillance—the control of information and the superintendence of the activities of some groups by others—is in turn the key to the expansion of such resources."[50] In the shift from absolutist state to nation-state, Giddens identifies a need for the "internal pacification of states" to mitigate the class struggles that emerged from rapid industrialization. While the modern state successfully monopolized the means of violence through the military, as Max Weber suggests, and shifted the military's objective from the internal population to foreign countries, surveillance arose as a new means of regulatory force toward the internal population by the government.

This replacement of state violence with surveillance overlaps with what Foucault proposes as the withdrawal of extreme violence against internal populations by absolutist states. Similarly, as Foucault asserts that disciplinary power helped industrial capitalism grow by creating docile bodies, Giddens contends that the monitoring of the workplace and the control of deviance became a primary object of internal pacification in liberal democratic states. Those surveillance activities inherently require the expansion of administrative coordination to collect, retain, and use data on the population, which in turn facilitates the growth of bureaucracy, regulatory techniques, and statistical knowledge of peoples' lives.

In contrast, Edward Higgs finds external reasons for state surveillance in the modern era. He agrees that state surveillance of the internal population in Britain began with modern bureaucracy in the early nineteenth century, coinciding with the first national census taken in 1801 and civil registration in 1837.[51] But then his study shows how the late nineteenth and early twentieth centuries saw the real foundation of the modern information state, which grew out of concern over the loss of British hegemony.[52] Against Giddens's view of state surveillance as an internal pacifier of class struggle emerging from industrialization,[53] Higgs proposes "international geo-politics" and the "imperial crisis" as principal motivations for centralized state surveillance. "National efficiency" was pursued on the basis of demographic data to ensure industrial and military mobilization of the population when facing external "threats."[54] This gave rise to centralized information systems in the police and security services during the same period and in pension and welfare systems during and after two world wars. For Higgs, imperial competition over colonial acquisition, not class struggle, is the major reason bureaucrats undertook surveillance activities. Police and security agencies tried to uncover foreign agents, and the public health and welfare systems emerged directly from two world wars that mobilized the entire population. On the whole, Higgs shows that modern state surveillance systems developed from a number of demands on and consequences of the imperial growth of nation-states and wars. External crises facilitated the internal surveillance of British citizens in service of strengthening state power.

Thus, it was not coincidental that a mandatory passport system was invented around the time of World War I.[55] The imperial clash among European powers fostered xenophobia and gave the state the ideal opportunity to reinforce its control over people's movements during a state of emergency. In Germany, passports were not only issued to the nation's citizens; "foreigners" were also required to carry them. France also mandated that all foreigners carry ID cards. The passport, a cross-national ID card, became the backbone of documentary substantiation of identity used to register and track the movements of aliens. John Torpey argues that the modern state monopolized the legitimate means of movement, paralleling its monopolization of the legitimate means of violence.[56] Nation-states—the state of assembled people—not only monopolized weapons and air fighters but also invented the administrative technique of using passports to check the movements of nationals and nonnationals in the war.[57] This deprived people of the freedom to move across certain spaces and forced them to "depend on states and the state system for the authorization to do so—an authority widely held in private hands theretofore."[58] The state obtained the authority to prove a resident's identity, and personal identity was inseparably tied to the state through the passport system, regardless of how weak the tie was, how little the person's nationality corresponded with their identity, or whether or not the person supported state authority. The passport inscribed a national logo on one's personal identity.

These sociohistorical studies together show that modern state apparatuses came into being in conjunction with imperial competition outside of national borders. The rise of the information state was facilitated by conscription, production, taxation, and welfare when the state pushed the political economic interests outward from its existing territory. In turn, imperial battles consolidated nationality and citizenship within the country. It is important to understand the modern

formation of identification or identity against the backdrop of the internal and external affairs of the imperial nation-state. However, the
studies referenced here look at the formation of identification or identity only within Europe, not outside Europe, including its then newly
acquired territories. As a result of its imperial wars, European borders
extended to other continents, and a new group of people became the
object of imperial power. What types of identities were given to the
conquered people, and how were they classified in the new social order
within the empire?

IMPERIAL SCIENCE ON BIOLOGICAL BODIES

The intellectual ethos of the nineteenth century rapidly expanded the
use of "scientific" methods of identification that focused on the population's biological bodies. In centers of European industrialization, the
police deployed visual technologies to regulate the growing presence of
a chronically unemployed working class beginning in the 1840s, and the
photographic documentation of prisoners was routinized from the 1860s
onward.[59] In France, Britain, and the United States, criminal portraits
became a central way for police to identify, classify, and differentiate
"habitual criminals."[60] The collected visual and measured information
on criminals' bodies was carefully studied to identify typologies of deviance and social pathology. The face and head were especially believed
to show outward signs of inner character, such as in the practices of
physiognomy and phrenology, in which optical and statistical technologies merged to define and regulate the criminal nature of individuals.

Anthropometry, a method of criminal classification using rigorous
bodily measurements and record keeping by card filing, had also developed in metropolises by the mid-nineteenth century.[61] Bertillonage, the
most popular method, named after the French police official Alphonse
Bertillon, involved a prisoner being subjected to exact body measurements in eleven different categories. The operator filled out a "Bertillonage card" to describe the subject's eyes, ears, lips, beard, hair color,
skin color, ethnicity, forehead, nose, build, chin, general contour of head,
hair growth pattern, eyebrows, eyeball and orbit, mouth, physiognomic
expression, neck, inclination of shoulders, attitude, voice and language,
and clothing.[62] After categorizing each of the prisoner's body parts, the

Bertillon cards were cataloged by sex in the archive. Then they were classified according to whether the subject's head length was "small," "medium," or "large," and subclassified by head breadth, and then by middle finger length, and so on, through foot, forearm, height, and little finger.[63] Despite the meticulous measurements and classifications, Bertillon's instruction manual was translated into seven languages and rapidly spread to police departments and penal institutions in the United States, Canada, Argentina, and Britain.

Bertillonage clearly exemplifies the scientific drive to find objective truths about criminals and suspects through biological data obtained using statistical and mathematical methods. However, Bertillonage was far from automating identification. In particular, colonial officials were less enthusiastic about such anthropometry because it was difficult for European eyes to find and describe physical differences among colonized people.[64] Officers also faced language and literacy barriers. The clumsy white gaze gave rise to the technology of fingerprinting after the 1880s as a single bodily identifier. The invention of fingerprint identification set the course for Japan's colonial identification systems, so the developmental processes are closely examined here.

Henry Faulds, a British physician serving at Tsukiji Hospital in Tokyo, Japan, during the late 1870s, discovered fingerprints on ancient Japanese ceramics and published his observation in *Nature* in 1880. Faulds also wrote a letter to Charles Darwin, who had already published *On the Origin of Species by Means of Natural Selection*, and Darwin forwarded the letter to his cousin Francis Galton, one of Britain's imperial scientists. Galton believed that fingerprint patterns might be a useful technology for the empire to avoid "the great difficulty in identifying coolies either by their photograph and measurements."[65] He formalized the technology of fingerprinting in the last decade of the nineteenth century, in competition with Bertillonage.

Galton presumed that fingerprint patterns might be the elusive visible markers of heredity. His interest in finding evidence to support his belief in white racial superiority led him to join in the search for a biologically determined "criminal type,"[66] and he would later propose a concept of eugenics through evolution. Galton classified fingerprint patterns into three groups: arch, loop, and whorl. Edward Henry, the commissioner of police in Bengal, visited Galton's London laboratory in 1894 and was convinced that fingerprinting could reduce both errors and costs in identification. His assistants Azizul Haque and Chandra Bose did research to improve Galton's classifications. They reduced the three types to two (loop and whorl); classified ten fingers in five paired sets, each of which could be one of four possible classifications (e.g., LL, LW, WW, WL); and with some other changes, established a method called the Henry Classification System.[67] In 1897, Henry convinced the governor-general of India to switch from anthropometry to fingerprinting.[68] Within a few years, fingerprinting was implemented not only for record keeping but also for criminal investigations and later as legal evidence.

South Africa offered a springboard for both Galton's and Henry's careers. Galton traveled around South Africa in 1850 and published *Narrative of an Explorer in Tropical South Africa* in 1853.[69] Emphasizing that Black people of South Africa were "brutal and barbarous to an almost incredible degree,"[70] he produced an influential account of African inferiority and the pivotal claims of social Darwinism in Britain. He repeatedly rejected the humanitarian critique of slavery because he believed that Black people were suited to slavery. He inaugurated eugenics with biostatistical concepts, inspired by his experiences in South Africa. Keith Breckenridge points out that "Galton's two biometrics—eugenically motivated statistics of human biology and the technologies of fingerprint identification—have common roots in the project of Empire."[71]

Edward Henry was sent to South Africa in 1900 by Joseph Chamberlain, the British secretary of state for the colonies, to establish a new Criminal Investigation Department in Johannesburg and "to introduce a scientific system of identification."[72] The most important task he faced there was to deal with the mining corporations' demand for systematic identification to bind migrant workers to their long-term contracts. Henry designed the police force around the particular needs of the mining industry and initiated the enforcement of the Pass Law, which prepared the foundation of the notorious passbook systems of South Africa's apartheid policies. Henry created many fingerprint repositories in different locations and built the pass control system linked with fingerprints, "with funds raised from the wages of hundreds of thousands of mine workers, [which] was more intrusive and more long-lasting than any similar fingerprinting regime on the planet."[73] The Pass Law generated a notorious pattern of incarceration among the colonial population: Black men found without passes were subjected to weeklong imprisonment to allow for the identification of deserters.

According to Breckenridge, the owners of the mining industry in South Africa, like their Japanese counterparts in China, had no interest in understanding or memorizing the names of indigenous workers and called them by common English names, such as "Charlie," "Sammy" or "Jonnie," so that when the workers moved to another workplace, their names also changed.[74] The owners wanted automatic identification and tracking of the workers' profiles, and Henry responded by introducing fingerprinting registration. Although the indexing system Henry introduced produced results that were contradictory, messy, and expensive, it was imposed on miners in order to satisfy economic demand by the imperial businesses.

A few years later, seventy thousand Chinese men became the first successful models for this method in South Africa. In the 1900s, many Chinese workers migrated to South Africa, partly because their seasonal jobs were halted by the Russo-Japanese War (1904–5). The imperial wars and colonial industries created a transnational migration of Chinese workers as cheap labor power. The Foreign Labor Department first used photographs and then Bertillonage to identify Chinese workers upon their arrival in South Africa, but it found this system time-consuming and ineffective for immediately distinguishing one worker from another. Foreign Labor Department officers followed instructions Henry had left behind and found that fingerprinting was much more efficient and cheaper. The department fingerprinted about thirteen thousand Chinese workers a year and covered all Chinese single workers within five years—and eventually every Chinese or Indian adult male in the Transvaal, known as the gold-mining center.[75] Their fingerprints were organized in relation to all administrative aspects of recruitment and control, including fees and wages charged to the mines. In 1906, the department registered more than ten thousand newly arrived migrants, identified twelve thousand Chinese workers released from prison, fifteen thousand who appeared in court, and five thousand who were repatriated, all from fingerprints.[76] Breckenridge analyzes how this model served the initial development of the biometric state of South Africa and was looked back on by bureaucrats as a triumphant legacy: "The Chinese episode seemed to offer disciplinary possibilities that would dissolve the most persistent barriers to the proper organization of an enormous colonial labor force. These obstacles, first cultural—'the Chinese aptitude for prevarication'—and second, linguistic—'no one of the finger print experts spoke the Chinese language'—collapsed under a regime where officials confronted the migrant exclusively 'through his finger prints and the classification under which they fell.'"[77]

In 1907, the use of Henry's fingerprint registration extended from the confines of the mining district into the general population and the whole of the Transvaal, as the universal ten-fingerprint registration. Among many social engineering projects tested in the British colonies under imperial progressivism, Breckenridge concludes that the technology of fingerprinting most powerfully bound India and South Africa.[78] While some critics warned that the techniques of imperial governance would find their way home, fingerprinting was not adopted for the purpose of labor control in Britain. Breckenridge says, "It was precisely because it contradicted the long-established patterns of respectability that were associated with written civil registration."[79] This point is relevant when we contrast the registration systems of Japan, the *koseki* system (chapter 2), with the biometric ID system in Manchuria (chapter 3 and 4).

The colonial technology of fingerprinting traveled quickly to other empires. Japan strove to catch up with Western imperialism in East Asia, and Japanese elites—including Yoshida Shigeru, who was a high-ranking diplomat in the prewar years and became a prime minister postwar—admired Britain as the world leader of imperialism.[80] Japanese mining companies adopted fingerprint identification toward local and migrant workers in China. Just as Galton's view on Africans was fiercely derogatory, the Kwantung Army similarly treated the Chinese with no respect. Crucially, this racism gave birth to biologically focused methods of identifying each human body, and the positivist knowledge produced from these methods reinforced racism, like a self-fulfilling prophecy. Galton's dream of biometric governance came true in the colonies because of the covert relationship between racism and science during the imperial era.

THE COLONIAL IS CRIMINAL: RACIALIZING SURVEILLANCE

The previous section illuminates an interesting contrast. Though fingerprinting most often conjures up images of criminal investigation, it was born in European colonies as a technology to identify masses of civil populations, whereas photography and anthropometry were implemented to identify criminals and predict criminality in individuals in Europe.

In other words, for the imperial governments of the nineteenth century, "colonial" and "criminal" were interchangeable categories in that they were both suspect identities. Colonizing authorities assumed that colonized populations bore not only intrinsic inferiority but also potential criminality. In 1871, the Criminal Tribes Act was passed for the registration and surveillance of certain tribes in India.[81] For this legislation, British ethnographers applied the idea of the "habitual" and "professional" criminal to suspected tribes. One of the major purposes for implementing fingerprint identification in India was to prevent pension fraud by the local population. As such, Indians were perceived as liars and deceivers by British officers, in the same manner as officers described the Chinese miners in South Africa as "prevaricating." The imperial state attributed the category of "suspect identities" to the entire colonial population. Western epistemology inscribed potential criminality in the biological bodies of the Indigenous population and racialized them as Others who did not deserve respect equal to White subjects. Biometrics embody this colonial epistemology.

North America is not immune from this trend. In the United States, bodily identification techniques were developed alongside the establishment of slavery. Simone Browne describes how the transatlantic slave trade generated numerous methods of surveillance of Black bodies: chains and cuffs, branding, slave tags, slave passes, runaway notices, slave patrols, and slave catchers.[82] The system of slavery would have been impossible without surveillance practices, and from the very beginning, slavery was experienced not only as incarceration but also as "slow-motion death" by African captives.[83]

Christian Parenti also contends that the plantation system produced the earliest form of bodily surveillance in the United States, and he situates the slave pass, wanted posters, and newspaper advertisements for runaway slaves and servants as the information technologies of slave surveillance.[84] Under the pass system, enslaved people were arrested when they were found outside their master's domain without a pass or were not in the company of a white person. The slave pass system, like the pass system in South Africa, strictly regulated African people's mobility as the property of European descendants in the United States. In any case, if a slave escaped from total control, the runaway notice detailed their biological features, as in this ad about an enslaved person named Tom: "blubber Lips, yellow Complexion, his Hair is neither right Negro nor Indian, but between both," "His eyes very full, as if they were starting out of his head," "his great Toes have been froze, and have only little pieces of nails on them," and so on, with a promise of monetary reward when securing him.[85] The written description was the means of spreading information and identifying the fugitive, but it also reduced him to these biologically focused identifiers, as seen through the White master's gaze.

Browne conceptualizes all these institutionalized practices against Black people as "racializing surveillance."[86] She defines racializing surveillance as "a technology of social control where surveillance practices, policies, and performances concern the production of norms pertaining to race and exercise a "power to define what is in or out of place.'"[87] Thus, the systematic act of surveillance has continuously created and normalized social categories of race, contrary to the assumption that the biological differences necessitated surveillance in the first place. The effect of racializing surveillance may vary depending on the time and place, but in Browne's view, it "most often upholds negating strategies that first accompanied European colonial expansion and transatlantic slavery that sought to structure social relations and institutions in ways that privilege whiteness."[88] Clearly, institutions of slavery criminalized African people who acted as if they had agency. Surveillance techniques and technologies were mobilized to punish slaves "out of place" and send fugitives back to the plantations. Enslavement required numerous techniques and technologies of surveillance for its maintenance, and those surveillance technologies reified the problematic ideology of racial superiority and inferiority.

Browne's intersectional approach to the generative forces of surveillance is applicable to social categories other than race: "as operating in an interlocking manner with class, gender, sexuality, and other markers of identity and their various intersections."[89] In building on Black feminist theories, Browne's argument resonates as a discursive mechanism of gender identity. Under this construct, no one could ever become the pure concept of woman, because, as Butler writes, it is created discursively.[90]

Interestingly, Browne finds less effect on the construction of subjectivity in racializing surveillance than in self-surveillance practiced by individuals who try to fit into heterosexual gender normativity. Countless runaway slave notices prove that Black people refused to be the docile slave their master expected or to be completely commodified in the plantation economy. Browne proposes "dark sousveillance,"[91] a gaze from the bottom to the top of social hierarchy, which suggests the limitation of the panoptic gaze internalized within the subject.

Slavery ended in the United States before the biological focus of imperial science moved to the stage of fingerprinting. But the abolition of slavery did not mean the end of racializing surveillance against non-White bodies. Fingerprinting was proposed as a way to help identify Asian immigrants after the Chinese Exclusion Act was passed in 1882. In 1902, an American identification expert noted, "[T]his system [fingerprinting] would be of great service . . . in the official identification of Chinese, negroes, and other races, the features of which, at least to the Caucasian eye, offer hardly sufficient individuality to be at all times trustworthy."[92] Though this plan was never realized, Chinese descendants already residing in the United States were subjected to registration and routine surveillance.[93] As Simon A. Cole put it, "[F]ingerprinting seemed like part and parcel of the new, rationalized bureaucracies, scientific management, mass production, [and] Progressive era technocracy," which perfectly fit into industrialization of the society.[94]

North of the U.S. border, an Act of Respecting Chinese Immigration came into effect on July 1, 1923, to completely halt Chinese immigration to the Dominion of Canada. All Chinese Canadians, many of whom were children, were required to register with the Department of Immigration and Colonization. Though the registration certificate issued by the department did not employ fingerprints, the photographed ID card is undeniably an act of racializing surveillance designed to check on their movement. Many children photographed in the certificate are nicely dressed in Western clothing, implying their parents' intention to show how much they had been already assimilated to white Canada, but the ID card states, "This certificate does not establish legal status in Canada." The ID card did not play any role in protecting children, most of whom were born in Canada; rather, it marked them as racial Others.[95]

Chinese immigrants and their descendants were not the first bodies to be racialized through registration and identification in Canada. First Nations people were required to register for the Pass System. Though the Pass System was not codified in any specific law, it was practiced in the Canadian west in the late nineteenth and early twentieth centuries.[96] The Indigenous peoples had been enclosed in "reserves" by the white settler government and had to ask the Department of Indian Affairs for passes and permits to leave their reserves and visit other places. Nakoda (Assiniboine) Chief Ochankuga'he (Kennedy) remembers: "In the early days of reservation life, the Indians were plagued with all kinds of restrictions, imposed on them by the guardian government. We could not sell grain, cattle, horses, wood, hay, etc., unless we got a permit from the Indian Agent. We also had to get passes from the Indian Agent to go anywhere on social visits or business trips. The Indian reserve was a veritable concentration camp."[97]

Around the same time that the Chinese Exclusion Act was passed in Canada, government officials also discussed with the Royal Canadian Mounted Police taking the fingerprints of Inuit peoples in the Northwest Territories.[98] This plan was never deployed. Instead, in 1941 the government began to register the Inuit persons with the Eskimo Disk List System and issued leather discs for them to wear around their neck or wrist or attach to their clothing. The disk was printed with a four-digit code, starting with E to identify each Inuit body, such as "Annie E7-121," though her name was Lutaaq, Pilitaq, Palluq, or Inusiq to her parents and elders.[99] The missionaries had trouble pronouncing traditional Inuit names properly, so they attached biblical names to Inuit people. In the same way that Chinese mine workers were given common English names in South Africa, Inuit cultural identities were ignored and molded into the Western style and enumeration. Thus, biometric bodies are reduced to information to be understood efficiently by colonial authorities,[100] and the Indigenous populations in imperial margins are continuously marked as racial Others.

In summary, obsessive measuring of the body, typically seen in Ber-tillonage, arose out of an academic enthusiasm to search for the origins of crime in the European nation-states, involving biology, anthropology, and eugenics.[101] In colonies, the occupiers searched for universal signs of inferiority in racial Others. Race became a focus of scientific research that aimed to diagnose the nature of the human species. Colonial anthropologists looked for the missing link to human origins in "savages," and evolutionary theories were supposed to prove an objective difference between the races and the superiority of Caucasians. They were, in the end, not successful in discovering a reliable physical indicator of inferiority in racial Others, but they established a way of thinking that attributed social phenomena to biological nature. Biometric identification stems in part from such biological reductionism, as well as from the Western epistemology of "truth finding" that claimed to prove its own superiority.

In turn, departing from criminal investigation and colonial management, the contemporary revival and proliferation of biometrics contribute to inscribing criminalities on bodies in the wider categories of the marginalized, whether in antiterror measures, immigration and refugee screenings, or welfare applications. In such margins of neoliberal systems, the obsessive ethos of colonialism to single out physical identifiers is still alive, and it further spreads as part of a larger movement "to use quick-fix technologies as the solution to complex social problems,"[102] and it diminishes the language of social identities. As Shoshana Magnet comments on biometrics, "The assumptions about gender, race, sexuality and disability are encoded by scientists directly into the operational elements of the technologies, revealing the inseparability of science from culture" to this day.[103]

A CRITIQUE OF BIOPOWER

Having uncovered the oppressive practices of colonial surveillance against Brown, Yellow, Black, and Red bodies, it is difficult to simply accept existing theoretical frameworks that were developed based on European models. The colonial case studies demand that researchers not only modify dominant frameworks and critically apply popularized concepts, but also decolonize the knowledge that was produced through such prevailing frameworks. While Foucault's biopower may be valid in explaining how surveillance facilitated the political economic growth of Western nation-states, it cannot meaningfully reflect the contemporary experiences of Others in the colonies, where many people were exposed to the power of death.[104] Eurocentric epistemologies not only block the public from knowing what happened to people in the colonies because of Western imperialism. They also reproduce colonial knowledge that disproportionally represents the interests of White men who ruled Europe and beyond, and the biased methods and data that emerged from imperial sciences and racist technologies. To proportionally acknowledge the oppressive impacts of hegemonic surveillance exercised outside the West, and to decolonize the existing knowledge that accumulated in conscious and unconscious racism, what kinds of theoretical interventions are possible?

An alternative approach I explore for colonial surveillance begins with bare life, a concept by Giorgio Agamben. In the shadow of the productive aspect of biopower, Agamben sheds light on the exclusion of the biopolitical body and how that exclusion becomes prevalent.[105] Bare life is categorized by the sovereign power as not needing, or invalid to live among the population. This process is given the form of "a state of exception" in the juridical order, because the sovereign can suspend the validity of the law and legally place individuals outside the law, often in a state of emergency such as a war or armed conflict. The bare life is excluded from the normal provision of the law, but this doesn't mean escaping the rule of the sovereign. On the contrary, the bare life is exposed to the direct exertion of sovereign power. Thus, the state of exception is *inclusive exclusion* from the general rule of constitutional protections, and it treats the individual only as a biological being, stripped of the political, legal, or social status of a full subject. In other words, bare life is legitimately abandoned by the law, that is, "exposed and threatened on the threshold in which life and law, outside and inside, become indistinguishable."[106]

The strength of Agamben's theoretical intervention to biopower is in finding a threshold of the dual character of sovereignty: productive and repressive, inclusive and exclusive, simultaneously. And in this duality, he reveals the hidden technique of biopower within juridical systems of the apparently democratic nation-state. It reserves a domain where

sovereignty can freely act for the right to kill, within the general principles of economic productivity and civil rights, the right to foster life.
In that state of exception, law merely legitimates sovereign violence.[107]
His discussion finds the principal paradigm in the Nazi concentration
camps as well as the U.S. Guantanamo Bay detention camp.[108] German
citizens were sent to Auschwitz after all their citizenship rights and
properties were legally rescinded because of their socially constructed
biological categories, such as "Jewish," "homosexual," or "disabled."

Similarly, during the War on Terror, Muslim men in Guantanamo,
a territory in Cuba leased by the United States, were deprived of their
legal protections as prisoners of war under international humanitarian
law and designated as "enemy combatants"—a category that does not
exist in the Geneva Conventions.[109] The detainees of bare life, including
U.S. citizens, are placed in maximum indeterminacy at Guantanamo
and other hidden U.S. foreign facilities—as in the case of the Canadian
citizen Maher Arar, whom American agents sent to Syrian prison, referred to in the preface[110]—and are vulnerably exposed to sovereign
violence. The U.S. government takes the stance that American constitutional rights do not apply in these U.S. facilities abroad, and this state of
exception legally turn the detainees into "enemy aliens." They are rendered ineligible for rights and protections and disqualified their agency.

Most importantly, the state of exception is not an exception in predatory politics of globalization in the twenty-first century.[111] In fact,
Agamben sees the state of exception to be the "original nucleus of sovereign power" throughout Western politics.[112] The bare life of the citizen
has been reproduced everywhere under biopower, and the exception
increasingly becomes the rule. Thus, *"The original relation of law to life
is not application but Abandonment."*[113] The concept of bare life helps understanding the contradictory phenomenon of abandoned lives under
biopolitics, not in spite of but because of productivity and efficiency.

This theoretical intervention to biopower also calls into question
the normative historical view of modern nations as progress in human
civilization: Why and how has the massive destruction of human lives
repeatedly taken place under the political and economic rationale of a
population's biological well-being? The normative view not only under-
acknowledges the destruction of lives in the past and present but also
offsets destruction with the construction of a new order in the future.

The decentering of the mass destruction of human lives in favor of the "restoration" of a country and "reform" of political systems immediately dominated the news on the invasions of Afghanistan, Iraq, or Palestine, carried out in the name of peace, democracy, or gender equality. The quick shift of the political agenda from destruction to construction wore an air of humanitarianism and contributed to the reproduction of a Eurocentric worldview, trust in hegemonic power, or social apathy for those who had initially opposed the mass destruction of human lives. Bare life attempts to subvert such normative views of "a just world" or historical progressivism. It points instead to the dual structures of Western democracy, double standards of a modern nation, or paradoxical effects of biopolitics, which incorporated all lives into the productive forces of capitalism and nation-states and simultaneously disqualified certain lives from judicial protection. Bare life illuminates the double standards of Western democracy and helps to uncover hidden relations between colonial surveillance and violence.

NECROPOLITICAL ENDS OF COLONIAL SURVEILLANCE

In my next step of theoretical intervention, Achille Mbembe's concept of necropolitics more directly reflects on colonial experiences as the original nucleus of sovereign power, replicated outside of Western soil. Knowing the dominantly violent rule of colonization, Mbembe suggests necropolitics as the ultimate expression of sovereignty that dictates who *may* live and who *must* die.[114]

Mbembe criticizes biopower as insufficient to account for contemporary forms of the subjugation of life to the power of death. Population control starts by dividing people into those who must live and those who must die. In the division and subdivision, a biological label is constructed, which is what Foucault calls racism. The murderous function of the state is enabled in the racialized categories of Others, through appeals to exception, emergency, and a functionalized enemy. All these appeals serve to dehumanize racialized Others and to legitimate the taking of people's homes, their rights over their bodies, and their political status. Mbembe echoes Agamben in arguing that the sovereign right to kill is the origin of modern terror and exemplifies the formation of modern terror in the slave trade, South African apartheid, and the

Israeli occupation of Palestine. Thus, biopower is understood in concatenation with the state of exception and the state of siege. Mbembe spec-
ifies: "Crucial to this concatenation is, once again, race. In fact, in most
instances, the selection of races, the prohibition of mixed marriages,
forced sterilization, even the extermination of vanquished peoples are
to find their first testing ground in the colonial world. Here we see the
first syntheses between massacre and bureaucracy, that incarnation of
Western rationality."[115]

Mbembe clearly states that colonies are zones where the guarantees
of judicial order can be suspended at any time in the service of "civilization,"[116] and the sovereign right to kill—necropower—is ubiquitous.
This resonates with Hannah Arendt's work on totalitarianism: Such
syntheses between massacre and bureaucracy were deployed in colonies.[117] Like fingerprint technology that inscribed suspect identities on
Indian, Chinese, and South African bodies, the systematic methods of
massacre perpetrated against racialized groups were first implemented
on colonial soil. Serial techniques for putting people to death were later
brought back to the gas chambers and ovens of Nazi extermination
camps, in Mbembe's view. This was the integration of technological rationality with the machinelike bureaucracy of the modern West. The
political techniques that enabled Auschwitz, which is seen as an exceptionally cruel event in the history of Western civilization, were invented
and evolved in colonial territories, simply through quotidian forms of
rule. Mbembe states, "The colony represents the site where sovereignty
consists fundamentally in the exercise of a power outside the law and
where 'peace' is more likely to take on the face of a 'war without end.'"[118]
Under such a normalized state of exception, surveillance as a regulatory
technique of population control becomes synonymous with violence. In
Mbembe's term, bare life is the living dead in colonies.

Such theoretical defects of biopower are increasingly exhibited in
social scientific literature on colonial surveillance.[119] In his studies on
Palestine, Ellia Zureik points out that "Israel as an occupying power is
less interested in the management of the population (in the Foucauldian sense) than it is in controlling and appropriating the territory on
which the population resides."[120] Palestinian individuals have often
been exposed to extrajudicial brutality, torture, executions, and ubiquitous surveillance, but the Israeli government does not care. Alfred

McCoy demonstrates that the United States developed a powerful intelligence apparatus that first contained and then crushed Filipino resistance during the American occupation of the Philippines from 1898 to 1935.[121] Obviously, the intelligence apparatus did not serve to empower the colonial population in any productive way. While the occupation transformed the United States into a surveillance state, the security apparatus itself has persisted in the Philippines since its independence and has maintained its extrajudicial power to this day.[122]

Back in colonial South Africa, Breckenridge's study found more of an absence of information on the population than a presence, so he named this administrative indifference "No will to know."[123] Universal registration had failed in the countryside, and the Black population, especially women and children, had never been of national interest to the colonizers. This neglect, or lack of interest in people as agency, in both Palestine and South Africa, can be seen as another expression of racism, in tandem with imperialism. Arendt would support this understanding of South Africa, as she observed the marriage of racism and bureaucracy in South African society and called it "culture-bed of imperialism."[124] The notorious apartheid system grew out of the imperial marriage. Importantly, South African colonizers paid a high cost to maintain the racial pyramid even when their practices contradicted economic rationality and profits, even "at a terrific price," argues Arendt.[125] The apartheid system taught the colonizing power that profit motives are not holy and can be overruled, and that such a society can function according to principles other than economic ones, through sheer violence.[126] Necropolitics invented systematic methods of massacre via the integration of technological rationality with productive administration. The marriage of racism and bureaucracy did not necessarily work for productivity, but it did for white sovereignty.[127]

Though originally developed outside the West, many techniques of dehumanization and technological rationalities for massacres have also spread in Western countries, along with the state of exception. Some call the proliferation of these necropolitical techniques the "boomerang effect,"[128] and surveillance systems are central to the techniques. For example, American unmanned aerial vehicles, or drones, that had performed unilateral, effective killing in Afghanistan and Iraq, were also used against Black Lives Matter protesters by the FBI in Baltimore.[129]

The actions metropolises take in colonies change the metropolises themselves sooner or later.[130] This again unveils the making of racism in which the racialized Others are the product of an imaginary, as are nation-states,[131] where the technological rationality of necropolitics transgresses borders and consumes whoever the bare life is. This proliferation does not mean that technology flattens the world toward equality. Breckenridge reminds us that there are still obvious imperial legacies in identifying and policing a target population today: "[T]he most powerful biometric surveillance systems are being developed in the poorest countries, the former colonies of the European empires."[132] American, Japanese, and Israeli technology companies are enthusiastically selling their biometric products to the Global South in humanitarian logics and charity gestures, such as ID4Africa.[133] Chinese and Indian enterprises are also participating in these rapidly growing markets and exporting biometric identification technologies to other countries.[134]

In conclusion, to unpack the violent consequences of colonial surveillance, I bring in the concepts of bare life and necropolitics as theoretical interventions to biopolitical understanding of modern governance. Given the popularity of biopower and Foucauldian approaches in social sciences and humanities in general, this intervention is my theoretical contribution to surveillance studies, science and technology studies, communication and media studies, sociology, and history to push for a more balanced view of the nation-state, capitalism, and civilization. The genealogy of identification technologies in transnational perspective suggests that colonial experiences are often missing from the conceptualization of modernity. When European powers increased productive strength through nation building and industrial capitalism, the conquering and dispossession of the colonies was the springboard for the accumulation of wealth. From transatlantic slavery to the use of fingerprinting in India and South Africa to the Pass system to contain Indigenous peoples in Canada, identification systems racialized colonial populations, reduced them to biological beings or statistics, and exposed them to the power of death using the state of exception the metropolis permanently set in the colonies. The necropolitical ends of biopolitical surveillance in colonized societies demand new social theories to warn of the potential harms of identification systems automated by digital technologies, as we see in the ongoing imperial projects of the twenty-first century.

A few concepts I coined and refer to later in this book, such as colonial threshold (chapter 3) and bodies as risky resources (chapter 4),
respond to this demand and point to the intertwined processes of nation
building and colonial practices. The contours of nation-states have
always been refined and negotiated along with the internal and external making of the empire. Thus, rather than separating nation building
and colonialism and placing nation building as central to—and colonialism as a side effect of—modernization, the two processes are examined
together throughout this book. Such a separation, often seen in popular
historiographies, fails to grasp the global experiences of surveillance
technologies as a whole.

On the same horizon, I intend to bring this case study on Japan's colonial ID systems to the central arena of ongoing identification debates
and eschew views that excuse it as an exception to modern civilization,
a misuse of Western technology in the Far East, or as a technology that
is essentially neutral but could be harmful in the wrong hands. The genealogy of identification, laid out in this chapter, proves that biometric
technologies have been transmitted from one owner to another across
empires and have similarly served biological determinism, categorical
suspicion, and imperial dispossession in different locations.

As in Brecht's description of the passport system at the beginning
of this chapter, my hope is to draw out a piece of truth about ID systems that is normally hidden in the unity of civilization and cruelty.[135]
I also hope to challenge normative views of historical progressivism
and a world in which good and evil are balanced. An alternative understanding of technology can begin only after discovering such a marginalized fact. Regardless of how much technology and rationality have
progressed, it should *not* be a goal of progress that the human becomes a
mechanical device to carry a piece of ID, as Brecht's Big Man assumed.

CHAPTER TWO

CONSTRUCTING "JAPANESE" AND INTERNAL OTHERS

The Koseki *System as Surveillance*

> Japanese people are descended from the same ancient mythology; since the establishment of the nation, the people have resided on the same national land and had the same language, habits, customs, history, and so on; they have never been conquered by any other nation, and so formed a big group of lineage that struck roots throughout the ancient land of Japan.
>
> *—(Inoue Testujirō, The Interpretation of The Imperial Rescript on Education, 1899)*[1]

Japan's modern nation building began in response to Western demands that the country open itself to a global market in the mid-nineteenth century. The Tokugawa (Edo) regime (1603–1867) had established an isolationist policy when it came to power in 1603, which banned people from going abroad, restricted exports and imports to only the port of Nagasaki, refused entrance to Christian missionaries, and punished Christians. In the early nineteenth century, Western nations frequently sent ships to request international trade with Japan. Among them was the United States, which threatened the country by showing up in a battleship in 1853, thus forcing an end to the 250-year isolationist policy.

The Tokugawa shogunate signed friendship treaties with the United States in 1854, with Russia in 1855, and with other countries later, to form diplomatic relations and initiate trade. But Japan soon found itself in an unequal position in those treaties, which denied its government judicial authority over the Westerners staying in the concession.

Facing drastic changes in national policies, the ruling class warriors of the Tokugawa regime were divided over whether to seek Westernization—a divergence that ultimately plunged the country into civil war. The rebel group won the internal conflict, and restored the emperor to sovereign power in the Meiji Restoration of 1868. The Meiji regime launched a constitutional monarchy around which political, economic, and cultural institutions were hurriedly constructed in the Western style. The goal was to achieve Japan's recognition as a civilized nation by its Western counterparts, maintain its independence as other parts of Asia were rapidly colonized, and renounce unequal treaties with the West.

Westernization meant nothing but building a nation-state—a state that would supposedly consist of one kind of people. Until the early nineteenth century, such an idea of sovereignty had never been common in East Asia.[2] International orders had been shaped by suzerain relations, in which a powerful country granted less powerful countries titles to govern themselves, and, in turn, the less powerful paid tribute to the powerful. Such was the relationship between the Chinese Min Dynasty (1368-1644) and the Korean Joseon Dynasty (1392-1897), for example. National borders were not strictly defined or disputed in suzerain relations. But for a nation-state, national borders bear importance because they demarcate the sovereign territory. As Benedict Anderson famously defines, a nation-state is imagined to be constituted of a homogeneous population within a limited territory.[3] In other words, the place where a homogeneous group of people resides can be claimed as a territory of the nation-state. National consciousness or nationalism is vital to bind people to a nation-state, and the mechanisms through which nation-state is accomplished are constantly updated.

For the Tokugawa shogunate, such a national consciousness was not only unnecessary for a feudal lord to govern their own territory but also dangerous, because it could flatten the hierarchical relations of occupational castes in the Edo era.[4] If shogun, feudal lords, farmers, merchants, and underclass people were all equalized as "Japanese," how could the distinctions among them be maintained? But the Meiji government needed to adopt the Western-style nation-state, define who the "Japanese" were, and plant a national consciousness among its people. Therefore, the Meiji government launched the process to construct "Japanese" in 1871, in the early stage of nation building, through the creation of a centralized registration and identification system, called *koseki* (戸籍).

The *koseki* system remains Japan's national identification system to this day. Residents are required to register with municipalities as a family unit. Registration is the first step for the individual to be recognized and identified on the basis of collected personal information. Once registration is complete in the file, identification becomes possible by matching registered data with the individual or data carried by the individual. Together, national registration and identification transform the population from unknown individuals into subjects legible to the state.

This chapter examines the *koseki* national identification system as surveillance, including how it constructed nationals and controlled the population while Japan's territory grew via imperial wars. The *koseki* system was implemented in both the center and the periphery of the Japanese empire, but it brought different effects of surveillance to each place. To demonstrate the consequences, I first describe the prehistory of modern *koseki*, prior to the Meiji era. Second, I explain the significance of *koseki* as a tool of population control that classified individuals within a patriarchal family framework and led them to pledge supreme loyalty to the emperor. The *koseki* became the very basis of defining the relation between the monarchical state and its subjects, not only administratively but also moralistically. It is centered on male lineage, imagined as the biological connection with the emperor, and it contributes to the myth of the Japanese people as a sole, unique, and pure race. As seen in the epigraph to this chapter, the myth was widely distributed through the media and in schools, particularly after the promulgation of the Imperial Rescript on Education in 1890. The *koseki* embodies the patriarchal and patriotic value system that molded the people into a new being, in symphony with Japan's major imperialist policies.

Third, I move on to how this *koseki* system was applied to colonial populations, mainly in the cases of Taiwan and Korea. While *koseki* kept including the newly conquered people into the emperor's property lists, it also branded racial marks onto the colonial populations and strictly prohibited them from merging with the Japanese. Finally, *koseki*'s disciplinary effects as surveillance are comparatively discussed between the metropolis and colonies. I analyze how the colonial *koseki* was not as constructive as the Japanese one in producing a national identity and contributing to the new market system.

The whole discussion of *koseki* as surveillance in this chapter posits that internal nation building and external colonialism are historically simultaneous, intertwined processes. Classifying the colonial population as second-class subjects solidified the proud identity of the "Japanese" as the highest category in the racial hierarchy of the empire.

PREMODERN CHARACTERISTICS OF NATIONAL REGISTRATION

The first national registration to be found in Japanese literature appears in the seventh century, when a leading clan defeated competing clans and established the first centralized nation.[5] The head of this leading clan ascended to the emperor's throne. Other clans, which had previously ruled their own territories, submitted to the emperor their private lists of properties, including records of human households attached to their lands. The aggregated registry was named *koseki*, originally a Chinese term, meaning "house membership." The first nation of Japan compiled *koseki* to distribute land to each household to grow rice and to tax each household on the basis of the size of its land. The ancient *koseki* consisted of lists of the national properties of the emperor and represented the population via economic and inhabitant units. Thus, the national registry was born with the first establishment of the sovereign state by the emperor; however, listed individuals were not considered the subjects of the nation. Rather, the properties were.

After the ninth century, land was partly privatized and redistributed with the emergence of the aristocratic and warrior classes, and so was the registry. The ruling groups privatized the land and compiled their own registries, which gave rise to a feudal system under the warriors' regimes. In 1591, the conqueror of the Civil Wars, Toyotomi

Hideyoshi, investigated the land and population throughout Japan to internally pacify and disarm the farmers to prevent rebellion.[6] The registry Hideyoshi started was completed under the subsequent Tokugawa regime. It was called *ninbetsu-chō* (人別帳), meaning "human category book" in old Japanese.

The main category in *ninbetsu-chō* was occupation—at that time most subjects were farmers—which was equivalent to social class. Nobody was allowed to change occupations or to move or work outside of their registered places. This limitation prevented any reduction in the tax revenues remitted to feudal lords, which were based on land and products. People were even required to get permission from the lord to marry someone from another village or move out of the domain. *Ninbetsu-chō* helped restrain people's movements and tied them to the land in order to maintain tax revenue and social order. In 1670, the Tokugawa regime added the function of religious surveillance to *ninbetsu-chō* to search for hidden Christians.[7] Every year, local officials verified the religion of each villager: They required each villager to step on a picture of Jesus Christ, recorded the name of the Buddhist temple that guaranteed the person was not a Christian, and submitted aggregated lists to the central government through the feudal lord. The government scrutinized the lists every six years until the end of the Tokugawa regime. This combined book of occupational and religious registries is called *shūmon ninbetsu-chō* (宗門人別帳).

Both *ninbetsu-chō* and *shūmon ninbetsu-chō*, compiled separately in feudal territories, chained people to the land and the same occupation over generations. The national economy relied on the production of rice, so farmers were particularly mandated to stay in one location and cultivate the land for the warriors. When the ruling class abandoned its isolationist policy to join the global market in the mid-nineteenth century, industrialization of the economy became the immediate agenda. The restriction of people's movements contradicted industrialization, for which an independent labor force—free to move at the demand of capital—was essential.[8] The Meiji government needed to invent a new registration system that would support both the creation of a nation-state and industrialization—a departure from the role played by ancient property lists and strict bondage to land and occupation. Yet, a new ideology came into play to shuffle and shackle the people.

MAKING UP MODERN JAPANESE

With the Koseki Act of 1871, the Meiji regime started registering people as subjects of the new nation. The preamble of the act stated: "It is the most urgent and important task for the government to grasp the details of *koseki* members, because protection of the people is the central task for the government. . . . *Thus, if someone evades to register and be counted [by koseki], this person does not receive the protection from the government, and he almost chose by himself to be outside of the nation.*"[9] With a threatening tone, this message attempts to convince people to register in order to be included and protected. Though it is doubtful how exactly the government protects them afterward, protection of subjects by the state was the rationale for the creation of a national identification system. Interestingly, the government describes anyone who does not register as an outsider, although they may remain inside Japan. *Koseki* drew internal boundaries of Japanese membership among people and in turn territorialized the population through forced inclusion.

As such, *koseki* was a tool not only to enumerate the national population but also to contain, find, and use the subjects who were available for the government. *Koseki* went through several reforms after the 1871 act, and the 1886 version is considered the foundation of today's *koseki* that focuses on family relation.[10] But each *koseki* reform has been closely associated with major nation-building policies, such as taxation or conscription. *Koseki* collected more information to support these policies and employed a specific framework to make up people who could be useful for the new sovereign power.

Koseki uses a patriarchal family frame for registering units,[11] whereas its European counterparts use an individual-based frame. It requires all residents to register as a family unit at the municipal office of their address. One *koseki* file consists of a master of the family and all members who belong to the master. Each family member is defined with a title—for example, father, wife, and first son—in relation to the master. In other words, one has to belong to a family to be registered and to be categorized as a member of a family from birth. *Koseki* imposes a hierarchical order among the members, such as older over younger, lineal over collateral bloodline, and male over female.[12] Under the imperial

Constitution (1889-1946), these social orders ran parallel to the Civil Law, which stated that the master of the family had the right and duty to supervise his family members, that females did not have legal competence, and that the first son exclusively succeeded his father's mastership and inherited all the family property. The early modern *koseki* sometimes covered several generations under the same surname, making the file resemble the ancient *koseki*—the property list of the master's humans and nonhumans.

The address to register for *koseki*, called *honseki* (本籍), did not and still does not necessarily correspond to the residential address of the actual household or cohabitant members. It can be any real location, including the address of the Imperial Palace. Many register the master's residential address or an ancestor's address as a symbol of the patriarchal family group. Accordingly, the family unit registered in one *koseki* does not reflect the residing members, either. Some members of *koseki* are often distant from where the master resides and is registered. They may study, work, or even have their own households. *Honseki* represents nothing but the imaginary unity of a patriarchal family where every member belongs hierarchically. It can track who belongs to which families, their titles and ranks within the family, and relational changes among families by marriage and adoption. On the other hand, *koseki*'s structure was not adept at precisely tracking the movements of each member.

Thus, the imaginary character of *honseki* exposes *koseki*'s symbolic meaning. *Koseki* does not really reflect the actual being of the family in everyday life. Rather, it places the private entity of the family into a hierarchical relationship, incorporates it into public and social domains, and remakes it into a formal component of the modern state, with certain moral guidance. The *koseki* family is given the status of the smallest unit in the state apparatus. The family is no longer a private entity, but rather becomes a public one. *Koseki* is by definition publicly open for identification purposes, for business or marriage, though access by third parties has been increasingly restricted in recent practices.[13] The information was of course used for taxation and conscription. It aptly helped implement the national slogan of the time: "Enrich the Nation, Strengthen the Soldiers" (*fukoku-kyōhei*, 富国強兵).[14]

In this way, *koseki* goes much further than just counting people. At the heart of the *koseki* system is the establishment of a patriarchal order, which prepared the very basis of constructing new nationals in the everyday setting of the household. Though all nationals were newly given the same status as subjects, they were not equal to each other in *koseki*'s hierarchical disposal of memberships. *Koseki*'s patriarchal frame defines the position of the person, not only within the family but also within a larger social structure. How, then, does *koseki* involve inclusion and exclusion in society at large?

PATRIARCHY AS A VEHICLE TO SUPREME LOYALTY

First, *koseki* determines who are the legitimate members of the family: who can be included and excluded from *koseki* within the male-centric succession of the family. Under the Koseki Act and the Civil Law, a marriage became effective only when it was registered by the state, after it was agreed upon by the masters of both families, not by the couple. The woman was transferred from one family to another, and joined into another family of *koseki* by replacing her surname. This was known as "entering *koseki*"—referring to legitimate marriage in which the common surname of the couple was a determiner of legitimacy. In turn, *koseki* excluded women and children who did not share the master's surname and classified them as illegitimate family members. Though the official patriarchy was abolished in postwar Japan, the exclusion by surname remains in the present *koseki* system. *Koseki* defines a title for each family member in relation to the master, so it scrutinizes whether a woman has a legitimate husband or whether a child has a legitimate father.

A child born outside a legitimate family is socially stigmatized as a "private child" (*shiseiji*, 私生児), or "child outside marriage" (*kongaishi*, 婚外子) in legal terms, from the moment of birth registration. In the birth registration, the parent is required to check the box indicating whether the newborn is "legitimate" or "not legitimate," even today. If the father's surname is different from the mother's, the municipal office refuses to register the child, asks to erase the father's name, and then registers the child, leaving the father's name blank.[15] The father does not exist on legal record unless he takes the procedure of legal acknowledgment of the child as his own (and he can take this proce-dure without the consent of the mother). But a father's acknowledgment does not really remove the stigma attached to the "private child," as it is publicly inscribed in both the father's and the child's *koseki* that the child was born outside a legitimate marriage. To avoid such exposure, children born outside wedlock are sometimes fictitiously registered as children of their grandparents. Thus, *koseki* records biological family relations not accurately but rather symbolically.

The classification of (il)legitimate women and children exposes *ko-seki*'s gendered structure, too. For a woman, all her children are un-questionably legitimate, whether inside or outside of wedlock. The legitimacy of a child matters only to the succession of male-descended headship and inheritance. Thus, the (il)legitimacy box on a newborn's birth registration is a double inquiry because it unveils whether the mother is legitimate or illegitimate to reproduce a legitimate family for a man. It presupposes binary categories of women: all mothers are either a legitimate wife or illegitimate mistress to a man. Unregistered relationships are classified as deviant, corrupt, or behavior rebellious to the social order through *koseki*. Illegitimate women and children are produced and excluded through *koseki*'s patriarchal categories.

Second, as a social effect of *koseki*, the patriarchal frame has pro-moted an ideology of guarding male bloodlines and a culture of hon-oring surnames. Surnames play a fictitious role in male bloodlines in *koseki*, as already discussed, and were central to the succession of the family mastership from father to son in the warrior's tradition during the feudal era. People in other classes did not have surnames under the Tokugawa regime. Surnames were considered an honorary gift from the emperor, as warriors were delegated power to rule through surnames awarded by the emperor. That is why the emperor and his family never had a surname because it contradicted his existence as ruler.

In 1870, the year before the first Koseki Act was enacted, the gov-ernment permitted all classes other than warriors to take a surname. This permission became an order in 1875 that everyone must have a surname, because the surname was necessary to categorize a family by *koseki*.[16] The surname is technically attached not to the individual, but to the *koseki*. In fact, no one has a surname in the *koseki* file, includ-ing the master, where only first names of the members are listed. The surname is used as an index that enables the state to distinguish family units and to find individuals in the unit. Correspondingly, the emperor and his family without surnames are not included in *koseki.*

The Meiji government declared that all people were equal with the right to surnames. But surnames disseminated the ideology of male-centric bloodlines across the social classes and paradoxically facilitated competitions in the social classes for the honor of the family. For example, family members are expected not to merge with lower social classes through marriage in *koseki,* where the outcast class of the previous feudal system was most carefully avoided. This community is now called *hisabetsu-buraku* (被差別部落) but was called "nonhuman" in the Tokugawa regime and often searched out and exposed by Honseki, where their communities historically exist. *Koseki* has made it possible to trace lineage back over generations of the bloodline and identify who belonged to which blood, or classify which blood is noble or untouchable. *Koseki*'s patriarchal framework has caused the social exclusion of the outcast, and it continues the caste system through bloodline tracking. A hidden market that detects someone's social class through *koseki* still exists today and is used for preventing marriage with or employment of people from *hisabetsu-buraku.*

Third, as a social consequence, *koseki* created a fictitious picture of Japanese biological unity: All Japanese are connected to one another through bloodlines and share the same ancestor, ultimately the sacred emperor. As already discussed, family relations recorded in *koseki* do not necessarily reflect biological facts, but rather the surname masqueraded as bloodline and was treated as biological succession in and among families. As a result, the whole of *koseki* files symbolizes an inherent unity of the nation and reifies the myth that Japan consists of one race or ethnicity. This myth fits comfortably into the notion of the nation-state and persists today as a common misunderstanding that there are no ethnic minority groups in Japan. So, supported by biological unity, it is assumed that all Japanese share the same interests and destiny, led by the sacred leader.

For this reason, Bunmei Satō, the pioneer of critical studies on *koseki,* argues that patriarchy was incorporated into the constitutional monarchy for "educational" purposes, by embodying an imagined connection between the emperor and his subjects, implanting morality into the family sphere, and extending it to the state system.[17] The patri-archy *koseki* institutionalized was an instant vehicle for loyalty to the authorities in the state apparatuses. Loyalty to the emperor arose on the same horizon in constructing moral subjects: As sons and daughters obeyed their father, Japanese subjects should obey their emperor. As a father takes the best care of his children, the emperor gives his best to his people. Thanks to the emperor's wisdom and mercy, his subjects can make a good life, so they owe a debt to him. This was taught in school, in the workplace, in the family, and in the military, often with the rhetoric that all Japanese are The Emperor's Baby (*sekishi*, 赤子).[18]

This patriotic moral education was officially coded in the Imperial Rescript on Education in 1890 and even more reinforced along with the expansion of war. Children and youth were taught to happily die for the emperor, and dead soldiers became gods at the Yasukuni Shrine, so no worries. Dying for loyalty to the emperor was superior to all other moral values, and the dead were honorably discharged from other moral duties.[19] *Koseki*'s patriarchal order contributed to constructing a strong ideology of national unity and nationalism that dissolves any other moral virtues.

Ruth Benedict remarks that family is the first place the Japanese learn social order, unlike in the American family, where one does not have to behave formally.[20] In her book *The Chrysanthemum and the Sword: Patterns of Japanese Culture,* written to contribute to the Ameri-can policy of remaking post–World War II Japan, she observes that Japa-nese society is hierarchically organized from top to bottom, and people believe in hierarchy. Children grow up watching the wife bow to her husband, and the younger brother to the older brother. They learn a hierarchical value system based on gender, age, and the monopolized right of the first son to inheritance. Family members are trained to obey their family's will out of loyalty to the family. "For the exact same reason why the Japanese respect the family, they do not respect each family member or ties between the members," Benedict writes.[21] The individual applies this experience to the wider sphere of social life and automatically shows respect to anyone who is given a higher position than their own.

In sum, modern *koseki* remade the private family into a public entity and a moral model, within a male-centric classification of bloodlines.

It socially excludes women and children born outside patriarchal marriage and codifies "untouchable" bloodlines into a social class. Both
gender and class discrimination were institutionalized and automated
under *koseki*. At the same time, patriarchy was a successful vehicle for
bringing people into the fictitious biological unity of a "Japanese" race
and for worshipping the emperor and obeying state leaders to whom the
emperor delegated power. As the first modern national identification
system, *koseki* played a central role in constructing subjects of imperial
Japan whose identity was built on loyalty to authority. But the imagined
unity of subjects was also constructed against Others.

MARKING INTERNAL OTHERS: THE *KOSEKI* IN COLONIES

Benedict Anderson finds that Japan's imperial wars with China (1894)
and Russia (1904) and the annexation of Korea (1910) contributed more
than anything else to shaping the imagined identity of the "Japanese"
among its people and legitimizing the emperor and government as rep-
resenting the new nation.[22] The new nation-state in East Asia achieved
all these victories within fifteen years. The imperial wars consolidated
Japan's national identity as the "excellent student of Asia" and authen-
ticated the success of "go-fast imperialism."[23] Japan's nationalism was
typical of official nationalism from above, in Anderson's view. At the
same time, nationalism usefully concealed the inconvenient truth of
inequalities among the population, especially the extreme poverty produced by rapid industrialization. Spreading the myth of Japanese one-
ness and pureness, the government described the Japanese as an elite
and supreme race, in contrast with other neighboring Asians, who were
depicted as "backward" in a Eurocentric view.

   While *koseki* defines the Japanese, it simultaneously defines the
non-Japanese, who do not surrender to or belong to the emperor. The
first *koseki* registration of 1872 was mandated to register all residents
in its territory; those registered were all categorized as "Original Japanese" (*gen-nihonjin*, 原日本人) in terms of nationality.[24] Since that time,
Japanese nationality has been essentially passed only to the children of
those "Original Japanese" (*jus sanguinis*), and new residents have rarely
been included in *koseki*, even if they were born in Japan (*jus soil*).

   Oddly, the Nationality Act was enacted in 1899, more than a quarter
century after the first Koseki Act registered the members of the modern

state.[25] This indicates that *koseki* had overridden nationality, and the Nationality Act was written in accordance with *koseki*'s patriarchal membership. To safeguard the male bloodline, only children born from a Japanese father, not mother, could receive Japanese nationality until 1984.[26]

Consequently, foreigners have been strictly excluded from *koseki*. They are synonymous with a potential enemy of the emperor or an object to be conquered. Along with imperial expansion, the conquered were added to the emperor's property lists. Before Japan began waging an external war, internal colonization was already underway. The first *koseki* registration in 1872 covered the geographical area of Hokkaido, the northern island, where the Indigenous Ainu people had fought against Japanese invasion for centuries but had come under Japan's rule during the feudal era.[27] The Meiji regime sent a mass migration of armed settlers and forced strict homogenizing policies, including *koseki*, onto the Ainu. The Ainu people were forced to register their names in the Japanese style, which was linguistically different from their original names. In the south, the Meiji regime invaded the Kingdom of Ryūkyū and annexed it as the Okinawa Prefecture in 1879. The southwestern islands were included in *koseki* in 1886, and Okinawan names were also compulsorily converted to the Japanese style. The Indigenous people there, who had kept their own languages and cultures for centuries, were compelled to speak "standard" Japanese and assimilate their lifestyle to the Japanese way, as the gatekeepers living at the edges of Japanese territory. *Koseki* continued to construct the mystical unity of Japanese identity in the midst of policies that repressed ethnic, linguistic, and cultural diversity among the population.[28]

Upon Japan's victory in the first official war of the Meiji regime, the Sino-Japanese War of 1894-95, China ceded Taiwan to Japan, and Japan detached Korea from Chinese suzerainty. The Russo-Japanese War of 1904-5 solidified Japan's presence in Korea and Northeast China to block Russian interference and establish political and economic hegemony in the region. Japan then annexed Korea in 1910, at which point those populations, previously Others, became Japanese, as they were given Japanese nationality, but with unequal status vis-à-vis the "Original Japanese."

Japan deployed the *koseki* system in the new territories but separately from the Japanese *koseki*. First of all, the government chose a governor-general system to colonize Taiwan and Korea. Both governors-general in Taiwan and Korea were appointed by Japanese military officers and held de facto legislative power.[29] Japan promulgated the imperial Constitution in 1889, and the colonies came under its jurisdiction. The imperial Constitution gave legislative power only to the Diet, and its laws were endorsed by the emperor in the constitutional monarchy system. Thus, giving legislative power to the governor-general was unconstitutional and escaped democratic checks and balances, as was heatedly debated in the Japanese Diet.[30] Nonetheless, the early period of colonization in Taiwan and Korea particularly faced constant armed resistance by the local people, in which the Japanese military claimed emergency power to create laws for security purposes. This exceptional power essentially endured until the end of Japanese colonial management.

The laws created by the governor-general were not called law—*hōritsu* (法律) in Japanese—but *ritsuryō* (律令)in Taiwan and *seirei* (制令) in Korea.[31] The governor-general could choose to enact some of laws created by the Japanese Diet but constructed an independent legal system, separate from the Japanese one. These legal tricks were obscured by the ambiguous administrative terms that detached the colonies from Japan: "inside land" (*naichi*, 内地) referring to Japan, and "outside land" (*gaichi*, 外地) referring to colonies. The imperial Constitution applied to both *naichi* and *gaichi*, which made all residents Japanese nationals on those territories, but people in *gaichi* were placed outside constitutional protections and legal rights by the governor-general system. Through this legal trick, the Japanese were able to claim sovereignty over conquered lands while containing the constitutional rights of newly created Japanese subjects.

As a result, the Koseki Act was never implemented in Taiwan and Korea, though the *koseki* system was adapted. Each colony had a different regulation about the *koseki*. The major files compiled under the Great Empire of Japan are as follows: Japanese *koseki* (of the "Original Japanese," including the Ainu and Okinawa), Taiwanese *koseki*, Korean *koseki*, and Sakhalin *koseki*.[32] The extended *koseki* systems listed the new members of the empire but simultaneously stratified the population into hierarchically organized racial/ethnic categories.

A distinctive marker of this inclusive exclusion was *honseki*. As mentioned earlier, Honseki does not have to be a residential address in Japan and often only symbolizes the patriarchal origin of the family, but in the colonies, it needed to be a residential address. The Taiwanese were able to register only in the Taiwan *koseki* and Koreans in the Korean *koseki*, even if they lived in Japan. Because the Taiwanese and Korean *koseki* were created by the pseudo-law of the governor-general system, there was no legal bridge between the Japanese and colonial files to facilitate the exchange of registered people. This absence of such a legal procedure was intentionally left out until the assimilation policy promoted intermarriage, at which time the government allowed Koreans to marry Japanese and move into the Japanese *koseki*.[33]

In Taiwan, the preliminary investigation of households took place in 1896, the year after the founding of the Taiwan government-general. While in Japan the family head had legal responsibility to register, in Taiwan the police investigated and recorded household information. The police collected more data about Taiwanese households than the Japanese *koseki* did, such as race, behavior, criminal record, and opium habit. The preliminary *koseki* was combined with a community-based policing system in 1899: the *hokō* (保甲) system, created to "suppress the bandits."[34] Only the Taiwanese were subjected to both registration and policing systems; Japanese residing in Taiwan and ethnic minorities were exempted. In 1902, the Japanese imperial Diet passed the Census Act, which was first implemented in Taiwan in 1905, before the homeland. While the census for the homeland was designed to collect household data on eight items, Taiwan households were subjected to twenty-two items for policing purposes.[35] The first census in Taiwan was the foundation of Taiwan *koseki* and a police state.

In 1933, the Taiwanese governor-general issued an order that elevated the household investigation to an equal position with Japanese *koseki*, as Taiwanese *koseki*.[36] For the government, it was a solution to the problem of intermarriage between Japanese and Taiwanese. Because the Taiwanese had not had *koseki* until then, many couples did not register their marriages. In the event that a married Taiwanese person moved to Japan with a Japanese spouse, he or she was not able to move the Honseki to Japan. Similar to Korea, the governor-general allowed marriage as an exceptional reason for a Taiwanese person to move their Honseki and enter the Original Japanese *koseki*. By doing this, the government could track the relationships and movements of colonial individuals, too.

In Korea, Japan had taken over political power before the 1910 annexation and initiated household investigations in the name of the Korean government and the Civil Registration Act of 1909. Household data was passed on to the Korean *koseki* in 1923, by the Korean Koseki Order. Some Korean lawyers demanded that the Japanese government implement a Koseki Act in Korea, instead of a Koseki Order, so they could change Honseki by marriage, remove the racial/ethnic boundary, and be treated equally to Japanese subjects. In a petition written in 1936, they claimed that it would promote the government slogan, "the Unity of Mainland and Korea" (*naisen-ittai*, 内鮮一体), and that "because of the desire to become a *naichi* person, Koreans would compete with each other to marry Japanese, become Japanese, and give birth to genuine Japanese, which is also beneficial for both governance and conscription."[37] But the government responded apathetically: "Implementing the Koseki Act in Korea means removing the distinction between the mainland and Korea, which sounds ideal for the future, but is too early. Some Japanese may move their *honseki* to Korea to escape conscription."[38] Japan did not implement a conscription system in Korea until the very final stage of World War II, because of the fundamental suspicion of Korean loyalty to the Japanese emperor.

The Sakhalin *koseki* also started with a preliminary police investigation of the household and then was elevated to *koseki* like other colonies. It first included only Japanese who resided in Sakhalin, and then the Ainu people. Other Indigenous peoples, such as Gilyak, called "savage" (*dojin*, 土人), were left out of *koseki*, similar to the Indigenous peoples called "barbarian" (*banjin*, 蛮人) in Taiwan. Sakhalin *koseki* merged with Japanese *koseki* in 1943 with the integration of governmental sections.[39]

ASSIMILATE BUT SEGREGATE

In all the colonies, people were very aware of the unequal status they were given in the colonial *koseki*, so they demanded equal application of the law. In the colonies, the police most likely retained *koseki* documents for policing purposes, while in Japan, the municipal offices stored *koseki* for administrative purposes. *Koseki* imposed the Japanese nationality on the colonial population and legitimated racial and ethnic segregation within the empire. The Ainu and Okinawans in Japan had also been segregated by *koseki* at the beginning. Their files were organized separately and inscribed with their racial/ethnic origins. This can be understood as an inclusive exclusion,[40] because *koseki* included the colonial population but classified it for exclusion from the constitutional principle through governor-general system. Being placed into the state of exception, the colonial population was deprived of the right to vote and to work for the military or government. But the social repercussions of the racial/ethnic marks that *koseki* inscribed on the colonial population were much broader and deeper when linked with cultural repression.

The impact of racial/ethnic segregation by *koseki* should be contextualized with assimilation policies that were rolled out in tandem. To remake the colonial populations as "Japanese," the government deployed strict assimilation policies in Taiwan and Korea, as it had in Hokkaido and Okinawa. Those policies typically pressured or required people to speak Japanese, to change their names to the Japanese style, to participate in Shinto worship of the emperor as the national god, and eventually to behave, think, and live like Japanese people. However, no matter how much they conformed to the imaginary unity of the Japanese, they were still clearly tracked and marked as internal Others in *koseki*. *Koseki* included Others but classified them as second-class nationals, through exclusionary categories. Inclusion in exclusionary categories produces and reproduces Others, against whom discrimination is rationalized. *Koseki* represents the deceptive, dual structure of assimilation policies that allude to equality but scrutinize the colonized as Others over generations through unavoidable inclusive exclusion.

Along with mobilizing the colonial population for war, the government needed to modify the unequal distinction between Japanese and internal Others. In Korea, the volunteer soldier system was established in 1938, and it moved toward conscription in 1942.[41] The government attempted to apply the Mobilization Act to the colonies in 1944, forcing people to work in factories and in other industries to support the war. Equalizing colonial *koseki* with Japanese *koseki* was occasionally proposed within the government, but government leaders never removed the racializing distinctions or allowed Korean people to move their Honseki to Japan even though they lived in Japan. According to a note by the Ministry of Internal Affairs, moving Honseki was more than just a simple legal procedure. Rather, it would cause "a fundamental problem of mixing ethnicities and threatens assimilation policies and the Japanese purity."[42] Conversely, the idea that Japanese people would move their Honseki to the Korean or Taiwanese *koseki* was even more unacceptable to the government, because doing so would imply assimilating Japanese with Taiwanese and Korean culture.

After all, Otherness never merged with the purity of the Japanese as defined in *koseki*, even though that purity was a complete fiction. Through the racializing distinctions in the national ID systems, Japan established a racial order among the population. *Koseki* noted their Otherness and underpinned ethnic rankings devised by the empire: Original Japanese at the top, followed by Ainu and Okinawa, then Taiwanese and Koreans, and at the bottom, the smaller groups of Indigenous peoples from the northern and southern Pacific islands.[43] In terms of identity formation, this racial hierarchy never allowed the colonial individual an identity equal to Japanese; rather, it imposed the inadequate identity of second-class Japanese. Through racial sorting, colonial subjects remained internal Others within the Japanese empire.

In April 1945, four months before the downfall of the empire, the government finally gave its colonial subjects the right to vote. But the expansion of the franchise was never put into practice and was suspended in December 1945, under the Allied Forces' occupation, to prevent Koreans and Taiwanese from voting.[44] Masataka Endō points out that even though the Japanese government needed to concede the right to vote to its colonial subjects—facing a serious shortage of soldiers and workers—it never compromised the application of the Koseki Act to the colonies until the end of the imperial era. Endō writes: "Even in the context of political reform for the colonies, the wall between *naichi* and *gaichi* in *koseki* was solidly guarded. The distinction was treated as the sacred and untouchable part of the Japanese colonial governance."[45]

KOSEKI'S DISCIPLINARY POWER IN JAPAN

Koseki brought different effects of surveillance to the metropolis and colonies. *Koseki* clearly shows a disciplinary characteristic that works on individual bodies as surveillance in the metropolis.[46] *Koseki* first invented people who fell into the category of "Japanese" and eventually constructed the subjects that embodied and represented the nation with a collective identity.[47] Although *koseki* does not physically provide visual supervision, to this day it sets people in panoptic relation with the state. *Koseki* embodies the state's inward gaze and automates soul training, which is defined as grooming the objects of its gaze to become loyal subjects of the supreme authority. This not only is compelled at an abstract level and repeatedly practiced by the government but also is embedded in thousands of eyes among the people who also internalize patriarchal morality. *Koseki* extends the effect of panoptic surveillance to two other dimensions: lateral and synoptic.

First, *koseki* sets up internal monitoring among family members in the same file. Because any individual changes in *koseki* may affect other member's social rank, the members laterally check one another to ensure that nobody hurts the family name. Members can easily notice and intervene in the behavior of others because the file is *their own record*. Any individual actions against the social order that may evoke shame, dishonor, or sanction toward the whole family are repressed or removed. For example, if a member of an upper-class family wants to marry someone of a lower class, it is not uncommon for other members to blame them via the rhetoric of "soiling the *koseki*." If someone divorces, they have "damaged *koseki*," family members would say. *Koseki* can thus facilitate spontaneous, mutual surveillance among family members.

Second, in theory, *koseki* is open to the public since the family is not a private entity but rather a public one, and a model for morality.[48] The wider society, not just the state, can watch over the individual and the family from a patriarchal vantage point. It becomes synoptic surveillance when many watch over a few through institutions and media and condemn the delinquency of the individual and the family. Accusations against a family's morals disrupt the family's protection of an individual member. A person is more likely to gain support from their own family when supported by society. Once society opposes or denounces them, the family has to punish the individual for having damaged the family's name. Otherwise, the whole family is synoptically punished by society. "Approval of the outside society is important in Japan incomparably to any other countries" because the public eye penetrates the family and the individual.[49] *Koseki*'s structure contributes to exposing the individual's and the family's lives to the public eye, which views them as deviant and metes out punishment for going against the social order.

Thus, *koseki* automates three dimensions of monitoring for the patriarchal social order: panoptic, lateral, and synoptic. These triple cross-checks make the Japanese social culture of surveillance perhaps more powerful than the Western model of the panopticon. Surrounded by light from three windows, self-discipline is multiply secured and intensified. One is not even sure where self-discipline originates: from the state, the family, or society? Or perhaps one does not even think about the source, because disciplinary thinking is already so much a part of oneself, even before establishing one's agency. Benedict notes how exhaustively Japanese youth are trained to observe their own behavior: constantly calculating how other people will respond to them and judging how they should behave.[50] The probability of being monitored by others—whether monitoring is present in reality or not—creates spontaneous self-surveillance. This three-dimensional surveillance in Japanese society builds extreme obstacles and social isolation around a person who decides to take action against the status quo.

Additionally, it should not be overlooked that nation building, begun with *koseki* registration, was a response to an external demand triggered by a new political economy to remake the agricultural population into an industrial one. *Koseki* was also implemented as a technique of population control and social sorting for the modern regime. It enlists, counts, and sorts members of the imagined community.[51] When Western countries demanded that Japan open its market for trade, the Meiji regime needed to ease the bonds tying the population to land and occupations that restricted movement under the feudal system, and instead to make people available as mobile labor power for industry in the locations where they were needed. The government gave people freedom of occupation and movement, but it shackled them to the patriarchal family and a new moral code of conduct to maintain the social order.

Foucault states that disciplinary society is indispensable to the development of modern capitalism.[52] Disciplinary power repeatedly trains the human body on an individual basis, having "'got rid of the peasant' and given him 'the air of a soldier,'"[53] and it remakes the individual into a docile body for certain patterns of behavior demanded in the factory and at school. Disciplinary power capitalizes on, and disposes of, the individual's time, space, and body, for maximum production on a mass scale. Giving the population mobility with disciplinary ties to patriarchy enabled the Meiji government to make the population available for rapid industrialization, exploit women and children positioned at the bottom of patriarchal order, and gain competitiveness to adapt to the global market. Japan's modern economic development came into being along with the new form of surveillance represented by *koseki*, that is, "thousands of eyes posted everywhere, mobile attentions ever on the alert, a long, hierarchized network," in Foucault's words.[54]

This economically productive aspect of modern power is more clearly articulated by the concept of biopower.[55] For Foucault, the creation of individual docile bodies is not enough to sustain the systematic development of capital on a mass scale, which led him to analyze how power incorporates a population into the economic process as a technique of population control. Especially for the availability of free labor power, capitalism requires "methods of power capable of optimizing force, aptitudes, and life in general without at the same time making them more difficult to govern."[56] Thus, biopower works on both ends of an anatomopolitics of the human body and a biopolitics of the population.[57] In that sense, *koseki* as surveillance in the metropolis reflect both ends of biopower: It creates docile bodies by using patriarchal moral codes and surveillance, and it makes the population available as mobile labor power for industrialization.

KOSEKI'S DISCIPLINARY POWER IN COLONIES

However, *koseki*'s productive aspect as biopower was rarely demonstrated in the colonies, where disciplinary power was also exercised differently than in the metropolis. *Koseki* was central to controlling the colonial population via policing and assimilation, but not to increasing productivity or optimizing the labor force.

First, the colonial population was not allowed as much mobility as was the group at the top of the hierarchy in Japan. In both Taiwanese and Korean *koseki*, the residential address was registered as the *honseki* by police, unlike the Japanese *koseki*, in which the *honseki* can be imaginary and registered by the family master. Taiwanese and Koreans were not allowed to move their *honseki* to Japan, even if they physically lived there. To track their movements, the government implemented a supplemental registration system, the Temporary Residence File, in 1914.[58] This file was initiated to capture the locations of colonial and foreign subjects who did not have *honseki* in Japan. But the system later expanded to encompass the whole population for wartime mobilization. It was also necessary for Taiwanese and Koreans to obtain permission from the police to visit Japan or go abroad. The government particularly restricted Taiwanese from visiting the Chinese continent to prevent them from meeting Chinese nationalists and members of the growing anti-Japanese movement. For strict identification purposes, photos were used in Taiwanese passports before they appeared in Japanese ones.[59] Novel techniques of population control are often first tested on colonial subjects, as we saw with the census first implemented in Taiwan. Under tight regulation, colonial subjects were never free to move to produce wealth; rather, they were banned from traveling, left to life in poverty and starvation.

Second, in terms of *koseki*'s repressive role, the colonial population was essentially placed in a state of exception vis-à-vis the imperial Constitution and other legal rights, including the Koseki Act. Colonial subjects did not possess equal status to participate in the modern market system. Their lands and natural resources were taken away by Japanese colonists, and their wages were almost always lower than those of their Japanese counterparts. As *koseki* was institutionalized, the colonial population was stratified at the bottom of the socioeconomic structure. *Koseki* was less used to protect listed members on colonial soil, contrary to the preamble of Koseki Act of 1871, which promised to protect members of the nation. It was not used for their entitlement or welfare, only for policing and assimilation. On the same track, the Japanese Nationality Act was also not applied to Korea.[60] This law provides the right to secede from Japanese nationality or change nationality. The Japanese government was afraid that Koreans would secede from Japanese nationality and obtain other nationalities if the law was applied to Koreans, in which case Japan would not have full authority to capture and punish Korean dissenters. The government used nationality as a means to seize its colonial subjects—a case of inclusive exclusion.[61] Japanese nationality given to Koreans was a legal cage and invalid as a right.

As a result, in the colonies, *koseki* did not construct as many loyal identities as it did in the homeland. *Koseki* succeeded in internalizing the gaze of the state as surveillance among individuals in the top group of the racial hierarchy, but the privileged Japanese identity was constructed against Others, the rest of the hierarchy. For these internal Others, becoming a loyal "Japanese" created a deep contradiction, as the internalization of an inferior identity.

Leo T. S. Ching's *Becoming "Japanese"* delves into the existential contradiction and identity crisis experienced by Taiwanese intellectuals who needed to navigate their lives in the midst of Japan's colonization and assimilation policies.[62] One of the original texts Ching used for his analysis, *The Orphan of Asia*, presents an allegory of both the inevitability and the impossibility of obtaining a fixed and autonomous identity under internal colonization.[63] In the novel, a Taiwanese teacher whose experience overlaps with the life of author Wu Cho-liu (Go Daku-ryū, 呉濁流) goes on a journey from colonized Taiwan to imperial Japan and to war-ridden China, but he always finds himself in contradiction and alienation, eventually returning to Taiwan, where he goes insane. *The Orphan of Asia* expresses the internal struggles of colonial intellectuals whose identities were split and who found no place to belong because the Taiwanese were fundamentally categorized as second-class subjects in the imperial order and exposed to harsh assimilation policies and social exclusion.

A similar contradiction has been passed on to Korean and Taiwanese descendants residing in present-day Japan, where they have lived their whole lives. Many of them conceal their ethnic identities to avoid social discrimination in education, employment, and marriage. Such outer conditions become inner struggles to obtain a fixed and autonomous identity as Korean, Taiwanese, or Japanese. This identity crisis can be so serious that it sometimes triggers suicide or violence against others.[64] Coercive categories are neither completely internalized nor lead necessarily to resistance and change. These struggles reaffirm the ongoing power of identification and categorization over marginalized social groups.

If disciplinary power is most successful in achieving the spontaneous internalization of authority among individuals and eventually
constructing a person who supports the authority, the automated mechanism of identifying with authority is less likely to function in the colonies than in the metropolis. How, then, could the government control
the colonial population without a united, national identity? Evidently,
through exclusion and violence.

Therefore, the *koseki* system as surveillance brought different results
to the metropolis and to the colony. In the metropolis, the patriarchal
ideology inscribed in *koseki* was instilled and internalized among individuals through its three-dimensional surveillance mechanism, and
so it constructed loyal subjects as a disciplinary power. But in the colonies, the internalization of *koseki*'s ideology was much more limited and
twisted, since it classified the colonized as internal Others. For colonial
subjects, identifying with the Japanese was a contradictory, self-alien-
ating experience. While the productive aspect of biopower is unseen in
the colonial state of exception, the disciplinary power of *koseki* is mainly
used for more direct surveillance of individuals for policing, assimilating, banning, and punishing.

SUTURING NATION BUILDING AND COLONIALISM

In summary, as the first centralized ID system, *koseki* defined who was
Japanese and who was Other in order to construct the new nation-state's
population as loyal subjects of the emperor. *Koseki* adopted a patriarchal
framework of family, marriage, bloodline, surname, and inheritance,
and thus it constructed a people who perceive themselves through the
gendered hierarchy. The vehicle of patriarchy, at the same time, brought
people to worship authority in other social relations. A Japanese person
who is expected to be a loyal son within the family order, a loyal student
for the school, or a loyal worker for the company should most importantly be a loyal subject for the emperor. Self-devotion and collective
sacrifice were inscribed on docile Japanese bodies.

Koseki has exerted disciplinary power as surveillance over individuals by internalizing the sovereign gaze toward the self. Yet far beyond
visual oversight in the panoptic model, *koseki* mobilized thousands
of eyes among the people in three dimensions—panoptic, lateral, and

synoptic—to watch and check one another through internalized patriarchal and imperial categories. Any deviants were referred for social pressure, segregation, ostracism, and expulsion—and at worst, physical death during wartime. Despite the nation as an imagined community,[65] the reified institution is real. *Koseki* contributed to economic production by freeing people from their feudal tie to the land, but it bound them instead to the system's patriarchal ideology to follow authority, whether that of the family master, the factory manager, or the emperor. The national identification system indeed constituted "Japanese" through categories of loyal subjects who monitor one another in their everyday lives.[66]

Koseki also included the colonial population but marked them as internal Others or an enemy within.[67] The inclusion of the Ainu, Okinawans, Taiwanese, Koreans, and other racially categorized people to *koseki* did not mean equal treatment as Japanese, and the categories were stratified according to the racial/ethnic order of the empire. For those new subjects, joining Japanese *koseki* was strictly prohibited in order to protect the purity of the imaginary "Original Japanese." The colonial legal manipulation placed them under the state of inclusive exclusion, where people did not have freedom to move, travel, or participate in nation building.

It is important to note that inclusion in national membership did not guarantee equality for the included, nor did assimilation policies. Rather, they were inscribed as inferior subjects in the national identification system. But because of this exclusionary treatment of internal Others, *koseki*'s effect of constructing loyal subjects was limited in the colonies. As the Japanese police collected personal data from Taiwanese and Korean households for policing purpose, Japanese imperialism was challenged by armed and unarmed resistance in the colonies. Japan's disciplinary power was at the forefront in the colonies, but not all-powerful, and troubling to their identities.

Obviously, the registration helped the government to identify who was available to fight in wars and to mobilize the population for national interests. In the West, state apparatuses were already shaped by imperial competition and conflict, which consolidated the information state as discussed in chapter 1.[68] The growth of the internal information state enabled external battles over colonial lands and resources, and in turn, the acquisition of colonies nurtured national pride. In the Japanese case, too, the government obtained new forms of knowledge about the population through *koseki*, which enabled it to fight imperial wars and construct a collective identity in opposition to Others.

In this sense, *koseki* exposes a simultaneous, intertwined process of nation building and imperial competition in modern Japan, which defines who is Japanese and how they should be. The national ID system binds the two sides of internal classification and external expansion to establish a new social order. Internal and external politics together draw the boundaries of Japanese identity. One cannot stand without the other. This must be reiterated because the bright achievements of modernity tend to overshadow the misery and violence of colonization, as well as experiences of colonial identification and surveillance that were previously overlooked, unrecorded, or hidden in the history of nation-states. The two sides must be sutured together to provide a view of the whole. The next three chapters shine light into the shadows of modern Japan.

Koseki reveals the social structure of modern Japan that centers the holy emperor is founded on gender, race, and class segregation. *Koseki*'s categories, therefore, have deeply grounded and naturalized a patriarchal way of thinking among the people. The panoptic, lateral, and synoptic effects are correspondingly alive and have helped reproduce hierarchy-friendly male dominance in postwar Japan. Even more crucially, how the Japanese citizen-subjects describe, act, and react to neighboring Asians through a colonial lens has been contained within the epistemological framework of the national identification system. The *koseki* system still stands as the major source of imagined homogeneity of Japanese society in the twenty-first century.

CHAPTER THREE

JAPAN'S MAXIMUM
SURVEILLANT ASSEMBLAGE

*Separating "Bandits" from "Innocents" in the
Colonial Threshold of "Manchukuo"*

Conditioned by the advent of the nation-state, industrial capitalism, and other revolutions of the modern age, imperialism
became increasingly multidimensional, mass-mobilizing, and
all-encompassing. The relationship between modernity and
empire, moreover, was dialectical: just as modernization conditioned the growth of empire, the process of imperialism shaped
the conditions of modern life.

—*(Louise Young, Japan's Total Empire, 1998)*[1]

Fingerprint technology was first widely incorporated into Japan's identification systems in Northeast China for the purpose of population
control. Why was the forerunner of biometrics adopted in a mass scale
there earlier than in Japan and its colonies of Taiwan and Korea?

To answer the question, we must unfold a large map of Japanese surveillance activities in Northeast China to see how fingerprints worked
in concert with these surveillance activities. In other words, a fingerprint was meaningless without files of personal data collected through
registration, interrogation, or other means. Japan's occupational force

Kwantung Army, its intelligence agents, and other colonial institutions operationalized people's fingerprints as individual identifiers to match or unlock their personal data. To understand the significance of fingerprint identification, it is first necessary to know who used the information and how they attached it to ID cards that connected prints to personal files. This relationship between ID cards and surveillance systems presaged contemporary interactions between individual digital devices and networked databases.

This chapter lays out the big picture of surveillance activities deployed for policing and security in Manchuria. Kevin D. Haggerty and Richard V. Ericson theorize the "rhizomatic" character of electronic surveillance as the surveillant assemblage (chapter 1).[2] Building on this notion, I call the convergence of discrete surveillance agents and systems Japan's "maximum surveillant assemblage." Although Japan covered Northeast China with surveillance dragnets before the computer age, the concept is useful for unpacking the complex interactions between different agents, institutions, and technologies of surveillance. It sheds light on the multiple actors who participated in policing through separate systems and who assembled once-discrete data sets to create meaning out of the different kinds of personal data collected. The police, military agencies, labor organizations, and other colonial apparatuses mushroomed in Manchuria, engaged in mass surveillance for their own organizational goals, and together shaped the maximum surveillant assemblage. The plurality of surveillance practitioners and the interoperability of personal data predate the digitization of technologies, though there is no question that the capacities of data mining were enhanced by digitization.

The characteristics of the pseudo-state of Manchukuo indicate why Japan deployed fingerprint identification there specifically. The historian Louise Young calls Manchukuo *Japan's Total Empire*. Like a total war, the "total" in this context refers to "a process of empire building that was multicausal and multidimensional, all-encompassing and, by the end, all-consuming" Japanese imperialism took every opportunity to consume the colonial population for its own supremacy while repressing it as a future risk for the empire.[3] For Young, Manchukuo was unique in its total mobilization for the benefit of a sovereign power. Both capitalist and state systems were rapidly constructed by various agents of the imperial imagination, freely drawn on continental soil, and seized from Others.

In what follows, I begin with a brief historical overview of Japan's involvement in Northeast China and the declaration of Manchukuo. Next, the paradoxical characteristics of Manchukuo will be discussed as settler colonialism,[4] and as what I call the "colonial threshold," in which people are simultaneously placed inside and outside the law. Then, I explore Japan's policing agencies and the Kwantung Gendarmerie's leading position in the surveillance assemblage. To immediately eliminate "bandits," Manchukuo imported the technique of "thought crime" investigation, including various tortures, from the Tokkō (特高) police in Japan. Security laws and decrees were rapidly compiled in the name of civilization and conferred colonial agents with expansive surveillance power over the population.

After identifying the major agents of Japan's surveillant assemblage, I discuss the institutions charged with registration and community surveillance. The identification techniques already tested in other Japanese colonies, described in chapter 2, were also brought to Northeast China, but Japanese agents took them much further in the colonial threshold. Villages were displaced from strategic points and residents' fingerprinted ID cards were regularly checked to cut off the flow of materials and communication between the armed resistance and the people. Last, through the words of Wang Xuancai—a farmer I interviewed in Heilongjiang Province—the chapter contextualizes how local people experienced the agents and institutions of mass surveillance all at once or sequentially. Wang Xuancai's parents survived Japan's maximum surveillant assemblage, but his uncle was caught by the dragnets and ended up in Unit 731.

THE MAKING OF MANCHUKUO

As seen in the previous chapter, Japan's imperial expansion, in parallel with its nation building, encompassed Northeast China after the Russo-Japanese War (1904-5). Japan managed to win the battle but took tremendous losses: More than one million soldiers were mobilized, and eighty thousand were killed.[5] Through the Treaty of Portsmouth in 1905, Japan took over Russian leases in the south of Changchun in the region called Manchuria, including the management of railways, attached areas, and mining concessions. Japan named the leased territories in Lüshun and Dalian Kwantung Province and established the Kwantung Government-General, which was split into the Kwantung Government and Kwantung Army in 1919.[6] When Japan annexed Korea in 1910, the colonizing power expanded its political and economic interests into the Chinese territory adjacent to Korea.

The railway was the central conduit by which the imperial state transferred people and goods, developed industries, and pushed territorial boundaries. The Japanese government founded the South Manchuria Railway Company in 1906, commonly known as Mantetsu (満鉄) in Japanese. Mantetsu—a joint agreement linking corporations and the government—overlaid a corporate model onto Japan's colonial management, much like the relationships between the East India Company and British government. Mantetsu not only built the railways but also operated air-conditioned express trains and fifteen Western-style hotels, as well as several universities, archives, and libraries in major cities.[7] As the leading developer in early twentieth-century Northeast China, it owned the coal mines, seaports, and steelworks, and grew into the biggest Japanese stock company of the time.

The company's administrative services along the railways were particularly valuable as Japan turned its economic presence into political authority in the region. Mantetsu developed a large research section for economic planning and hired academics and social engineers who had not been able to find suitable jobs in Japan under the surge of antisocialist policies and purges.[8] Those Japanese researchers and technicians found Manchuria to be a place of opportunity and brought novel ideas for urban design, modern architecture, and the latest technologies to the experimental site. Mantetsu's research section turned into a sort of think tank for the architecture of Manchukuo. It established a corporate-state model that ran the state for capital development, while internally competing against the Kwantung Army and Kwantung Government-General over colonial management. The Kwantung Army was garrisoned in the railway linked areas to secure a privileged position in Northeast China. Seeing it as an opportunity to take over German leases in China, Japan took part in World War I (1914–18) and sent troops in the name of protecting Japanese residents of Shandong Province, located in the south of Manchuria.

Meanwhile, the Chinese Revolution of 1911 overthrew the Qing dynasty and established the Republic of China. Growing nationalism began to challenge Japan, the late imperial power. In 1928, the Chinese Nationalist Army and the Japanese Army fought in Jinan, the capital city of Shandong Province, which alarmed the Chinese, who saw Japan as a major invader competing with the British and other Europeans to divide up the country.[9]

On September 18, 1931, the Kwantung Army blew up a railway line near the city of Shenyang (called Fengtian until 1945) and opened fire against the regional warlord Zhang Xueliang (張学良), blaming him for the blasting.[10] The plot enabled the Kwantung Army to occupy the three northeastern provinces of Jilin, Heilongjiang, and Liaoning within a few months.[11] In that time, it placed thirty million people under its control.[12] Because the General Staff of the Kwantung Army, Ishiwara Kanji, Itagaki Seishirō, and others, secretly initiated the attack without the permission of the Japanese government, Japan never formally declared war against China and called the takeover the "Manchurian Incident." The invasion marked the government's loss of civilian control over the army and the further acceptance of the illegal expansion of battle lines in China for the next fifteen years.[13] The growing military presence in the government eventually destroyed Japan's fragile democracy, which had achieved "universal suffrage" in 1925. Despite the exclusion of women, the political party system had been up and running, and Diet members had been elected by popular vote. The Kwantung Army's military adventurism made no sense of deliberate debates in the Diet and superseded diplomacies in the landsliding invasion of China.

Ishiwara and Itagaki explained that the Manchurian Incident was meant to help local Chinese people who were struggling for independence from corrupt Chinese warlords. But they eventually gave up their original plot to annex this region to the territory of the Great Empire of Japan due to increasing Chinese resistance and international pressure against Japan's aggression.[14] As a compromise, in March 1932, Japan declared the creation of the state of Manchukuo as a multiethnic and multicultural nation. The Kwantung Army appointed the Qing dynasty's last emperor, Puyi, as head of state and set its capital in Changchun, renaming it Xinjing (新京), or "new capital." Japan publicized it as Heaven on Earth, where people would see a "kingly way of governance" and "racial harmony among five ethnic groups"—Manchurian, Han,

Mongolian, Korean, and Japanese.[15] Puyi became emperor of Manchukuo two years later, after changing its name to the Empire of Manchukuo, as the Kwantung Army had promised him.[16]

In the beginning, the Manchurian government consisted of four divisions: legislative, administrative, judicial, and auditorial. But the legislative division, which supposedly produced laws, like Parliament or Congress in a republic, was never realized because people were not enfranchised.[17] The auditorial division was soon abolished. Thus, the administrative division of the Department of State (Kokumuin, 国務院) and the courts of law constituted the government, and the Department of State monopolized legislative power. Laws and regulations were proposed and settled in the Council of Department of State (Kokumuinkaigi, 国務院会議) and endorsed by Puyi. The Council of Department of State consisted of the prime minister, other ministers of Manchukuo, and the heads of administrative bureaus. Although the ministers were Chinese, the preliminary assembly of the council consisted of the General Staff of the Kwantung Army and Japanese bureaucrats, who carefully selected the subject matter for the council.[18] This unofficial but systematic screening was called "internal guidance" (naimenshidō, 内面指導) by the Japanese, who always took the lead in important decision-making for the supposedly independent Manchukuo.[19] This skewed concentration of administrative power characterized the governing structure of Manchukuo.

Despite its government's claim to be a modern, civilized nation, Manchukuo was clearly a puppet regime, as it allowed a foreign army to occupy its area, and all administrative decisions had to be approved by the army. The League of Nations did not admit Manchukuo's statehood. The Lytton Report, an investigation by Victor Alexander Lytton, proposed that Japan jointly manage the three northeastern provinces with other foreign powers.[20] Dissatisfied, Japan left the League in 1933. The chief delegate to the League at the time was Matsuoka Yōsuke, who had worked as vice president of Mantetsu from 1927 to 1930, on mining resources. With increasing international isolation, Manchukuo remained in a state of internal war, as the Kwantung Army fought armed resistance by Chinese Nationalists, Communists, local warlords, and guerrillas. Despite the facade of modern urban planning and technology, Manchukuo remained under the military regime of the Kwantung

Army until 1945. The continuous internal war and instability of the puppet regime prompted it to impose various surveillance methods on the population.

How was it possible for the Japanese to execute such a reckless plan: to invade another country and create a new "nation" within it while completely ignoring the outrage and criticism of the Chinese and international society?

"Defend the Manchurian Lifeline!"—the popular slogan, coined by Matsuoka, became widespread in Japanese newspapers and magazines.[21] Japan's first two wars had contributed to the rapid growth of the mass media.[22] Its people were infected with war fever after the Manchurian Incident by the mass-produced image of "Manchuria as a lifeline for Japan."[23] Print media reminded readers of their collective sacrifice in the Russo-Japanese War, and claimed Japan's legitimate right to territorialize Northeast China due to the loss. Northeast China became a major battlefield in the Russo-Japanese War, referred to as a place that should be redeemed by "100,000 spirits of dead soldiers and 20 billion [yen] of national expenditure."[24] Although Manchuria belongs to the Republic of China, this rhetoric of a lifeline blurred Chinese sovereignty and connotated an organic connection with Japan. In this sense, the Manchurian Incident was in effect a replay of the Russo-Japanese War.[25] Several published stories on war heroes during the Manchurian battles urged readers to defend their foothold in Northeast China, which had been built on the loss of their fathers, brothers, and comrades in the Russo-Japanese War. The media reduced Chinese resistance to nationless "bandits" and portrayed them as backward people in a lawless wasteland.

Matsuoka was again involved in Mantetsu as its president from 1935 to 1939.[26] His lifeline rhetoric reflected another reality of the Japanese economy. Because Japan had enlarged the imperial map, colonies had become situated as the source of strategic trade and materials and symbolized the industrial umbilical cord of the nation's destiny. After the rice riots of 1918 in Japan, rice imports from Korea and Taiwan grew to such large amounts that Japan came to depend on the colonies for domestic food supplies.[27] The Great Depression of 1929 intensified public uncertainty regarding a severe economic recession. The media stressed Japan's shortage of resources and dependency on imports and spread "fears of economic blackmail into the language of imperialism," as

Louise Young has put it.[28] Thus, the lifeline metaphor was appealing to the public in both tapping collective memories of the imperial past and speaking to the economic insecurities of the present. A collective sense of victimization from the past war and economic distress incited war fever throughout Northeast China and raised emotional support for the Kwantung Army's unlawful invasion.

SETTLER COLONIALISM AND THE COLONIAL THRESHOLD

Young lists Japan's three major projects in Northeast China: military conquest, economic development, and mass migration.[29] After the military conquest, Japan targeted the natural resources of Manchukuo to feed its metropolitan population and as a market for consumer products imported from Japan. In addition, Japanese economists proposed to solve domestic agrarian issues through migration to Manchuria. Japanese peasants had suffered extreme impoverishment during its rapid industrialization. More than a million Japanese agricultural migrants, entrepreneurs, and soldiers crossed the ocean to the promised land to create a self-sufficient production sphere, or "Japan-Manchuria bloc economy."[30] Manchurian economic development became Japan's top priority as it exploited opportunities in the Chinese market. Politically, mass migration aimed to replace part of the local population and establish the Japanese as the ruling group.

Military conquest, economic development, and mass migration are the typical processes of colonization, as seen in European precedents. The mass migration of Japanese people to replace the local Chinese population amounts to what we now call settler colonialism.[31] Japan not only conquered the land militarily but also shipped in groups of Japanese civilians to stay and establish new lives on the land under the guise of state policy. As Patrick Wolfe famously defines, settler colonialism pursues elimination, rather than assimilation, of the Indigenous population. He asserts: "As opposed to enslaved people, whose reproduction augmented their owners' wealth, Indigenous people obstructed settlers' access to land, so their increase was counterproductive. In this way, the restrictive racial classification of Indians straightforwardly furthered the logic of elimination."[32] Indeed, local farmers' lands and houses were forcibly taken away and given to Japanese settlers coming into Manchukuo, as I detail in chapter 4. The mass migration policy itself was devastating to the farmers who made their living there. The settler colonial logic of elimination undeniably guided Japan's policing operations in Manchuria.

Yet Japan also struggled to carry out its settler colonial policies because of a conundrum stemming from the political duality of Manchukuo. It was officially created outside Japanese sovereignty, the product of a political compromise with Chinese nationalism and international criticism against Japanese military adventurism. Diplomatically, Japan needed to treat Manchukuo as a foreign allied country, on the one hand. On the other hand, Japan wished to maintain its dominance and fight the internal war within the region. As a result, numerous political techniques were invented to maneuver the administrative and judicial systems of Manchukuo in accordance with the military occupation and the appearance of an independent state. In this sense, Manchukuo was a *colonial threshold* between inside and outside of imperial Japan. Manchukuo was designed as a nation-state by Japanese hands, not as a colony.[33] The Manchurian population was located inside of Japan's imperial map politically and economically but legally outside of Japanese membership. Colonies were all too often exempted from the constitutional rights of nation-states, as seen in Japan's official colonies of Korea and Taiwan in chapter 2. Manchukuo was even more so because it was defined outside of Japan's imperial constitution and its jurisdiction from the outset. Manchuria was seen as both the front line and the margin of the empire, as unsecured and dangerous to govern.

Thus, the local population in Manchuria was in a more vulnerable position: attacked by Japan to subordinate and conquer and pushed to live bare life without citizenry protections.[34] Like it or not, the people in Northeast China were included in Japan's settler colonial project but excluded from equal opportunities, benefits, and rights. This inclusive exclusion was the source of Japan's regional power in its race against Western imperialism. Indeed, the people under the occupation were "exposed and threatened on the threshold in which life and law, outside and inside, become indistinguishable," as Agamben describes bare life.[35] To navigate the threshold of inclusion and exclusion, surveillance was cultivated and woven into every administrative and judicial practice in Manchukuo.

In fact, the ambiguous nature of the colonial threshold between the inside and outside irritated the Kwantung Army. Itagaki, the mastermind of the Manchurian Incident, ordered Japanese policymakers to satisfy three conditions in constructing the legal foundation of Manchukuo: it should be a completely independent country that followed Japanese rule and relied on Japanese defense, though this was called "joint defense."[36] In the fulfillment of these contradictory requirements, Itagaki commented that he would not care what kind of constitutional body it would result in—republic, kingdom, or empire. He was constructing an independent puppet state—an oxymoron that was, in the end, never translated into legal terms.

This colonial threshold created a profound contradiction in defining Manchurian nationals at the heart of the imperial project. Manchukuo lacked a Nationality Act and a constitution that defined who its subjects were and what their rights and duties were.[37] The Kwantung Army and the Mantetsu Economic Research Department played central roles in drafting bills to define who the nationals of Manchukuo were in 1935. While both groups tried to include all who were born in Manchukuo into the nationals, no matter their ethnicity, they tried to allow only Japanese residents to keep the dual nationalities of Japan and Manchukuo, which was intended to guarantee their absolute privilege as the ruling group. However, because this would give only the Japanese extraterritorial rights, it obviously contradicted the official principal of a "kingly way of governance," which promised equal status for five different ethnic groups. Even the Chinese ministers, appointed by the Japanese, contested the idea of allowing dual nationalities only to the Japanese.

While including as many local Chinese residents as possible, the nationality bill was meant to exclude migrant workers from other parts of China by labeling them as foreigners, to prevent the local population from uniting and to block the formation of a collective Chinese identity, both of which would counter Japanese colonization. But after much debate among Japanese bureaucrats and army elites, Manchukuo failed to define and construct its nationals. This was a real enigma for the settler colonizers who did not officially run the state but wanted to formalize their privilege as the ruling ethnic group at the colonial threshold. During the nationality debates,

Japanese elites abandoned the egalitarian mask and blatantly expressed eugenic ideology to maintain the purity of Japaneseness.[38] Thus, the utopian banner of a "kingly governance" was not substantiated by laws, though egalitarian images were abundantly disseminated through the media.

Crucially, Japan's failure to define the nationals of Manchukuo did not limit their power over the people. On the contrary, the Japanese exerted force directly on the population of the colonial threshold, in a state of exception from the constitutional protection. While the Japanese elite failed to make up Manchukuo nationals on a legal basis, they continued to write a number of laws and regulations at a fever pitch to establish their dominance in Manchuria. The Manchurian population was positioned under these repressive laws but abandoned by constitutional protections. Such lawmaking, meant only to justify and conceal the reality of military occupation, again exposed "the peculiar characteristic that it cannot be defined either as a situation of fact or as a situation of right, but instead institutes a paradoxical threshold of indistinction between the two."[39]

In sum, the colonial threshold is a place where the paradox, or duality, of modern sovereignty resides along with a violent reality, contrary to the utopian discourse of imperial multiculturalism. I will come back to this point at the end of the chapter. Here, to frame my analysis against the historical backdrop of Japan's expansionism, I find Manchukuo at a colonial threshold where the rule of law and seamless brutality appeared together in the construction of a pseudo-nation-state. It set the conditions for the development of an extensive surveillance apparatus and new techniques of identification that would be used to mask and maintain armed rule behind a civilized facade.

KWANTUNG GENDARMERIE: TOP OF THE MANCHURIAN INTELLIGENCE NETWORKS

Surrounded by unconquered people and afraid of the enemy within, Japan built powerful policing networks "to achieve the high-level defense state" in Northeast China.[40] The major apparatus of the policing networks was the Kwantung Gendarmerie, the military police of the Japanese Kwantung Army. Under the command and "internal guidance" of the Kwantung Gendarmerie, three other apparatuses were also involved in state surveillance: the Foreign Affairs Ministry Police, the Kwantung Police Department, and the Manchukuo Police. Furthermore, other intelligence agencies mushroomed in both the military and the civilian sections of the Manchurian government, normally under the obscure name "Special Mission" (Tokumu, 特務). The boundaries between those multiple surveillance agencies were ambiguous and competitive, and they comprised an overlapping and layered structure of all-encompassing surveillance. All these policing apparatuses utilized the notion of thought crime not as an Orwellian metaphor, but as a real administrative term that was already appearing in Japanese criminal law at the time and that merged into counterinsurgency measures in Manchuria. To search out suspects of thought crimes, the intelligence networks expanded to place the entire population under scrutiny. They were collectively inscribed suspect identities, just as the Indians under British rule (chapter 1).[41]

The Kwantung Gendarmerie was founded in 1905, when Japan took over the Russian leases in southern Manchuria as a result of the Russo-Japanese War. It placed the headquarters in Lüshun, the southern city of Liaoning Province, and put branches in five other cities. The Gendarmerie's official task was to police the military: investigating crimes by military personnel, violations of military disciplines, and antiwar tendencies among soldiers. But the Kwantung Gendarmerie played a completely different role from the beginning, focusing instead on maintaining and enlarging Japan's political economic interests in the leased regions in competition with the Chinese and Russians.[42] In 1918, along with the United Kingdom, United States, France, and Italy, Japan sent troops to Siberia to intervene in the Russian Revolution. There, the Kwantung Gendarmerie "first encountered the intelligence war against communism."[43]

The Manchurian Incident of 1931 definitively altered the Kwantung Gendarmerie's role from policing the military to policing for the military. Although Ishiwara, Itagaki, and other Kwantung Army elites waged an unofficial war against the chain of command, and without the permission of their commander in chief, Emperor Hirohito, the Kwantung Gendarmerie did not investigate this severe violation of military discipline. Despite the controversy within the organization, the senior gendarmes eventually took a stance in support of military adventurism.

A former gendarme commander described the shift in the agency's attitude:

> Given the circumstances under which our army has been already making all efforts to attack the Northeastern military powers, lost its own soldiers, and could no longer reverse the situations, we should not make accusations of conspiracy [about the Manchurian Incident], and should rather cooperate with it now. Taking a broader perspective of the military efforts, we should let go the conspiracy and restrain ourselves to make a case on this matter.[44]

By swiftly deploying their units and expanding battle lines throughout Manchuria, Itagaki and Ishihara succeeded in silencing the opposition within the army and made most of the faits accompli to escape discipline. This trend of bellicose leadership receiving no punishment continued and contributed to the perpetual expansion of the front lines until the end of the war with China. The role of policing *for* the Kwantung Army, not policing the army, was enhanced the following year when the Kwantung Gendarmerie was detached from the central gendarmerie headquarters for the whole Japanese military and came to directly serve the Kwantung Army. The army was still expanding the battle lines outside occupied areas in China, and so wanted the gendarmerie to gather information for its acts of aggression.

After the Manchurian Incident, the number of Kwantung Gendarmerie officers grew from about 200 to over 690 by 1933.[45] The Kwantung Gendarmerie spread branches throughout the occupied area, from the Imperial Palace to watch over Puyi, to towns and villages, to listen to residents' conversations. In parallel, the Manchukuo Police was crafted as part of the Civil Policy Section (Minseibu, 民生部) under the Department of State. Its first police head was Amakasu Masahiko (甘粕正彦), former gendarmerie captain in Tokyo, who was known for murdering anarchist leader Ōsugi Sakae(大杉栄), his partner Itō Noe(伊藤野枝), and Ōsugi's young nephew Tachibana Munekazu (橘宗一) under martial law in the aftermath of the Great Earthquake of 1923.[46] Amakasu was convicted of the murders and sentenced to a 10-year imprisonment but was released three years after and moved to Manchuria.[47] Not only Amakasu, but other military and police officers joined the Manchurian policing apparatuses from Japan and constructed the foundation of total policing in the Manchurian government.

In 1937, the Manchukuo Police was transferred to the Security Section (Chianbu, 治安部), for more thorough security operations under
the unification of military and police and two other major police agencies: the Foreign Affairs Ministry Police and the Kwantung Department
Police.[48] Combined with the Manchukuo Police, there were one hundred thousand officers in total. Japanese individuals held fewer than
10 percent of the positions in the Manchukuo Police but occupied the
major lines of command and the thought-crime sections, especially the
Japanese gendarmes.[49] The police organizations were incorporated into
the military structure, which obscured the boundaries between internal policing and external war. In fact, the two were understood to be the
same and practiced on the same horizon at the colonial threshold.

It was not only the policing agencies that cooperated with the army
but also judicial authorities like prosecutors and judges. The Justice
Section in the Department of State were similarly filled with legal professionals moving from Mantetsu and the Ministry of Justice in Japan.
They called their mission "judicial subjugation" of the "Chinese bandits,"
stating, "We, who engaged in thought regulations in Manchukuo, sometimes armed ourselves, rushed to dangerous zones, and processed cases
under the army's protection of bayonets."[50] They invented ad hoc courts
in battlefields, called the Security Court (*chiantei*, 治安庭) and Special
Security Court (*tokubetsu chiantei*, 特別治安庭 after 1941), to efficiently
respond to the army's sweeping operations. These ad hoc trials were set
up outside the regular court system to quickly "process" a large number
of Chinese suspects captured as thought criminals in military operations, and to give the appearance of lawful capital punishment to their
deaths. The Special Security Court was held without any attorney for
the suspect, the first judgment was final, and most of the convicted were
immediately executed. The entire criminal justice system assisted in the
military subjugation of the local population through rituals created by
legal professionals. The judicial department of Manchukuo did not over-
see police nor military actions, but merely approved them. Japan's total
empire of Manchukuo was indeed all-consuming, as Young suggests,
consuming even the judicial systems to support military operations.

In sum, the Kwantung Gendarmerie stood above all other competitive policing agencies in Manchukuo. The main objective of Japan's

surveillant assemblage in Manchuria was not criminal investigation, in the sense of finding a suspect of theft or murder, but subjugation of those opposed to Japan's occupation. Policing activities were disguised as criminal investigations, but they operated under military command for territorial interests. The vast and intricate policing networks were optimized for security intelligence, guided by the logic of elimination in settler colonialism, and their brutal policing was legalized as national security in the colonial threshold.

WHO ARE THE BANDITS?

So, who were the actual targets of the surveillant assemblage woven by the Kwantung Gendarmerie?

Even though the major warlords were subjugated or subsumed into the Manchurian government within a few years after the Manchurian Incident, the "anti-Manchukuo and resisting-Japanese" (Hanman Kōunichi, 反満抗日) guerrillas and Chinese patriots never disappeared; rather, they kept fighting. By 1930, the Chinese Communist Party had organized the Chinese and Koreans to counter Japanese imperialism in Northeast China,[51] and the Soviet Union supported unifying them with non-communist groups, which resulted in the formation of the Anti-Japanese Northeast United Army in 1936. The Anti-Japanese Northeast United Army was estimated at about forty thousand at its peak in 1937.[52] It reflected a vast alliance, from landowners whose properties were taken by the Japanese, to Kim Il-song, who led his army around the border zones with Korea, Jiandao, and later became prime minister of the Democratic People's Republic of Korea in 1948.[53] Their resistance actions relied on the help of local farmers and villagers, who provided food and resources to the soldiers, as agriculture had been the major industry in Northeast China.

Japan labeled the wide range of Chinese participants in the armed resistance as "bandits," synonymous with "terrorists" in the twenty-first century. *The Manchukuo Annual Report*, published by the Manchukuo News Service in Japanese in 1933–43, introduced seven categories of the population: political bandits, religious bandits, communist bandits, indigenous bandits, Korean bandits, Mongolian bandits, and half-farmer, half-bandits.[54] Intriguingly, the article begins by describing those categories of dissidents as a natural disaster:

> Manchuria gives us instant images of running bandits and a red sunset. Bandits and Manchuria—they are seen as inseparable. But bandits were actually not new and came into being naturally, with the special transition of the long history and social institutions in Manchuria. They are not seen in other countries, particularly never in Japan. They are beyond the imagination of Japanese nationals who have consistently had profound history and social thought.[55]

While this news article refers to the uniqueness of history and social institutions in Manchuria, it also naturalizes bandits as biological beings inherent to the region. It does not examine how bandits were historically shaped or why they opposed Japanese occupation. Rather, they are as much a part of the natural landscape as the red sunset. They are described as wild creatures, born with no allegiance to authority, in comparison with the loyal Japanese who understand and appreciate the mercies of the emperor. Loyalty in this context represented civility, and civility implicitly gave the Japanese the legitimate right to remove bandits and own the land, within settler colonial logic.

The article goes on to detail the different categories of bandits. According to the writer, "political bandits" are ones who attempt to subvert Manchukuo and are often supported by the warlord Zhang Xueliang. "Communist bandits" are organized and trained physically and mentally by the Russian and Chinese communist parties, so the most severe counterinsurgency measures should be deployed against those tough militants. "Korean bandits" demand independence for Korea from Japan, and are active near the Korean border. "Half-farmers, half-bandits" is a category open to any resident who could possibly join the armed resistance after "being influenced by the environment."[56] Interestingly, when it comes to this final category and the threshold of bandit identity, the article admits the challenge of identifying bandits and distinguishing them from innocent civilians:

> In this sense, *all bandits* can be categorized as half-farmer, half-bandit ... It is difficult to distinguish good residents from bandits. When the concept of half-farmers, half-bandits includes informants to bandits, too, it causes a headache for the Japanese and Manchurian

governments, how to identify these kinds of subjects and contain them. This will increasingly demand more complicated measures of internal policies under the kingly way of governance.[57]

This article discloses two aspects of Japan's colonial policing. First, despite the detailed matrix of bandit categorizations offered up front, the article confesses "all bandits can be categorized as half-farmer, half-bandit," which means that all bandits are local residents and farmers who have been living on their traditional land. Given that the main occupation for the local population in Northeast China in the 1930s was farming, a bandit could be anyone—or potentially everyone in Manchuria—to Japanese authorities. The policing agencies categorized bandits to construct and justify the objects of policing, but those categories were somehow left open with regard to nonbandits. In the eyes of the Kwantung Gendarmerie, any Chinese person was a potential suspect of banditry, and the entire population was suspicious. Japan's total empire rested on the inherent fear of being surrounded by potentially undefeated people and doubting their obedience. The open categories of bandits display the all-encompassing character of Japan's surveillant assemblage.

Second, because of the difficulty of locating bandits in farming villages, the article mentions the need to bring in an efficient means of identification. How to identify the population individually was the central issue for the colonial policing and counterinsurgency measures in Manchukuo. The reporter of *The Manchukuo Annual Report* claims the need for a national identification system to facilitate colonial management. When the categories of bandits were expanded to include supporters and bystanders, that meant any Chinese person could be one, so an ID system was needed to track and trace everybody. The ID system enabled the Japanese to sort the population, single out the subversives, and punish them. The national ID system began to be imagined as a necessary institution to sort the population into "desirable" and "undesirable" for security purposes. Fingerprint identification was proposed as an effective, scientific solution in the early stages of nation building in Manchukuo.

Still, when bandits were cultivating their land during the day, how could Japanese agencies know if they were armed at night or providing food and fuel to the guerrillas behind the backs of the Japanese police?

They didn't carry any physical mark of connection with bandits. How could the occupiers read people's minds and predict their future actions?

TECHNIQUES OF POLICING THOUGHT CRIME

Japanese policing agencies employed the notion of thought crime, which had already been put into practice to criminalize and oppress socialists and communists in Japan, to identify "bandits" in Manchukuo. Among dissidents opposed to the rapid modernization and emerging inequalities of nation building, socialists and communists were considered a particular threat to Japan's "national body" (*kokutai*, 国体), the political and social order of the imperial state that deified the emperor. To guard the ambiguous and hierarchical concept of *kokutai*, the Special High Police (Tokubetsu Kōtō Keisatsu, 特別高等警察)—in short, Tokkō (特高)—was founded in 1911, following the mass arrest of socialists and anarchists in the Taigyaku Incident (大逆事件) in 1910. The Taigyaku Incident was a crackdown on the growing Japanese socialist movement. Twenty-six socialists and anarchists who had allegedly planned to assassinate the Meiji Emperor were prosecuted for treason, twenty-four were convicted and sentenced to death, and twelve were actually executed, including Kōtoku Shūsui (幸徳秋水) and Miyashita Takichi (宮下太吉).[58] The whole criminal justice process of the Taigyaku Incident took place only within about six months, and the police immediately developed a nationwide dragnet to search out anarchists, socialists, communists, and anyone else who might challenge the national body.[59] As a result, the Tokkō section was independently founded in the Tokyo Metropolitan Police (Keishichō, 警視庁) and other provincial police agencies, focusing on the thoughts, rather than actions, of people in the criminal investigation. The surveillance of foreign visitors and the censorship of print media were also institutionalized in this period.

Nonetheless, Japan continued to see a surge in labor disputes and strikes, and the inauguration of the Japanese Socialist League in the 1920s. In response, the Ministry of Internal Affairs and provincial polices increased the number of Tokkō officers surveilling the "persons who require observation." The Peace Preservation Act (Chian-ijihō, 治安維持法) of 1925 provided the comprehensive legal basis for Tokkō to criminalize those who formed groups or acted individually to reform the national body or deny the private property system. The Diet and media criticized the bill as unconstitutional because it would severely restrict freedoms of the press, speech, and expression, which were framed as gifts from the emperor under the imperial Constitution, albeit in a limited form.

Despite public opposition, the bill passed and was first applied on a massive scale on March 15, 1928, to arrest 1,600 people who were suspected to be communists and proxies. This crackdown leveraged a revision of the Peace Preservation Act of 1928, which enabled Tokkō to charge suspects of thought crimes with the death penalty and led to the creation of a thought prosecutor and thought gendarmerie.[60] The revision provided Tokkō with an extraordinary power to surveil and punish on the basis of what people thought, and thought-crime agencies were widespread in the 1920s. Publications that allegedly profaned the honor of the emperor and his family, called for the abolition of the monarchy, or promoted strategies and tactics for socialist revolution were banned, including films and theater plays.[61]

While no Japanese was sent to death row under the Peace Preservation Act, two thousand Japanese people are estimated to have been tortured by the Tokkō and to have died in prison.[62] Socialists and communists who publicly voiced criticism against Japan's imperial wars remained major targets of state oppression until 1945. Yet people who resisted Japan's expansionist policies and demanded independence from the empire shaped new categories of threats to the national body. Korean dissidents were added to the Tokkō's watchlists of "persons who require observation," as the government and media often insultingly called the recalcitrant Koreans (*futei senjin*, 不逞鮮人). Under the application of the Peace Preservation Act, forty-eight Koreans—allegedly leaders in the movement against Japanese imperialism—mounted the gallows. The different effects of the same security law between the Japanese and Korean dissidents suggest that the law brings more direct violence to the population in the colonies, revealing an asymmetrical experience of colonization between the colonizing and the colonized.

The oppressive techniques of thought-crime investigation were imported to the settler colonial threshold of Manchukuo, where the entire population was suspected of potentially being anti-Japanese. When Tōjō Hideki came into the position of commander in chief of the Kwantung

Gendarmerie in 1935,[63] he founded the Policing Control Committee to unify the thought-crime policing and military operations and to enhance the leadership of the Kwantung Gendarmerie over other policing agencies. Tōjō, who later became prime minister (1941-44) and led the Pacific War, mobilized both the Kwantung Gendarmerie and the police for joint operations targeting communist groups in Northeast China. He gave instructive comments: "The core mission of the Policing Control Committee is to exterminate the northeast branch of the Chinese Communist Party and the mixed armed groups led by them."[64] As a military elite, Tōjō must have seen more continuity than change in security policing of Japanese socialists versus Chinese communists. The Policing Control Committee absorbed intelligence data through various channels of the military operation.

The historian Fujio Ogino contends that the Kwantung Gendarmerie was the springboard for Tōjō's career, demonstrating his initiative in sweeping out political opposition to Japanese imperialism. The settler colonial threshold allowed him to unleash preemptive techniques of thought-crime policing toward the unprecedented realm; such techniques operated more covertly and indirectly to persecute dissidents in Japan under more effective legal constraints and in the public eye. What Tōjō established was maintained and reinforced after he left his position as commander in chief of the Kwantung Gendarmerie. In 1937, Tōjō's successor Fujie Keisuke pushed the mandate farther by ordering all gendarmerie branches "to enhance the surveillance to bandits' information, to arrest and process the underground bandits and communicators severely, while thoroughly repressing communist organizations and preventing interventions from abroad."[65]

In Japan, Tokkō relied primarily on spying for intelligence gathering. Similarly, the Manchurian policing apparatus hired many Chinese informants and forced others to become informants by threatening their political and economic stability. Typically, prior to military operations by the Kwantung Army, it was routinized to gather information and identify potential enemies in the region by harassing and torturing the local Chinese. For example, before invading Jehol Province (熱河省) in 1933 to expand its territory in southwestern Manchukuo, the Kwantung Army sent forty gendarmes with four or five spies and translators to collect regional data. Looking back, a gendarme said, "Because information was most precious, the gendarmerie tortured the Chinese by any means [to obtain information . . .] Before occupying Jehol, the gendarmes had killed more than 100 people for this purpose. They also forcefully levied 500 horses for logistics, from ordinary people who were relying on the horses for their living, and burned down 500 houses."[66]

A thought-crime section was expanded to every gendarmerie branch in 1936. The officers wore Western suits or Chinese-style clothes to walk down streets and detect their targets. Torture was in fact the only weapon they could use to find out anything valuable from the Chinese, who had no reason to support the invaders. The gendarmes normally took steps to "capture someone who has nothing to do with the communist party, torture him to get some kinds of clues, and then dig into the clues."[67] While such a scheme was like looking for a needle in a haystack, and presumably misidentified communists and harmed innocents, the Kwantung Gendarmerie tried to turn the captives into their spies. What they needed for this tactic was money. The Kwantung Gendarmerie captain Yoshifusa Torao states, "In February or March of 1944, I secured 600,000 yen per year as a budget for forming an organization that employs about 250,000 Chinese as spies, distributed these spies to the gendarmerie branches, and instructed them how to use the spies."[68] Tokkō's thought-crime policing techniques catalyzed the vast surveillance networks as war tactics at the colonial threshold, where the internal pacification and external war were indistinguishable.

Equivalent to the Peace Preservation Act in Japan was the Temporary Bandits Punishment Act and the Temporary Rebel Punishment Act, enacted in Manchukuo in 1932. The two provided the legal basis to criminalize the Hanman Kōnichi movement and eventually merged into the Manchurian version of the Peace Preservation Act in 1941. The two laws legalized killing suspects at the time of arrest without sending them to court.[69] It was called "severe punishment" (genjū shobun, 厳重処分) in military code—the hidden but normalized imperative of counterinsurgency operations. The two laws typically created a state of exception, among other laws the Japanese wrote for colonial management. The law and rogue violence were embodied as one, as severe punishments committed in an orderly fashion. In other words, the real intention of the two laws was to legalize the illegal violence already practiced by the army, which would have been punished in the normal application of criminal law as slaughter without due process of law, or as war crimes in international law.

The Kwantung Gendarmerie was aware of the arbitrary nature of severe punishment, so they wanted to avoid it in cases where the suspects had government jobs, or student status, or were of the intellectual class for fear of criticism from the international community. The commander ordered his subordinates "to deceive the international eye, avoid immediate severe punishments, and send suspects to court temporarily, as a way of making the guise of due process."[70] Then, to process them quickly, the aforementioned Security Court and Special Security Court were set up on an ad hoc basis alongside military operations and carried out severe punishment with a more lawful appearance.

Lawful massacres, along with counterinsurgency operations, were repeatedly reported to the Policing Control Committee. Two hundred thirteen people were arrested in 1936 as members of the Manchurian Communist Party in the Harbin area. The committee categorized 40 percent of the captives as "intellectual elements," like schoolteachers, and so decided to spy more intensively on educational institutions. In 1937, the Kwantung Gendarmerie and Manchukuo Police arrested 346 suspects of the Chinese Communist Party in Dalian and other cities, and 126 people were sent to death row. Fujio Ogino estimates that, in total, at least 2,000 people identified as "communist bandits" were given the death penalty and immediately executed through the Special Security Court.[71]

Like the Korean cases, Ogino remarks on the enormous gap in the number of death penalties executed between Japanese and Chinese people, involving similar security laws and policing techniques. Although many postwar Japanese intellectuals recognized Tokkō and the Peace Prevention Act as a significant part of the war machine that smashed opposition to the war in Japanese society and contributed to the totalitarian regime and its catastrophic end, the massive scale of bloodshed resulting from the same security legislation and policing techniques in the colonies has been largely ignored in postwar Japanese intellectual discussions. This omission again uncovers the more brutal impacts of the security law and surveillance in the colonies, where the state of exception became the rule. The surveillant assemblage in Manchukuo clearly served the sovereign right to kill, not to foster life.[72]

In other words, Tokkō's necropolitical techniques fully bloomed at the settler colonial threshold, without compromise to biopolitical citizenry protection. The Kwantung Gendarmerie reigned over surveillance networks throughout Manchukuo with fewer legal constraints or even with legal support. Nonetheless, Japan still did not achieve total conquest in Northeast China. Tokkō's infiltration and torture were inadequate to separate bandits from innocents in the unknown population of the disputed land.

SEPARATING "BANDITS" FROM "INNOCENTS": THREE SYSTEMS OF COMMUNITY SURVEILLANCE

To identify an entire population of potential "half-farmers, half-bandits," Japan brought registration and identification systems to Northeast China, as to its other colonies. Household investigation and census were used to register the population and combined with multiple systems of community surveillance. I unpack three examples of community surveillance in this section: the civil registry, the *hokō* system, and the concentration village. Each of them was associated with the other and created opportunities for the colonizers to collect personal data on residents. These intertwined systems acted as dragnets for Japan's surveillant assemblage, against which biometric ID cards tracked residents' movements.

Civil Registry: Making Up Manchurian Nationals

A feature of occupied Northeast China was that Japan did not implement the *koseki* system. As discussed in chapter 2, the patriarchal *koseki* system has historically played a central role in defining who the Japanese are and subsumed the Nationality Act in the civil law system. People obtained Japanese nationality through membership in a patriarchal family that was registered in *koseki*. In the colonies of Taiwan, Korea, and Sakhalin, *koseki* integrated the colonial population into the emperor's property lists and classified people in a racial hierarchy, always positioning them below the top group of "Original Japanese." *Koseki* was conceived as the fundamental basis of the national body, and symbolized unity and loyalty for the Japanese empire. For that reason, Japanese military elites and bureaucrats gave up bringing *koseki* to the colonial threshold, which was supposed to be a country independent from Japan. *Koseki* was not suitable to directly tie the local Chinese to the Japanese emperor, unlike in other colonies. Furthermore, as seen in the previous section, Japanese policymakers failed to establish the Nationality Act in Manchukuo due to the same contradiction of making an oxymoronic independent puppet state. It remained a major conundrum to create equal memberships for five different ethnic groups while simultaneously upholding absolute Japanese privilege.

Still, Japan wanted to list the people residing in Manchukuo for purposes of population control. The process of registering and identifying the Manchurian population was in fact very similar to the process of launching the *koseki* system in Taiwan.[73] First, the police investigated households, then the government conducted a census for a larger scale of data collection, and last it was legitimated as the national registry of the population for identification purposes. In Japan, *koseki* was the foundation for constructing the subjects of the nation-state and for fostering a sense of loyalty, nationalism, and patriarchal social order. But in the colonies, it was intended primarily as a means of policing dissidents. The Manchurian case shows this contrast even more clearly: Japanese policymakers in Manchukuo commented that "the national registration would support crime investigation, make people careful about their own actions, and prevent them from joining with bandits."[74]

The comment intriguingly suggests that colonial planners expected the panoptic effects of self-surveillance in the registration system. They imagined national registration as a proactive counterinsurgency measure: sorting the population into desirables and undesirables and isolating uncertain individuals from each other to curtail resistance. At the same time, colonial policymakers were aware that registration would play less of a role in constructing loyal subjects for the Japanese emperor among the Chinese population than the role played by *koseki* in Japan. In the colonial threshold, disciplinary surveillance does not necessarily automate soul training through internalization of authority's gaze or create docile bodies.

Like the Japanese police in Taiwan, the Manchukuo police began to visit individual households in 1933, a year after the declaration of Manchukuo, to collect data on each household member's name, age, address, occupation, place of birth, race, religion, relation to the family head, and other "items necessary for policing." Many more personal details were collected to analyze every individual characteristic, compared to Japanese *koseki*, and that data was updated every six months. If the police found "anyone who needs special attention" in a household, such as potential anarchists, communists, socialists, "anti-Manchukuo" followers, political and labor "extremists," the sick and pessimistic, or tramps, the police monitored them every month. The wide range of data, the frequency of police visits, and the focus on thought crimes characterized the registration system in Northeast China. The patriarchal frame of *koseki* was only partially observable in the format of data collection, which provides more proof that the soul-training function of *koseki* was not really envisaged in the occupied land.

After the Manchukuo Police came under the Security Section in 1937 to work as an arm of the military, it became compulsory for the household head to update changes in individual data with the police, such as changes in a household members' address and marital status. The Temporary Civil Registry Act enacted in 1940 turned household investigation data into "national" registration and supplemented the miscarried Nationality Act with official lists of Manchukuo subjects. To detail personal information, the government conducted the first census within the same year. Fifteen items of data were collected on each individual: name, family head's name and address, parents' names and relations to the person (e.g., first daughter, second son), sex, date of birth and age, marital status, occupation, race, residing address, dates of entry to Manchukuo, conscription record, and so on.[75] As a result of the census, 43.2 million people were not only counted as the population of Manchukuo but also registered as "Manchukuo nationals" in the civil registry (*minseki*, 民籍) while still lacking the legal definition of nationals. Most of the population was of course Chinese: 94.5 percent were categorized as the ethnic group of Manchurian (Han, 85.3 percent; Manchu clan, 6.2 percent; Mongolian, 2.5 percent; Muslim, 0.5 percent), 5.3 percent as Japanese (Japanese, 1.9 percent; Korean 3.4 percent), and 0.2 percent as no nationality (asylum seekers from the Soviet Union and other diasporas).[76] Only Japanese and Koreans—as Japanese nationality holders at the time—were allowed to register dual nationalities in the civil registry.

The civil registry collected data on an individual basis, unlike *koseki*, which did so on a patriarchal family basis and attempted to record the actual locations and lives of residents in the household. Fingerprinting was also proposed for inclusion in the civil registry. Fingerprint identification was in fact suggested as a symbol of modernity from the very beginning of the making of Manchukuo. A Japanese encyclopedia published in 1932 anticipated that "Manchukuo is the top runner in a world that combines fingerprinting schemes into the *koseki* system. This is truly suited to the new nation. It will turn the formal *koseki* system into a genuine [identification] system, which must be most accurate all over the world."[77] Japanese policymakers passionately pursued designing the "perfect" national ID system that would enable them to watch over every individual through biological identifiers.

The shift to an individualistic focus for the registry was first motivated by policing, but later by conscription and for labor purposes.[78] For such a multidimensional mobilization, the Japanese needed to invent nationals for Manchukuo and foster a positive feeling about Manchurian nationality, even as the people who lived on the occupied land did not care for nor have an incentive to be loyal to their nationalities. While unable to resolve the conundrum of the Nationality Act, Japanese colonizers hoped that the civil registry would do the work of a customary law defining who Manchukuo's subjects were. But for security purposes, they wanted to do it selectively. All migrant workers from other parts of China were excluded from the civil registry, even though they resided in Manchuria at the time of the census, to prevent them from forming a collective Chinese identity and fomenting nationalism, potentially countering Japanese imperialism. Migrant workers were subject to the most intensive scrutiny of their movements: from entering Manchukuo, to moving from one workplace to another, as we will see in the next chapter. While its leaders feared their resistance, Japan desperately needed their labor power to run its colonial enterprises. Thus, individual data were needed to find, select, and mobilize workers.

In comparison with Japan's other colonies, it is unclear how the civil registry was used for assimilation policies in Northeast China. Because Manchukuo was internationally advertised as an equal utopia for five ethnic groups—Han, Manchurian, Mongolian, Korean, and Japanese—assimilation to Japanese culture was difficult to rationalize. But Japanese privileges were crystal clear in all aspects of the occupation, and some of my Chinese interviewees said that they were forced to speak Japanese at school, like in other colonies, and the teachers spanked them when they rejected it.

Colonial planners also repeatedly discussed how to preserve the "pure" Japanese bloodline in Manchukuo during mass migration programs from Japan, which aimed to replace the Han population. In 1932, the government initiated migrations of farmers and young men who were trained in farming or soldiering. The Manchuria Migration Association, an extragovernmental body, recruited and sent 2,400 women as "continental brides" from 1938 onward to couple with Japanese men.[79] Japanese policymakers believed that if a Japanese person was assimilated into Chinese culture through intermarriage, it meant that the Japanese person "fell down" the hierarchy to form part of an inferior ethnic group, and this was not acceptable.[80] In their view, assimilation should take place in just one direction: from the Japanese to others, not the reverse. Japanese settlers in Manchukuo eventually numbered about three hundred thousand by 1945.[81] Policymakers believed that the racial marker in the civil registry could differentiate Japanese individuals from other ethnic groups and help preserve the "blood purity" of what they believed was the superior group while deterring mixing with other groups.

The Hokō System: Lateral Surveillance and Collective Punishment

Parallel to conducting the household investigation, Japan institutionalized a vigilante system based in local communities, called the *hokō* (保甲) system in Japanese and *baojia* in Chinese.[82] The Temporary Hokō Act was enacted in 1933, with the establishment of the Peace Preservation Association at all provincial and municipal levels. The *hokō* system consisted of three levels of units: About ten households make the first level of a unit called *hi*; several units of *hi* made the next unit level called *ko*, and the assemblage of *ko* made *ho*, the area covered by a police branch.[83] The term Baojia comes from the ancient Chinese structure, but the *hokō* system the Japanese brought back was updated for community-based lateral surveillance, to supplement the Manchukuo Police apparatuses. Surveillance by *hokō* disguised a form of "co-responsibility" for crime

and subversion. If anyone was found to be a criminal or related to bandits, all households in the same unit were punished or fined. The *hokō*
units were also compelled to organize armed vigilante groups of men
between eighteen and forty years old.

This collective punishment and vigilante system was naturally expected to search out potential members and supporters of the Chinese
resistance in the community. The police evaluated the *hokō* system as
a highly effective way to cut off local support for the Anti-Japanese
Northeast United Army, which was actively attacking the Kwantung
Army and Manchukuo Police in 1935–37. To counter it, the police had
formed more than 440,000 *hi*, the first-level unit, by 1936, and 9,861
vigilante groups covered almost the entire region of Manchukuo.[84] The
household investigation and *hokō* systems became the two wheels of the
operation separating "bandits" from people by the Kwantung Army. As
a result of the two systems working in tandem, potential bandits were
found and killed on sight, lawfully, in the name of "severe punishment"
or "immediate disposal."

Concentration Village: Prison Without a Ceiling

In addition to the two wheels mentioned in the previous sections, the
Kwantung Army constructed an even more aggressive vehicle for community surveillance. The concentration village (*shūdanburaku*, 集団部落)
was a little-known proactive tactic of occupational surveillance. The
army destroyed villages in locations that were strategically important
to them and relocated the villagers to new places the army selected.
There, biometric ID cards were used to check residents' day-to-day
movements.

Concentration villages started to be built in 1933, beginning in
the Jiandao region bordering Korea, to counter the armed Korean independence movement.[85] The governor-general of Korea ordered that
nine concentration villages be built in the first year to house Korean
residents. As the Kwantung Army saw the effectiveness of this tactic to
separate "bandits" from residents, Manchukuo adopted this egregious
method and expanded the subjected area in 1935. Typically, the Kwantung Army told villagers to leave their homes and take their things with
them immediately—sometimes within a week, but other times within
an hour. The army burned down houses and forcefully moved people to

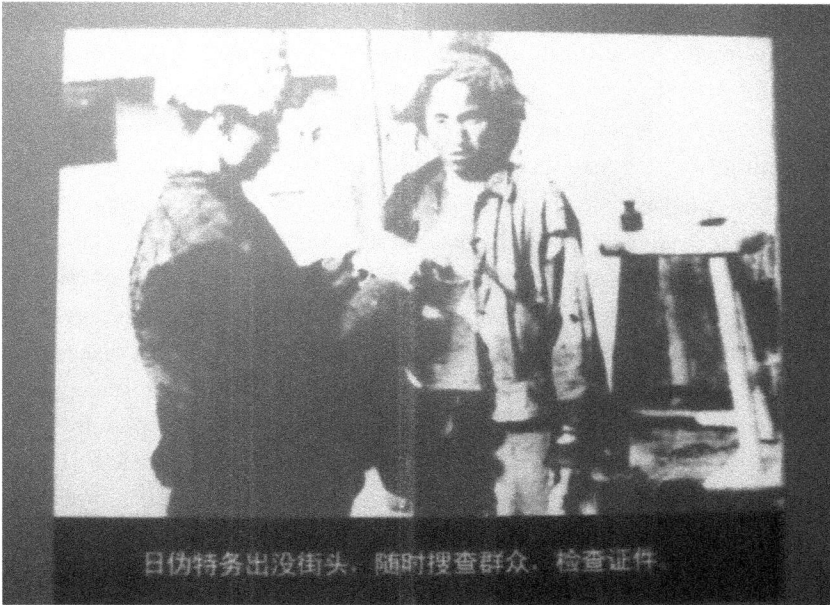

FIGURE 3.1. A Japanese soldier checks the villager's identification card at the gate of concentration village. Public exhibition in Museum of Imperial Palace of Pseudo-Manchukuo, Changchun, Jilin Province, 2016. Photo by Ken Mizokoshi.

a new location. According to a resident, "The people living in the upper mountain were relocated to the lower, the people spread on the prairie were collected to the center," for easy police access.[86] Another resident commented: "There was no choice for villagers to refuse moving, as the army would behead dissenters, or kill them in other ways."[87] The army also deprived the villagers of their livestock and crops and destroyed their furniture, fields, and farming tools, so as not to leave any resources for the guerrillas.

Normally, thirty to one hundred households composed one concentration village, containing up to a thousand people.[88] Residents were also coerced into building mud walls of about three meters in height, surrounding the village, four watchtowers and two gates. The gates normally were open from six in the morning to six in the evening, and there, soldiers or vigilantes checked the people entering and leaving the village. To prevent guerrillas from visiting the village, resident ID cards and travel permits were issued to villagers over age eighteen; the cards and permits included photographs and fingerprints.[89] Villagers had to show their ID card whenever they left or returned to the village. They were allowed to cultivate only the fields nearby and could not travel without travel permits. Their personal belongings were also strictly checked—food, shoes, and clothes—again, to keep them from offering anything to the guerrillas. A resident in Jiandao commented that because of this restriction, "We couldn't buy more than a pair of shoes without a reason."[90] The villagers were also forced to serve the army as vigilantes and in construction. The army also imposed harsh tax rates on residents, who were already malnourished; further deprivation meant starvation and the increased prevalence of infectious disease.[91]

In total, more than seventeen thousand concentration villages were constructed from 1935 to 1945, and about five million people were confined in the panoptic villages.[92] For the army, the creation of concentration villages was often simultaneous with the invention of "uninhabited regions" following the elimination of the people around the guerrilla bases. Everyone across the uninhabited regions were assumed to be guerrillas and spies and were subject to punishment. The Japanese Army pursued the same strategy in other parts of China outside Manchuria, in its obsessive attempts to separate "bandits" from local communities. The army used aircraft to check from the sky that everyone had moved out of the mountains and prairies.[93] If they found anyone remaining, soldiers were dispatched to attack and force them to leave.

The concentration village was the ultimate way of placing daily life under Japan's total policing, integrated with a military operation. It was a world crafted for maximum surveillance from scratch, a prison without a ceiling. All kinds of identifying and classifying techniques—the civil registry, *hokō* system, concentration village, and fingerprinted ID cards—were combined and configured to proactively exterminate collective resistance by cutting off human ties within and among communities. A location was selected prior to a sweeping operation, and numerous civilians were killed in the process of destroying their villages and making residents move to a new and dismal prison. It was a space artificially designed for 24/7 panoptic surveillance. If anyone did anything suspicious, they were readily arrested and tortured in the name of political crime, thought crime, economic crime, or as a smuggler or spy, because they were regularly identified and their behavior tightly tracked. The villagers' misery was inscribed in a song: "We must register when getting out of the gate and must report when returning. If we make any mistakes, it threatens the whole family's lives."[94] The Japanese called these places "model villages" or "safety farms" and depicted them as a symbol of modernity, civility, and security accomplished by the progressive leaders of East Asia.[95] But the Chinese described the new residences as prisons and internment camps.

Japan's military operation in China has been called Three Sweeping Tactics (Sankō sakusen, 三光作戦), referring to "sweeping kill, sweeping burn, and sweeping dispossess." Surveillance activities comprised a significant part of the notorious tactics. Registering personal details, checking ID cards, removing people from their residences, and making them surveil each other were not mere observation but tactical violence. It is unknown how many Chinese civilians were murdered, raped, and abused through these merciless tactics. Survivors were confined in the concentration villages and lived bare life under the ever-expanding surveillance assemblage. A manifesto written by the Anti-Japanese United Army, in Hulin, Heilongjiang Province, in 1936, aptly grasped the purpose of the concentration villages:

1) to cut off the relationships between the people and the Anti-Japanese Army, and naturally exterminate us by taking our residence, food, and information,
2) to arm you to shoot your brothers,
3) *to spy on you. If you don't obey their (Japanese) words, they can capture you easily. No place to hide.*[96]

THE LIVED EXPERIENCE OF JAPAN'S MAXIMUM SURVEILLANT ASSEMBLAGE

How, then, did these different agents, institutions, and techniques of surveillance work together as an assemblage? During my field research in China, Wang Xuancai (王选财), who lives in Jidong, Heilongjiang Province, told me about his family's lived experiences with the *hokō* system, concentration village, and the loss of his uncle as a result of the Tokumu's spying activities and Kwantung Gendarmerie's classification of bandits. His family story contextualizes the impacts of Japan's maximum surveillant assemblage and unpacks how the local population experienced it on the ground.

FIGURE 3.2. Wang Xuancai (王选财), standing beside the grave of his ancle Wang Mingshen (王明生), who was placed under "Special Transfer" to Unit 731 biological war facility. The tombstone says, "born in 1916," "killed at 731 in 1941," and "patriot who resisted fascism." Heilongjiang Province, 2016. Photo by Ken Mizokoshi.

His uncles, Wang Mingshen (王明生, or Wang Zhenda, 王振達, stated in the Kwantung Gendarmerie's file, Figure 3.3A&B) and Wang Mingde (王明德), joined the Anti-Japanese Northeast United Army in 1933, covertly collected information on Japanese soldiers and military facilities, and crossed the border to deliver the information to Russian intelligence to obtain their support.[97] The village head where Mingshen, Mingde, and his family lived noticed that some youth might be involved in the United Army and reported it to the Kwantung Army. The Japanese officer and Chinese vigilantes visited their house while they were away on their mission and told their parents, "Bring your sons back soon, otherwise, we kill everybody in your household." Their father did not take their words seriously, but the same group of vigilantes came back later with the village head and Kwantung Gendarmerie, and confirmed it: "This is the last chance. If you can't find your sons in the next three days, we will kill you all." The next day, their mother left home with a basket full of eggs, pretending to go to the market to sell the eggs. She visited a communist base in the neighboring city of Mishan and asked what she should do. The following morning a messenger from the base visited her at home and said, "You should leave home with your stuff tonight after dark and move to the United Army's base in the mountains. Because of the *hokō* system, if you escape, nine other households will be punished. So, you should bring all these families to the base together." Then, the ten households disappeared from the village overnight.

According to Wang Xuancai, who heard the story from his parents and grandparents, it took two days to reach the United Army's base in Boli, walking through the mountains, across rivers, plagued by gnats and mosquitos. The Anti-Japanese Northeast United Army distributed guns to the young men to become soldiers and asked the elders to cultivate the fields for food production and the women to sew clothes in the factory. They lived there for about two years, until the Kwantung Army found them in the winter of 1938. Because their soldiers were absent when they were discovered, the women managed to convince the Chinese interpreter to tell the Kwantung Army that they were not part of the United Army. The Japanese destroyed everything at the base, from the houses and sewing factory to the plates and bowls, but spared their lives. Xuancai's parents and others were eventually sent to a concentration village nearby.

In the concentration village, the resident ID cards—called "Good People Certificates"—were issued and required to be carried at all times.

"Whenever you left the village to work, you had to bring it to the Japanese soldiers, leave it with them, and get it back on your return," Xuancai told me. Xuancai's parents suffered starvation in the concentration village: His mother became a beggar, and his father and grandfather served the local landowner. The Japanese soldiers strictly checked their movements every day using their ID cards, and asked them what they were doing and where they were going every day. The villagers had to give the army their fingerprints for the ID cards. Xuancai said, "If you didn't give them your fingerprints, you were not 'good people.' Fingerprinting was the way the Japanese controlled the Chinese. The Japanese trusted only Japanese, not Chinese." Xuancai's parents were able to return to their home in 1941.

That same year, his uncle Mingshen was detained by the Kwantung Gendarmerie and sent to Unit 731, Japan's secret biowarfare facility. A community member who worked for the Tokumu reported that Mingshen and his close friend Zhu Yunxiu (朱雲岫) had been involved in the United Army, and the two were captured together on May 3, 1941. Mingshen's parents heard of his detention in a prison in Mishan but lost track of him after that. In 2000—almost sixty years later—they learned that the Kwantung Gendarmerie files on Unit 731 included Wang Mingshen's name and photos.[98]

The file unveiled that the gendarmerie tailed Mingshen and got to know Zhu Yunxiu who was also involved in the United Army.[99] Furious with their imprisonment, Zhu Yunxiu's brother Zhu Yuntong (朱雲彤) roughed up the Tokumu informant with kicks and blows, and the heavily injured informant also turned in Zhu Yuntong to the gendarmerie. The Zhu brothers' names were also found in the files of "Special Transfer" to the biological testing site.[100]

Both Wang Mingshen and Zhu Yunxiu seemingly did not compromise with the gendarmerie in the face of brutal interrogation. In Mingshen's file, he was assessed as "cunning characteristic," "inherently lazy," and "anti-Japanese bandit in the past, who barbarously attacked a village and committed to kidnapping."[101] Zhu Yunxiu was similarly described as "no feeling of repentance."[102] They were classified as having no value for the Kwantung Army and killed for imperial science. Wang Mingshen was twenty-five years old, and Zhu Yunxiu was twenty-three years old, as recorded in their files.

Without knowledge of her son's whereabouts, Mingshen's mother kept waiting for his return, often standing on the street in the late afternoon and looking for his shadow, remembered Xuancai. Respecting his uncle's extreme courage and commemorating his forced death, Xuancai erected Mingshen's tombstone without remains to bury—a traditional way to mourn missing people in this region (fig. 3.2).[103]

In summary, this chapter has illustrated the convergence of different agents, institutions, and techniques of colonial surveillance uniquely developed in the pseudo-nation of Manchukuo. Importing the precedent techniques of registry, census, or thought-crime investigation from Japan or Taiwan, Japan's imperial ethos spread the rhizomatic arms, wove intricate layers of intelligence, and executed brutal counterinsurgence tactics under settler colonialism. Because settler colonialism prioritizes settlers' access to lands and resources over that of the Indigenous population, Japanese colonial managers showed little hesitation about practicing the logic of elimination in the occupied land. In all aspects of the occupation—military conquest, economic development, and mass migration—Manchukuo was a colonial threshold between the inside and outside of imperial Japan. It supposedly had statehood, but within the reach of Japan's imperial rule. Together with the contradiction and the legal manipulations to cover that contradiction, the Manchurian laws served only to turn the local population into bare lives exposed to sovereign violence, such as "severe punishment," or to disguise sovereign violence as lawful. It was not rule of law, but rule by law, saturating the colonial threshold.

In the eyes of the Japanese occupying force, the colonial margin was most insecure and dangerous, and the unconquered people had to be highly surveilled. For this reason, Japan's surveillant assemblage was obsessed to distinguish different categories of "bandits" and separate them from the rest of the population. Yet the policing agencies struggled to conduct rigorous classifications, and the categories of bandits eventually dissolved to encompass the entire population: Any Chinese could be "half-farmer, half-bandit," given the suspect identity as a racialized Other. Colonial was criminal, after all. The Japanese colonial managers launched a household investigation, census, and civil registry to collect personal data on the entire population and implemented the *hokō* system and concentration village to automate lateral surveillance in communities.

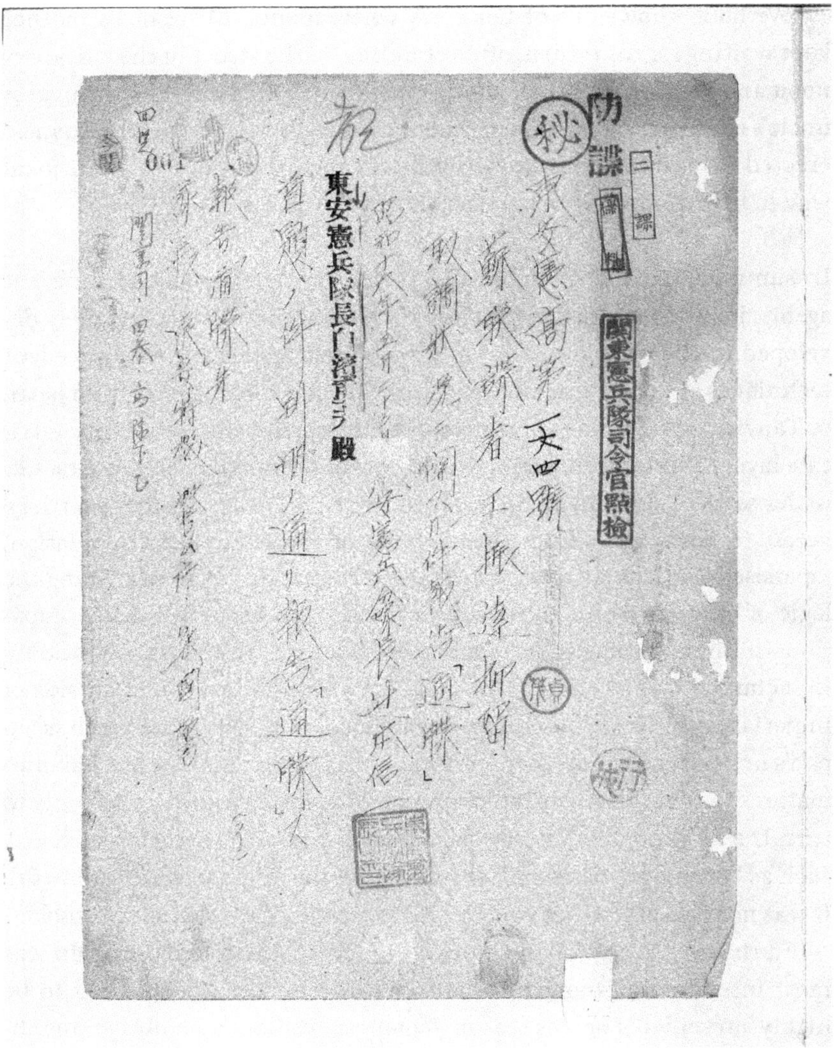

FIGURE 3.3A. Wang Mingshen (王明生)'s Special Transfer file, written by the Tongan Gendarmerie Branch Head to the upper gendarmerie head (May 25, 1941). The cover page, with red stamps of "secret" and "counterintelligence." From Heilongjiang Provincial Archive, Heilongjiang People Foreign Friendship Association and ABC Project Committee. *The Iron-Clad Evidence of "Unit 731" Criminal Activities—The Kwantung Gendarmerie Special Transfer Documents* (China: Heilongjiang People Publishing, 2001). Reprinted with permission.

FIGURE 3.3B. Photos of Wang Mingshen in the file. From Heilongjiang Provincial Archive, Heilongjiang People Foreign Friendship Association and ABC Project Committee. *The Iron-Clad Evidence of "Unit 731" Criminal Activities—The Kwantung Gendarmerie Special Transfer Documents* (China: Heilongjiang People Publishing, 2001). Reprinted with permission.

FIGURE 3.4. Photos of Zhu Yunxiu (朱雲岫) in his Special Transfer file. He and Wang Mingshen (Figure 3.3) both participated in the Anti-Japanese Northeast United Army, were placed under surveillance by the Kwantung Gendarmerie, detained and sent to Unit 731. From Heilongjiang Provincial Archive, Heilongjiang People Foreign Friendship Association and ABC Project Committee. *The Iron-Clad Evidence of "Unit 731" Criminal Activities—The Kwantung Gendarmerie Special Transfer Documents* (China: Heilongjiang People Publishing, 2001). Reprinted with permission.

The fingerprinted ID cards, detailed in the next chapter, were operationalized as surveillant power to track individuals' movements, in exchanges with these networked data of the preelectronic age. These discrete collections of personal data flowed into the maximum surveillant assemblage, which rendered residents increasingly vulnerable to intrusion by authorities in an uncontestable form. The surveillant assemblage moved as the arms of colonial law and violence worked in unity, captured, and punished those who protested, Wang Mingshen, Zhu Yunxiu, Zhu Yuntong, and many others.

CHAPTER FOUR

BODIES AS RISKY RESOURCES
Fingerprinting for Labor Control

Japanese evils are cruel and brutal

They persecute us the workers ruthlessly

We were frozen, starved, fell, and die, so Fengman has pits of ten thousand corpses

The iron pillars are made of our bones, the concrete is made of our flesh,

The water is our blood, and the dam is made of our bones and flesh.
— *(The Song of Fengman Dam Workers)*[1]

In 1923, The South Manchurian Railway Company, Mantetsu, published a report titled *Chinese Labor in Fushun Mine*. The report is the oldest Japanese-language source that references the use of fingerprinting for identification purposes in Northeast China. Mantetsu detailed how it had sorted workers into different categories in this report and mentioned that the migrant coal miners from the neighboring region had been already required fingerprinting in the recruitment process before coming to the Fushun Mine. The report suggests that fingerprint identification was practiced before the making of Manchukuo and disseminated from the colonial labor management.[2]

The Group Saying "No" to Fingerprinting (GSNF, 指紋なんてみん なで"不"の会) found this report in the 1980s and performed the most detailed ethnographical research on Japanese practice of fingerprint-ing in Manchukuo. Why did the investigation happen more than forty years after the collapse of Manchukuo? The civil group formed in Japan in the 1980s because there was a growing social movement to abolish fingerprinting for the Alien Registration System in post-World War II Japan. The GSNF supported non-Japanese citizens who refused to be fingerprinted for the Alien Registration System—the successor to the colonial biometric system—and advocated for the abolition of crimi-nal-like treatment of colonial descendants and foreign citizens (see the conclusion).[3] To uncover the historical genesis of compulsory fin-gerprinting, the group conducted field research in Northeast China in 1987 and published the outcomes in the book *Resisting Japan, Our Pride* (抗日こそ誇り——訪中報告書——). The team of nineteen scholars, lawyers, journalists, workers, and Chinese community leaders visited Shenyang, Fushun, Changchun, and Yanbian Korean Ethnic Autono-mous Prefecture (former Jiandao area), interviewed twenty colonial survivors who experienced fingerprint identification by the Japanese, and gathered documents with help from Chinese professors and youth groups. This collaborative investigation guided my field research thirty years later.

Against the backdrop of Japan's maximum surveillant assem-blage depicted in chapter 3, this chapter focuses on the development of biometric identification cards to classify the Chinese population in Northeast China. Japan's application of fingerprint identification to the colonial threshold strongly resonates with the Western trend of scien-tific rationality legitimizing racism. Mimicking British imperial social engineering, Japan went on its own path to extend fingerprinting from its use as labor control to leverage it to mobilize the entire population in Manchukuo.

First, the chapter probes the Manchurian origin of fingerprinting practices, which predates Japan's military occupation and declaration of Manchukuo. It was in 1920s at the Fushun Mine in Liaoning Province that the Japanese began to use fingerprints to identify workers and keep track of their movements. Fingerprinting was much more useful than existing ways to track where individuals came from, where they were

going, and what they had done before. Even on paper, long before com-
puterization, this form of identification functioned well for employers
to carefully select workers on the basis of reliability and to prevent resistance in the interest of economic efficiency. Recognizing its positive
effects for management, other large businesses put fingerprinting into
practice, which prompted some collective resistance from workers.

Following this background, I pull together the discrete threads of
Manchurian fingerprinting identification systems—sometimes used for
security purposes and other times for labor control—and observe how
they were gradually configured into an all-encompassing national
ID system, along with the pseudo-nation building of Manchukuo. The
major site of surveillance remained in mining and other heavy industry, but the objectives of the ID systems grew as Japan's war in China
expanded outside the Northeast and eventually into the Pacific and
Southeast Asia.

The institutionalization of biometric ID systems is divided into three
phases for close examination in this chapter. The first phase is the early
period of 1932-36, when the ID card systems were used to reduce the
numbers of migrants and restrain their movements. The Manchurian
government, under the Kwantung Army, restricted migrant workers
from coming into the occupied Northeast from neighboring provinces,
due to the suspicion that they would unite local resistance and spur Chinese nationalism. But this policy was modified in the second period,
1937-40, because of a shortage in labor power. The Industrial Development Five-Year Plan to develop a Japan-Manchuria bloc economy, and
the subsequent outbreak of the Chinese-Japanese War demanded more
labor to increase production and mobilization for the war. The fingerprinted Labor Card System was established in this middle period, as
was the Fingerprint Management Bureau, founded in 1939, as part of
the Security Section of the Manchurian government. The Fingerprint
Management Bureau matched fingerprints for both employers' screening of employees, and the Kwantung Army's scrutiny of potential enemies within.

During the final period of 1941-45, the two streams of fingerprint
identification converged in the National Passbook System in 1944, to
mobilize the population completely for total war. Desperately seeking
labor power, the Japanese leaned more on forcing farmers to serve their

"nation," abducting "vagrants" from the street, and placing prisoners of war into slave labor. The National Passbook symbolizes the meticulous way the imperial regime exhaustively classified and mobilized the population as human resources. Although a serial emergency law legalized these practices as a state system, the people who were subject to forced labor experienced them as nothing but terrorizing violence.

FROM EUROPEAN TO JAPANESE EMPIRE

Fingerprint identification was first introduced to Japan in 1908 by Ōba Shigema, an attorney who had traveled to Germany to study. On his way, Ōba stopped in Singapore and Egypt, where he visited prisons and police offices and witnessed the practices of the latest technologies for scientific identification: photography, anthropometry, and finger-printing.[4] Both Singapore and Egypt were under the rule of the British empire. After his return to Japan, Ōba strongly advocated for the implementation of fingerprinting and published a book titled *Individual Identification Method* in 1908. In his book, Ōba discussed the Hamburg method of fingerprinting, which had been developed in Germany based on the British Henry System (chapter 1).

The Hamburg method simplified the Henry System in categorization and index systems. It first categorizes fingerprints into three shapes—arch, loop, and whorl—and then further categorizes the loop into five kinds and whorl into three. In total, including lack of fingerprint, ten categories are created, and each category is given a number from 0 to 9. This way, each finger can be enumerated, and ten fingers creates a unique combination of numbers with which a person can be identified. Typically, the combination of numbers is stated in the form of fraction, in which the numbers of right fingers is stated as denominator and left fingers as numerator, such as $\frac{25375}{58651}$.[5] The ten-digit number in the form of fraction became a person's ID number, used to search, find, and mine their data.

The Japanese government first adopted fingerprint technology via a 1908 executive order mandating that fingerprints be taken from prisoners sentenced for fifteen different crimes. In 1911, the Metropolitan Police Department of Tokyo founded the Identification Laboratory in the Criminal Investigation Section, and extended fingerprinting to criminal suspects for the purposes of investigation. Soon, the method diffused to other police departments nationwide.

Today, most Japanese people believe fingerprinting is a tool specific to criminal investigation. However, Ōba proposed its use not only for criminal justice; he repeatedly suggested that it be applied to many other governmental purposes, such as policing vagrants and identifying mentally ill citizens and dead soldiers.[6] He claimed that fingerprinting should be combined with the *koseki* system for general administrative procedures. Ōba criticized *koseki* because it could update only personal data and could not substantially identify individuals in motion. His proposal of fingerprinting for mass identification was never realized in Japan but was implemented twenty years later in the colonial threshold.

In her book *Fingerprints and Modernity: The Technique to Control and Govern Mobile Bodies*, the sociologist Asako Takano traces the historical trajectory of fingerprint identification from the British to Japanese empire. Japanese bureaucrats mainly imported various schemes of colonial management from the leading empire. A government economics journal translated and published an English article, "The Chinese Miners in South Africa," in 1915. The article described how mining companies registered Chinese workers by fingerprinting them and attaching metal tags with numbers to them (chapter 1).[7] Mantetsu published *The Miners in Manchuria*, which narrates how Britain, France, and Germany recruited Chinese workers in Shandong Province during a World War I–era labor shortage and British took the fingerprints of workers. The way Mantetsu recruited Chinese workers in Shandong and Hebei Province in the 1920s is analogous to the British method.

THE ORIGIN STORY IN THE PRE-MANCHUKUO PERIOD

According to *Resisting Japan, Our Pride*, about fifty thousand coal miners were working at Fushun Mine near Shenyang in the 1920s.[8] Mantetsu hired workers in different categories: The upper classes were "employee" and "regular Chinese worker," and the lower were "Chinese coal miners" and "temporary Chinese workers." The latter, precarious categories numbered more than twenty thousand predominantly migrant workers. To recruit them, Mantetsu sent recruiters to several cities in

Shandong and Hebei Provinces, gathered potential workers at the offices, and "conducted a bodily examination, selected only the workers who looked adequate to handle the heavy job of coal mining, registered them, took their fingerprints, sent them to the accommodation, and arranged their transportation to the mine."[9]

On July 21, 1924, at the site of Fushun Mine, Mantetsu officially imposed fingerprint identification on the "Chinese coal miners" to "research the psychology of their movement, know the reasons for their movement, and regulate Chinese workers' movement in general."[10] Movement in this context referred to changing the site of employment from one place to another. Because the workers were migrants, employed on a daily or weekly basis, their wages were set lower than those of their Japanese colleagues. They constantly moved among the mines, looking for better wages and labor conditions. Fushun Mine consists of several different mines, so workers moved among those mines, too. But their constant workplace changes made it hard for Japanese managers to secure a consistent labor supply. Another report by Mantetsu in 1924 states that "a fingerprint scheme was applied to the police investigation in Japan, but it has never been used to regulate workers. The mining company implemented it on the Chinese coal miners on July 21, to protect the diligent, skilled Chinese workers on one hand, and on the other hand mend the bad habit of movement by others and prevent it."[11] Japanese employers were frustrated with the constant relocation and disappearance of Chinese workers and aimed to restrain it.

The processing of fingerprint identification in the Fushun Mine worked in the following way. "Regular Chinese workers" and "Chinese coal miners" had to give their left index fingerprint on two "employment cards" at the time of employment. The Chinese Worker Section of the company verified the fingerprints on the employment card with the person and then composed a "fingerprint card" by taking ten fingerprints to store in the office. The Chinese Worker Section retained an employment card and returned another to the worker's workplace.[12] If the office found fingerprints that matched anyone in the following categories, the person was not hired:[13]

1) Workers who were already hired and had not completed dismissal procedures.

2) Workers who were dismissed in the last two months, except for being laid off by the company.

3) Workers subject to disciplinary action by the company, or determined as "wicked" based on their profile.[14]

As a result, at least 1,640 people were excluded from the hiring list, and 26,954 workers were hired.[15] Mantetsu took one year to collect the fingerprints of forty-five thousand workers who had already been hired and saw the positive outcome of reducing to twenty-one thousand workers while maintaining the same productivity.[16] The Fushun Mine administration was satisfied: "We had not known the profiles of Chinese workers we hired every day, and unable to recognize when they gave us false names or records. But as a result of the fingerprint scheme, we are now able to infer false records and profiles."[17]

For Japanese colonial industries, fingerprint identification proved an efficient way to classify potential labor power, hire usable bodies with clean profiles, and exclude undesirable and suspicious bodies. It quickly spread to other mines run by Mantetsu, and other colonial industries, like iron and steel. Even though it was done only with ink and paper, and not by digital devices, ten-digit fingerprint technology provided the information needed by the industries. In 1937, Fushun Mine screened 31,997 personnel for hiring purposes and did not hire 7,879. Among them, 2,031 (25 percent) were excluded based on fingerprint identification: 389 were already hired and registered by other mines, 1022 have not yet passed two months after dismissal in other mines, 304 were found to have formerly received disciplinary actions by the company, or to be "wicked" from their profiles, 161 showed a high rate of movement, and 155 had been injured during work.[18] The reasons for disciplinary actions by the company were "organized disobedience," "following immoral situations," and "intentionally inciting a crowd." In short, any workers who had organized resistance to the employer or shown any potential for disobedience to the employer were carefully eliminated.

Thus, originally, fingerprint identification was used in the workplace to select diligent workers, make them stay to maximize productivity, and restrain potential resistance. A regional picture of labor migration explains the fear of Chinese resistance, shared by Mantetsu and other Japanese industries at that time. Shortly before Mantetsu introduced fingerprinting to Fushun Mine, there were several strikes against Japanese factory owners as workers sought increased wages, an end to violent abuse by Japanese managers, and the return of dismissed workers in Dalian, Yingkou, and Shenyang. Some of those strikes won victories for workers. The wave of labor disputes reached Fushun Mine by the end of 1923, and about 1,400 coal miners out of 1,500 went on a nine-hour strike against reduced wages and increased food prices in the mine.[19] Nine hundred coal miners went on another strike against the new wage system and to abolish the rule requiring workers to pay for damaged mining tools. Both instances of organized resistance saw some positive outcomes. But the labor movement presumably motivated Japanese employers to conduct more rigorous background checks on workers.

CHEAP LABOR AND RESISTANCE FROM WORKERS IN THE 1920S

In 1926, the South Manchuria Industrial Society was formed in Shenyang, and owners agreed to establish a common fingerprint identification system across industries, basically following the Fushun Mine scheme. The effected industries varied from tobacco to spinning, from mechanics to electricity, all of which faced constant strikes. Each company sent the South Manchuria Industrial Society offices one of two employment cards, with the original fingerprints of all employees. The companies were required to report to the office whether any employees committed crimes or undesirable actions. Then, the office would send a photo of those workers' fingerprints to all related agencies. Any workers found to be negligent or "wicked" in the records of previous workplaces, and whose fingerprints matched them, were to be dismissed immediately. If the fingerprint suggested that the worker was still employed by another employer, the company had to get the former employer's permission to hire that worker. Companies could buy employment cards and other fingerprinting materials from the Industrial Society's office, and the office maintained a close relationship with the Shenyang Police, Kwantung Government, Mantetsu, and other entities.[20] Clearly, the basic scheme of collecting, retaining, and using fingerprints mimicked the method used in Fushun Mine, but the scale of data exchange expanded to the major Japanese industries in Manchuria. Employing this fingerprinting system across industries helped colonial business owners exclude troublemakers.

For their part, Chinese workers did not seem to welcome biometric identification. A strike against fingerprinting occurred in a factory of the Japanese wool-spinning company Manmō Keori (満蒙毛織) in Dalian in October 1926. Manmō Keori introduced fingerprint identification based on its agreement with the South Manchuria Industrial Society. Initially, it required fingerprints of new employees, and later, from employees already working in the factory. Trouble erupted even before the end of the first day. Many workers refused to give their fingerprints. Some interpreted the fingerprinting as an agreement to sell family members. Others, after giving their fingerprints, demanded that the company give them back. The next day, angry workers did not follow the daily inspection of the body and baggage; many Japanese factories checked workers' bodies at closing time, suspicious that they may smuggle out the factories' property. This turned into a physical confrontation with the factory's Russian security guards. The factory tried to punish these dissidents the following day, and eventually 470 workers went on strike.[21] In collective bargaining after a week on strike, the workers demanded that the company abolish fingerprint identification, raise wages, stop hiring Russian guards, and guarantee their right to a year-end bonus. Manmō Keori refused all the requests and fired all the workers.

The Group of Saying "No" to Fingerprinting interviewed another former Shenyang worker in 1987, during which the worker explained the cultural connotations of fingerprinting in China. "We had to give our fingerprints when selling our daughters, lands and other properties to the landowners and capitalists," he said. "It tends to happen with unequal relationship. When they forced someone vulnerable to contract with them, they took the fingerprints as evidence of the consent."[22] Although the comment referred to cultural customs and not to the intent of Manmō Keori and other Japanese business owners, dissenting workers intuitively sensed that the compulsory fingerprint would further restrain their freedom and reinforce existing inequalities between employers and employees. The workers' early resistance to fingerprint identification remarkably shows that workers understood fingerprinting as another means of oppression in their workplace.

In 1927, Mantetsu expanded the categories of businesses required to take fingerprints from new Chinese employees, and fingerprinting became part of the regular hiring process in colonial industries in Northeast China. It was established as a model of biometric labor control before Manchukuo was declared in 1932. This is the prehistory of the Manchurian biometric ID system, and it demonstrates how the colonization of Northeast China commenced long before it took the governmental form of Manchukuo. Economic colonialism tested racializing biometric technologies on the local population and gradually adapted the classification system to larger circles of industries in interactions with the imperial interests of the time. The fingerprint identification scheme tested by Mantetsu in Fushun Mine became the default for population management in all of Manchukuo.

Practitioners of the new technology were aware that it could be applied to manifold workplaces and help underpin their power in colonial management, both economically and politically. A Japanese fingerprinting professional in Mantetsu said in 1934, "Fingerprinting is a kind of dragnet like when you catch fish. Fish can be captured any time if you set the net everywhere."[23] In this context, the Chinese population were the fish: they did not have to be suspects at the moment of fingerprinting, but whenever the Japanese found them suspicious, the fingerprinting made them easy to seize. This illuminates the same motives and effects of digital mass surveillance practiced in the twenty-first century.

Multipurpose biometric dragnets were not just for show or to deter people. The GSNF interviewed a former miner in Fushun Mine who had witnessed many colleagues killed by an explosion and who escaped in terror from the mine. He changed his name and found another job at a construction site. But twenty-two days later, he was identified and sent back to Fushun Mine thanks to fingerprint identification. Biometric identification enabled the colonizers to contain runaways, strikers, and dissenters across industries. The dragnet captured human beings—as the Mantetsu fingerprint professional confidently described—as evidence of its efficacy.

The classifying power also helped supply colonial industries with hundreds of thousands of cheap workers and subjected them to extremely unequal conditions. According to the Mantetsu statistics, in Fushun Mine, when a Japanese manager or skilled employee earned 2.75 yen in 1925, the Chinese counterpart earned 0.72 yen, the "regular Chinese worker" earned 0.44 yen per day, and the "Chinese coal miner" 0.7 yen.[24] On average, Chinese workers received only a quarter of the wages received by Japanese workers in the official record, which is already an extreme gap, but the GSNF estimated an even larger gap from interviews with former miners. The wage disparity continued under Manchukuo and naturally increased labor conflict and instability within the workforce. Evasions and protests by Chinese workers against routinized inequalities became more probable than possible, and fingerprint identification served to prevent adversary actions in advance, bind workers to specific workplaces, and stabilize colonial extraction. Another former miner aptly summarized the purpose of fingerprinting to the GSNF: "I think that the Japanese used fingerprinting to exploit the Chinese."[25] This sentiment must have been largely shared among workers at the bottom of the colonial labor structure.

Therefore, the economic desire to manage cheap labor power by preempting risk of resistance gave rise to the fingerprint ID system in Japanese colonial industries in the 1920s. Labor control in Fushun Mine, run by Japan's biggest corporation at the time, established a biometric scheme to which only racialized Others were subjected. We will see in the next sections how the same method was integrated into the "national" ID systems in Manchukuo.

FINGERPRINTING TO RESTRAIN CHINESE MIGRATION, 1932–36

In April 1932, one month after the declaration of Manchukuo, the Japanese daily newspaper *Manshū Nippō* reported, "Manchukuo will enact the Fingerprint Act as a supplemental measure to the Koseki Act and apply it to 30 million nationals."[26] In fact, the fingerprinted national ID system was not put into practice until 1944, nor were the Koseki and Nationality Acts realized on the colonial threshold (chapter 3). But the *Manshū Nippō* article shows how fingerprinting technology represented the efficiency, productivity, and security of modern systems. Fingerprinting identification was expected to prove Japan's leadership in East Asia and its legitimacy to create an ideal nation in the militarily acquired land. Technology was supposed to advance Japan's positive image and even justify the occupation. The *Manshū Nippō* report detailed the following plans: The Manchukuo government would set up the Human Rights Protection Agency (Jinken hoshōkyoku, 人権保障局) to enact the Status Registration Act (Mibun tōkihō, 身分登記法) that would add fingerprints to *koseki*. As the first step to implementing the original plan, the government would hire one hundred female officials to be trained as fingerprint technicians.

Similarly, a draft paper for the Status Registration Act written by Mantetsu Economic Research Association in March 1933 listed all possible reasons every single Chinese person had to be identified and profiled. Namely, to find anyone who did something against the government and attach the indicator of wrongdoing to those elements; to prevent them from being hired in the government, military, or police; to prevent others from joining them in case of insurgency; to prevent fictitious or false names; to teach people the decisive force of the new government; to teach criminals that the government could find them anywhere, and so on.[27] Fingerprint identification was not only incorporated into the planning of quasi-state systems from the very beginning; it was also expected to demonstrate Japan's modern, technological, and disciplinary power in a tangible way to the local population.

The Status Registration Act was defeated, however, because the Police Department apparently did not have enough human resources to cover the entire population with the fingerprint ID system. Instead, in September 1934, the police started fingerprinting only for criminal investigations. But a similar idea of thorough surveillance was immediately practiced in household investigations and the *hokō* system (chapter 3). The colonial and criminal were treated synonymously as categories of people, as they had been in India and South Africa. The *Manshū Nippō* article shows that the sovereign desire for a biometric national ID system was very present from the beginning of pseudo–nation building, and advanced continuously over the next thirteen years, while the Japanese legal elites struggled to resolve the enigma of Manchukuo nationality (chapter 3).

Early attempts to control the population in Manchukuo focused heavily on restricting Chinese migrants' entry for national security reasons. The Kwantung Army organized the Labor Control Committee with the Korean governor-general, Mantetsu, and other major companies in September 1933, to "establish the fingerprinting section to thoroughly control the movements of the workers" coming from other parts of China.[28] The military and police saw the working class as particularly suspect. The Metropolitan Police in Changchun expressed its adversarial view: "It is an obvious fact who the subversive elements are in getting the public attention, threatening and giving anxiety to ordinary people, or attempting any actions of the anti-Manchukuo and resisting-Japanese. They all belong to the working class, or pretend to be them."[29]

In the first meeting of the Labor Control Committee, the Kwantung Army asserted the clear vision that Japan should restrain Chinese migrants, increase Japanese immigration, and eventually aim to make labor supply meet demand within the occupied area *without* Chinese migrants.[30] The business side claimed that it needed cheap migrant labor, because, for example, construction companies "pay the [migrant] Shandong coolies two-thirds of the wages paid for the local coolies. So, if reducing their entries into the country and using only local labor, it will delay construction plans and raise costs."[31] This comment reveals how under capitalism, racism—or racialization of workers—provides a source of profit, and security measures may undercut economic gains. But at last, the army got its way. Security for the occupying power overruled the profit motive in the aftermath of the Manchurian Incident and in the face of Chinese protests.

In the first phase of Manchurian labor control, establishing racial hierarchy and political privilege for the occupying Japanese was prioritized over economic rationality. This was an unexceptional decision in colonial management, as Hannah Arendt finds in the South African case. She points to the grave impact of racist Western rules on totalitarian governments in Africa and states "that profit motives are not holy and can be overruled, that societies can function according to principles other than economic."[32] Arendt argues that because of politics, even if an action runs counter to economic principles in the short term, a state can eventually use sheer violence to create an exploitable economic class.

What the Kwantung Army intended was not dissimilar from South African white supremacy, with its early blueprint for a population ratio plan. Despite Japan's economic principles and internationally projected image as a racially harmonious nation, the army tried to establish Japanese privilege through a mass migration plan from Japan to Manchuria. The related elite discourses were disguised in the language of a "civilization mandate," like the "white man's burden" rationale for British rule in Asia.[33] At the Japanese-Manchuria Labor Issue Meeting in 1934, a Japanese official from the Ministry of Internal Affairs (Naimushō, 内務省) said, "The superior race of Japanese should come to Manchukuo and show the ideal model of constituting the state and the leaders."[34] The concept of mass migration included Koreans. Elites viewed Korean migration to Japan as increasing the unemployment rate there, so labor experts found a solution in relocating them to Manchuria. Korean migrants, as Japanese nationals, were used to push the imperial boundaries toward China.[35]

The restriction of Chinese migrants was in fact linked with the plan for Japanese settler migration. Before the declaration of Manchukuo, most "free migration" plans for Manchuria had lacked government support and had failed, although the government had propelled farmers to migrate voluntarily. The Chinese protested Japan's economic encroachment in China, and Japanese farmers were less competitive than Chinese farmers in the global market. Instead of admitting the demerits, the Kwantung Army and Mantetsu doubled down by inaugurating a pilot project recruiting armed immigrants through the veterans' association from 1932 to 1936. About five hundred households arrived in Manchuria in the first two years.[36] The second group encountered an armed protest by thousands of Chinese farmers, and the Kwantung Army killed five thousand Chinese farmers in this incident. Although images that sold migration as reclaiming a Chinese wasteland were widely distributed for recruitment, the land that Japanese migrants actually settled in Manchuria was already under cultivation by Chinese farmers whose homes were taken away.[37] The Kwantung Army also chose settlement locations strategically—less for farming than for defense. The migrants were allocated to the northeast, closer to the conflict zones near the Russian and Korean borders, rather than in the warm south, which is more suited to agricultural production. The army deliberately used Japanese migrants as human shields to block potential attacks from Russia and counter anti-imperial movements by the Koreans and Chinese.

The pilot project was completed in 1936, but continuous Chinese resistance meant the Japanese sought a different form of migration, on an even more massive scale. The Manchukuo government, Mantetsu, and the industrial conglomerates of Mitsui (三井) and Mitsubishi (三菱), jointly founded the Manchuria Reclamation Company (Manshū Shokutaku Kabushikigaisha, 満州拓殖株式会社). The Manchuria Reclamation

Company planned to send one million households to Manchuria beginning in 1937 and over the following twenty years, or about five million
Japanese in total.[38] The plan was for one hundred thousand households
to migrate in the first five years (1937-41).[39] Japanese settler colonialism
clearly aimed to change the demographic ratio of the Manchurian population to stabilize the Japanese ruling position. The two initiatives, the
pilot program of armed immigrants and the subsequent larger scale of
family migration, were undertaken while restricting the entry of Chinese migrants to Manchukuo.

To regulate the number of Chinese migrant workers, the Labor Control Committee codified the process of recruitment: The Civil Policy
Section of the Manchurian government set a quota of migrant workers for each industry annually; the recruiting agency Daitō Company
(大東公司), located in Shandong and Hebei Province, inspected recruited workers and issued visas allowing them to enter Manchukuo;
and the police checked their visas upon their entry to Manchukuo in
the border cities of Shanhaiguan, Andong, Yinghou, and did not permit
workers to enter without a visa. Although fingerprinting was not included at this point, this was the same process that Mantetsu had established a decade earlier to recruit coal miners for Fushun Mine using
fingerprints. To formalize it as a "national" institution, the Daitō Company was founded as the official recruiting agency under the Tianjin
Special Mission Agency of Kwantung Army in April 1934. The Foreign
Workers Policing Rules of 1935 went into effect to restrict migrants'
access to the recruitment resources and to police the recruits.

The officialization of migration channels saw some troubles at the
beginning. The Republic of China did not recognize Manchukuo, the
Daitō Company, or the Manchurian government representative and
intervened in the process. As a result, the number of Chinese workers
entering Manchuria increased from 568,768 in 1933 to 627,322 in 1934,
contrary to the policy goal.[40] Frustrated, the Labor Control Committee
required workers to also get an ID card certified by the Daitō Company,
and the ID card needed to be stamped by the police in the city of entry.
Fingerprinting was not required yet, apparently due to the shortage of
human resources, but the ID card collected more information from the
visa: home address, name, age, category of labor, places of entry and
visit.[41] Workers were required to carry their ID card at all times. This

strict identifying process helped reduce the number of workers from 444,540 in 1935 to 364,149 in 1936.[42]

Meanwhile, the use of fingerprinting for labor control was discussed from this early stage of building Manchukuo. Mantetsu drafted the Laborer Fingerprint Control Act in 1934, to expand administrative control from migrants to all workers, with fingerprint identification.[43] It was not immediately passed, but the nation builders incubated the idea for the Labor Card system that was realized later. The bill required all workers *within* Manchukuo to register with fingerprints and hold work permits. Mantetsu assessed the direct benefits of the system to be the policing of false names and aliases and the prevention of anti-Manchukuo elements from entering the region. One of the indirect benefits was that the demographic data gathered through registration would supplement a future enactment of the Nationality Act. Labor control, security operation, and construction of the nation were closely intertwined from the beginning.

ESTABLISHMENT OF FINGERPRINTED ID CARDS, 1937–40

Two historical events in 1937 mark the second period of national labor control: the Industrial Development Five-Year Plan announced in April and a clash between the Japanese and Chinese armies in Lugouqiao in the southeastern suburbs of Beijing in July, which broke out into the full-scale Chinese-Japanese War. The Industrial Development Five-Year Plan aimed to boost the Japanese-Manchurian bloc economy and thus situate Manchuria as the industrialized repository of natural resources for Japan. The Japanese government was initially reluctant to approve this plan, as it required the massive national investment of 2.5 billion yen.[44] Yet the Chinese-Japanese War dramatically changed the situation. Manchuria was located on the war's margins, and the budget was increased to 4.8 billion yen to support the war. Manchukuo faced serious demand for labor to fulfill the planned production. To recruit more workers, the Manchuria Workers Association (Manshū rōkō kyōkai, 満州労工協会) was founded in January 1938, jointly by the Manchurian government, Mantetsu, the Manchurian Construction Association, and private companies. It absorbed the Daitō Company in 1939 and centralized the screening

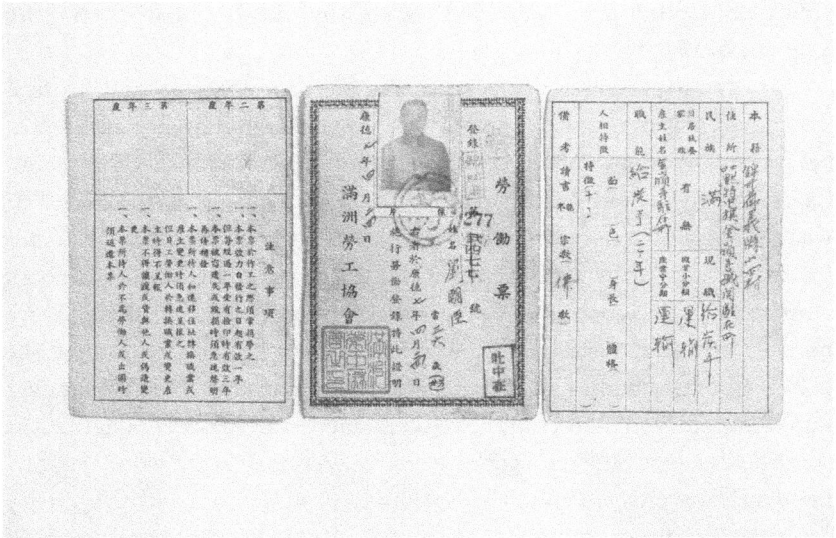

FIGURE 4.1. The Labor Card, issued to a worker by the Manchurian Labor Association in 1940. It shows the bearer's personal information, such as address, ethnicity, occupation, category of occupation, employer, skills, bodily features, literacy, and religion. Photo by Ken Mizokoshi.

system for both migrants and local workers in Manchukuo by having them fingerprinted and issuing them a work permit called the Labor Card (*Rōdō hyō*, 労働票).

The policy shifted to mobilize the entire Manchurian population to win Japan's still undeclared but no longer deniable war, the battle lines of which were advancing toward inland China. The National Total Mobilization Act was enacted in February 1938 in Manchukuo two months earlier than its counterpart in Japan. A series of regulations creating a temporary Labor Card and ten-digit fingerprinting followed and culminated in the Labor Control Act in December 1938. The Labor Control Committee, led by the Kwantung Army, was replaced by the Labor Committee in July 1938, under the State Department of Manchukuo. The Manchurian government's new imperative was to hire as many workers as possible. The policy change in labor control, though, did not relax Japanese scrutiny of workers; instead, it intensified individual identification, due to increased suspicion of people arriving from other parts of China. Biometric ID systems played an even more important role as gatekeepers of Manchukuo.

The Labor Card was first required for workers in factories, mines, construction, transportation, and forestry. These fields were the dominant enterprises of the Industrial Development Five-Year Plan and were directly related to military operations. The Temporary Labor Card Regulation required employers who had more than thirty employees in the workplace to register them at the Workers Association; 562,105 employees were registered in the first year.[45] Fingerprinting was then added to the registration, and the Workers Association collected about two hundred thousand sets of workers' fingerprints by the next year.[46] The Workers Association organized an agreement with 240 companies to identify workers and not to hire them if they were already employed by another company.[47] The Workers Association played the role of internal gatekeeper across industries, while the Daitō Company played the external gatekeeper for entry into Manchukuo, collecting workers' profiles and watching their movements. The practices exactly followed the pattern established by Fushun Mine and the South Manchuria Industrial Society in the 1920s.

Finally, to centralize indexing and matching systems for this enormous batch of fingerprints, the Fingerprint Management Bureau (Shimon kanri kyoku, 指紋管理局) was established under the Security Section of the Manchurian government in January 1939. Its headquarters was located in Changchun, with branches in the provincial police. All fingerprints collected by the Workers Association were sent to the Fingerprint Management Bureau, and merged with fingerprint records for criminal investigation in the repository. The Bureau had amassed 2.7 million sets of fingerprint records in the two years since its establishment.[48] To process the high volume of data—without computers— the government built a training center for fingerprint technicians. The first year, the Bureau hired 155 technicians in the Headquarters and 227 in local branches, and the number grew to 211 in the Headquarters and 460 in the branches by the end of 1940.[49] The national institution of fingerprint identification, dreamed of at the beginning of quasi-state building, finally took shape with the establishment of the centralized Fingerprint Management Bureau.

Biometric labor control kept growing under new legislation continually produced by Japanese bureaucrats in this period. As described in chapter 3, Manchukuo had no congress or parliament, so

the Manchurian government produced laws quickly, without democratic debate. More precisely, the Japanese bureaucracy kept producing
decrees it called laws. In a democratic government, legislative power
resides only in a congress whose members are selected by the people,
but these decrees had no such democratic basis, and were instead anon-
ymously created by bureaucrats and freely applied by government
officers. Rule by decree is distinguished from the rule of law in this
sense, and resembles despotism, as Arendt discusses.[50] Rule by decree
naturalizes a state of exception in the legal system. The Manchurian
legislation shows how rapidly bureaucracy and decree could move as vehicles of imperialism to enable lawless despotism in a civilized, efficient
manner. Efficiency was maximized under a political structure that did
not allow adversarial views and democratic pluralism. The "iron fist" of
the bureaucratic machinery, as characterized by Max Weber,[51] seized
workers' movements through fingerprint identification, uniting labor
control and racializing surveillance in favor of wartime state monopoly
capitalism.

To mobilize the entire workforce for full-scale war, the Labor Control Act was enacted in February 1939 to remove limits on the size of
workplaces subject to registration, and to compel all workplaces related
to heavy industry to register. Following the Fushun Mine and Daitō
Company schemes, local workers had to give their ten fingerprints at
the offices of the Workers Association, and they received a fingerprinted
Labor Card. Migrant workers were required to receive ID cards prior
to entry into Manchukuo, have the cards stamped by the police in the
entry city, bring them to the Workers Association, give their ten fingerprints there, and finally receive the stamp of the Association. ID cards
were treated as Labor Cards. The cards expired after three years, but
workers had to go to the Workers Association every year to get a stamp,
otherwise the cards lost their validity. The Workers Association shared
fingerprints with branches of the Fingerprint Management Bureau,
and the branches sent copies to the headquarters. The headquarters
and branches contacted the Workers Association if they identified any
dual registrations and searched profiles upon the Workers Association's
requests.[52]

It was a massive operation that collected more than one million
sets of fingerprints annually but did not yet cover the entire adult

population. Who, then, was prioritized for fingerprint identification? Takano finds that categories of occupation determined the Labor Card requirement. Nationality, ethnicity, sex, or age did not affect the conditions of biometric registration.[53] Thus, by definition, Japanese individuals were also subject to labor control, but in reality, they rarely required fingerprinting. Chinese men were the majority group fingerprinted. Out of 1,075,122 workers fingerprinted by the bureau in 1940, 540,963 were migrant workers from other parts of China, and 505,117 were workers residing in Manchukuo.[54] In total, 97.3 percent of those fingerprinted were Chinese. Only 2.6 percent, or 28,609, were Japanese, but most were in fact Koreans. Thus, Japanese were less than 0.1 percent of those fingerprinted, or 1,053 people, because most Japanese migrants were engaged in farming, which was not subject to biometric registration. For Takano, this shows that only people in movement or mobile bodies were seen as risky and requiring control. Yet in an intersectional view of race and class, the gap between definition and reality reveals more: By using occupational categories, Japanese bureaucrats were able to scrutinize only Chinese workers without referring to racial categories in regulations. Policymakers avoided using overtly discriminatory language and racial identifiers, as those words would spark critique and protest by Chinese and Koreans. Of the occupational categories, construction was the biggest group, followed by factory production and mining. Workers in those occupations were predominantly Chinese individuals who undertook short-term contracts and constantly changed places of employment in response to job insecurity and a volatile market. The working class was largely stratified by race, so Japanese agents did not have to specify which races were particularly suspected and subjected to fingerprinting.

To understand the racial demographics of the labor force, it is worth tracing the trajectory of the Japanese government's mass migration plan in this period. A five-year pilot project prioritized the migration of armed immigrants until 1936. Then, the Japanese government announced a scaled-up plan to send one hundred thousand Japanese households to Manchuria over the next five years: seventy thousand for collective farming and thirty thousand for individual farming, commerce, and industry.[55] However, this was already unachievable in 1938 because of the high labor and production demand in industries on the archipelago—military industries monopolized the labor market with the Chinese-Japanese War. Japan did not have sufficient free or flexible labor power to export to Manchuria. Then, the Japanese government founded the Manchuria Youth Reclamation Volunteer Army to supplement the decreasing number of migrants; it recruited males over sixteen years old who had not yet been conscripted.

The Japanese and Manchurian governments redefined migration policy to reinforce the unity of Japan with Manchukuo, fortify defense capabilities against the Soviet Union, and improve farming and industry in Manchuria. The mass migration plan's purpose morphed from economic to being a security safeguard. But the plan still had to be modified a few times, and eventually it achieved only 36 percent of the goal of the five-year migration plan and 45 percent of the goal for the Youth Reclamation Volunteer Army.[56] A second migration plan was launched in 1942. Before seeing its completion, Japan lost the wars and its colonial lands. When the Soviet Army came down across the Manchuria border on August 9, 1945, the Kwantung Army was already withdrawing, leaving civilians behind.[57] With no guards, Japanese settlers were attacked and retaliated against by the Chinese, whose land had been stolen. Many died of starvation and lack of medicine and transportation in flight back to Japan. On the way, many parents left their babies and children in the hands of Chinese villagers who cared for the children. In total, 318,000 Japanese from 106,000 households had migrated to Manchuria by 1945. Only an estimated 110,000 migrants were able to repatriate to Japan after the war was lost.[58]

Overall, though the Japanese government promoted Japanese mass migration to Manchuria, it hardly changed the demographic of the Manchurian workforce. Heavy industry especially still relied on Chinese migrants, who had no choice but to work in the most miserable conditions, for the lowest wages, and under the most severe surveillance—the Labor Card. Japanese technocrats occupied top positions in Manchurian industries, and Japanese bureaucrats dominated directory roles in the administration, while Japanese settlers were allocated remote land as farmers and soldiers. Although the labor control policy shifted from restricting to increasing Chinese migrants, they were still positioned at the bottom of the Manchurian economic structure, which was increasingly characterized as a wartime state monopoly. The government upheld the principle of providing the Japanese with leading positions and skilled labor, relegating the Chinese to subordinate and unskilled labor. Most Japanese were immune to the intensive surveillance embodied in the Labor Card System, because of the socioeconomic structure stratified by race.

On another note, the use of fingerprint identification of Japanese settlers in an exceptional case nuances our understanding of ruling relations between the metropole and colonial threshold. Because the Japanese military industries tried to primarily anchor skilled workers in Japan, few skilled workers moved to the Manchurian workforce. The Japanese also did not want to share knowledge with or train a large number of Chinese professionals. As a result, Japanese skilled workers were subjected to fingerprint registration in October 1937 as rare human resources. The Professional Technique Registration Order required that engineers in 107 professions related to the military be fingerprinted for total war mobilization. While eliminating the potential resistance of low-wage workers in the Labor Card System, fingerprint identification enabled the government to proactively find and leverage specific skills for the war agenda. The Labor Control Act also allowed the Workers Association to request that heads of local municipalities recruit workers. This indicates the transitional character of the second period, from recruiting for "free employment" (at least in terms of contracts, though under the worst conditions) in the early period to organizing compulsory labor as a national service in the last period. Throughout, fingerprint identification prevailed as a settler colonial tool that bolstered racial privilege.

As part of the Security Section of Manchukuo government, the Fingerprint Management Bureau also worked closely with the Kwantung Army on military operations. The fingerprints accumulated in the bureau were used to single out potential enemies. Before specific sweeping operations, the bureau issued ID cards to residents in the targeted regions, such as in the concentration villages (chapter 3), and sent a team of fingerprint technicians to work in battlefields during the operations. For example, in the Special Security Operation in the Southeast Area in 1939, the bureau planned to issue residential ID cards in the subject area in August, sent forty fingerprint technicians, trained police officers in fingerprint identification, and issued

590,144 single-fingerprinted ID cards to residents by the end of the fiscal year.[59] Then, the bureau organized a Mobile Fingerprint Unit for the army, which worked to identify residents and "bandits" at checkpoints. The same pattern of operations was repeated the next year, when 742,688 fingerprinted ID cards were issued before armed attacks on the region and 1,304 people were arrested as suspicious.[60] If a person's fingerprint matched with the lists of bandits, they were "severely punished," which in some places meant execution. If the person did not have their ID card, they were assumed to be bandits and given the same punishment.

Finding the invisible enemy within was an unbending, essential strategy used by the Kwantung Army to conquer the colonial population. It identified elements of armed resistance, isolated them, and cut off their support from village people. The Mobile Fingerprint Unit even took up arms during operations. Yang Jingyu (杨靖宇), general of the Anti-Japanese Northeast United Army, was killed in February 1940 in this Special Operation in Southeast Area. The Kwantung Army identified Yang's corpse and performed an autopsy. They found little food in Yang's stomach—only some grass and bark from his time hiding in the mountains. The autopsy illustrated the severe impact of Japan's identification and isolation tactics on the Chinese resistance: Chinese soldiers lost access to local community support, and thus to food, water, clothes, fuel, and other essential resources, due to how the maximum surveillant assemblage tracked people's movements.[61]

Northeast China was not the only place where Japan issued fingerprinted Labor Cards and residential ID cards. I saw various kinds of ID cards preserved in the Jixi City Museum: a temporary group travel permit, a temporary resident certificate, a Chinese worker recruitment card, a normal labor exit and border-crossing card, and a skilled professional card (see fig. 1.1). There are no official lists that clarify how many and what kinds of ID cards Manchurian agencies issued, but these examples demonstrate the meticulous networks used to control the movements of the Chinese. Every time a Chinese person moved from one point to another in and out of Manchukuo, they had to get permission, or register themselves, and obtain, carry, and show their ID cards at checkpoints. During this period, the Fingerprint Management Bureau integrated labor control and counterinsurgency measures, both technically and politically, into a national system that tracks every body on the move.

THE NATIONAL PASSBOOK FOR TOTAL MOBILIZATION, 1941-45

In September 1941, the Manchurian government announced a new policy establishing the New Labor Structure (Rōmu shin taisei, 労務新体制), demarcating the final period of the use of fingerprint identification systems to track the entire population in Manchukuo. The discrete streams of identification practices converged in a mandatory National Passbook meant to mobilize the entire population for total war. Despite efforts to increase the numbers of migrant workers coming from neighboring provinces in China, the reform was not straightforward. It required the involvement of more Chinese agents as recruiters, caused the outflow of wages migrant workers had earned in Manchuria, and incited labor conflicts and strikes by low-wage workers over inflation.[62] Fingerprint identification could not solve these structural issues of the labor market under the wartime economy.

The term "New Labor Structure" in fact framed private work as public duty. The "Labor" part in the name of this new policy is written 労務 in Japanese, rather than 労働, which normally refers to labor. While 働 simply refers to work, 務 connotes duty or service. The term 労務 was often used by the government in relation to labor management. This choice of language reflects a policy shift from labor as private work to labor as a public duty linked to moral conduct. The amalgamation of private work and public duty was indeed maximized in the last stage of total war, and the public announcement of the New Labor Structure did not hide it. Its goals included "Respect Labor," "Every National Works," and "Bring Prosperity to the Nation through Labor," and it proclaimed to "place all the energies of nationals' labor under the strong control of the state, and develop it to the full extent of state control."[63] It particularly aimed to establish a national service system, generate a spirit of self-sacrifice among youth, and initiate a volunteer labor movement from the bottom of the economic structure.[64] The Labor Control Act was revised in October 1941, and it dissolved the Manchuria Workers Association and put direct management of fingerprint registration and the issuing of Labor Cards to workers under government. It also founded the

Labor Vitalization State Association (Rōmu kōkoku kai, 労務興国会)—
under the Civil Section's control—to promote "service spirit" and thus
mobilize the entire population to work for the nation. This campaign
was launched to indoctrinate people of all age groups, from youth to the
elderly, in this principle and to make already cheap labor into unpaid
work as an honorable service to the quasi state. Manchukuo desperately
needed labor power to maintain the expanding wars in the Pacific and
Southeast Asia and defend Japanese advantages at the battlelines. But
there is no evidence that this official nationalism convinced the Chinese
people, since they were always classified as Others, enemies within, or
at best, second-class subjects on settler colonial land. As a result, Chinese adults, youth, and children experienced the worst kinds of forced
labor in the last few years of the occupation.

As springboards to mobilize the entire population, three new laws—
the National Soldier Act, Census Act, and Civil Registry Act—were enacted in 1940. The conscription system of the National Soldier Act was
not as exhaustive as the one in Japan, due to persistent doubts about
Chinese loyalty to the Japanese empire. The law limited conscription
to men, to those who had a "suited personality," came from a wealthy
family, and were physically tough.[65] The rest of the young men were sent
to labor in factories and construction sites. For this purpose, the Census
Act was designed to exhaustively collect data on who lived where and
the civil registry tentatively defined residents as national subjects of
Manchukuo who could be mobilized as human resources. Together,
those laws extracted more data from the population, enriched the data
linking biometric identification, and engineered a new database for
total mobilization.

The New Labor Structure clearly reflected an even more dire labor
shortage than before. The Japanese Army enlarged the occupied area
in China to include neighboring Shandong and Hebei Provinces, the
hometowns of most migrant workers in Manchukuo. It generated competition within the Japanese Army between Manchuria and the neighboring regions to obtain workers. To ease the pressure, the North China
Workers Association was founded in April 1941 to regulate the processes
to recruit, transport, and distribute migrant workers from those provinces and Inner Mongolia under an agreement with the Manchurian
government.[66]

Another factor in the extreme labor shortage was the Kwantung Army Special Exercise (Kantōgun tokushu enshū, 関東軍特種演習, in short, 関特演). Disguised as an exercise, the Kwantung Army secretly planned to attack the Soviet Union in the summer of 1941, soon after the German invasion of the Soviet Union in June. Japanese war leaders expected that some units of the Soviet Army around the Manchurian border would be relocated to the Western front lines in response to the Nazi's surprise attack. As Japan signed the triple military alliance with Germany and Italy in September 1940, the German invasion was an opportunity, in the Kwantung Army's view, to catch the Soviet Union in a pincer attack with Germany. The Kwantung Army Special Exercise amassed 500,000 to 850,000 soldiers to the Russian border.[67] To build military facilities, trenches, and transportation lines, the phantom attack mobilized four hundred thousand workers in July and August and maintained the same scale of labor power even after the plan was eventually abandoned, when the Soviet Union did not reduce the troops allocated around the Manchurian border as Japanese leaders had hoped.[68] Every new military operation necessitated the recruitment of local workers, but especially for this record-breaking mobilization. It exacerbated the labor shortage and slowed economic plans for Manchukuo.

In December 1941, Japan's Pearl Harbor attack demanded yet more labor power. To exhaustively recruit people of all ages who could physically work, a series of new regulations emerged in 1942, including the Emergency Labor Regulation, Wage Control Regulation, National Labor Service Act, and Student Labor Service Act.[69] While still heavily relying on migrant labor from the Southern provinces, those regulations focused on cultivating labor power within the local population. For example, the youth population in Manchuria became one of the newly targeted categories for internal mobilization. The National Labor Service Act and Student Labor Service Act were modeled on Nazi youth organizations, stating their purpose: "to have imperial youth devoted to constructing a highly defended state, train them with labor, foster a genuine sense of labor, promote a spirit of service for the state, and keep them moving forward to accomplish the ideals of the national foundation."[70] The tone of the description demonstrates that spiritual rhetoric and totalitarian indoctrination disguised forced labor. The law required men aged twenty to twenty-three who were not conscripted and not physically or mentally disabled to belong to a service team and work for twelve months in total. About 130,000 men were subject to this law in 1943: 36,000 men allocated for transportation and logistics, 20,000 for military construction, and 17,000 for waterworks, and so on. In total, 99,400 people served this program that year.[71]

The total mobilization eventually gave a birth to the biometric National Passbook. It was designed to categorize all individuals who had able bodies and to track records of the work, service, and movement of each. The National Passbook Act came into effect on New Year's Day in 1944.[72] The law required all men over age fifteen to register with fingerprints and carry the fingerprinted passbook at all times. The purpose of this law was "to grasp the human resources necessary to fully exert the national power, benefit the imperial subjects' identification, and serve the smooth administration of national policies, especially to assist the mobilization for national service."[73]

The passbook system amalgamated the civil registry, temporary residence registry, and Labor Card systems. The civil registry, implemented in 1940 (chapter 3), could not track the movement of people as a surveillance tool, like the *koseki* system. So the Temporary Residence Registry Act of 1943 required anyone who was away from the address registered in the civil registry for more than ninety days and who did not have a registered address to register the place where they were staying. This temporary registration of residential address allowed the government to track people's geolocations. A similar registration system

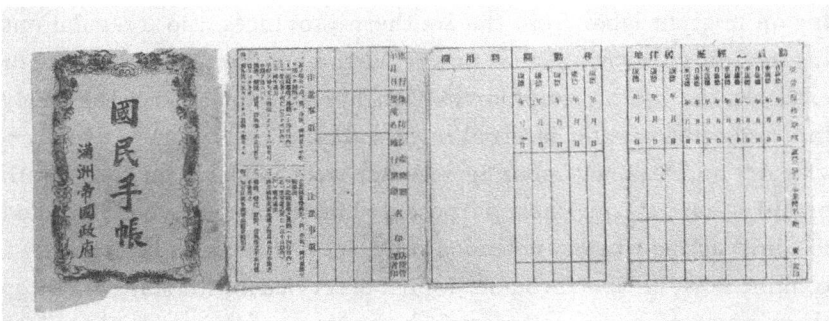

FIGURE 4.2A. National Passbook issued by "Manchurian Empire Government." Front: bearer's record on public service, residence, movement, vaccine, and notes saying that bearer is required to update information, and that fabrication of National Passbook is punished. Photo by Ken Mizokoshi.

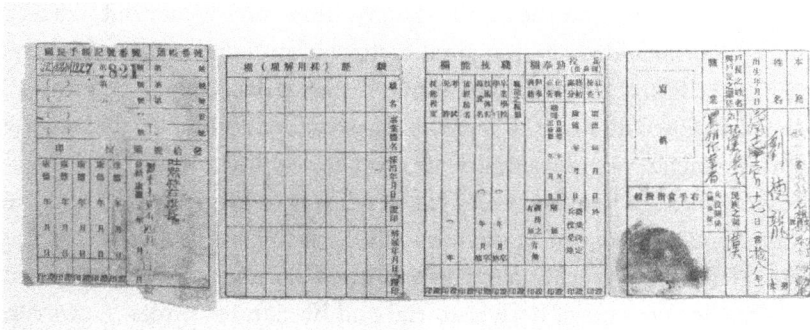

FIGURE 4.2B. Back: Honseki, name, date of birth, family head, ethnicity, occupation, military service, skills, job history, National Passbook number, issuer, and the right index fingerprint. Photo by Ken Mizokoshi.

was in effective in Japan, too, to supplement the *koseki*, but the Manchurian version included migrants who did not register with the civil registry. In fact, it mainly targeted migrant workers, who—even during the shortage of labor power—counted 918,000 in 1941 and 1,069,000 in 1942.[74] This extended registration suggests the Manchurian government's intention to use the temporary residence registry as a step toward counting migrant workers as Manchukuo nationals and eventually including them in the civil registry, as Takano points out.[75] It would give the Manchurian government legitimate power to mobilize non-resident migrants just as it did nationals. The National Passbook Act merged the ID systems respectively developed for labor control and security, in both private and public spheres, and for Japanese rulers' economic and political interests.

It was the Fingerprint Management Bureau, the longtime advocate for the biometric national registration system, that oversaw issuing the National Passbook. Various formats of passbooks were developed, depending on the region and the time. They typically included a photograph and fingerprint (right index) and recorded many items of personal information: residential address, name, date of birth, name of family head, ethnicity, occupation, conscription record, occupational skill, employment history, labor service history, moving history, and vaccination record. The one I obtained in China, issued in Jehol Province in April 1945, has eight pages. One I saw in the Jixi City Museum has twenty-six pages. More data were aggregated by the National Passbook than by the Labor Card, and they built the profiles even further out, tracing past residential addresses, personal history of national service, and the carrier's skills and abilities as a human resource available to the state.

It is unknown how far the National Passbook was disseminated among the Manchurian population, due to the policy's short life. It was legislated only twenty months before Japan's defeat in World War II and the simultaneous collapse of Manchukuo. It is reasonable to assess that the National Passbook was applied to a limited number of people, due to the extreme shortage of both material and human resources. However, it was the culmination of identification technologies that mobilized the entire population in Manchuria for the Japanese occupation. All people were required to participate in the imperial project, from free employment to voluntary service to forced labor. How, then, were the Chinese residents and migrant workers brought to the sites of forced labor?

LÜ GUIWEN'S STORY: FORCED LABOR IN FENGMAN DAM

In each village, the government assigned a quota of workers to participate in labor service teams. Typically, the prefecture demanded that every household choose a person suited for labor service and register them at the labor registry with ID numbers. Then they were ordered to join a labor team at the government's behest; the teams varied in size depending on the number of workers needed.[76] The heads of labor teams were normally government officials at the prefecture level, and school teachers and village heads at the village level. At schools, from elementary schools to colleges, students were mainly mobilized for farming, as one of the major strategic industries supporting the war. When farmers were sent to mines and construction sites, youth were mobilized to work in the adults' absence. Labor Service emerged in school activities as early as 1939, when the government struggled to increase labor power to meet the goals of the industrial development plan. It was officially incorporated into university curricula in 1942 and in elementary and middle schools in 1943. In 1941, a total of 332,107 people were mobilized to work in the fields of military, farming, mining, and road and land development.[77]

I interviewed Mr. Lü Guiwen (吕贵文) in 2016 in Jilin City, Jilin Province. He was one of the farmers who was forced to work to satisfy the government's quota. Lü, age ninety-five, was born in Shandong Province, where his family faced starvation. His whole family of fifty people moved together to Jilin Province and settled down to cultivate the land. In 1941, every family in his village was required to choose someone for labor service, and Lü was randomly selected. He believes someone rigged the drawing to send him to labor. He did not want to go, but the Chinese officer under the Kwantung Gendarmerie captured him at home and brought him to the construction site of Fengman Dam (Hōman Dam, 豊満ダム), about fifty kilometers from his home. Fengman Dam was one of the largest infrastructure projects of Japan's settler colonialism in Manchukuo. Construction started on the dam in 1937 and was completed in 1942.[78] It is estimated that more than 150,000 workers were mobilized for the construction during those six years.

Lü was twenty years old, married, and had a child at the time. He was put into a shed called the "labor shelf" and ordered to carry baskets of rocks and sand, along with other workers, to reroute a river. They worked from dawn until after dark. They were fed cornbread and were paid no wages. The Chinese managers, government officials, and Japanese gendarmerie always watched the workers from fortress-like watchtowers. The managers hit Lü with a whip or stick when they thought he was slow or not productive enough. The worst punishment he suffered was a blow to the right side of his chest with the butt of a gun, which broke his ribs and deformed his torso. But he said that the most horrifying violence he saw in the labor camp was against the "workers from the south," who came from outside of Manchukuo. If those workers escaped and were captured, they were punished with death. He witnessed a worker who was lifted by a crane and dropped in the middle of the river as punishment for not completing a task.

Lü escaped twice from the forced labor camp at Fengman Dam. The first time, he ran away by himself but was soon captured by a government official, brought back to the dam, and heavily punished. The second time, the opportunity presented itself during a worker riot. Workers from the south were fed up with the brutal treatment and planned to escape in small groups in different directions. The night they made their attempt, Lü ran, walked, and eventually returned home. Lü and his wife knew that he would be killed if captured again, so she sent him to her relative's place about twenty-five kilometers

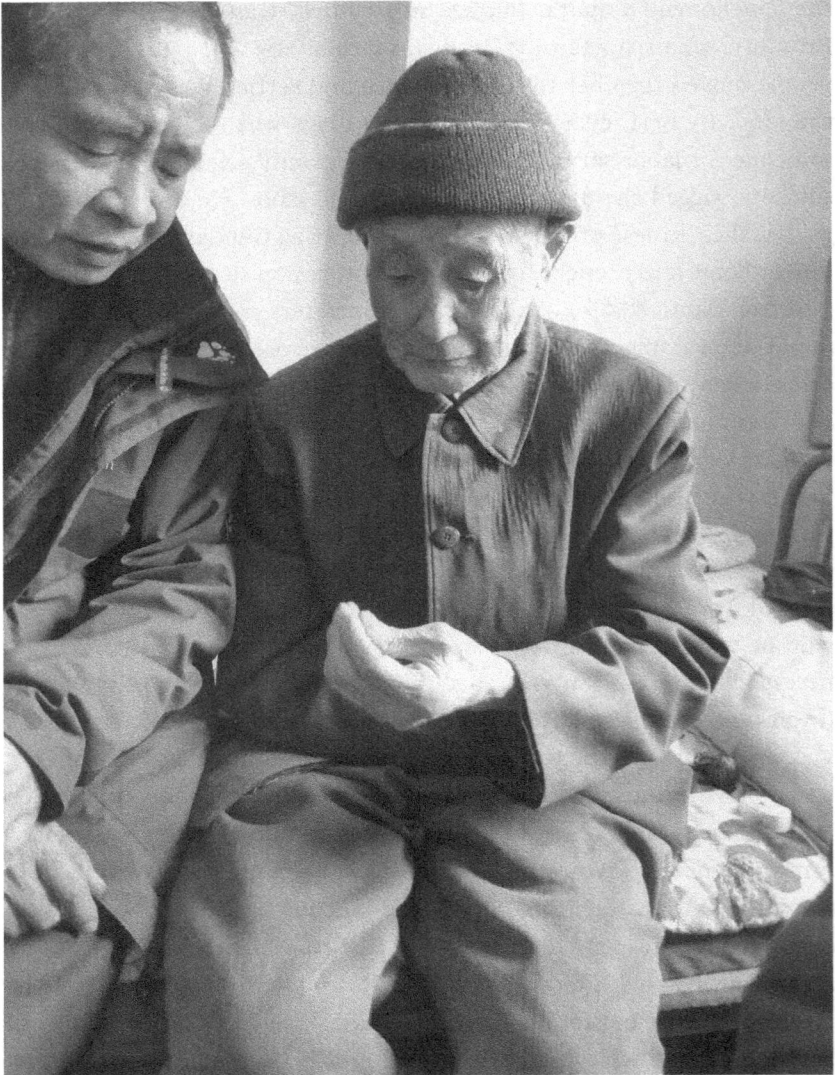

FIGURE 4.3. Lü Guiwen (吕贵文) looking at the fingers while commenting fingerprint identification he experienced. He had his ten fingerprints taken for forced labor in Fengman Dam. Jilin Province, 2016. Photo by Ken Mizokoshi.

away to hide. After a year had passed and no one had come searching for him, he returned home. He later heard that not many people who fled with him were able to get back home, and that most were captured and killed.

Mr. Lü Guiwen had suffered a stroke in 1990, and could not speak clearly when I interviewed him. Two of his sons assisted my communications with Mr. Lü at his home. They had heard the same stories repeatedly from their parents since childhood. Their father did not want to tell them the most brutal part of his one-year experience in Fengman Dam. But when I asked him about the fingerprinted Labor Card, Lü clearly answered, "I had the Labor Card" and "I had ten fingerprints taken."

As reflected in his story, it was common for workers to try to escape from the conditions of slave labor. Identifying runaways had been an important role of fingerprinted ID cards ever since the original implementation of ID cards in Fushun Mine. Japanese employers tried to make runaways as visible as possible, like slave owners did in the United States. Forced laborers were visually identifiable in their appearance: They covered their bodies with cement sacks and other construction materials because their employers did not provide them with proper clothes and shoes. Their miserable outfits made forced laborers visible to anyone's eye. A history museum in Heilongjiang Province exhibited photos showing how the Japanese shaved workers' hair and eyebrows, to deter escape and find runaways. These bodily assaults were equivalent to tattoos on enslaved people. Yet only the person's fingerprint could identify a person exactly. Fingerprint identification was a biometric tattoo inscribed on the worker's body.

Fengman Dam is a historical site where visitors can observe both Japan's colonial project and its collective abuse of the local population. Construction of Fengman Dam, proposed in 1933 by the Manchurian government, was central to the Industrial Development Five-Year Plan of 1937: to increase electricity production, stabilize the water supply for factories and irrigation and to prevent flooding.[79] Hoshino Naoki, the top bureaucrat in the State Affairs Section, believed that it was the "monumental project of the foundation of Manchukuo."[80] It was meant to showcase Japan's superior technology to the world. Among other megaprojects, dam construction embodies modern planning and technology mobilized to rule over the natural environment.[81] In Hoshino's view, it symbolized the modern civilization Japan brought to the region—a manifest destiny to the construction of East Asia.[82] But Hoshino

FIGURE 4.4. Construction of Fengman Dam, for which approximately 255,000 workers were mobilized. Public exhibition in Jilin City Labor Memorial Museum, Jilin Province. Photo by Ken Mizokoshi.

never saw its completion before he left his dream land and wrote his memoir on Manchuria, *The Infinite Dream*:

> Fengman Dam is the great monument of Manchukuo. I can't help but feeling moved when thinking how we could accomplish it in the [Manchukuo's] short life of thirteen years. We can no longer use it or even see it because of the historical change. But there is no doubt that this dam raised the standard of Manchurian culture to one level higher. There is no doubt that the dam is one of the pillars of splendidly reported Chinese communist construction. It at least comforts us that our efforts contributed to increasing the happiness of 50 million people in Manchuria.[83]

The exhibitions in the Jilin City Workers Memorial Museum that sits by the dam today preserve evidence against his one-sided, narcissistic view. The visitors see the handcuffs, fetters, and "wolf-teeth sticks"—studded with nail heads—that security guards used against the workers, and the worn-out jackets, cement sacks, and thin soles (not whole shoes) the workers wore. Among those, I found a Labor Card issued by the

Daitō Company that was required for workers from the south to enter Manchukuo in the early stage of the dam's construction.

It is estimated that at least fifteen thousand workers died under the harsh conditions of slave labor in Fengman Dam.[84] The Manchurian government allocated 250 million yen for the whole construction project, but used only 6.4 percent of the budget for labor costs and 2.8 percent for land acquisitions and compensations, meaning that they treated the Chinese land, resources, and labor as almost free.[85] The workers' song in the epigraph of this chapter, therefore, is apt: "The iron pillars are made of our bones, the concrete is made of our flesh, the water is our blood, and the dam is made of our bones and flesh."

Around the museum, numerous workers' skeletons were discovered underground after the Japanese left. Thirty-five bodies were moved and lined up on the ground for an exhibit. According to the exhibition panels, those skeletons are assumed to be men aged twenty to forty years old, but they are not individually identified. Twenty-seven of them had no injuries and seem to have died of starvation, cold, sickness, and excessive work. The other eight bodies had clear signs of torture or corporal punishments. Some had been struck on the back of the skull with a hammer, nails had been driven into others' skulls, and some had been tied with iron wires. The staff in the museum told me that skeletons of workers were still being found in the ground around Fengman Dam, and similar discoveries were reported at other sites of Japan's colonial projects in China. Those mass graves of unknown, abandoned bodies are called *wanrenkeng* (*man'ninkō*, 万人坑), meaning "pits of ten thousand corpses" in Chinese.

Japan's forced labor within China has rarely garnered public attention in Japan, compared to the laborers forced to Japan. While about 39,000 Chinese were shipped to and forced to work in Japanese coal mines and factories between 1942 and 1945, it is estimated that 7.9 million Chinese were sent to Manchuria from the south, and 8.5 million were mobilized within Manchuria for forced labor between 1934 and 1945—in total, 16.4 million people.[86] A top-secret file composed by the Japanese trade company Nichiman Shōji reports the terrifying mortality rates of the Chinese workers at fourteen sites of Japanese industry in Manchukuo in 1943, including Fushun Mine and Shōwa Steel factory. On average, from the time Chinese workers began to work at the site, 6.7 percent of them died within fifteen days, 20.6 percent within one month, 51.3 percent within three months, 75.9 percent within six

FIGURE 4.5. *Wanrenkeng* (万人坑; pits of ten thousand corpses) near the Fengman
Dam. Skeletons of Chinese workers who died of malnutrition, harsh labor
conditions, fatigue, or punishment during the dam construction. Their bodies
were dumped to ground near the dam, and the site is preserved as part of Jilin City
Labor Memorial Museum. Jilin Province, 2016. Photo by Ken Mizokoshi.

months, and 87 percent within one year.[87] These statistics indicate that
workers were almost completely replaced within one year, their bodies
abandoned to *wanrenkeng*.

Journalist Shigeru Aoki, who visited forty-two sites of *wanrenkeng*
in China between 2000 and 2019, states that this massive number of
the dead produced by Japan's industries reveals that profit was the real
objective of colonization. It was not only the Japanese Army, but also
Japanese capitalists who killed a multitude of Chinese people through
their colonial businesses.[88] The violent consequences of forced labor
have been concealed in the shadows of modern projects to this day. Japanese popular discourse has reproduced positive images of Manchukuo
as an ambitious invention, embellished with nostalgia for colonial privilege and benevolent intent, including *The Infinite Dream*.[89] Nonetheless,
thousands of skeletons—among what the Jilin City Workers Memorial

Museum calls the "mountainous testimonies of blood"—quietly but elo-quently protest Hoshino's hubris.

MAXIMIZING FORCED LABOR: STREET HUNTS AND PRISONERS OF WAR

While many farmers like Lü Guiwen were assembled from villages to fill the compulsory quota of labor services, others were hunted down on the streets and in urban spaces. Those people had fled to the cities because their family businesses had gone bankrupt under the govern-ment's strict economic control, because they were dodging compulsory labor in the villages or because they had escaped from deadly working conditions in mines. The government called them vagrants to justify sweeping them out of the cities.[90] For example, the metropolitan police in Changchun hunted vagrants in May 1943 by raiding homes and ver-ifying residents with data collected in household investigations, and arrested about 1,300 people, including those from the streets. Among the detained, eight people were sent to Unit 731. That night, the de-tainees broke through the windows and more than a thousand escaped. The police shot eight dead, and two hundred were sent to construction sites.[91] The police in Shenyang cleared six hundred vagrants from lodg-ings, streets, and markets between August 1944 to August 1945 and sent them to the Mishan Mine in Heilongjiang Province.[92] In Fushun in April 1944, three hundred police officers blockaded the city center, set up checkpoints, and captured eight hundred men who did not have government ID cards or Labor Cards. After the inspection, about six hundred were sent to a "correction center" to work in a coal mine.[93]

To legitimate the massive street hunt, the Security Correction Act (Hoan kyōsei hō, 保安矯正法) and the Thought Correction Act (Shisō kyōsei hō, 思想矯正法) were enacted in September 1943. The former created a legal mechanism enabling the government to send "anyone who has the possibility of committing crimes" to correctional facil-ities, which provided them with soul training of self-discipline and compelled them to work.[94] The latter enabled the arrest of anyone who might potentially commit political crimes and forced them into labor. Importantly, "preventive detention" (*yobō kōkin*, 予防拘禁) was legiti-mated by these laws, because they criminalized people who had not yet committed any criminal actions on the basis of the possibility that they would take such action against any Japanese authority figure, such as the imperial family, state, Shinto religion, resources of national defense, or military secrets. The notion of preventive detention was stretched almost infinitely by police searches for potential criminality in the colonial population. For the colonizers, this logic killed two birds with one stone: It confined the Chinese for security purposes and used them for slave labor.

To detain workers hunted from the streets, "correction centers" (*kyōsei hodōin*, 矯正輔導院) were quickly set up in at least fifteen cities. These were supposedly places for the "care and protection of inmates," including opium users, but in reality, they were no better than prison and labor camps.[95] Many centers reused existing facilities within or near the sites of mines and factories. I saw one of those ruins in Didao Mine in Jixi City, Heilongjiang Province. About thirty thousand Chinese were estimated to have been detained in the correction centers from 1943 to 1945, and their "incomes belonged to the national treasury."[96] Japan's major corporations, such as Shōwa Steel, Fushun Mine, Manmō Keori, were involved in trading workers and wages with the Manchuria government. Xueshi Xie suggests that although the proportion of prisoners in forced labor was relatively low, the level of exploitation was maximized. Their labor power was truly "created" by the Japanese rulers, "to restrain the fluidity of the population, improve the coal output rates, and secure the planned economic objectives" under "the labor structure built for total war."[97]

Another group maximally surveilled for systematic slave labor were Chinese prisoners of war (POWs) sent from outside of Manchukuo. Under an agreement with the Kwantung Army in April 1941, the Japanese Army sent Chinese POWs to benefit Manchurian industries, thus linking military operations with labor recruitment. They were called "special workers" (*tokushu kōjin*, 特殊工人) and were strictly segregated from the rest of the labor force and placed under maximum surveillance and violence. This may be the group of "workers from the South" that Lü Guiwen described as having been treated most violently in places like Fengman Dam.

Special workers were also caught inside of Manchukuo. This category of people had actually been used in the Manchurian labor force before 1941, as "subjugated bandits" (*kijunhi*, 帰順匪). In addition to being fingerprinted, they were tattooed on the inside of the left arm and required to carry the Subjugation Card at all times.[98] They had to show up at the police station more than three times a month to express their penitence. If they were identified as still associated with the resistance, the police and military placed them in "severe punishment" immediately. In 1939, Shōwa Steel, Fushun Mine, and other Japanese corporations used subjugated bandits from the south in numbers exceeding ten thousand in 1941.[99]

As such, the forced labor of POWs preceded the military agreement of 1941, but the agreement legitimated and objectified the purpose of seizing POWs for labor. One of the "hunting-workers operations" took place in the border area of Shandong, Hebei, and Henan Provinces in June 1942.[100] The soldiers of two divisions encircled the area and slowly moved to close the circle. They rounded up the farmers who happened to be in the circle, interrogated their personal details, and classified the men as being in strong shape for labor. The army slaughtered one thousand farmers in this operation and sent two hundred to Manchuria and Japan. Subsequently, in "rabbit-hunting operations" in the neighboring area, the Japanese Army captured 1,300 Chinese farmers, and sent 500 men to Jinan for labor. Four hundred men were selected to labor in Japan, and 150 women were sexually abused.[101] The labor hunt operated not only for Manchuria but also for Japan and other parts of China, and it almost always entailed considerable numbers of murders and rapes.

Thus, the category of special workers was, in the end, not necessarily former Chinese combatants; it often included civilians. About sixty thousand people are estimated to have been victims of human trafficking in 1941–43, although data are limited by the nature of military secrecy.[102] Special workers were strictly segregated from the rest of the workers in the workplace and accommodations. Japanese managers tagged them with numbered pieces of metal and threatened them with weapons. Fearing rebellion, the Japanese infiltrated the Special Workers and developed spy networks to prevent their escape.[103] Identification was also conducted most strenuously against this group. Despite the most intensive surveillance against the special workers, their runaway rate was higher than other groups of workers. Workers usually ran away in groups of a few, tens, or sometimes more than a hundred.[104] They also resisted Japanese managers and guards by sabotaging and rioting in the mines or steel factories.

Xie notes that although the number of forced laborers did not exceed the scale of free employment by private corporations, the government relied on forced labor to secure wartime production.[105] Forced laborers tended to be sent to military construction projects and wartime emergency mobilizations while freely employed workers remained in general industries in this last phase of Manchukuo. However, even hired by private industries, workers lost their last bit of freedom of work and movement in this period. From the biometric National Passbook to the metal tag around the neck to the tattoo on the arm, workers' bodies were visibly marked and heavily surveilled. The draconian security measures took over economic policies and labor markets in the wartime state monopoly.

BODIES AS RISKY RESOURCES: BIOPOLITICAL MEANS AND NECROPOLITICAL ENDS

In sum, Manchukuo embraced fingerprint identification technology throughout its existence on two fronts: labor control and security operations. The first practice of fingerprinting, imported from the British empire, predated the construction of pseudo-nation. At the Fushun Mine, colonial industry used fingerprinting to trace and restrain the movements of migrant workers and to profile their backgrounds. Industrial interests were formalized as compulsory national identification card systems under Manchukuo, linking security measures. The Fingerprint Management Bureau was established as a state apparatus, which formally amalgamated the labor control and security measures of fingerprint identification. Labor Cards and other ID cards used to track residents were merged into the National Passbook system to mobilize the entire population for the wartime labor shortage. The national ID systems eventually suffocated workers' freedom to work, quit, escape, hide, or resist, and brought them under the direct surveillance of the police and military. Applying ID systems to surveillance enabled the colonizers to intervene in individual lives, turn people into available resources, and sort them out for exhaustive use. Fierce recruiting and violent measures coerced Chinese farmers, "vagrants," prisoners of war, and dissidents to work under conditions approximating enslavement.

As the original fingerprinting case in Fushun Mine illustrates, fingerprinted ID cards were introduced to Manchuria as a biopolitical technique to maximize productivity in colonial industry. The technique was authorized by the state apparatuses of Manchukuo as a flexible means of population control for both labor and security. At both sites, fingerprinted ID cards contributed to sorting the population into desirable and undesirable categories, and preempted the risk of resistance. Proactive surveillance was developed to foster colonial industries and strengthen sovereign power. In this sense, the Manchurian ID systems embody the productive characteristics of a modern nation-state, as Foucault emphasizes in his notion of biopower. In Japan's path of "go-fast imperialism" in East Asia,[106] Manchuria became its cutting-edge laboratory of colonial technologies. The Japanese literally called Manchuria "Japan's Lifeline," from an economically strategic viewpoint, and wanted to make the most of its resources to benefit the metropolitan market. Yet, the colonial frontier was—probably always is—conflicted.

Thus, the biopolitical means of surveillance—the fingerprinted ID card systems—emerged from the duality of modernity: simultaneously productive and repressive, inclusive and exclusive. Accordingly, the fingerprinted ID cards handled dual tasks: classifying people as desirable or undesirable and exploiting them as different categories of resources. The entire Chinese population looked potentially suspicious to the Japanese eye and so was never trusted. But the colonizers needed their labor power, which was cheaper than in the metropolis and competitive on the global market, to kick-start the capitalist system in the region and cultivate the benefits of the new territory. The Chinese were not trusted as supporters of the Japanese empire, but their bodies were still useful and actually necessary for economic development: They were a risk, but also a resource. Biometric ID cards had the rare, dual capability of watching over the movements of Chinese bodies as sources of potential resistance while mobilizing the same bodies as profitable labor power and a source of wealth. In the former process, the body is reduced to a fragment of data that tells the colonizers who the person is, and in the latter, the body is reduced to a resource for the colonizers to appropriate.[107] Biometrics reduced a person to a single bodily identifier and cut off their other components. It only paid attention to the corporeal body and its untrustworthy soul and ignored the complete individual living in a historical, social, and cultural context. This degrading tool came from the colonies, where the Indigenous and racialized population were suspect in the colonizers' gaze. The Chinese were never fully respected as people, or trusted as capable subjects. They were treated as biological resources, but risky ones—as risky resources.

In this sense, although ID systems classified the population into desirable and undesirable for sovereignty, no one ever became perfectly desirable. This is because the categories the colonizers used were imaginary, not based on the substantive beings of individual subjects. As Judith Butler reveals in the context of gender identity (chapter 1), biological difference is discovered and defined by the dominant ideology of the time.[108] The categories of people, whether women or loyal nationals, were imaginarily constructed and imperatively imposed. It was impossible for a person to become a category collectively and compulsorily constructed.[109] No matter how hardworking and obedient a Chinese person was, he was never fully innocent or treated equally by Japanese officers and employers. The entire Manchurian population was distrusted and discursively marked as suspicious and biologically inferior.

This is more evident in contrast to the use of the *koseki* system in the metropolis. As discussed in chapter 2, *koseki* demonstrated the powerful effect of constructing loyal subjects for the Japanese empire by assigning patriarchal categories to families. The social orders *koseki* imposed on everyday life enabled multidimensional surveillance among members. And it instilled a hierarchy-friendly bias in the Japanese populace. Surveillance was internalized onto the self, as in Foucault's panoptic model. Social sorting helped create the individual identities of loyal subjects who would serve the nation-state from their assigned positions. On the other hand, it is hard to imagine that the Chinese (or Koreans and Taiwanese) adopted identities loyal to the Japanese empire, considering they were clearly racialized as second-class subjects and disconnected from imperial benefits. Rather, under continuous assimilation policies, racialized Others were implanted with a sense of inferiority and alienated from their own cultures. It was impossible for them to finally become Japanese, no matter how well they assimilated and behaved.

The category of loyal subject was, in the end, fictional, collectively and compulsorily constructed.

In other words, the panoptic mechanism of soul training was limited in the colonies despite the centralized and all-encompassing structure of surveillance. Colonial ID systems were not as successful as *koseki* in constructing loyal subjects. Evidently, the Japanese encountered constant defiance in the colonial threshold, from inside and outside imperial Japan. So, what made the biometric ID systems a powerful tool of surveillance there?

My field research indicates that is sovereign menace, implicated in identification. This was what my interviewees witnessed and what Chinese sources suggest. Workers didn't see the surveillance acting behind the violence. They did not know exactly how their fingerprints were classified to exclude them, because the surveillance was hidden. But the violent menace was very palpable and ubiquitous in the acts of the Kwantung Army and Japanese occupation, as we saw in the resistance to the fingerprint identification by the Manmō Keori workers in this chapter. The workers' intuitive understanding of fingerprinting or tacit knowledge of Japanese colonization was right; the fingerprint technology and ID systems effectively captured the entire population in a dragnet and exposed them to sheer violence, whenever and however the policing agencies wanted. The surveillance systems watched over individual movements, identified armed groups, classified risky subjects, reduced people to resources, deprived them of ways to resist or react as able subjects, and finally exerted abusive force toward individuals.

Thus, the biopolitical ID system resulted in a necropolitical experience at the settler colonial threshold. While in the metropolis the ID system served to construct loyal subjects for the nation-state by internally automating surveillance within the self and society, the ID systems in the colony functioned as direct surveillance, externally exercised to restrain and mobilize the population. The internal and external functions of surveillance in the imperial state obviously brought advantages to one side and disadvantages to the other side. The colonial population was incorporated into this global system of imperialism but excluded from its advantages. Thus, the colony was caught up in inclusive exclusion, in Agamben's concept,[110] in which the sovereign right to kill is preserved in the excluded zone as the state of exception to the biopolitical right to foster life. In Manchukuo, the unilateral process of inclusive exclusion was legitimated by the rapid production of colonial laws and the classification of the population through the fingerprinted ID cards and corresponding surveillance apparatuses. The National Passbook turned its bearers into bare life, ever legally exploited by the Japanese bureaucracy, racism, and technology.

Agamben reiterates that the state of exception is the original nucleus of Western politics, where repressive violence is the source of sovereign power. The democratic nation-state normally certifies constitutional rights and legal protections for its citizens. But these rights were totally nullified in its colonies. Colonies were the source of wealth and prosperity for the imperial nation-state, exploited as a resource. Biopolitical prosperity in the metropolis drew out necropolitical dispossession in the colonies. Hence, though Agamben's discussion focuses on Europe, his insights are relevant to colonies: *"The original relation of law to life is not application but Abandonment."*[111] The abandoned subjects and their miseries on the margin were driven by the productive forces in the center—not in spite of productivity, but because of productivity.

Productivity and abandonment can and did operate together in a state of exception. This was the space racialized workers were thrown into through mass surveillance by the fingerprinted ID cards in Manchukuo. The various forms of forced labor in particular were not meant to let the workers live, but rather to exhaust them. The Japanese did not treat workers as sustainable labor power, so they did not provide proper food, clothes, or a place to stay. They punished the Chinese anytime and used them until they died, to which the *wanrenkeng* testify. To the colonizers, laborers were a dispensable resource to consume infinitely. Labor and murder became very close categories to each other in wartime forced labor.

During my visits to the ruins of Japanese colonial industries, such as Fengman Dam and Fushun Mine, I repeatedly heard the phrase "forcing work to kill" from local people. In the workers' lived experience, the colonial labor was not the means of making living, but of hastening their death. Many workers resisted it. Perhaps they knew that their body was seen as risky resource; they refused being exhausted as resource for Japanese imperial hubris and fought for their dignity.

CHAPTER FIVE

FATAL CLASSIFICATION FOR IMPERIAL SCIENCE

Unit 731 and Japan's Secret Biological Experiments

> From the moment the [Chinese] patriots were captured by the Kwantung Army, they ceased to be human. . . They became just a "log", treated like lumber for construction. Because they were "logs", they did not need individual names. Each of the "logs" sent to Unit 731 was given a three-digit number, sorted into a different team in the unit, and used as a living ingredient for that team's research purposes.
>
> —*(Seiichi Morimura, The Devil's Gluttony, 1981)*[1]

In August 1999, the Heilongjiang Provincial Archive in the People's Republic of China held a press conference about a dossier compiled by the Japanese Kwantung Army from 1941 to 1944 during its occupation of Northeast China.[2] The sixty-six files were presented as "iron-clad evidence" of war crimes committed by Unit 731, which had secretly engaged in biological warfare and medical experiments.[3] The dossier included lists of Chinese men the Kwantung Gendarmerie had detained on suspicion of spying on the Japanese military and participating in anti-Japanese activities. The military police identified and classified the detainees for different treatment: to be released, turned into

161

informants, or transferred to Unit 731. Those sent to Unit 731, based in a suburb of the city of Harbin in Heilongjiang Province, were subjected to bacterial experiments. They were infected with plague, typhoid, dysentery, or other kinds of bacteria, and scientific data was collected on them and used in the production of biochemical weapons by Japanese medical professionals and academics. No one subjected to these tests returned from Unit 731. All the prisoners transferred to the test facilities were killed there.

Though Japan's human experimentation and war crimes had been publicly recognized in China, the identities of victims had rarely been made public until the 1999 discovery of the Kwantung Gendarmerie files in the Heilongjiang Provincial Archive. Who was targeted, captured, and victimized? The top-secret files identified fifty-two victims by name, and more cases were revealed later. The Jilin Provincial Archive followed in September 2001, announcing that more than four hundred newly found Kwantung Gendarmerie files showed that 277 Chinese, Russian, and Korean individuals were sent to Unit 731.[4] Previous studies estimated that at least three thousand people were killed in Unit 731.[5] More than a half century after Japan's defeat in the Chinese-Japanese War (1937-45), victims' family members were shocked to learn how and where their loved ones' lives had ended. This was sadly the moment when the victims' names were restored, along with their personal backgrounds, and they could be remembered as people rather than abstracted as numbers.

The interrogation files showed how the military police intensively scrutinized its victims over a long period of time before selecting them for germ experiments. The gendarmes wrote documents to describe the process of interrogation, justify the accusation, and obtain permission from senior officers to place specific individuals in "Special Transfer" (*tokui atsukai*, 特移扱い), the code name for sending people to Unit 731. Most of the documents were burned or buried by the Kwantung Army when they rushed to leave for Japan in August 1945. But they were dug up by Chinese hands after liberation at the sites of the Kwantung Gendarmerie Headquarters and its branches. The files suggest that Special Transfer was not a contingent operation, but a carefully planned and institutionally authorized outcome of military intelligence activities and bureaucratic classification, determined by specific criteria.

The violent consequences of identifying and classifying power in occupied Northeast China were multifarious, not limited to the labor mobilizations and economic exploitations shown in chapter 4. People who
opposed the Japanese occupation and potentially took part in armed
resistance constantly fell into Japan's surveillant assemblage and were
deprived of their lives. Among them, thousands of Chinese who were
secretly sent to the Japanese Army's biological warfare facility should
be understood as victims of Japan's total policing and population control at the colonial threshold. This chapter analyzes how technological rationality facilitated extremely unethical scientific experiments
on living human bodies—one of the worst consequences of colonial
surveillance.

In the following, I first give an overview of my sources to clarify
what has already been uncovered with regard to this controversial issue
and what I am going to add to these disturbing discoveries. Next, I lay
out Unit 731's major operations and how the Kwantung Gendarmerie
organized Special Transfers for Unit 731. Third, I closely examine the
classification chart the Kwantung Army used for Special Transfers: a
tool to rationalize systemic slaughter in the name of imperial science.
Then, I move on to individual stories revealed by the Kwantung Gendarmerie dossier and my interviews with family members of the victims identified in the files. Last, I analyze how people were converted
into expendable resources in the colonial laboratory after they were
caught up in Japan's maximum surveillant assemblage.

DISCOVERIES AND COVER-UPS OF JAPAN'S SECRET OF SECRETS

Japan's atrocious war crimes are not new discoveries but have been controversial amid the tension between historical justice claims and historical revisionism. Primary sources on Japan's biological warfare facilities
are still very limited due to the Japanese Army's deliberate destruction
of evidence and the international cover-up. It is worth noting how Japan
and the Allies coordinated to conceal Unit 731, as well as elaborating
the sources this chapter draws on, before delving into the connections
between Unit 731 and surveillance.

Unit 731's founder, the army surgeon Ishii Shirō, was fully aware that
the Geneva Protocol of 1925 prohibited the use of biological weapons.

Thus, the existence of Unit 731 was deeply hidden during the operations, and its mission was disguised as epidemic prevention. Nonetheless, historical documents indicate that the Allied Forces, including their military intelligence, chemical warfare, and public health authorities, as well as the war crimes prosecutors for the International Military Tribunal for the Far East (Tokyo Tribunal, 1946–48), were aware that hundreds of Japanese medical scientists committed these crimes.[6] Unit 731 was never held accountable in the Tokyo Tribunal, which had been set up by the Allied Forces.

The U.S. Army produced four confidential reports on Japan's biological experiments and attacks based on interrogation of Unit 731 Captain Ishii and other members between 1946 and 1947. In response to the Soviet Union's request to deal with Unit 731 crimes in the Tokyo Tribunal, U.S. officials stated in confidential documents that since "any 'war crimes' trial would completely reveal such data to all nations, it is felt that such publicity must be avoided in the interests of defence and national security of the U.S." Furthermore, they expressed that the knowledge gained by the Japanese from their human experiments "will be of great value to the U.S. BW [biological weapons] research program," and "the value to U.S. of Japanese BW data is of such importance to national security as to far outweigh the value accruing from war crimes prosecution."[7] In exchange for the data they had produced in Unit 731, Ishii and his superiors and subordinates in the army were granted immunity from prosecution for war crimes.[8] A nine hundred-page top-secret file on human experiments with plague, anthrax, and *Antinobacillus mallei*, compiled by Unit 731, was later discovered at the U.S. Army's testing site for chemical weapons in Utah.

The Soviet Union independently tried the division head of Unit 731, Kawashima Kiyoshi, in the Khabarovsk War Criminal Trial in 1949.[9] It also transferred 969 Japanese prisoners of war to the newly established People's Republic China, including Yoshifusa Torao and Kamitsubo Tetsuichi, in July 1950. The Japanese detainees lived in the Fushun War Criminal Control Center in Liaoning Province, and were investigated by Chinese prosecutors after 1954. Eventually, thirty-six generals, high-ranking gendarmes, judicial officers, and major administrators of Manchukuo were indicted by the Special Military Tribunal of China's Supreme People's Court (the Shenyang War Criminal

Tribunal), held in June and July 1956.[10] Testimonial statements written by Unit 731 members for the two trials in Khabarovsk and Fushun are the major sources of my analysis in this chapter.

All the detainees in Fushun had been released by 1964. Once back in Japan, they formed the Association of Returnees from China (中国 帰国者連絡会), or Chūkiren, in 1957.[11] While most former Japanese soldiers kept silent about their war crimes in postwar Japan, the Chūkiren members have spoken out about the emperor's sacred army's shameful murders and rapes in China. *The Three Sweepings* and *The Invasion* are selected collections of those statements and the only firsthand information available to me.[12]

There are several published works on Japan's biological war and medical experimentation by Japanese, American, and British journalists and academics.[13] In Japan, the high-profile novelist Seiichi Morimura did an extensive investigation into Unit 731, interviewed thirty-one former unit members, and published *The Devil's Gluttony* in the 1980s, which brought the greatest attention to the gruesome practice of vivisection. Around the same time, the veteran journalist John W. Powell Jr.'s article "Japan's Biological Weapons: 1930–1945, a Hidden Chapter in History," appeared in the *Bulletin of Atomic Scientists* (1981), sparking the allegation that Japan had used American prisoners of war (POWs) as "human guinea pigs" in Manchuria.[14] Together, they led a public uproar to the extent that the Japanese government needed to comment on the issue. The government admitted in the Diet for the first time that Unit 731 existed and that it committed heinous war crimes.[15] It also revealed that Ishii had been given a handsome retirement pension, despite government knowledge of his illegal and immoral conduct.

Since the Kwantung Army documents were discovered in Heilongjiang and Jilin provinces around the year 2000, Chinese researchers have taken the initiative to identify who was placed in Special Transfer and how the massive medical crimes were organized. Japanese academics and civil researchers have worked with them to support a lawsuit by the victims' family members against the Japanese government for compensation since the 1990s.[16] I build on the findings of those sources, written in different languages, and shed new light on how colonial surveillance helped institutionalize the illegal and unethical operations of Unit 731.

ISHII'S ILLEGAL LABORATORY

Unit 731 had its origins in the Army Medical School's epidemic prevention team, founded in April 1932 following the declaration of Manchukuo. Ishii Shirō, a first-class army surgeon, had traveled to European countries, Egypt, Turkey, Soviet Union, Australia, the United States, and Canada in 1928–30 to gather data on biological and chemical warfare. He was particularly interested in the devastating impact of plague in Europe. Back in Japan, he was appointed instructor of the Army Medical School, where he convinced his superiors to research bacteriological weapons and poison gas, despite the fact that Japan had signed the Geneva Protocol in 1925, which forbade their use.[17]

In 1932, the army founded a Bacteriology Laboratory in the Army Medical School, which was later renamed the Epidemic Prevention Laboratory. Receiving a lucrative budget secretly from the army, Ishii expanded his lab from Tokyo to Beiyinhe (背蔭河), southeast of Harbin, in 1932–33. The antecedent of Unit 731 was named the Kamo Unit (加茂部隊). It is reported that Kamo Unit used "bandits" for its experiments using poison gas, electric shock, and potassium cyanide.[18]

After a mass prisoner escape in 1934, the secret test site was relocated to Pingfang (平房) in southwest of Harbin in 1937, to keep its activities deeply secret. To increase security, the military classified 120 square kilometers around the site in Pingfang as a special military district, and four villages were removed. Residents over fourteen years old living in this special district were issued resident ID cards, and the police checked their movements and the activity of all visitors through the ID cards. The new facilities, completed in August 1939, employed state-of-the-art modern technologies, electrical infrastructure, railways, an airport, a prison, and experimental rooms. In 1940, Ishii Unit began using the Kwantung Army Epidemic Prevention and Water Supply Department as its official and cover name. It grew to have four branches in Manchuria, securing more than 4,500 personnel by 1945.[19] Led by Ishii, sites of biological warfare experiments were built throughout China, including in Changchun, Beijing, Nanking, and Guangzhou, and beyond. Not limited to China, they also proliferated to other places, such as Korea, Malaysia, Singapore, and Thailand. Between 1938 and

1945, Japan established a total of sixty-three epidemic prevention and water supply units—actually biological warfare facilities—in East Asia and Southeast Asia.[20]

Unit 731 cultivated bacteria of the plague, anthrax, typhoid, dysentery, cholera, and other diseases, and infected human bodies with them. It also repeated frostbite experiments in the field and conducted vivisections. Ishii recruited many Japanese medical doctors from top universities such as Kyoto Imperial University, Tokyo Imperial University, and Keiō University, and they joined Unit 731 to boost their careers.[21]

The scientists were constantly involved in human experiments and "consumed" the living bodies of prisoners at a rapid pace. For example, Ueda Yatarō, an assistant in Unit 731, described how human bodies were central to a comparative experiment on plague bacteria: his team

FIGURE 5.1.   Boiler tower, the symbol of Unit 731, showing its abundant budget and secret biological war facility built in the suburb near Harbin. Though the unit blew up the facilities to hide the war crimes when they left the site in August 1945, the ruin is preserved as part of Unit 731 War Crime Exhibition Hall, Heilongjiang Province, 2016. Photo by Ken Mizokoshi.

injected 0.1 gram of plague into five victims, 0.2 gram in another five, and 0.3 gram in a third group of five. They produced a table with the results of their comparative observations. They then gave 0.1 g, 0.2 g, 0.3 g of plague bacteria to other groups of five victims by embedding them in the tissues and formulated another table for the results. The third table compiled the data on groups of five victims who took 0.1 g, 0.2 g, and 0.3 g of plague orally.[22] Yang Yanjung at the Unit 731 International Research Centre of the Harbin Academy of Social Sciences infers, "The total of 45 subjects used in one single plague experiment provides testimony to the vast scale of human experimentation by Unit 731 and the huge numbers of victims."[23]

It was vital for Unit 731 to ensure a steady flow of resources for human experiments. The security agencies in Manchuria, led by the Kwantung Gendarmerie, were the major suppliers of these resources. The processes of victimization are documented as Special Transfers in the top-secret files. The Special Transfer files show that the largest group subjected to this secret process were Chinese dissidents who were allegedly involved in anti-Japanese intelligence activities, from the Nationalist Party, Communist Party, or the Anti-Japanese Northeast

FIGURE 5.2. Ruin of the special prison, secretly built in the center of Unit 731 facility. The victims of Special Transfer were detained in the small cell. Unit 731 War Crime Exhibition Hall, Heilongjiang Province, 2016. Photo by Ken Mizokoshi.

United Army. The rest of the people were from the streets and villages, as we saw in chapter 4, rounded up in labor hunts.[24]

The Gendarmerie branches normally sent detainees by train to Harbin station after approval by the Kwantung Gendarmerie Commander. The victims were called *maruta*, meaning "log" in Japanese, and counted as one log or two logs. They were indeed dehumanized and treated like construction materials, but the code word also served to conceal war crimes. The Harbin Gendarmerie Branch received the *maruta* and drove them to Unit 731 in a specially covered truck. Not only was the Kwantung Gendarmerie centrally involved in this process, so were other policing agencies such as the Manchurian Police, the Army Intelligence Agency, the Japanese Consulate, and the deepest secret entity called the Peace Preservation Bureau.[25] Together, the policing agencies in Manchukuo relayed suspects to Unit 731's secret of secrets: the special prison, built into the center of the facility and completely hidden from the public view. Once part of Unit 731, the victims' names were taken away and they were given three- or four-digit numbers.

FROM SEVERE PUNISHMENT TO SPECIAL TRANSFER

The number of victims put into Special Transfer has been estimated to be at least three thousand from 1940 to 1945, based on the confessions of Kawashima Kiyoshi—the division head of Unit 731—to the Khabarovsk War Criminal Trial in 1949.[26] Kawashima testified that Unit 731 had never experienced a shortage of experiment subjects and that about six hundred subjects were sent to Unit 731 through the Special Transfer per year.[27] This implies a total of at least three thousand victims in five years. Yet the actual number of prisoners remitted to Unit 731 between 1932 and 1939 remains unknown. Yoshifusa Torao, an adjutant of the Kwantung Gendarmerie Command, stated that at least four thousand people were killed in Unit 731 between 1937 and 1945.[28]

However, recent studies on the Special Transfer files discovered in the Heilongjiang and Jilin provincial archives imply a significantly larger number of victims than this estimated three thousand or four thousand. Xin Peilin found that each of the Special Transfer files was given an "order number," which suggests how many times the Special Transfer orders were made in each year. For example, the file as of September 22, 1941, is given the order number 936, meaning that a Special Transfer had taken place 936 times by that date from the beginning of the year, and that more than 936 people were sent to Unit 731.[29] If the frequency held between 1938 and 1945, it would add up to almost eight thousand people in total. Additionally, one order often placed two people under Special Transfer, and sometimes seven or eight people, or even tens together. For example, order number 224 in 1939 placed ninety POWs of the Communist Army under the Special Transfer; thirty went to Unit 731 and sixty to the branch in Songo.[30] Furthermore, when it comes to the total number of victims, Special Transfer was not the only way to deliver subjects to the biological war facilities. Undocumented people, detained contingently and used for human experiments in those facilities, must also to be taken into account. Thus, the actual total number of victims could very possibly exceed ten thousand between 1932 and 1945.

The Kwantung Gendarmerie was the main agency supplying subjects to Unit 731. Yoshifusa explains that Special Transfer to Unit 731 played a crucial part in the chain of command, and was introduced as a substitute for the "severe punishment" discussed in chapter 3:

> After the September 18 (Manchurian) Incident, the Japanese imperialists deployed "severe punishment" policy in the Northeast, which allowed Japanese soldiers to kill Chinese citizens arbitrarily. But, because of the Chinese vigorous resistance, this severe punishment had to be banned at least outwardly in 1937 . . . then, instead of the severe punishment, another plan of slaughter secretly proceeded, which seized the Chinese as living ingredients of bacterial cultivation, easily and limitlessly.
>
> At the end of 1937, the Army commander circulated a secret order, a "Special Transfer Rule." It enabled the Gendarmerie and Manchurian police to arrest Chinese illegally, judge them guilty of felonies without trial, send them to Unit 731, and kill them as the ingredients of bacterial experiments.[31]

Yoshifusa also described how he deliberately sent as many Chinese as possible to Unit 731 in the interest of his own promotion within the army. He encouraged his subordinates in the Gendarmerie branches to use counterintelligence operations to find suitable suspects and rewarded the officers who captured them. His subordinates responded well to his order, like "leopards looking for prey,"[32] and they competed to keep good records, obtain awards, and receive promotions by putting innocent Chinese into Special Transfer. Yoshifusa further describes a specific frame-up by the Gendarmerie, who pretended that some Chinese had learned confidential Japanese information so that they would be arrested and sent to Unit 731. Others were sent because they refused to cooperate with the Japanese as double agents or because they had been so severely damaged by the torture that the Gendarmerie did not want to send them home and allow them to go public.[33]

Yoshifusa's confession reveals that Special Transfer was not a contingent or exceptional operation, but one of the major missions of the Kwantung Gendarmerie. Utilizing the surveillant assemblage, the gendarmes hunted people and framed them to keep supplying Unit 731 with subjects. These operations were not random hunting. So, how were victims selected for Special Transfer?

CLASSIFICATION CHART FOR RATIONALIZATION

In his investigation in the 1980s, Seiichi Morimura found there were three main sources of "logs" for Unit 731.[34] The first were Chinese POWs: These intellectuals and workers had participated in anti-Japanese resistance and were captured throughout China and transferred to Harbin on the military train. The second were Soviet intelligence agents and White Russians arrested in Harbin and nearby. They were detained in the city and sent to Unit 731. The last were Chinese citizens arrested for petty crimes, deceived, or accidentally captured in military operations.

Yang Yanjun further explored the victims who were recorded in the Kwantung Gendarmerie's Special Transfer files and found that most of the Chinese detainees were categorized as "Soviet spy" (蘇連諜者, in short 蘇諜or ソ諜) in the files. As the Kwantung Army was preparing to attack the Soviet Union, they built numerous facilities, including seventeen fortresses, eighty thousand permanent fortifications, and thousands of underground warehouses, power stations, telecommunications hubs, and water purification stations in Northeast China between 1933 and 1945. Especially from 1938 to 1944, the Kwantung Army built gigantic military fortifications along the Chinese-Soviet Union and Chinese-Mongolian borders, which commanded the attention of Chinese and Soviet intelligence agencies.[35] The Soviet Union also supported the Anti-Japanese Northeast United Army. Irritated, the Kwantung Gendarmerie deployed aggressive counterintelligence activities to keep those facilities' locations secret and arrested hundreds of Chinese and Russians who they suspected of spying activities in the region.[36] "Soviet spy" constitutes the main categorization of the captives listed in the Special Transfer files in the Heilongjiang Provincial Archives.

The Kwantung Gendarmerie officially documented the Special Transfer selection criteria in March 1943 (fig. 5.3), to follow up on the original order issued in January 1938 (undiscovered). As Unit 731 had been operating since 1932, they had already been capturing and using people for human experiments for about a decade, but apparently there had been no clear documentation of criteria or justification of the Special Transfer operation. In other words, any captives who fell into the Japanese Army's hands could have been sent to Unit 731, so the creation of selection criteria aimed to specify who could be subjected to Special Transfer, given the very serious consequences for anyone placed under

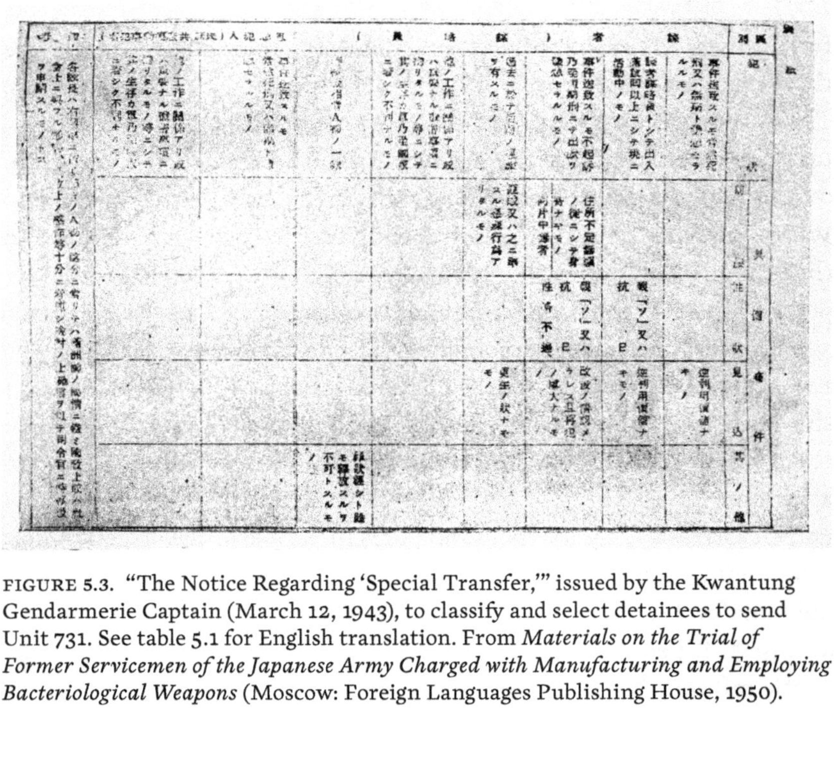

FIGURE 5.3. "The Notice Regarding 'Special Transfer,'" issued by the Kwantung Gendarmerie Captain (March 12, 1943), to classify and select detainees to send Unit 731. See table 5.1 for English translation. From *Materials on the Trial of Former Servicemen of the Japanese Army Charged with Manufacturing and Employing Bacteriological Weapons* (Moscow: Foreign Languages Publishing House, 1950).

Special Transfer. The documentation of the selection criteria was argu-ably intended to clarify and narrow down what kinds of people would be sent to Unit 731, rather than blurring and delimiting the categories of people.

In table 5.1, the selection criteria anticipate two groups of people as potential subjects of Special Transfer: spies and thought criminals. As obstacles to Japanese occupation, these were the categories of people subjected to the most severe punishment. Under these two categories, suspects were further examined to determine whether they fell into any of eight "character of crime" categories, and other supplementary con-ditions ("biological facts," "personal characteristics," "our appraisal," and "others") were also taken into consideration. For example, the first category of character of crime described "persons who will be sentenced to death or life imprisonment if legal proceedings are taken," and "no value for reverse use as a spy" under "Our appraisal" supplementarily conditioned the decision to subject that person to Special Transfer. The first category aligned with the gendarme's testimonies on the transition from severe punishment to Special Transfer, discussed in the previous section, in the army's effort to give a more judicial appearance to un-lawful killing.

Similarly, the second category of spies—"persons who have crossed into Manchuria more than several times as a spy or saboteur and are currently engaged in spying activities"—were also sent to Unit 731 when they had "personal characteristics" of being "Pro-Soviet or anti-Japanese minded" and "no value for reverse use as a spy." But the third category of spies—"persons who will not be prosecuted or only sen-tenced to a short-term imprisonment if legal proceedings are taken"—seems to have determined that a subject had not caused serious sabotage against the Japanese Army, contrary to the first and second categories. Then, the decision of whether to send the people in this category was conditioned by three other supplementary conditions: "vagrants with no definite residence or family. Opium users" (biological facts), "pro-So-viet or anti-Japanese minded. Recalcitrant character" (personal char-acteristics), and "persons who show no feelings of repentance and have possibility of committing the crime again" (our appraisal).

As such, the classification chart was structured to focus on spies and thought criminals, precluding others, and carefully specified the

Table 5.1 English translation of Figure 5.3, "The Notice Regarding 'Special Transfer,'" issued by the Kwantung Gendarmerie Captain (March 12, 1943). Translated by the author.

Category	Character of Crime	Other Supplementary Conditions			
		Biographical facts	Personal characteristics	Our appraisal	Others
SPIES (SABOTEURS)	Persons who will be sentenced to death or life imprisonment if legal proceedings are taken			No value for reverse use as a spy.	
	Persons who have crossed into Manchuria more than several times as spy or saboteur and are currently engaged in spying activities		Pro-Soviet or anti-Japanese minded.	No value for reverse use as a spy.	
	Persons who will not be prosecuted or sentenced to only short-term imprisonment if legal proceedings are taken	Vagrants with no definite residence or family. Opium smokers.	Pro-Soviet or anti-Japanese minded. Rebellious character.	Persons who show no feelings of repentance and may commit the crime again	
	Persons who have been engaged in spying activities in the past.	Bandits or persons who were engaged in the similar harmful activities.		Persons who have no hope of being reeducated	

	Person who are related to other forms of operations, or engaged in important, confidential matters, and whose survival will extremely harm our military or state.		Persons who are guilty of minor crimes but should not be released.
	Persons who belong to the same group that comes under the category of special transfer.		
THOUGHT CRIMINALS (Criminals involved with the Nationalist and Communist movements)	Persons who will be sentenced to death or life imprisonment if legal proceedings are taken		
	Person who are related to other forms of operations or engaged in important, confidential matters, and whose survival will extremely harm our military or state		
Note	In deciding how to deal with any given person in conformity with the above-enumerated standards, chiefs of gendarme units should take full consideration from the point of view of the internal situation of Manchukuo, what impacts their decision will make on state policies, society and public morale, and must have confidence to apply to the Chief of the Kwantung Gendarmerie for permission to employ special transfer.		

personal types applicable to Special Transfer. The table's categories provide the reasons used to justify placing subjects in Special Transfer via
ostensibly clear, administrative, and rigorous standards. The rigorous
standards allowed the Kwantung Gendarmerie to check every aspect of
the suspect against their potential to work for the gendarmerie's benefit, and if the gendarmerie found no benefits or use for the person, the
chart let the gendarmerie send them to Unit 731.

The classification chart also rationalized the deadly effect of Special
Transfer by equating it with the most severe judicial punishments—
sentencing to death or life imprisonment—or the potentially existential
threats caused by "persons who are related with other forms of operations, or engaged in important, confidential matters, and whose survival
will extremely harm our military or state," the fifth category of spies. In
their military rationale, these categories of people had to be eliminated
anyway. They were living dead, so there was little difference to the
Kwantung Gendarmerie between death by hanging, shooting, or on an
operating table. This internal logic gave the gendarmes emotional relief
and an ethical refuge from their cruel decisions and maltreatments of
the captured. Thus, the rationale allowed Special Transfer to normal-
ize their actions as part of the military bureaucracy without question,
hesitation, or limitation. Furthermore, using captives' bodies for scientific progress—seeing their bodies as resources—could be rationalized as
a better option than wastefully executing them. The living dead could
thus, the logical went, contribute to the war and medical science and die
a more meaningful death.

In service of this rationalization, the Special Transfer conditions
listed in the chart contain a tone of moral judgment and victim blaming.
The chart lists categories identifying the most harmful and unforgiv-
able subjects, who thus deserve to be dissected for medical data, such as
"persons who have crossed into Manchuria more than several times as a
spy or saboteur and are currently engaged in spying activities," "persons
who show no feelings of repentance," and "persons who cannot be hoped
to be reeducated," or "recalcitrant character." These moral judgments of
personal characteristics do not appraise military damages caused by the
person, but rather rationalize who was invalid to live: spies, guerrillas,
saboteurs, vagrants, opium users, pro-Soviet, anti-Japanese, rebels, and
anyone who did not cooperate with the Japanese military. In any case,

the table created a mirage in which Japanese authorities had repeatedly given captives the chance to work for the Japanese side, but they had repeatedly, stubbornly refused. They were immoral and unsavable because they did not understand the emperor's grace and mercy or Japan's righteousness in modern civilization, so there was no remedy for them nor a chance for them to live. Terms like "recalcitrant character" and "cannot be hoped to be reeducated" refute this moral judgment and clearly blame the victim.

As a result, the criteria in the table create the appearance that victims of Special Transfer were selected rigorously and that exceptional decisions were made for inevitable reasons. The table framed Special Transfer as a more rationalized and scientific form of violence than severe punishment. By classifying the severity of rebellious activities, the table provided a moral argument for the Kwantung Gendarmerie to make its victims responsible for the cruelest type of punishment and human rights violations. The chart set the fatal classification automatically, removing the moral responsibility from individual gendarmes and offering them the rational justification that captives would be killed anyway, so Special Transfer would make no difference to their fate. Morimura repeats in his book *The Devil's Gluttony* that this rationalization was more than a slippery slope to the demoralization of military actions; rationalization facilitated modern barbarism for infinite killing.

Yang Yanjun identified 876 victims of Unit 731, most of whom were sent to the biological war facilities through Special Transfer.[37] Many were involved in intelligence activities that aimed to end Japan's invasion and settler colonialism. They tended to be educated, courageous young Chinese, Korean, Mongolian, or Russian men and women. In the classification chart, those people typically fell into the categories "persons who have crossed into Manchuria more than several times as a spy or saboteur and are currently engaged in spying activities" and "persons who are related with other forms of operations, or engaged in important, confidential matters, and whose survival will extremely harm our military or state."

But there were also other categories of victims who did not fit the criteria. Those were farmers, workers, merchants, and children who had not really taken any rebellious actions, but were suspected of being anti-Japanese. In this logic, the entire population of the occupied land was suspected of disloyalty to the rulers. The logic also created another infinite end of scientific human slaughter, which is discussed later in this chapter. The realities that emerged from my interviews with Special Transfer victims' family members were more ambiguous and arbitrary than what the selection chart suggests. Let's listen to their stories.

THE PORTRAITS OF THE SPECIAL TRANSFER VICTIMS

Li Houbin (李厚宾)

Li Houbin, a former Manchurian police officer in Heilongjiang Province, was arrested in 1941, when he was thirty-two years old. The Special Transfer files discovered in 1999 show that Li Houbin had been under Japanese surveillance for a long time, as the file reports his personal meetings.[38] According to the file, he graduated from middle school and became a police officer for Manchukuo. When he was working for the Daomugou Police Branch in 1937, the branch head, Liu Rixuan, recruited him as a spy for the Soviet Union, and Li Houbin worked as part of an intelligence network Liu Rixuan had developed in the border town with the Soviet Union. Li Houbin entered the Soviet Union, just on the other side of the Ussuri River, four times to provide Japanese military information.

Li Houbin's son, Li Gang, told me that his father was deputy head of the Daomugou Police Branch. Japanese gendarmes showed up at the branch in 1937, coming down on the river in two speed boats, and requested a meeting with the branch head, Liu Rixuan. Sensing tension, Liu Rixuan ordered his translator to invite the Japanese police group to a lunch in the branch before the meeting. While the gendarmes were eating, Liu and his family took a boat across the Ussuri River and landed in the Soviet Union one hundred meters away. Local people remember this successful escape as the Daomugou Incident.

But that was not the end of the story. The angry gendarme leader ordered all villagers to gather in a public square, including five-year-old Li Gang. The gendarmerie pointed guns at the gathered people from the four corners of the square and searched every house in the village for the suspects. Unsuccessful, the gendarmes threatened to shoot all the

FIGURE 5.4. Li Gang (李刚) in my interview. His father Li Houbin (李厚滨 or 李厚彬), the former Manchukuo police officer, participated in the anti-Japanese resistance and was secretly sent to Unit 731 by the Kwantung Gendarmerie. Heilongjiang Province, 2016. Photo by Ken Mizokoshi.

villagers with their machine guns if they did not share Liu Rixuan's whereabouts. Some of the adults cried and begged for their lives, as no one knew where the police chief had gone. Li Gang remembers that his mother held his hand tightly so that he would not move. The village head made an emergency call to the local government and pleaded for forgiveness for the innocent villagers. At dusk, the Japanese military released the people and left the village. Li Houbin also returned home and told his wife that all the police officers had been threatened together in another location. The Japanese gendarmes had interrogated him all day long, but he was eventually allowed to go home.

Because of this ignominy, the Daomugou Police Branch was dismantled and its officers were transferred to other branches, including Li Houbin. The Daomugou Incident seemed to end with the hilarious story of the great escape. However, the total policing networks developed by the Kwantung Gendarmerie did not forget Li Houbin or forgive him.

On August 8, 1941, the Hulin Gendarmerie Branch arrested Li Houbin for helping the then police head and Soviet spy Liu Rixuan and for visiting the Soviets four times to pass information. Li Houbin was no longer a police officer and had changed his residential address a few times by then, but the gendarmerie found him and watched his every move for four years.

Li Gang had not known that his father had been part of anti-Japanese intelligence activities but did remember how his father was taken away. Two gendarmerie officers (one of them was Korean) in civilian clothing, not uniforms, visited their house, and told his father to come with them to the gendarmerie branch. Li Houbin left with them and never came home. His family tried to find out what had happened to Houbin, and his wife sent some people to the gendarmerie branch and police. A Chinese person working for the police told the family to no longer search for Houbin because he had upset the Japanese officers, they had thrown him into the cage of military dogs, and he was dead. Neighbors asked the family why they remained in town, as they could be in danger soon. Li Gang and his family moved to his grandparents' place in another town, where it was even more difficult to trace his father's whereabouts.

The truth was that Li Houbin had been sent to Unit 731. A top-secret document, written by Hulin Gendarmerie Branch head Nagashima Tsuneo, states: "He is under detention, has no value of reverse use, and

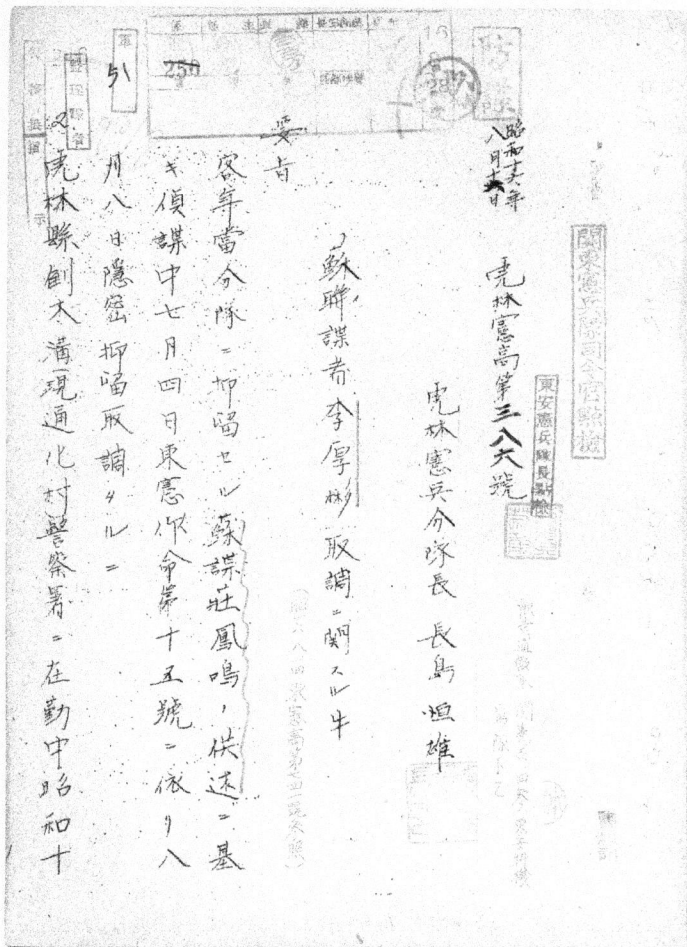

FIGURE 5.5A. Li Houbin's Special Transfer file (August 16, 1941). The cover page, written by the Hulin Gendarmerie Branch Head Nagashima Tsuneo, shows red stamps of "secret," "counterintelligence," and "special transfer." From Heilongjiang Provincial Archive, Heilongjiang People Foreign Friendship Association and ABC Project Committee, *The Iron-Clad Evidence of "Unit 731" Criminal Activities—The Kwantung Gendarmerie Special Transfer Documents* (Heilongjiang People Publishing, 2001). Reprinted with permission.

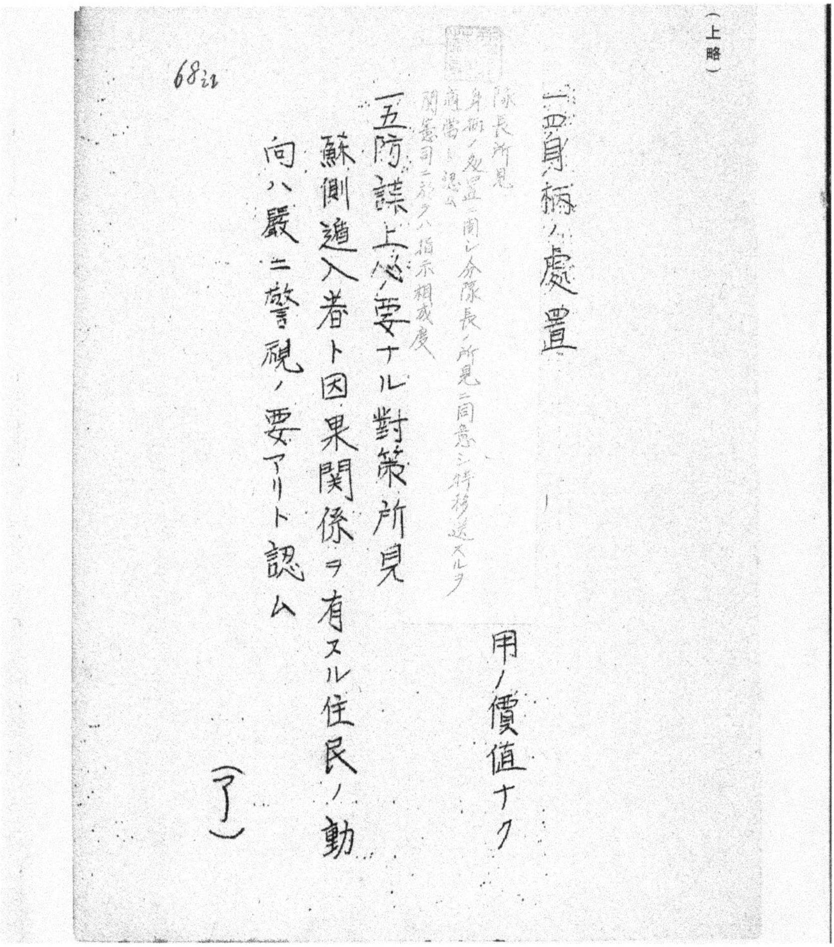
(上略)

(四)身柄ノ處置

用ノ價値ナク

隊長所見
身柄ノ処置ニ関シ分隊長ノ所見ニ同意シ特移送スルヲ
適當ト認ム
関憲司ニ於テハ指示相成度

(五)防諜上必要ナル對策所見
蘇側逆入者ト因果関係ヲ有スル住民ノ動
向ハ嚴ニ警視ノ要アリト認ム

(了)

68註

FIGURE 5.5B. In the file, Nagashima concludes, "[Li Houbin] has no value of reverse use, and so is suited to Special Transfer." His upper branch head endorsed Nagashima's view, and his comment is added by a slip attached on the file, written in red ink. From Heilongjiang Provincial Archive, Heilongjiang People Foreign Friendship Association and ABC Project Committee, *The Iron-Clad Evidence of "Unit 731" Criminal Activities—The Kwantung Gendarmerie Special Transfer Documents* (Heilongjiang People Publishing, 2001). Reprinted with permission.

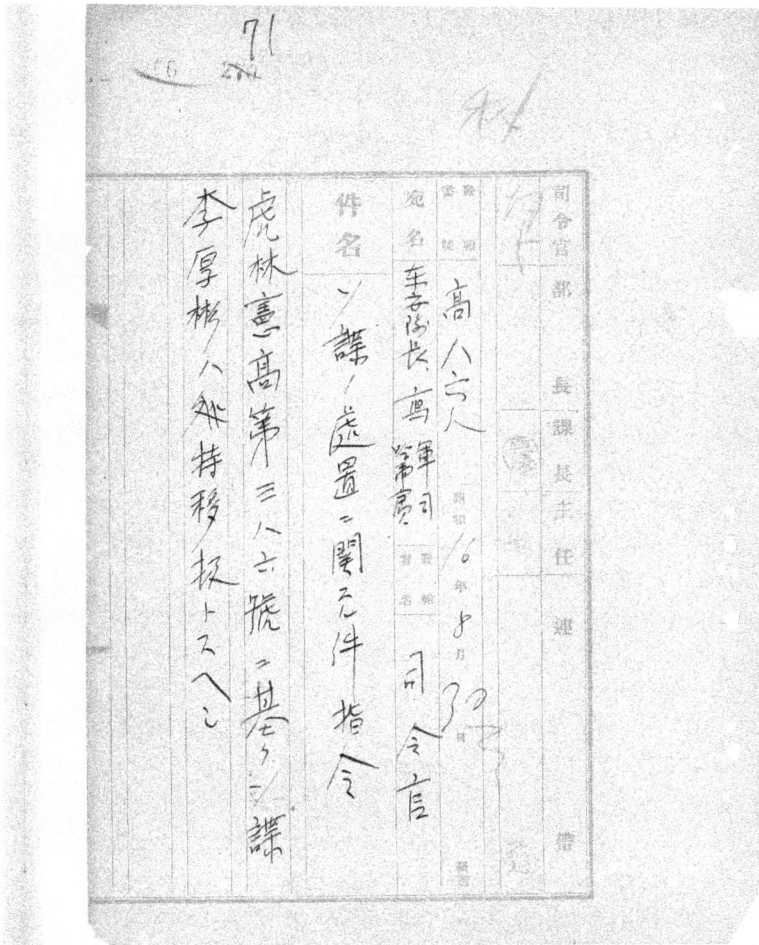

FIGURE 5.5C. In response, the Kwantung Gendarmerie Captain ordered Li Houbin's Special Transfer (August 30, 1941). From Heilongjiang Provincial Archive, Heilongjiang People Foreign Friendship Association and ABC Project Committee, *The Iron-Clad Evidence of "Unit 731" Criminal Activities—The Kwantung Gendarmerie Special Transfer Documents* (Heilongjiang People Publishing, 2001). Reprinted with permission.

so is suited to Special Transfer."[39] The upper gendarmerie branch head penned his approval in red ink and stamped the documents. As a counterintelligence measure, the branch head added, "behaviors of the residents who have relations with potential Soviet spies should be placed under strict surveillance."

Li Gang believed that his father had been killed in the dog cage until 2000, when researchers from the Heilongjiang Provincial Archive identified some Unit 731 victims in the Special Transfer files and informed the victims' families. After losing their breadwinner, Li Gang, his mother, and his four siblings experienced extreme hunger continuously in the postliberation period, even after the Japanese left. Li Gang wiped the tears from his eyes when he told me how his four younger siblings had died of illness, malnutrition, and lack of medicine.[40] His family was stigmatized as a Manchukuo police officer's family that had supported the Japanese occupation. Li Gang had a job auditing for Hulin City but had been restricted from opportunities for promotion because of his ambiguous family background. Seen as a traitor, he was forced to wear a sign reading "descendant of a fake Manchukuo police" and dragged around town during the Cultural Revolution.

Ironically, the Special Transfer files cleared Li Houbin's name in the communities. It proved that he actively took part in the resistance against imperial Japan, and was a true patriot. But it was never easy for Li Gang to accept that his father was placed in Special Transfer: "If my father died a normal death, I would not get angry. But he was used for bacteriological experiments and died. Japanese militarism is too cruel and inhumane. I am furious." He visited the Unit 731 War Crime Exhibition Hall twice, learned how the prisoners were treated, and cried so hard that he hurt his eyes during the visits. "So, I do not want to go back to the place," he declared. Gang's mother, always longing for her husband's return, died in 1990, murmuring that he never came back, and never knowing the truth.

Yuan Meizhen (原美臻)

On August 17, 1941, several days after Li Houbin was captured, the Kwantung Gendarmerie arrested Yuan Meizhen, age forty. Yuan Meizhen had run a restaurant in the city center of Hulin since 1939. When I interviewed his son, Yuan Wenqing, he told me that some gendarmerie officers visited Yuan Meizhen to ask him to come to their office to check a lamb they had bought, and he left with them. He never returned home. When his wife went to the gendarmerie branch to look for him, she was told that military dogs had killed him.

It was only in 2005, after his wife's death, that his family learned from the gendarmerie's document that Meizhen was a Special Transfer.[41] The confidential document classified him as a double agent for Japan and the Soviet Union.

The file details how Yuan Meizhen came to work for two powers. He was first hired as a soldier for the Manchukuo Army in Mishan in 1933, but his unit turned into "bandits and traitors"—or was radicalized, in today's parlance—and joined the Anti-Japanese Northeast United Army.[42] Yuan Meizhen left the unit and opened the restaurant in Hulin. He was recruited by another double agent, Li Manchu, in 1936 and worked within Li's intelligence network. Li and Yuan met a high-ranking Soviet Intelligence officer and took an oath to work for the Soviet Union, but the Mishan Special Mission team detected their spying activities in 1938. Under the condition of bringing information about the Soviets to the Japanese, the two were released. But Li did not return after entering the Soviet Union in 1940. The Hulin Gendarmerie Branch Head Nagashima Tsuneo decided that Yuan Meizhen had stopped spying for the Japanese and concluded, "He has no value for reverse use, and so is suited to Special Transfer."[43] The Kwantung Gendarmerie Commander approved it in another document.[44]

Researchers at the Heilongjiang Provincial Archive found that Yuan Meizhen's restaurant was an underground intelligence center for the Anti-Japanese Northeast United Army.[45] The restaurant seemed to have been under the gendarmerie's surveillance for a long time, and every visitor was recorded as a potential suspect. The Special Transfer file warned, "[We] need to severely surveil behaviors of double agents, and to closely scrutinize their families and acquaintances."[46] The family moved out of Hulin and changed their name to avoid being tracked by the Gendarmerie.

Yuen Wenqing, who was ten months old when his father was taken away, has no memories of Meizhen. He said: "I am very proud of my father. He worked professionally as a spy and died resisting the Japanese invasion." But his mother had a very difficult life after being left alone with a newborn. Yuen Wenqing remembers that his mother burst into tears whenever she saw a baby and mother on the streets until her seventies. Even when she held her grandchild in her arms, she cried not for joy, but for the daunting memory.

Sang Yuanqing (桑元慶)

Anyone related to the resistance was at risk for fatal classification. Sang Guifang's father, Sang Yuanqing, was an accountant. They lived in a gated community with guards who protected Japanese colonizers in Jidong, Heilongjiang Province. Well-educated and able to speak Japanese and Russian, Sang Yuanqing had good relations with his neighbors and commuted with Japanese officers by car. Guifang's mother sometimes exchanged her dumplings for sweets the Japanese wives made.[47]

However, on a Sunday night in November 1944, when Guifang was seven years old, about twenty Japanese gendarmerie, including Korean and Chinese subordinates carrying spades and hoes, brought her father home; he had been thoroughly beaten. They broke the bed and smashed through the walls, apparently searching for something. When they did not find it, they left for Yuanqing's close friend Sun Futing's place to raid and search further. During the raid on Sang's household, Guifang and her mother wanted to run to the wounded Yuanqing, but the gendarmerie pushed them back, and told them not to move and to stay quiet. Guifang clearly remembered this final moment with her father and told me in the interview, "My father said to me, 'Put on your winter jacket, and warm yourself up.'" Because he said this, the gendarme beat him again.

Sang Guifang's mother was seven months pregnant and waiting for her husband's return. After liberation, she heard from neighbors that a Soviet military officer had been looking for her husband. His friend Sun Futing, who previously worked for the Japanese Special Mission, also visited the family and said that he and Sang Yuanqing had been detained in the same prison. He disclosed stories of how they had worked together in the anti-Japanese underground networks. Sun gathered information on policing activities from the Japanese Special Mission and shared the information with Sang, so Sang could notify Chinese suspects of planned Japanese raids or arrests, so they could flee. They also

FIGURE 5.6. Sang Guifang (桑桂芳) in my interview. The Special Transfer of her father Sang Yuanqing (桑元慶) was revealed by the confession of Kwantung Gendarmerie officer Kamitsubo Tetsuichi in the Shenyang War Criminal Tribunal in 1956. Heilongjiang Province, 2016. Photo by Ken Mizokoshi.

sent Japanese military information to the Soviets using a radio that was found in Sun's place on the night of the raid. Because the damage of their activities to Japanese interests was significant, the gendarmeries were outraged.

The Kwantung Gendarmerie attempted to turn Sang Yuanqing into an informant for their side, but he refused. In prison, Sang told Sun not to tell the Japanese anything in the interrogation, despite unbearable torture, and to blame Sang as the main organizer, so Sun could be released. Sang also asked Sun to take care of his wife, Sang Guifang, and the expected baby. To fulfill the promise, Sun visited the family to help after the liberation. When Sun was sentenced to life by the court and transferred to a "correctional center," the guard told him, "Sang Yuanqing is going to a place to die, but you are not."

Unlike Li Houbin and Yuan Meizhen, Sang Yuanqing's destination was revealed not by the Special Transfer files, but by the testimony of Kamitsubo Tetsuichi—the gendarmerie branch head—to the Shenyang War Criminal Tribunal in 1956.[48] Kamitsubo wrote a serial statement for the tribunal about his initiatives for Special Transfer while he was detained in the Fushun War Criminal Control Center from 1950 to 1957.[49] His statement dated July 29, 1954, revealed that his gendarme arrested approximately ninety people involved in the communist networks over time, including Sang Yuanqing and others, interrogated them using torture, sent ten people to the Ishii Unit under Special Transfer, and released the rest.[50] In the tribunal, Kamitsubo named Sang Yuanqing, as one of the victims he had placed in Special Transfer.[51] As of July 30, 1954, Kamitsubo stated:

> As the Jinei and Dongan Gendarmerie Head, the numbers of anti-Japanese underground agents I ordered my subordinates to arrest and severely interrogate by the use of torture are more than 150. Among them, sent to the Ishii Unit in Harbin under Special Transfer were forty-four people, and dead by torture were two people.
>
> However, taking into consideration the extent of my [unclear] memories, it is certain that there were a considerable number of people I have not yet reported [to the prosecutors]. Thus, I acknowledge that it [the fact] should be more than my reported numbers [of the Unit 731 victims] and apologize to the Chinese people.[52]

The confessions written by Japanese soldiers in the Fushun War Criminal Control Center were published in China in 2011. For Sang Guifang, it clarified where her father's life ended. Kamitsubo had processed her father for his military promotion in April 1945.[53]

Everyone put into Special Transfer was killed in Unit 731, without exception.[54] No victim survived to testify about what happened in the system of slaughter in the name of advancing science. When Unit 731 left Pingfang in August 1945, the Japanese bombed the buildings and experimental facilities, and killed all the detainees. This made it difficult for the Chinese and international society to investigate these extreme but routinized crimes, just as the killers intended.

Li Pengge (李鵬閣)

The above cases prove that there were active networks of anti-Japanese intelligence in Northeast China, widely supported by the Soviet Union. The participants occasionally crossed riverine borders, and some of them were educated in Moscow. Especially around the time of the Kwantung Army Special Exercise when the Japanese Army prepared to attack the Soviet Union in the summer of 1941, enormous amounts of weapons and resources were transferred to the northern borders of Manchukuo, which was valuable information for anti-Japanese intelligence. They collected data around the train stations and railways. The Kwantung Gendarmerie, in turn, realizing this opportunity to track the spies' increased activities, intercepted their radio communications, and arrested many railway workers.

Li Pengge was the deputy stationmaster at the Mudanjiang Station, where three rail lines intersected in Jilin Province, when the Gendarmerie captured him in May or June 1941. According to his daughter Li Fengqin, because he did not come home that day, his mother went to Mudanjiang Station. The stationmaster told her that the Japanese gendarmerie took him away somewhere. His mother and wife, pregnant with Li Fengqin, looked for him around the gendarmerie and police sites, but the gendarmes scolded his mother and came to her home. The gendarmes raided their house and broke his mother's leg with a blow from the butt of a gun.

Li Fengqin heard this story from her mother, as she was not yet born. In 2006, Li Fengqin and her brother learned that their father was killed in Unit 731: The name Li Pengge was found in the Special Transfer file.[55] The file had been burned to the extent that only the victim's name was recognizable and no other details could be recovered from the burned documents. But researchers and journalists investigated the case and found that he had been part of the well-known resistance known as the Mudanjiang Incident in China. Li Pengge took part in the international anti-Japanese imperialism network, and he possessed two radiotelephones to exchange data collected at the train station about the Japanese Army's logistics.

Li Fengqin is very proud of her father's contribution to the collective resistance and China's independence. Yet accepting the fact that her father was killed at Unit 731 was nothing but agony for her. She visited the Unit 731 War Crimes Exhibition Hall and saw her father's Special Transfer file. "Father!" she called, for the first time, in a flood of sorrow. After his disappearance, the family suffered from extreme poverty and begged for food on the streets. Chinese government scholarships supported Li Fengqin to go to school, but she always saved as much money as possible and sent it to her family. She found a job in bus services in Changchun, where she worked until she retired in 1992. Throughout that time, her family looked for Li Pengge. Li Fengqin's grandmother and mother died without finding any clues. These imperial atrocities have been inscribed in many family histories and still affect their lives today.

Li Fengqin visited Japan in 2010, met with Diet members, demanded an apology from the Japanese government, and compensation for the war crimes committed by Unit 731. The government never responded to her. She was deeply disappointed, and told me, "Please spread my story to create a more peaceful world."

RIGOROUS OR LOOSE? APPLICATION OF
THE CLASSIFICATION CRITERIA

The four people whose stories are told above fell into Japan's maximum surveillant assemblage and were categorized as "Soviet spies" by the Kwantung Gendarmerie. Armed resistance against Japanese imperialism continued in Northeast China in the 1930s and 1940s, and the intelligence networks among the Chinese, Koreans, and Russians were interwoven. However, researchers must interpret the gendarmerie files with care and read the words of colonial military police critically. As the category meriting the harshest punishment, the label of "Soviet spy" could have been attached to any captive, and thereby generate a relentless supply of "logs" for Unit 731. The information in the Special Transfer files was also often gathered through torture. Given the contentious imperial competition over Northeast China between Japan and Russia since the Russo-Japanese War (1904–5) and the Kwantung Army's repeated skirmishes with the Soviet Union—such as the Nomonhan Incident (1939) at the Russian border and the subsequent preparation for war against the Soviet Union—"Soviet spy" was a convenient category for the Kwantung Gendarmerie to use to define specific individuals as enemies, and to then punish them in the severest way. The category of "Soviet spy" was the best for fit the Kwantung Gendarmerie's classification chart for Special Transfer. Anyone who was labeled "spy" or "thought criminal" could become a living ingredient for biological experimentation.

In other words, the apparently rigorous criteria for Special Transfer were in fact quite loose or flexible at the point of application. It is important to point out this paradox between the appearance of careful standards and the actual productive outcomes, given that Special Transfer files were updated on a daily basis and that thousands of victims were systematically and relentlessly sent to Unit 731 between 1932 and 1945. Clearly, the Kwantung Gendarmerie did not use Special Transfer criteria to limit the number of Special Transfers; rather they routinely used it to keep up the supply of "logs" to the test facilities. So, what in the classification criteria helped the gendarmes to stretch the categories and loosen their application?

Two points should be noted. First, the gendarmes could interpret the thought, mind, or sentiment of the suspect however they wanted to fit into the categories defined by the chart. Both "spies" and "thought criminals" could include people who opposed the Japanese occupation, even those with only internal doubts who had not taken rebellious action. The technique of thought-crime investigation by the Kwantung Gendarmerie displayed the elastic character of the draconian laws and regulations in Manchukuo (chapter 4). Thought crime could be capacious enough to encompass the entire population and thus victimize any Chinese person. The notion of thought crime gave the military police room to use their discretion arbitrarily, beyond punishing subjects' actual actions, and regardless of one's classification by the chart. In other words, anyone who seemed suspicious in their thinking could be defined as a spy. Determining who seemed suspicious was left up to the gendarme's discretion, and no evidence was required for the claim. Spies and thought criminals became interchangeable categories. As the Peace Preservation Act in Japan did not directly send Japanese individuals to death row but did send many Koreans (chapter 3), the notion of thought crime had a brutal effect at the settler colonial threshold. Victims were sent to secret laboratories by Special Transfer instead of mounting the gallows or facing a firing squad.

Second, torture, which was the normalized technique for thought-crime investigation, created more human bodies that the military police could logistically hide from the public. According to Kamitsubo, the Kwantung Gendarmerie tortured all suspects in various ways: forcing victims to drink water and jumping on their stomach, giving them electric shocks, putting them in hemp sacks and kicking them, hitting them with clubs, and burning their skin with red-hot pokers.[56] If the Gendarmerie still couldn't find any criminal elements that fit the chart, even after torturing a victim—and because of the damage done in the course of torture—they sent the fatally injured suspects to Unit 731. The Japanese did not let the victims' families or the Chinese public know about their violence against innocent people or about the horrible marks torture left on their bodies.

Yoshifusa remembered internal competition among the gendarmes over how many Special Transfers they could produce.[57] Torture created a short cut to Special Transfer. Mori Sango, the former gendarme who was detained as a war criminal in Fushun, commented: "The only way to create the conditions for Special Transfer was cruel torture. We tortured anyone by using water, punching, electronic shock, placing pencils between the fingers and pressuring them, and forced them to confess that they were spies."[58] Tsuchiya Yoshio, a gendarme in Qiqihar, similarly stated, "We sent people who were subjected to severe punishment without trial, or whose bodies were seriously damaged due to torture, so we could not return them to their families, even if we found them innocent."[59]

Thus, in actual practice, the selection criteria for Special Transfer did not set any boundaries on the Gendarmerie's decision-making. It rather encouraged, rationalized, and even automated the most inhumane kind of administrative decision. Naganuma Setsuji, another gendarme, said:

> Special Transfer was easier than anything else. To send suspects to court, we had to write a formal statement as the evidence, but it is normally difficult to find clear evidence. The petty crime does not deserve it, and the hard-core rebels never confess. . . Special Transfer does not need the suspect's confession on record. All you need is our report for the Gendarmerie Headquarters, and Unit 731 will certainly process them. The suspects were never going to survive and resist again, so our bosses had encouraged us to use the Special Transfer[60]

The final determination before Special Transfer was whether the person could be useful to the Kwantung Army as an informant or not. Anyone not useful was judged as invalid to live but could still be useful in Unit 731 as a disposable body for experimentation. Under this criterion, anyone not useful for Japan's "national body" could rationally be sent in Special Transfer as living dead.

After all, the classification chart's systematic rationalization made Special Transfer easy, not difficult. The chart left a large margin for the Kwantung Gendarmerie's and other policing agencies' discretion. The gendarmerie even deliberately used torture to create victims who would fit the chart's criteria. Policing agencies conducted identification and classification not in pursuit of an accurate investigation but to justify the most inhumane ways of killing. This practice drew on the dual characteristics of colonial surveillance: While dissidents were the most severely targeted, anyone in the colonial population could be victimized at any time through rationalized but arbitrary classifications. The ostensibly rigorous selection chart helped imperial elites to legitimate the loose expansion of Special Transfer, turning a massive number of human beings into "logs" to be sent to Unit 731 as useless and unworthy of life.

ORGANIZED CRIMES BY SCIENTISTS AND UNIVERSITIES

The madness of the Kwantung Army and Unit 731 medical professionals
was rationalized as necessary to Japan's imperial victory and scientific
discovery. Otherwise, the systematic consumption of human bodies
could never have been sustained for more than ten years. Unit 731 is as
much a modern horror as Auschwitz in this respect. Much like the Jews
who were sent to extermination camps, the risky Chinese were deemed
invalid to live. Even if the "risky" part was indefinite, medical professionals consumed their living bodies to contribute to the country's war
effort and the advancement of medical science. Even after the war, few
medical professionals reflected on the ethics of their involvement in
dissecting live human bodies, planting deadly bacteria into otherwise
healthy bodies, or bombarding people with poison gas. Rather, presented
with the unimaginable opportunity to test their ideas on real human
bodies, the perpetrators competed with each other to get new scientific
data. In the postwar period, many Unit 731 scientists obtained doctoral
degrees after the war, based on data collected from those criminal experiments. Others started pharmaceutical businesses, opened medical
clinics, and obtained professorships at universities.[61] They justified
their involvement in Unit 731 as an act of diligently following military
orders, just like Adolf Eichmann excused his role in transferring the
Jewish people to death camps as the loyal work of a Nazi bureaucrat.[62]

The organized war crimes committed by imperial elites illuminate
the inherent asymmetry of colonial relations and the immense gap
of rationales between the colonizers and colonized. Biopolitical rationales, such as productivity and efficiency, convinced the colonizers to
reinforce their political privilege and economic accumulation, but the
same rationales never made sense to the colonized people. The Japanese
biopolitical rationalization of killing was simply unacceptable for the
Chinese or Koreans. This asymmetry of colonial relations is still un-
derrecognized in academia. The irrational experiences of the colonial
population are less likely to be discussed in the Global North than are
the "progressive" outcomes of modern history. Where does this dispro-
portionate recognition of colonial facts originate?

Racialization and dehumanization of colonial others are central to
this trend, indeed. But I would like to point to another palpable factor I

learned from my interviews: secrecy. The Special Transfer was deeply hidden due to its illegality and inhumanity, and the Kwantung Army burned and buried all its records in a rush. The systematic destruction of evidence—and the subsequent cover-up by the Allied Forces—blocked these grave international crimes from public view. The secrecy established by colonizers in the last century still feeds public ignorance of colonial crimes and harms and helps create the lopsided worldview of civilization today.

Surveillance contributed heavily to state secrecy. Surveillance serves to construct and maintain secrecy in order to create and sustain an unjust institution without public knowledge. The identification systems and surveillant assemblage not only collected the data of the colonized, but also protected the colonizers by keeping the colonized from knowing about sovereign activities—like a smoke screen. Knowing military information caused fatal punishment in"Manchukuo, since it was at the core of the sovereign force. That is why the Kwantung Gendarmerie's intelligence agency obtained the top status for governing "Manchukuo," and those who gathered information on the Kwantung Army for the resistance were sent to Unit 731. Secrecy provided protection for imperial elites, including medical professionals, to commit political violence and unethical human experiments.

TECHNOLOGICAL RATIONALITY AND UNHEALED SCARS

Japan perhaps killed fifteen million Chinese or more in the imperial wars up until 1945.[63] When the Kwantung Army began to rule the pseudo-state of Manchukuo, it legalized the killing of subversives without trial, in the name of severe punishment. This suggests that the state of exception was the principle for colonial lives, where law and violence worked in unity. Yet fearing that such naked brutality would damage the reputation of the "kingly way of governance" in the multicultural state, and further inflame armed resistance, the Kwantung Army switched the severe punishment of on-site murder to the Special Transfer of captives to a hidden killing facility. The maximum surveillant assemblage that Japan developed throughout Manchuria took selected victims to the final place, where Unit 731 made purposely abandoned lives useful for biological warfare and racist science. It was not contingent murder, but institutional utilitarianism aligned with technological rationality. The army's technological rationality was not to kill them simply as risks, but to use them secretly as resources until the moment they died. This calculation was coherent with the policy to replace the Chinese population with Japanese through mass migration. Japan's settler colonialism could not aim at the immediate extinction of all Chinese, but could slowly and efficiently deprive the local people of land, resources, and life within this ethos of eradication. As Young describes Manchukuo as the total empire, Japan's surveillance was infinitely all-encompassing, and its colonial violence was greedily all-consuming.

Identification, classification, and secrecy played out together as a biopolitical means of population control with the necropolitical result of sovereign violence in occupied Northeast China. Japan's biometric identification systems—used for surveillance—helped colonial sovereignty dictate who could live and who must die at the colonial threshold.[64] To manipulate the threshold of inclusion and exclusion, surveillance was woven into every administrative and judicial practice in Manchukuo.

Because surveillance protects secrecy around sovereign power, it is not easy in general to trace and point to violent outcomes of covert surveillance. However, this chapter finds that surveillance prepared a path to massive sovereign violence through technological rationality. The identification systems sought out colonial bodies, and the classification chart rationalized, and thus automated, systematic consumption of the bodies through Special Transfer. Courageous dissenters who countered Japanese imperialism were targeted, but at the same time, the victims could be any body. The colonial power saw the entire population as a potential threat to its dominance, and surveillance helped the colonizers to rationally select victims in an administrative manner.

This is not to say that colonial surveillance always results in sovereign violence. In theory, surveillance can be used for inclusion, entitlement, or participation, which is the normative face of surveillance systems today. But violent outcomes of surveillance should be taken into consideration as long as societies include populations made vulnerable by imperialism, colonialism, capitalism, patriarchy, and other structures of inequality. Identification and classification can irreversibly harm those vulnerable lives, and they reveal the nucleus of sovereign power in Western civilization.[65] Again, the harmful side of colonial actions tends to be concealed, while the harmless side is repeatedly emphasized and advertised by the architects of identification systems (e.g., governments, corporations). Technological rationality was a major societal condition that enabled the Nazi's concentration camps to grow out of the Weimar Republic, according to Zygmunt Bauman.[66] Since the administrative principle of technological rationality has persisted in postwar identification systems, there is no social safety net for potential victims of modern massacre in a democratic system. Under such circumstances, those in power may reduce all bodies to risky resources, subject them to a long and invisible process of secret surveillance, and ultimately to irrational violence.

Every narrative I collected from Unit 731 victims' families in China exposed deep, unhealed scars resulting from irrational colonial violence. Victims' families did not accept the rationalization of bare lives and forced death. At the end of the interviews, I always asked participants if there was anything they wanted to tell me, including things I had not asked. Wang Xuancai said clearly, "I want you to work harder, to the extent that the Japanese government admits this history. They cannot deny and erase the history, rather they should apologize for the invasive activities."

It should be noted that those victims have never been encouraged to speak up and claim justice in Chinese society. Covert surveillance and sudden disappearance complicated their family lives continuously after the liberation from Japanese occupation. The families never had political or personal stability after the loss of their loved ones and the torment continued. Thus, most of them keep an eye on Japanese politics and international relations, and are familiar with historical revisionists posturing in the Japanese cabinet. Li Gang said: "I cursed the Japanese for a long time. After receiving social education by the Communist Party at the age of sixteen, I learned to think of the state and people separately and was able to stop cursing. That's also how the Chinese leaders educated the Japanese war criminals in Fushun. The Japanese are also human, so they can change their way of thinking. It is the right thing to move forward toward making peace." His comment reflects the Chinese government's attitude on the war and colonial issues in the aftermath of liberation, which has been an exceptionally generous deal for the Japanese. But the rise of right-wing government and historical denialism in Japan make the families of war victims feel uneasy. Was it worth treating the Japanese leniently?

The victimization of Special Transfers to Unit 731 cannot be justified by any means for any system, because every life is the reason for its own living. Life, unique and singular, was irreversibly exterminated. And the consequences were not limited to that one life, but impacted many other lives to come for centuries. Every victim is part of their families' struggles, friends' mourning, and social loss, forever. The dead would refute the unilateral rationalization of sovereign violence, no matter what it achieved. No scientific discovery, technological advancement, or imperial dominance is comparable with one life. Every victim must recuperate their name from the "logs" for their dignity and for the peace of generations to come.

CONCLUSION

TROUBLES CONTINUED

Identification and Identity in the Post-Colonial Era

JAVERT: Now bring me prisoner 24601
           Your time is up
           And your parole's begun
           You know what that means
VALJEAN: Yes, it means I'm free
JAVERT: No, it means you get your yellow ticket-of-leave
           You are a thief
               —("Look Down," Les Misérables, 2012 film)

This book has narrated various technologies and experiences of identification, surveillance, and control in the nation building of modern Japan and its militarily acquired lands, traveling from the imperial center to the colonial margins, and exploring the major impacts of disciplinary, biopolitical, and necropolitical surveillance. To close my sociological investigation and contribute to a more historically informed discussion of the social effects of identification technologies, I pull discrete elements of each chapter's analysis together in this conclusion, drawing them together with a theoretical thread. I then offer some stories of the *koseki* and biometric ID systems as they have been used in post-World War II Japan. These encapsulate how persistently the covert relationship between surveillance and violence continues to this day.

In this way, my research, anchored in surveillance studies, is connected back to sociology, social sciences, and society at large through the study of identification and identity. I am frequently challenged by my readers, colleagues, and students who say: "People do not care about surveillance. They are aware of its negative aspects, but they keep using the internet and cellphone any way," "Many don't think surveillance will harm them. They tolerate surveillance because surveillance protects them, and they even enjoy using surveillance apps to watch other people's lives," or "We need to keep up with technology for work or for social life. After all, there is nothing we can do about it!" In response, I submit this book in the hope that my work not only makes the surveillance-violence nexus visible but also helps to change the public mindset—including apathy and despair—regarding the gravity of issues raised by surveillance. In fact, it is not difficult to change the way we think when we listen to marginalized voices, imagine ourselves in the shoes of the colonial Others, and *feel* it. Novelists know that one book can change people's worldview: They have recurrently picked up the theme of surveillance as an existential question for humanity—see, for instance, works by Aldous Huxley, Franz Kafka, George Orwell, Philip K. Dick, and Margaret Atwood, to name a few.

Less acknowledged as a surveillance novel, Victor Hugo's *Les Misérables*, published in France in 1862, is also a celebrated text that depicts how easily an ID card can reduce a person to a vulnerable figure, chain them to social sanctions, and take away their freedom. Jean Valjean stole a loaf of bread for his sister's starving child and was put in prison for nineteen years. When prisoner 24601 came out of prison, it was the beginning not of his freedom, but of days chained to the yellow ticket of leave, as the policeman Javert tells him in the epigraph. Because Valjean had to show his ID paper wherever he went, he was still treated as a thief and could not find a place to live. After stealing silverware from a bishop who kindly offered him food and lodging, and who told the police that he gave Valjean the treasures, Valjean repented and vowed to live a new life. He tore off the yellow ticket of leave that blocked his freedom, made him hate the world, and turned him into a real thief.

Why has this story been the subject of so many theater productions and films around the world? A novel has of course many different attractions for readers, but it is reasonable that audiences have sympa-thized with the protagonist in his servitude and unfair treatment and root for him to live a life free from repression.

Similarly, I hope readers will experience colonial surveillance from the side of Jean Valjean, not Javert, in this book. I will return to this point. First, I summarize the major findings of this book and tie to-gether the three different threads of Japan's identification systems: dis-ciplinary, biopolitical, and necropolitical.

DISCIPLINARY, BIOPOLITICAL, AND NECROPOLITICAL IDENTIFICATION

The family-based *koseki* system that has constructed modern "Japa-nese" subjects exhibits a disciplinary characteristic that alters individ-uals into docile bodies.[1] *Koseki* does not perform visual surveillance. Instead, it instills the social order the state upholds, and automates soul training to make the population into loyal members of the patriarchal family and loyal subjects of the emperor. It reifies surveillance in the eyes of thousands of people who internalize the patriarchal hierarchy, and who physically watch over one another in family, community, and society. In this sense, *koseki* constructs multidimensional surveillance: panoptic, lateral, and synoptic (chapter 2).

Importantly, *koseki*'s disciplinary characteristics helped the Meiji government to industrialize and join the global market. Japan's mod-ernization was originally a response to an external demand by Western powers for international trade. The Meiji regime rushed to release the population from feudal bondage to land, profession, and restriction of movement—all strictly controlled in the Edo era—so that people could move as free labor power for industry. Just as Foucault finds that cre-ating docile bodies is not enough for modern capitalism and points to the technique of population control as part of biopower,[2] so too has *koseki* functioned to mobilize the population for industrialization and productivity, while tying it to a patriarchal and patriotic code of con-duct. Disciplinary and biopolitical characteristics coexist in the *koseki* identification.

This productive character seen in biopolitical population control is, however, rarely observable in the colonial *koseki* implemented in Taiwan and Korea. The colonial *koseki* was strictly separate from the Japanese one. The plan was not to merge colonial individuals with "Original Japanese," but to establish a racial order within the expanding imperial population. Though Taiwan and Korea were counted as territories of imperial Japan, the imperial Constitution of 1889 did not fully apply to the colonies, nor did the Koseki Act. Taiwanese and Koreans were included in the *koseki* but marked as second-class subjects of the empire. Their registered information was used for more direct and physical surveillance: for policing, assimilating, banning, and punishing individuals. The colonial *koseki* could not convince people to internalize a mythical national unity, nor become loyal subjects of the Japanese empire.

When Japanese imperialism encroached on Northeast China, fingerprinted ID cards were adopted as a new technology of population control. The roots of this process go back to the 1920s, before Japan's military occupation and the subsequent creation of the settler colonial threshold Manchukuo. Fingerprinting technology, invented by the British imperial police team in India in the 1890s, was first successfully applied to Chinese miners in South Africa in the 1990s (chapter 1). The imperial wars and colonial industries generated transnational migration of Chinese workers as cheap labor power. Fingerprint identification chased them back to China, which was increasingly under Japanese political and economic occupation, as the spoils of the Russo-Japanese War. As the biometric identification system expanded from Chinese migrants to the Black population in South Africa, the Manchurian scheme began to track migrant laborers in coal mines and was then tested across other colonial industries as the Labor Card system (chapter 4). The fingerprinted Resident Card was also issued, closely related to military operations to sever links between residents and armed resistance, and to sweep out dissidents. Japan's Kwantung Army developed total policing networks by generating multiple intelligence agencies. This maximum surveillant assemblage drew necropolitical effects from biometric identification, seen in the Chinese survivors' attestations (chapters 3–5).

Toward the catastrophic end of the Greater East Asia Co-Prosperity Sphere, the Manchurian government had a serious labor shortage, and at that time the Labor Card and Resident Card converged into the National Passbook. The government used the passbook to force villagers to work in industries and farms, and even to hunt people down on the streets for the labor camps. Biometric ID cards in the settler colonial threshold advanced a repressive rather than productive aspect of modern administration. The biopolitical means of population control mobilized the entire population for labor and service, which threw people under necropolitical power. The numerous *wanrenkeng*, unknown mass graves of Chinese workers discovered in the Japanese-run mines and construction sites, testify to the difficulty that the workers were rarely able to escape from necropolitical power once they were set on the track of forced labor via systematic identification. Others, who resisted the Japanese occupation and were caught in the surveillant assemblage, were sent to Japan's illegal biological testing facilities and extinguished by the devil's gluttony (chapter 5).

In contrast with the patriarchal files of the *koseki* system, biometric identification individualizes the population and tracks the movements of each body. The Manchurian case exposes two primary purposes of colonial ID systems: mobilizing the local people as cheap labor power and preempting potential rebellion. The biometric ID systems became a powerful means of population control, which helped the Japanese to sort the colonial population into desirable and undesirable and exploit it as a resource. The Chinese and other colonial bodies were classified as a security risk for the empire, but still useful to the economy. Biometric technology had dual capabilities: monitoring the movements of colonial bodies as sources of resistance while mobilizing the same bodies as profitable labor power and a source of wealth. The colonizers reduced the body to a dispensable resource, not a subject, of the empire. Identification cards gave Japanese colonizers legitimate ways to identify, track, record, restrain, or ban the movements of colonial bodies, and single out and punish individuals who resisted.

Here, the popular concept of biopower in North American academia should be carefully applied to modern regulatory systems, not to overgeneralize experiences of imperial technologies and ignore their oppressive aspects. While biopower articulates the productive character of modern power,[3] it exposes the inadequacy of elucidating sovereign violence mechanisms within it. Agamben inserts the concept of the state of exception to explain these paradoxical mechanisms and shows how certain people are set in inclusive exclusion and deprived of legal protection within the democratic principle of a nation-state.[4] But Agamben's application of the concept does not go far enough outside of the Western Hemisphere. Mbembe, by contrast, directly casts light on the brutal result of biopower as necropolitics and the mass killings and threats administered by Western nation-states in colonial zones.[5] As such, a theoretical intervention to biopower is necessary to fully lay out the global consequences of surveillance techniques and technologies constructed by a modern power that is internally a nation-state but externally an imperial state, simultaneously. This holistic approach can operationalize major concepts of surveillance studies—such as social sorting, categorization, and population control—in a new research direction. It enables researchers not only to depart from the internal boundaries of analysis from a position of privilege but also to reach out to the marginalized effects of surveillance and map out the ruling relations of technology from the bottom of society, formerly an unknown or underrepresented truth.

STATE SECRECY AND VIOLENCE

My genealogical investigation has unpacked the relationship between surveillance and sovereign violence that is rendered invisible in two layers. In the first layer, surveillance activities operate covertly, and so the watched feel uneasy and left in uncertainty. Surveillance activities have been (often legally) protected by secrecy and blocked from public oversight for a long period in history, which constitutes the second layer of invisibility. Many family members of Unit 731 victims did not know that their loved ones were sent to Special Transfer until a half century later. It is still not easy to trace back the individual cases of Special Transfer since the administrative processes were top secret, and the collection of evidence was obstructed by the perpetrators. The secrecy has in effect shaped our understanding of world history and human experiences with technology to this day. That is why Chinese scholars and my interviewees did not understand the objectives of my research in the first place: to them, the ID card was only an insignificant part of the Japanese occupation or was even considered a relatively less harmful part of colonization, as physical violence and terror were at the forefront of the Chinese experience of Japanese occupation. To me, that is why I needed to write this book, to make visible the crucial and devastating role of surveillance in perpetrating violence.

The Kwantung Gendarmerie sent thousands of dissidents to the biological war and human experimentation facility of Unit 731 while hiding the operation behind the Special Transfer code name from 1938 to 1945 (chapter 5). The classification chart for Special Transfer helped the gendarmes to keep producing "logs" and to justify the selection of them. The criteria rationalized who was useless and reasonable to kill due to being sorted into the given categories: spies, guerrillas, saboteurs, vagrants, opium users, pro-Soviet, anti-Japanese, rebels, and anyone who rejected becoming a spy for Japan, and who "belong(s) to the same group that comes under the category of special transfer" (see table 5.1). It operated on the basis of technological rationality that squeezed the last drop of utility from a captivated body. Furthermore, despite the apparently rigorous criteria, the decisions were all-consuming in the end because the Kwantung Gendarmerie allowed a broad margin for discretion and the administrative processes did not require clear evidence. Japan's surveillant assemblage sorted out the colonial bodies according to their best use for the imperial political economy and its cruel, racist science.

Biometric technology turned people's bodies into sites of surveillance, to benefit the sovereign power that appropriated their bodies as dispensable resources and prevented their resistance. While the modern ID system was generated as a biopolitical means to construct nationals and develop a capitalist economy in the metropolis, it resulted overall in a necropolitical experience in the colonies. Through racialization and rationalization, colonial ID systems legitimated throwing people's bodies into a state of exception, where law and violence became indistinguishable.[6] Thus, the cruelest kinds of slaughter were systematically conducted in a civilized manner in the colonial threshold. This sharply contradicts Foucault's emphasis on the shift in the biopolitical character of the sovereign power vis-à-vis the population: from the ancient sovereign's right to kill to the modern sovereign's right to foster life. Japan's colonial ID system predominantly served as necropolitical surveillance, rationalizing who might live and who must die in Northeast China.

Conversely, this should be learned as a sociohistorical lesson: The practice of sovereign violence began much earlier than the destruction of individual bodies on a timeline, taking the form of surveillance. It began from the moment of identification in the occupied land. Identification is certainly the starting point of surveillance,[7] but it is also often the starting point of violence in colonial relations of rule, in the sense that it can curb or take away the agency of the subject, place it under institutional control, and turn the colonized body into a site of surveillance and violence carried out by the sovereign power. A similar phenomenon has been historically observed, for example, in the process by which the Nazis registered, identified, and sent Jewish people to the death camps,[8] how European settlers contained the Black population in the Homeland system in South Africa,[9] and how the Israeli government imposed a color-coded identification system on the Palestinian people.[10] Modern sovereign violence is a process shaped through bureaucracy and othering, and identification paved the way to sovereign violence in the noted cases. Much more critical attention should be paid to the role of identification and surveillance as an early stage of slow violence.

For this reason, I cannot emphasize enough that the invisible relationship between surveillance and violence, and the separate understanding of the two, are not naturally formed but deliberately constructed. It is terrifying that the deliberate erasure of the evidence on Unit 731 indeed succeeded in diverting public view from examining this massive crime against humanity in the contexts of identification, surveillance, nation-states, colonialism, torture, policing, science, technology, and eventually, the whole of civilization and humanity. The erasure and denial of the uncomfortable past directly affects our choices for the future, particularly in this case, on surveillance techniques and technologies. My work perhaps reveals only the tip of the iceberg of many violent experiences of identification and surveillance in modern history. It is necessary for researchers to be aware of hidden but deliberate attempts to subdue people's exclusionary experiences of surveillance technologies and to redeem marginalized voices from erasure, denial, and revision.

POSTSCRIPT STORIES: HOW COLONIAL IDENTIFICATION SYSTEMS REMAIN IN THE POSTCOLONIAL ERA

Japan lost all its colonies in its defeat in World War II in August 1945 and went through disarmament, land reform, and democratization of political, economic, and legal systems under the Allied Forces occupation until April 1952. The significant parts of identification systems and the function of surveillance discussed in this book, however, survived the postwar revolutionary reforms.

The Koseki *System*

The *koseki* system was reformed to dissolve official patriarchy as part of war machine in the postwar democratization of the civil laws. A *koseki* file over three generations was forbidden: One *koseki* file covers only up to two generations, usually a husband, wife, and unmarried child. Once the child marries, they are required to create and register a new *koseki* with the spouse. However, the nuclear-family-friendly format still requires people to identify the family head and the relationships of the rest of the members to the head. Although the postwar Japanese Constitution and civil laws state that men and women are completely equal, and marriage is valid only with the agreement of the couple, hierarchical positions within the family have remained the basis of all administrations. Only people with the same surname are allowed to be a *koseki* family. The couple can choose a surname from either the wife's or husband's side, but in reality, 95 percent of couples choose the husband's surname, and register the husband as the head of *koseki* family and his Honseki (imaginary address) as his family's. Unofficial patriarchy still governs family law and sustains male-centric society within democracy.

It is not coincidental that the emperor system also survived the lost war. General Douglas MacArthur, supreme commander for the Allied Powers who oversaw the occupation of Japan (1945-51), decided to preserve Japan's "national body" as a guard against communism, and the emperor was given a new status of "symbol of the nation" without political power, as defined in the pacifist Constitution of 1946. Just like Unit 731 Captain Ishii Shirō, Emperor Hirohito—the supreme commander of Japanese Army—was exempted from being charged as a war criminal among the war leaders in the Allied Forces' International Military Tribunal for the Far East (Tokyo Tribunal, 1946-48). Upholding the imperial family as the ideal at the top of the patriarchal structure, *koseki* continues to discriminate against women and children outside of institutional marriage, and against the people whose ancestors were classified as the untouchable class in the feudal era—Hisabetsu-buraku (被差別部落).

Today, *koseki* is still a list of "the pure Japanese" birthed by Japanese parents, and its exclusionary characteristic as a gatekeeper that creates nationals is consistent with Japan's restrictive immigration policies and the ban on dual citizenship. Yet, the *koseki* is clearly outdated as a surveillance tool in tracing individual movements, and its patriarchal aspect has been increasingly challenged by feminists and LGBTQ+ communities. Lesbian and gay couples have demanded their equal right to marry, claimed the Koseki Act and civil laws are unconstitutional, and sued the government for legislative change. They won two lawsuits at the level of High Court in 2024.[11] Civil lawsuits for married couples to each keep their own surname have also been ongoing and have disrupted the obsolete *koseki* system that dictates private and intimate relationships. Implementation of such legal changes has also been repeatedly advised by the Human Rights Council and the Committee on Elimination of Discrimination Against Women in the United Nations.[12] The right-wing government's stubborn refusal to hear those voices illuminates how much their governance relies on patriarchal relations of rule. For more than 150 years, from monarchy to democracy, *koseki* has continuously been a tool of soul training to instill an imaginary unity among the Japanese with one ethnicity, ensure their loyalty to the state, and erode the relationship between the state and people based on constitutional rights.

Fingerprint ID Card

Fingerprint identification and biometric ID card systems, implemented in occupied Northeast China, were incorporated into the postwar Alien Registration System. The Alien Registration Ordinance of 1947 altered the legal status of Koreans and Taiwanese residing in Japan to aliens overnight and required them to register. The Alien Registration Act replaced the last ordinance by Emperor Hirohito when Japan signed the San Francisco Peace Treaty and regained its sovereignty in 1952. Although neither the treaty nor the act directly stated the legal status of ex-colonial individuals, the government announced that it would deprive ex-colonial subjects of Japanese nationality permanently, by notification of the Ministry of Justice. At that point, 95 percent of registered "aliens" in Japan, approximately six hundred thousand people, were ex-colonial subjects.[13] The intent of this law was obviously not to regulate foreign citizens residing in Japan generally, but to continuously watch over the movements of the former colonial population.

The colonial *koseki* in fact helped the Japanese government in the transition to identifying, classifying, and excluding Taiwanese and Koreans from Japanese citizenship, and to subjecting them to the Alien Registration. Citizen or noncitizen status was determined on the basis of whether a person's *koseki* (more precisely *honseki*) existed in Japan, or in Korean or Taiwanese *koseki*. The colonial classification of the population enabled the government to draw a new citizenship boundary and to abandon its responsibility for the colonized population.[14] The Japanese ruling class, like former prime minister Yoshida Shigeru (1948-54), continued to view the ex-colonized as security threats (bandits or communists), and actively deny them any rights enjoyed by the Japanese.[15]

Furthermore, the Alien Registration System of 1952 officially restored fingerprint identification and incorporated it into the Alien Registration Card. The law required all foreigners over fourteen years old and staying in Japan for more than sixty days to be fingerprinted at registration and renew it every two years.[16] It was compulsory to carry the Alien Registration Card and show it to police if asked. If a person failed or refused, they were severely fined or arrested. This colonial technology of the ID card was whitewashed as scientific management in the postwar democratic system, while the Japanese police continuously watched over the ex-colonial population as potential suspects, enemy within, or, at best, internal Others.

For many Koreans and Taiwanese liberated from Japanese colonialization, this was unacceptable. A widespread protest arose in the 1980s, by mass refusal to fingerprint, in coalition with people of other nationalities. After a series of struggles in the courts and retaliation against protesters by the police and border control, the resistance eventually achieved a total abolition of fingerprinting of all foreigners in 2000.[17]

The colonial residual of biometric identification seemed extinct. However, it made a comeback within seven years, during the American War on Terror. Following the new border control scheme by the United States, Japanese immigration began to fingerprint almost all visitors to Japan at ports of entry in 2007.[18] The Koreans and Taiwanese with Special Permanent Residency—those who came to Japan before World War II and their descendants—were carefully exempted from the fingerprinting requirement at the border. Yet it is symbolic that the new imperial war brought the colonial technology of fingerprinting back to Japanese border control with the enhanced capacities of digital networks.

In 2012, the Alien Registration System was replaced with the New Foreign Resident Control System, which centralized the registration of non-Japanese citizens under Immigration Control in the Ministry of Justice, previously managed by the municipalities.[19] The Foreign Resident Card has a similar format to the Alien Registration Card, but requires updates with any change in personal details and collects more information. The colonial ID systems have transformed into a digitally centralized ID system through which the government can deal with all information about noncitizens and watch over their movements. The New Foreign Resident Control System has been continuously placing non-Japanese people in a state of exception to efficiently mark, track, and exclude them from Japanese constitutional rights.

Digitizing National Identification Systems

Fingerprinting was normalized as the main method of criminal investigation in postwar Japanese police systems. In 1961, the fiftieth anniversary ceremony of the police fingerprint system, held at the Tokyo Metropolitan Police Department, displayed the Japanese origins of biometric technology in colonial management. Five out of six fingerprint technicians who were awarded the highest honors had formerly worked for the Fingerprint Management Bureau in Manchukuo.[20] Those who trained in the colony brought back all the techniques for identifying colonial bodies and disseminated them widely in criminal investigations across Japan.

Postwar Japan continued to build new identification systems on top of the *koseki* system. Formally institutionalized in 1951, the Resident Basic Registration required all residents in Japan to register at their municipality of residence, including their residing address and household members. This registration system was intended to grasp the actual state of residents as a more practical grounds for municipal services, which is often different from *koseki* records, was originally paper-based, and managed separately in the municipalities. However, the 1999 amendment of the Resident Basic Registration Act centralized and digitized the Resident Basic Registration to build a completely new national ID system of Juki-Net (the Resident Basic Registration Network, 住民基本台帳ネットワーク) in 2002.[21] It is networked with the discrete files of the Resident Basic Registration that are stored in each municipality and has given the central government direct access to personal data for the first time. Juki-Net provides each citizen with a unique eleven-digit number and circulates fourteen items of personal data across different spheres.

The idea of a national identification system has been called the One Hundred Million Total Uniform Number System (一億総背番号制度) since the late 1960s, based on the image of a baseball player's number applied to the entire Japanese population. Business leaders, conservative politicians, and bureaucrats have been its main advocates, but many citizens have found it invasive to their privacy. When municipalities mailed the notification of the eleven-digit number to each resident, a nationwide protest commenced. People returned their ID numbers to the municipalities or tore up the notifications. Anticipating the citizens' vigilance with regard to invasions of privacy, the government stated in the law that Juki-Net is strictly used only by the government and does not share personal residential data with private companies. Contrary to the desire expressed by business leaders and bureaucrats, Juki-Net failed to grow into an infrastructure of e-government, from healthcare to banking, and its use has been limited to pension services.[22]

But this did not discourage the infinite appetite of scientific management for data. In 2014, the Common Number System (共通番号制度) was introduced over the failed Juki-Net, featuring interoperability with private databases. My Number—another number issued to each resident in Japan—attaches various kinds of personal data around taxing and social welfare. Not only the government but also employers collect and use the My Number of their employees. Thus, although the law does not require the individual to provide My Number to private companies, the Common Number System has a more compulsory characteristic pushing individuals to use it.

Both Juki-Net and My Number manifest a core idea of the old dream of the One Hundred Million Total Uniform Number System: a compulsory national identification card. Japan has never had a compulsory national identification card for citizens before, and it could be unconstitutional to force citizens to bear a national ID card under the postwar constitution that secures a wide range of basic rights, including the right to privacy. Thus, the Juki-Net and My Number systems offer only a voluntary photo ID card. The government widely advertised it to encourage people to apply for the ID card, but less than 20 percent of the population had applied for a My Number Card up until 2020, the beginning of the COVID-19 pandemic.[23] The long-term low rate clearly shows that most people don't need national ID cards. In fact, the government has implemented numerous pilot projects on electronic ID cards at municipal levels since the 1980s and subsidized technology companies with billions in tax money to test and build new data systems. The ID cards were so unpopular that none of the municipal experiments went well or remained.

So, to boost the issuing rate, the government adopted a neoliberal rewards policy, awarding shopping points called "Ma'ina points" to those who applied for My Number Cards.[24] If that is the carrot, the stick is the compulsory replacement of one's healthcare card with My Number Card, which began in 2024. The My Number Card is still voluntary in legal terms but is increasingly a de facto mandatory item for accessing bank accounts, buying insurance, and applying for essential public services. During the coronavirus pandemic, the Digital Agency was newly established as a government department to promote digitization and expand the use of My Number, linking up a wide range of personal data.

It should also be noted that since the rightist Prime Minister Shinzō Abe returned to power in December 2012, a series of surveillance and national security bills have been passed in parallel with the development of the Common Number System and the New Foreign Resident Control System: the Secrecy Act of 2013, the revised Wiretapping Act of 2015, the Conspiracy Act of 2016, and the Active Cyber Defense Act of 2025.[25] These laws give the state more ability to spy on residents and hide covert activities from the public. Under the new surveillance legislation, Japanese lives are rendered more transparent to the government, while the government surrounds itself with a smoke screen to hide surveillance activities.[26]

THE MEMORY AND FUTURE OF SURVEILLANCE TECHNOLOGY

As such, the biometrics, ID cards, and other identification systems tested and developed in occupied Northeast China have survived and been transformed into postwar administrative systems in Japan, despite the total collapse of Japanese colonial management. The recent digitization of identification systems, and the policing power that capitalizes on digital surveillance tools, demonstrate the continuation, rather than discontinuation, of surveillance practices since the imperial era and their transformation into new level of omnipresent surveillance. The transwar continuation means that the patriarchal and racializing techniques of identification systems have survived colonial wars. On a global scale, the same surveillance schemes have proliferated and augmented the technological capacities of data collection in the twenty-first century. So, it is reasonable to ask: Are we still living in a colonial regime? Or is this digital neocolonialism?

For the colonial survivors who still suffer the transgenerational impact of Japanese violence, history and memory are the actual site of their battle to transform their painful experiences into hope. Their suffering parallels the concerns about other modern atrocities, including Primo Levi who wrote about anxieties that, due to the extreme nature of genocide, Holocaust survivors' words would not be trusted or taken seriously.[27] The people I interviewed in China are the last generation who physically experienced and can testify to the Japanese occupation, and they are afraid that their experiences will not be passed on to future generations. In this sense, memory crucially involves social change.

We are perhaps in the transitional stage where living memory of colonialism turns into what Aleida Assmann calls cultural memory. Assmann states, "While individual recollections spontaneously fade and die with their former owners, new forms of memory are reconstructed within a transgenerational framework, and on an institutional level, within a deliberate policy of remembering or forgetting. There is no self-organization and self-regulation of cultural memory—it always depends on personal decisions and selections, on institutions and media."[28] Japanese institutions and mainstream media have turned their backs on the inconvenient truth of Japanese colonialism. The right-wing government erased the description of the Japanese "Comfort Women" system from history textbooks and discouraged teachers from discussing it in school. Particularly disturbing is the growing discourse denying Japan's past wrongdoings on the internet, by which younger generations are most likely to be influenced in the absence of the living memory of colonial survivors and war victims.[29] Those denials are growing together with hate speech, expressing perceptions that Koreans, Chinese, or other Asians living in Japan have received privileges that they have not deserved. This misinformation on Asian neighbors and the erasure of the colonial memory are linked and increasingly producing nationalistic agenda and jingoistic propaganda. It has also characterized the global trend toward authoritarian regimes and totalitarian societies that is prevalent in recent years, typically scapegoating migrants, immigrants, refugees, asylum seekers, and even international students from the Global South as the cause of social problem or security threats.[30]

Surveillance studies and social theories are not immune from such a reconstruction of collective memory. Marginalized experiences of being surveilled are not only underrepresented in research but also often silenced and erased at the immediate site of experience by deliberate decisions made to conceal facts. Surveillance deeply involves public relations, knowledge dissemination, and opinion making. In fact, the intentional distribution and manipulation of data are major objectives for intelligence agencies in democratic states such as the United States or Canada. Academics, journalists, and discourse producers, whether they like it or not, participate in the politics of knowledge production and memory construction. This is not only an academic subject but also a public issue of media control and the freedom to know and express.

For the future of surveillance, what we need is a more historically informed, humanitarian imagining for today's marginalized populations caught in surveillance capitalism and digital neocolonialism. This book encourages readers to wonder how people today experience mass surveillance, for example, in Palestine, Yemen, Afghanistan, Iraq, and Uygur or at the U.S.-Mexico border, on European shores, or in the urban centers of the prosperous Global North. As Hannah Arendt says of the diasporas of the twentieth century,[31] refugees from conflict and persecution—the twenty-first century's *Les Misérables*—are still treated as the scum of society, no matter where they are. Inclusive exclusion keeps happening along with the operation of surveillance cameras, facial recognition systems, spyware, drones, and other automated biometric technologies. It is logical to deduce that today's marginalized populations also experience surveillance systems as part of an overall, targeted discrimination and naked violence against them, just as the Chinese people experienced Japan's biometric ID systems. The colonial

experiences of mass surveillance strongly suggest the violent consequences of the present surveillance systems that are hidden from the
public eye.

Technology is often described as inevitable and unstoppable. Yet
in such a positivist view, the negative consequences of technology are
cleansed, masked, or at best offset by its positive aspects. Although it is
always uncertain where a technology will venture in the future, technology has its origin in certain political economic purposes, like other
social constructs. Technology is undeniably human made, so it is more
practical to reflect on who created the technology, for what purpose,
how it has been used, and what the outcome was for human lives. To
counter technological determinism, my work calls for the harmful consequences of past technology to be uncovered for the future of technology. The marginalized past suggests that an identification system has
the power to reduce individual bodies to risks and resources, and sets
people in a defenseless position from sovereign violence. A simple lesson
from the colonial experience is that we should not further let the same
systems go on. In this sense, a sociological account of an oppressed past
is as important as a contemporary analysis of technological novelties.
Scholars can and should challenge the positivist understanding of technology and untangle the invisible consequences of technology to create
a more equal, caring, and peaceful society.

Why peace? Because history shows that war and peace dictate the
course of major technological developments. My study proves that
conflict and suspicion feed surveillance technologies exponentially.
The more a conflict or crisis grows, the more a surveillant assemblage
spreads its rhizomic reach to peoples' lives and is immediately justified
in the name of national security without clear reasoning or lawful evidence. Without an effort to create peace, critical studies fall on deaf ears
and are unable to alter the future of technology. A plea for peace was the
resounding and profound message from the Unit 731 victims' families I
met in China to younger generations across the globe.

Identification represents, after all, the common question of identity
and humanity, to which everyone in any culture has a sense, claim, and
right, as seen in *Les Misérables*. Jean Valjean tore up his yellow ticket
of leave, but it did not really set him free. In the 2012 film directed by
Tom Hooper, Valjean, a mayor, struggles with whether to reveal his real

identity, knowing that an innocent man has been captured as Valjean. "If I speak, I am condemned. If I stay silent, I am damned." He asks, "Who am I? Who am I? . . . I'm Jean Valjean!" He runs to the court and declares that he is prisoner 24601. The chains of the ID system never let him live in freedom, but he broke them with his courage and conscience.

Why are we moved by such a story? The context and experience of systematic injustice, whether fictional or nonfictional, revives our sense of humanity and dignity. The marginalizing effect of identification is in fact widely understood and commonly shared among people. This shared sense can bring a more fundamentally ethical consideration to identification techniques and technologies. At least we can collectively raise the right question of whether we would like to live our life as a thief on parole, or live as a free person, a body with dignity. *Les Misérables* and my research would reply that no one should be reduced to a risky resource or fragmented data point for those in power. Ultimately, it should not be the ID system that decides who you are; it should be you.

APPENDIX

FIELD NOTES

I wrote this book based on a genealogical approach, institutional ethnography, and a fieldwork trip to China. As a methodology, my fieldwork stands out as the most significant part of this project, and it was very close to not happening for multiple reasons. It has been increasingly challenging for foreign researchers to enter and stay in China for the purpose of long-term academic research. So, I believe it is worth noting here how I managed to conduct a three-month fieldwork trip to China in September–November 2016, as a historical record and backstage narrative for present and future researchers. It would have been impossible without the help of many nonstate actors in every stage of this adventure. I hope my field notes are beneficial for other researchers to find channels for obtaining visas or permits and to maintain a persistent attitude, until the moment they can land at their research destination.

This appendix is also intended to remind of the unique value of fieldwork for researchers to tangibly understand people's lived experiences, including their emotion and everyday life, and, at the same time, to unambiguously recognize researchers' own positionality and epistemological limitations on the site of investigation. In postpandemic times, researchers are increasingly relying on digitally mediated communications, but fieldwork reminds us that there are still national borders and institutional barriers in the internet and social media, and the digital media cannot deliver wholesome social experiences. Fieldwork provides a vantage point for researchers to communicate directly with people, by physically going past international borders, and to witness the real issues and causes the people face, which are often covered up or modified by the media.

Last, this appendix is also a spinoff of my own ID troubles, about which my academic supervisor joked I could write another PhD dissertation, because of my labyrinthine experiences with Chinese visa and permit systems. Some personal circumstances—bringing my family to the fieldwork—can be additional information for researchers who have parenting obligation. Here, I unfold my troubles in this order: overview, administrative barriers, cultural challenges, and the importance of shock.

OVERVIEW

My fieldwork took place from September to November 2016 in the area formerly known as "Manchukuo," now consisting of three provinces (Jilin, Heilongjiang, and Liaoning) in Northeast China. I stayed on the campus of Jilin University in the city of Changchun in Jilin Province for two and a half months and visited Harbin, Jixi, Mishan, and Hulin in Heilongjiang Province, and Shenyang and Fushun in Liaoning Province.

During my stay in China, I met Chinese scholars of modern Chinese history, sociology, colonial studies, and war crime studies, and they connected me with relevant archives and prospective interviewees. To find and collect historical documents and published data, I visited fourteen historic museums and archives: the International Center for Unit 731 Research at Harbin Academy of Social Science, the Unit 731 War Crime Exhibition Hall, the Jixi City Museum of Japanese War Crime Evidence at Didao Coal Mine, the Jixi City Museum, the Hutou Japanese Fort Museum, the Jilin City Workers Memorial Museum, the Northeast Colonial History Museum, the Museum of Imperial Palace of Pseudo-Manchukuo, Jilin University Library, the 9.18 History Museum, the Special Military Tribunal of China's Supreme People's Court in Shenyang, the Fushun War Criminal Control Center, the Fushun Coal Mine Museum, and the Pingdingshan Massacre Memorial Hall.

At those sites, I was able to collect printed resources as well as visual data of different kinds of ID cards issued by the governmental bodies of Manchukuo. Importantly, the data included the Japanese Kwantung Army Gendarmerie's documents about investigating, selecting, and transferring Chinese victims to Unit 731. I conducted five semi-structured interviews with family members of the victims who were killed at Unit 731. I was also able to interview a survivor who was forced to work at a dam construction site in Jilin Province. Overall, my fieldwork yielded more fruits than I expected. I can confirm that the three methodologies were a good match for the fieldwork.

However, I also constantly encountered challenges from the preparatory stage of the fieldwork onwards, which modified my methodology. First, some administrative barriers kept me from researching in China. Those barriers were severe enough that I needed to abandon my original plan of fieldwork and eventually shortened the duration of my stay in China, which limited my data collection. Second, I faced cultural obstacles to get access to archival resources, to communicate the academic nature of my quest, and to interview people. These challenges ultimately stem from my objective and subjective positionality as a Japanese researcher. My positionality constrained my investigation but deepened my understanding of colonialism, too.

ADMINISTRATIVE BARRIERS

I started to prepare for research in China in December 2015, when I met the Chinese Liaison Officer for Queen's University, based in Shanghai. A foreign researcher needs an invitation letter from a Chinese research institute to apply for an academic exchange visa. I asked the liaison officer to search for any Chinese professor who might be interested in my project. Meanwhile, I planned to apply for the Mitacs Globalink Research Award to fund the field research, which requires a "host supervising professor" from a Chinese university for the application. The liaison officer recommended a professor at the Department of History at Jilin University who could help my visa and funding applications. Though the professor initially responded that Japanese ID systems during the occupation had never been researched in China before, and thus he was afraid that my fieldwork might not see positive outcomes, he agreed to become my host supervisor for the grant application. Because we communicated in English, it took four months to collect the required information from the Jilin University professor via the liaison officer and complete the application, but I was able to receive the Mitacs grant in May 2016.

The next step was to apply for a visa to conduct research in China. A Japanese citizen can stay in China up to two weeks without a visa, but I wanted to stay in China for four months, to establish relationships with resource persons, spend hours in archives, find prospective interviewees, and interview them. On June 21, by appointment, I submitted two application packages for an academic exchange visa, for myself and an accompanying child, to the Chinese Visa Application Center in Ottawa. My child's application was immediately declined, and the officer said it was only possible after I had obtained a visa. My application was accepted but compromised to reduce the duration from a category of six months to ninety days, because first-time research should be done within ninety days, according to the officer. I submitted my passport, too.

Within a few days, the center asked me over the phone to provide more detailed information about my research from the inviting party, Jilin University. I contacted Jilin University and asked for additional documents. I sent them to the center by fax. Yet the center declined my application for an academic visa and suggested that I apply for a work visa. I responded that I was not going to be employed by Jilin University or receive any income in China. No further response was provided. I drove back to Ottawa to collect my passport with no visa. My application package, including my photo, professionally taken, was not returned, although I requested it.

I canceled my flight reservations for the trip—the reservations were required for my visa application—and consulted with my academic supervisor and a Chinese history expert. The history professor advised me not to apply for a work visa, because it could demand more documents and time and end up with another refusal. Instead, she recommended that I apply for an exchange program between Fudan University in Shanghai and Queen's University, from September to December, as it might be easier to obtain a student visa based on an established program. I immediately tried this plan, though I wanted to stay in Changchun, not Shanghai. I was accepted by the program.

Meanwhile, my supervisor reported my case to the associate vice principal international for Queen's University, who contacted a few officers who worked for the embassy and consulates of the People's Republic of China. After a week, one of the officers responded to her, saying they could help process my visa application. On July 12, I got a call from the visa center in Ottawa, asking, "Are you still interested in a visa?"

It was only two days before my rescheduled flights to Japan and China. The officer told me that the center could issue my visa in one day if I brought my passport in the next day. But he forgot to tell me that I had to arrive by 11:15 a.m. for same-day processing. I discovered this at 9:30 the next morning, when confirming my visit to the center. My third trip to Ottawa within a few weeks became a dangerous road trip to make this very short notice. I received my academic exchange visa at 4 p.m. at the center, by paying the "visa rush" and "service rush" fees, double the normal fees, although I had time enough for normal process in the first place. I got home at 8 p.m., packed all my materials for my field research that night, and left home with my child for the Toronto Pearson International Airport at 6 a.m. the next day.

The university professor and administrator's intervention succeeded in getting me a ninety-day visa. Still, I experienced the similar pattern of trouble in the Chinese consulate in Japan, in this round, about my child and life partner's visa applications: requests for additional documents from Jilin University to prove our accommodations, and copies of *koseki* from the Japanese government to prove our common-law relationship, and so on. The process was suspended a couple of times, and the express fee was again charged in the last minutes. I was unsure if my field study could happen until three days before we took off from Tokyo-Haneda Airport to Shanghai on August 31, 2016.

In Shanghai, the visa struggle continued. Because I registered at the exchange program at Fudan University, I tried to extend my stay for another month until December, as I originally planned, based on my student status at Fudan until December. After standing daily in long queues on campus to complete the registration process, I went to the local police station to obtain resident permits. Then, with all these documents collected from the university and police in one week, we visited the Exit and Entry Administration Bureau for a visa extension. We were told that each of us must take medical exams, including a blood test, but the extension was not guaranteed. I was skeptical that medical exams were worth it for our ten-year-old child. I decided to retry the extension after moving to Changchun, where I would recruit participants in my interviews.

After experiencing the exhausting visa process in both Canada and China, I consulted a Jilin University administrator as soon as I arrived in Changchun. My host institution staff informed that I would be able to apply for a visa extension only in the last month of the duration stated on the current visa. So, I waited until late October and started the process over again at the police station, to obtain the Accommodation Registration Form for Overseas Personnel in Jilin Province—by law, foreign citizens need to get this kind of residence permit in every province they stay, which reminded me of the Japanese Alien Registration system.

As such, just to get one administrative document in China, it took a few days or a week. And in the end, all this persistent work, not only by the researcher, but also by my host professor who provided the letter of explanation about my visa extension, and by the university administrator who checked our required documents and put the data into CD-ROMs for submission, went in vain. I went to the Exit and Entry Administrative Bureau in the city center of Changchun on November 14, for our visa extension. But the officer at the Bureau requested the original copies of our *koseki*, issued by the Japanese government, with its official Chinese translation. We had already submitted the same documents in our initial visa applications. I had the photocopies of our *koseki*, but those were not accepted. To get the original copies of *koseki* in China, we had to visit the Japanese consulate in Shenyang and wait to receive them by mail for at least another week. Our initial visas would expire within two weeks.

I decided to no longer waste my time and energy in the Kafkaesque bureaucracy. Even if I continued this unpredictable game, I could end up with another request or denial of extension. I decided to end my field research in China on November 28.

In the end, one-third of my physical and emotional labor in my fieldwork were consumed by combating such administrative barriers. I must admit that it limited the depth and width of my data collection in China. I could have found more documents and data in the archives and recruit more participants in interviews, if the visa process was more open, clear, consistent, and proceeded in the way officially described. At each stage, it was hard to tell how much more time and money I should put into these administrative hassles. Yet administrative regulations premise what a researcher can do in the field, so I kept pushing the boundaries as far as possible. My persistence was worthwhile to bring me to my fieldwork. By choosing to end my own ID troubles, I was able to focus my final fourteen days on researching colonial ID troubles, not mine. It was very productive and stress-free. By then, Changchun was heading to a cold winter, already recording minus fifteen degrees Celsius, which began to restrain our mobility.

CULTURAL CHALLENGES

In addition to the administrative barriers, cultural differences allowed and restricted my field research. First, my host professor warned me that most Chinese public archives are not fully accessible for foreign researchers looking for unpublished documents, making photocopies, and taking them out of the country. I had a list of archives to visit, but he told me that some of those listed were very hard to access. The professor contacted a few scholars he knew, who worked for those archives, and helped me access the resources there. The Jilin University historian suggested that I focus on collecting published work, which is no problem to take out of the country (no border troubles!). He also wrote a reference for me to the manager of the Jilin University Library, where I was able to get special access to collections of Japanese publications regarding colonial policies from 1900 to 1945.

Thus, I focused on finding and collecting published resources, as a practical method for my limited time. Though I originally planned to discover unpublished documents, this was not a bad strategy because the published resources still brought tremendous new knowledge to me and were only available while I was in China. It was impossible to see those books and historical artifacts, such as pamphlets, reports, catalogs, and other printed matters written in Chinese, remotely from Canada or Japan. I purchased books and historiographical materials at museums and archives and took many pictures of exhibits. I collected relevant literature and data, more than I could directly incorporate into this book. Those resources turned out to be vital resources to discern Japan's colonial policies, which I had not known about before my fieldwork.

Thus, having helpful resource persons and their references mitigated the shortcomings of my limited access to Chinese archives. Given the merits, I should emphasize the significance of international exchange in civil society, people to people, not state to state. It makes sense for institutional ethnography, one of my methodologies, which attempts to lay out ruling relations from the bottom of society, on the basis of people's lived experiences.

Civil and scholarly networks fundamentally empowered my research since its preliminary stage one year before the fieldwork took place. In Japan, I met with Japanese researchers and citizens who formed the Japanese nonprofit organization, Unit 731 Biological War Research Center. Unit 731 Biological War Research Center has supported the family members of Unit 731 victims who sued the Japanese government for an official apology and reparations for biological warfare. The case was lost at the Japanese Supreme Court in 2007, but members of Unit 731 Biological War Research Center, scholars, lawyers, journalists, and civil researchers, are continuously investigating and disseminating knowledge about the hidden crimes of Unit 731, to hold Japanese government accountable.[1] Ms. Yukiko Yamabe, one of the leading members, lived in Manchukuo with her family and joined the Chinese People's Liberation Army after Japan's defeat in 1945, when she was sixteen years old. She worked for the Liberation Army until 1953.[2] After her return to Japan, Yamabe began researching Japan's war crimes and often visited China on projects with Chinese scholars. The eighty-seven-year-old woman, highly respected in China as a contributor to the revolution, handed me a few of her business cards to show to the resource people I would meet in China. She also wrote a reference for me by email to the director of the Unit 731 War Crime Exhibition Hall. Other members of Unit 731 Biological War Research Center in Japan also generously shared contact information on Chinese experts they had met in their own fieldwork in China. These contacts with resource persons set up a very effective starting point for my field research and made my research resilient in the face of administrative and cultural obstacles. In a sense, this book is a triumph of the international solidarity and trust established among those flesh-and-blood people who devoted themselves to transformative justice, and overcame political and bureaucratic tension between states.

I received valuable advice from them to effectively communicate with the Chinese resource persons. An Japanese expert, who had interviewed a number of former members of Unit 731 and was a visiting scholar at the International Center for Unit 731 Research at Harbin Academy of Social Sciences, suggested that I be *very* clear about what I want from the resource person, from the beginning of our communications; never hesitate or wonder if the request is too much or impossible, be assertive, and persuasively explain why I want it, showing my passion. This advice proved valuable throughout my fieldwork. In many cases, Chinese scholars and resource persons generously shared their documents and put me in contact with prospective interviewees, when they understand the purposes of my project. Coming from Japanese culture, I might have held back my request at the first meeting and made it later, to ensure a gentle introduction into the friendly relationship. The experienced expert advice helped me navigate communications in Chinese culture and brought me what I had looked for despite the limited time. Passion matters!

As such, grassroots partnerships of concerned citizens between China and Japan, against a political climate of historical revisionism, enabled my fieldwork to see success. It is of paramount importance to keep those private communication routes open and grow grassroots exchanges, no matter how much tension grows among governments. There are alternative ways to access resources and conduct field research when diverse networks of people exist when states seem to shut down windows. While the Western media typically keep producing stereotypes of total control by the Chinese Communist Party, researchers should not self-censor or back off before those popular images, and it is often rewarding to explore all possible communications with resource people and build relationships with them.

Finally, the last component of the cultural challenge was a colonial divide and its product of my own positionality and ignorance. As an investigative journalist and critical sociologist, I had actively read and written on Japanese war crimes and colonial ruling. However, growing up in Japan with the Japanese language as my mother tongue, I confronted the fact that my existing knowledge had been attenuated by nostalgic collective memory of the good old days for the Japanese colonizers in Manchuria. In my field research, I instantly noticed the fundamental difference between the local people and me in perceiving the face of the Japanese occupation. Most people I interviewed told me about various types of cruel violence by the Japanese who killed their loved ones. Brutality was forefront of their personal and collective memories. Because of this epistemological divide between the colonizers and colonized, the Chinese scholars and interviewees alike seemed puzzled as to the point of my questions on the ID systems, as even my host professor seemed at first doubtful of my research interests.

Under the circumstance, at least, one of my approaches to semi-structured interviews helped: listening to the entire story the colonial survivor offers, from beginning to end, without interrupting. I respected the interviewees' lived experiences and tried to relate their frame of significance, rather than pushing them to fit into my semistructured questions. I developed this approach from my past experiences interviewing several survivors of Japanese wartime sexual slavery, so-called Comfort Women. In 2000, I visited and interviewed some of the Korean women who were forced to serve the Japanese Army and were sexually assaulted during World War II. I prepared specific questions for the interviewees, such as where they were abducted, how they were deceived, or when they arrived at the "comfort stations." It was a journalistic routine to objectively describe what happened to the interviewee, along with shaping a story on the chronological timeline and geographical locations, which overlaps with academic survey. However, every woman had her own way of sharing her experience. It did not always follow a chronological order and sometimes lacked precise names of locations. I interrupted their stories and tried to clarify the years and places particularly, but I failed again and again. There were multiple reasons for this lack of information: they do not remember, or they were not told precise years and locations by the Japanese Army in the first place. Some women did not know when they were born. Their social status and educational backgrounds varied. But every woman intelligently structured her own personal experience that made sense to her, and create meaning for listeners. As soon as I got this, I stopped interrupting their stories. The narratives are constructed to carry the meanings of their experiences.

The objective data, such as time and place, certainly help journalists present the stories in a linear timeline and in association with other significant incidents of history, but those are not of primary importance to the narrators, rather such journalistic calculation and assumption deflect what the narrators want to present and represent.

Therefore, in my interviews in this 2016 fieldwork, I listen to all personal stories the interviewees were willing to offer until the end and then ask my questions to clarify and for my own interest. Although it seems a detour from efficient research, I assert that it is the most straightforward way to discover the marginalized meaning of the past with the proper context and nuance. Researchers should note that there is no short cut to the truth from the viewpoint of Others.

The colonial divide and my positionality cannot be easily overcome and indeed produce limitations on my research. However, my ignorance can be mitigated through some mindful approaches to the past, which ultimately demands that descendants of Japanese colonizers understand the full scale of Japan's violent colonization. While I tried to comprehend why my interviewees and Chinese scholars looked puzzled by my research questions, in turn, they gradually understood why I inquired about ID systems as an important part of colonial rule. In our last meeting, my host professor commented that he finally figured out why ID systems matter, and he would pay more attention to the theme for my future research.

THE IMPORTANCE OF SHOCK.

In summary, the administrative and cultural challenges I faced inevitably modified my methodologies of using a genealogical approach, institutional ethnography, and semi-structured interviews. My field research was limited because of the complexities. Nevertheless, the field yielded productive results overall. The most fruits were harvested from the trees of transnational civil and scholarly networks, and their will to uncover injustice and demand justice and peace. My interpreters for the interviews, graduate students studying Japanese at Jilin University, also contributed to creating friendly atmosphere and smoothing my conversations with interviewees. These support networks helped me both confront and accept the challenges, which were ultimately rooted in the colonial epistemological divide and my positionality as a Japanese descendant.

Arrested in this ambivalent relationship with the colonial Others, I cannot emphasize enough the significance of field research. It shocks the researcher. As quoted earlier in the introduction, Benjamin asserts: "Thinking involves not only the flow of thoughts, but their arrest as well. Where thinking suddenly stops in a configuration pregnant with tensions, it gives the configuration a shock, by which it crystallizes into a monad."[3] Field research creates a rare opportunity for a researcher to encounter Others, a monad of new thought, where they recognize the sign of "a revolutionary chance in the fight for the oppressed past," as Benjamin suggests.[4] During my three-month stay in China, I had more culture shock than any other place I had lived before, the United States or Canada, despite the geographical and cultural proximity of China and Japan. In the most epistemological sense, the shock came from realizing how long and far colonialism has been dividing the realities of the past throughout the postcolonial period.

The fundamental asymmetry is not only generated in the academic arena but also reproduced in popular discourse. As mentioned in introduction, Japanese publications on Manchuria prominently feature nostalgia. A diversity of writers, from soldiers and government officials to armed and unarmed settlers, commonly look back on better, sweeter days in the land of opportunity, without reference to their colonial privilege. They do not refer to the prehistory to when the Japanese "discovered" the wilderness or show interest in knowing how the Chinese experienced Japanese occupation. Japanese political and economic leaders involved in Manchukuo reluctantly admitted after the defeat, their complete failure to build "a kingly way of governance" and "complete equality among five ethnic groups" in Northeast China. But they never fail to dilute it by adding that there was nothing wrong with revolutionary bureaucrats having the brilliant idea to create heaven on earth by using modern technologies, and that they worked so purely, tirelessly, and devotedly to give birth to the young modern nation.

To be fair, there is a considerable amount of postwar Japanese intellectual writings that have critical views of Japan's aggression and colonialism, and I incorporated some of those significant works into this book. But many of Japanese narratives still tend to excuse the negative consequences of Japan's colonization as benign, a "gap" between goodwill and bad practice, or "light and shadow" of the regime, without having direct communications with colonial Others. This unilateral frame does not look back far enough to find the origins of the "gap," or of the totally different realities experienced by the colonized.

Thus, growing up in the long-term neglect of Chinese narratives in Japanese popular and academic discourse, it was necessary for me to physically go beyond this worn-out, one-sided epistemology and break it through. Again, I was shocked and ashamed. Shame and discomfort give a hard lesson for the researcher to understand colonial Others. Field research teaches the researcher about their ignorance as well as their objective and subjective positioning, how the outer world positions them in history, whether it corresponds to their subjectivity or self-identity, because the researcher is already embedded in ruling relations.[5] It is the moment of realizing who you are in the eye of Others, without a researcher's hat, which brings a profound ID trouble to you but finally transforms communication with Others from unilateral to bilateral.

Narratives in the colonial zone contradict what the researcher has gotten used to and pull them out of their comfort zone; direct and unfiltered exchanges with colonial Others can be sometimes powerful enough to demolish the existing framework of research. However, without out these cracks and struggles behind the scenes, alternative knowledge cannot be born. Shock in field research offers an indispensable opportunity to encounter Others and bring their marginalized voices to study.

NOTES

Preface

1. James Bamford, *The Puzzle Palace: A Report on America's Most Secret Agency* (Houghton Mifflin, 1982).

2. Glenn Greenwald, *No Place to Hide: Edward Snowden, the NSA, and the U.S. Surveillance State* (Signal/McClelland & Stewart, 2014), 107. This doesn't mean that only international communications fall into the NSA's dragnet. In 2005, Mark Klein, a former AT&T communications technician, discovered the NSA's secret room in an AT&T branch in downtown San Francisco. The 611 Folsom Street office had a similar facility to that of Special Source Operations to capture domestic telecommunication data. Mr. Klein became one of the earliest whistle-blowers on the NSA's unwarranted wiretapping programs, before Snowden. See Midori Ogasawara, "Collaborative Surveillance with Big Data Corporations: Interviews with Edward Snowden and Mark Klein," in *Big Data Surveillance and Security Intelligence: The Canadian Case*, ed. David Lyon and David Murakami Wood (University of British Columbia Press, 2021), 21-42.

3. Julia Angwin et al., "NSA Spying Relies on AT&T's 'Extreme Willingness to Help,'" *ProPublica*, August 15, 2015, https://www.propublica.org/article/nsa-spying-relies-on-atts-extreme-willingness-to-help.

4. Ogasawara, "Collaborative Surveillance with Big Data Corporations," 26.

5. Greenwald, *No Place to Hide,* 109-118. The NSA counted on these companies' tech power and utilized their private systems. Given the early development of the internet—the Arpanet, funded by the Department of Defense since the 1960s—it may not have been too strange for the NSA to ask Silicon Valley to share its big data in the databases.

6. Shoshana Zuboff, *The Age of Surveillance Capitalism: The Fight for a Human Future at the New Frontier of Power* (Public Affairs, 2019).

7. Glenn Greenwald, "Snowden Revelations 10-Year Anniversary: Glenn Greenwald, Speaks with Snowden & Laura Poitras on the Past, Present, & Future of Their Historic Reporting" *System Update #93*, June 6, 2023, https://rumble.com/v2sgyx2-snowden-revelations-10-year-anniversary-glenn-green-wald-speaks-with-snowden.html. There are many media reports on Pegasus spyware, developed by the Israeli tech company NSO Group. But one of the earliest exposures is the 2016 report by the Citizen Lab at the University of Toronto that Pegasus was used to target Ahmed Mansoor, a human rights defender based in the United Arab Emirates. Bill Marczak and John Scott-Railton, "The Million Dollar Dessident: NSO Group's iPhone Zero-Days Used Against a UAE Human Rights Defender," *Citizen Lab*, August 24, 2016, https://citizenlab.ca/2016/08/million-dollar-dissident-iphone-zero-day-nso-group-uae/. See also Bill Marczak, John Scott-Railton, Sarah McKune, Bahr Abdul Razzak, and Ron Deibert, "Hide and Seek: Tracking NSO Group's Pegasus Spyware to Opereations in 45 Countries," *Citizen Lab*, September 18, 2018, https://citizenlab.ca/2018/09/hide-and-seek-tracking-nso-groups-pegasus-spyware-to-operations-in-45-countries/.

8. International Civil Liberties Monitoring Group, "Canada's No Fly List," https://iclmg.ca/issues/canadas-no-fly-list/.

9. Maureen Webb, *Illusions of Security* (City Lights Books, 2007), 2, 10-12.

10. Commissions of Inquiry into the Actions of Canadian Officials in Relation to Maher Arar, "Report of the Events Relating to Maher Arar: Analysis and Recommendations," 2006, http://www.sirc-csars.gc.ca/pdfs/cm_arar_rec-eng.pdf.

11. David Cochrane, "Whitewash: Hassan Diab Attacks Report Concluding Government Acted Properly in his Extradition Case," *CBC*, July 26, 2019, https://www.cbc.ca/news/politics/hassan-diab-extradition-france-1.5226033. The French intelligence agency suspected Dr. Diab of being a perpetrator in a 1980 synagogue bombing in Paris. Though the Canadian judges were puzzled by the weak evidence, because the perpetrator's fingerprints and handwriting did not match Diab's, he was extradited in 2014 to France, where he was put into solitary confinement for most of his incarceration of three years and two months. In January 2018, the French court admitted the weak evidence and sent him home to Ottawa, where his wife and two young children awaited. Prime Minister Justin Trudeau commented, "I think for Hassan Diab we have to recognize first of all that what happened to him never should have happened . . . and make sure it never happens again." But that was not the end of the story. The French prosecutor appealed, the appeal was accepted, and the Paris Court of Assizes reopened the case in the absence of Diab, declared Diab guilty, and sentenced him to life in prison.

12. Among the new surveillance tools that emerged during the public health emergency, "vaccine passports" were particularly controversial in

Canada. In the British Columbia, where I live, all residents were required to show their vaccine passports to enter restaurants, movie theaters, sport facilities, and other indoor events from September 2021 to April 2022. To prove that the bearer had received two vaccine shots, the vaccine passports, both in print and on electronic devices, had a QR code, which linked to the public health database. Since no one likes rejection and exclusion, the vaccine passport system became one of the main causes for the Freedom Convoy movement, which occupied Parliament Hill in Ottawa in the winter of 2022, demanding the abolishment of COVID-19-related mandates. In response, Justin Trudeau's government used the Emergency Act for the first time since it had replaced the War Measure Act in 1988 to remove protesters from the capital. New ID systems have kept following crises, by installing latest technologies, being tested against mass population, and mobilizing political forces.

13. Walter Benjamin, "Theses on the Philosophy of History," in *Illuminations: Essays and Reflections*, ed. Hannah Arendt (Harcourt, Brace & World, 1968), 257. "The true picture of the past flits by. The past can be seized only as an image which flashes up at the instant when it can be recognized and is never seen again. . . . For every image of the past that is not recognized by the present as one of its own concerns threatens to disappear irretrievably."

14. Benjamin, "Theses on the Philosophy of History," 256.

15. Hitoshi Imamura, *Reading Benjamin's "Theses on the Philosophy of History"* (ベンヤミン「歴史哲学テーゼ」精読) (Iwanami Shoten, 2000), 99.

Introduction

1. Group Saying "No" to Fingerprinting (GSNF), *Resistance to Japan, My Pride: The Report of Visiting China* (抗日こそ誇り——訪中報告書——) (Research Group on Fingerprinting in Northeast China, 1988), 14.

2. According to *Population Stat*, the population of Jixi City in 2016 was 903,000, and it has kept growing (https://populationstat.com/china/jixi).

3. Japan took over the Jixi Coal Mine in 1933, which had operated since 1916. See Shigeru Aoki, *Visiting Wanrenkang: Unnamed Mass Grave in Manchukuo and Chinese Forced Labor* (万人坑を訪ねる―満州国の万人坑と中国人強制連行) (Ryokufū Shuppan, 2013), 205.

4. Zuboff, *The Age of Surveillance Capitalism: The Fight for a Human Future at the New Frontier of Power* (Public Affairs, 2019), 9, 12-14.

5. David Lyon, *Surveillance Studies: An Overview* (Polity, 2007).

6. Simone Browne, *Dark Matters: Surveillance on Blackness* (Duke University Press, 2015).

7. As mentioned in the preface, this approach is inspired by Walter Benjamin, "Theses on the Philosophy of History," in *Illuminations: Essays and Reflections*, ed. Hannah Arendt (Schocken Books, 1968).

8. Max Weber, "Bureaucracy," in *From Max Weber: Essays in Sociology*, ed. Hans Heinrich Gerth and C. Wright Mills (Oxford University Press, 1946).

9. Jane Caplan and John Torpey, introduction to *Documenting Individual Identity: The Development of State Practices in the Modern World*, ed. Jane Caplan and John Torpey (Princeton University Press, 2001), 1–12; David Lyon, *Identifying Citizens: ID Cards as Surveillance* (Polity, 2009).

10. Lyon, *Identifying Citizens*, 19–38.

11. Edwards Higgs, "The Rise of the Information State: The Development of Central State Surveillance of the Citizen in England, 1500–2000," *Journal of Historical Sociology* 14, no. 2 (2001): 175–97.

12. John Torpey, *The Invention of the Passport: Surveillance, Citizenship and the State* (Cambridge University Press, 2000).

13. Simon A. Cole, *Suspect Identities: A History of Fingerprinting and Criminal Identification* (Harvard University Press, 2001).

14. Christian Parenti, *The Soft Cage: Surveillance in America from Slavery to the War on Terror* (Basic Books, 2003).

15. Alfred W. McCoy, *Policing America's Empire: The United States, the Philippines, and the Rise of the Surveillance State* (University of Wisconsin Press, 2009).

16. Keith Breckenridge, *Biometric State: The Global Politics of Identification and Surveillance in South Africa, 1850 to the Present* (Cambridge University Press, 2014).

17. The so-called War on Terror was started by the American air strikes on Afghanistan in October 2001, as retaliation for 9/11, and named as such by the George W. Bush administration. However, the terms "terror," "terrorism," and "terrorist" do not have a legal definition that is internationally agreed on, despite the flood of uses in popular media, and they deflect attention from the political backgrounds and causes of murderous incidents. Because of the mystifying and sidetracking effects, I avoid these terms as much as possible in my writing and refer to the exact incident, such as 9/11.

18. Kevin D. Haggerty and Richard V. Ericson, "The Surveillant Assemblage," *British Journal of Sociology* 15, no. 4 (2000): 605–22.

19. David Lyon, "Surveillance as Social Sorting: Computer Codes and Mobile Bodies," in *Surveillance as Social Sorting: Privacy, Risk, and Digital Discrimination*, ed. David Lyon (Routledge, 2003); Lyon, *Surveillance Studies*.

20. Oscar H. Gandy, Jr., "Engaging Rational Discrimination: Exploring Reasons for Placing Regulatory Constraints on Decision Support Systems," *Ethics and Information Technology* 12, no. 1 (2010): 29–42.

21. Information and Privacy Commissioner of Ontario, "Biometrics." https://www.ipc.on.ca/en/privacy-organizations/data-and-technology-management/biometrics.

22. Irma Van der Ploeg, "The Illegal Body: 'Eurodac' and the Politics of Biometric Identification," *Ethics and Information Technology* 1, no. 4 (1999): 295–302; Shoshana A. Magnet, *When Biometrics Fail: Gender, Race and Technology of Identity* (Duke University Press, 2011).

23. Hiroshi Tanaka, "The Origin of Fingerprinting," *Asahi Journal* (October 9, 1987): 21–23.

24. Asako Takano, *Fingerprints and Modernity: The Technique to Control and Govern Mobile Bodies* (指紋と近代: 移動する身体の管理と統治の技法) (Misuzu Shobō, 2016), 51.

25. Pierre Bourdieu, *In Other Words: Essays Towards a Reflexive Sociology* (Stanford University Press, 1990), 480–81.

26. Seiichi Morimura, *The Devil's Gluttony* (悪魔の飽食) (Kōbunsha, 1981); Chengmin Jin, *Collection of Pictures on Japanese Military Germ Warfare* (日本軍細菌战图集) (Inner Mongolia Culture Press, 2010); Takao Matsumura, "The Special Transfer by the Kwantung Gendarmerie: To Reveal the Whole History of Biowarfare Unit 731," in *Resistance and Repression in "Manchukuo"* (「満洲国」における抵抗と弾圧), ed. Fujio Ogino, Toshio Kojima, Kenji Eda and Takao Matsumura (Nihon Keizai Hyōronsha, 2017).

27. Bunmei Satō, *Discrimination Koseki Makes* (戸籍がつくる差別) (Gendai Shokan, 1984); Bunmei Satō, *The Alternative History of Koseki* (戸籍うらがえ史考) (Akashi Shoten, 1988); Bunmei Satō, *The Life that Koseki Watches Over* (戸籍が見張る暮らし) (Gendai Shokan, 1991).

28. Tanaka, "The Origin of Fingerprinting"; Hiroshi Tanaka, *The Foreigners in Japan: Legal Barriers and Mental Gaps* (在日外国人 法の壁、心の溝) (Iwanami Shinsho, 1995).

29. China became the fourth great ally to the United States in World War II, but its actions in the war have been less recognized than other allied forces, as Rana Mitter writes in *Forgotten Ally: China's World War II, 1937–1945* (Houghton Mifflin Harcourt, 2013).

30. Midori Ogasawara, "The Daily Us (vs. Them) from Online to Offline: Japan's Media Manipulation and Cultural Transcoding of Collective Memories," *Journal of Contemporary Eastern Asia* 18, no. 2 (2019): 49–67. See also Kōichi Yasuda, *The Net and Patriotism: Searching the Shade of Zaitokukai* (ネットと愛国) (Kōdansha, 2012).

31. Tanaka, "The Origin of Fingerprinting"; Masataka Endō, *Nationality and Koseki in Modern Japanese Colonial Governance: Manchuria, Korea, and Taiwan* (近代日本の植民地統治における国籍と戸籍 満洲・朝鮮・台湾) (Akashi Shoten, 2010); Takano, *Fingerprints and Modernity* (Misuzu Shobo, 2016).

32. Michel Foucault, "Questions of Method," in *Michel Foucault: Power, Volume 3*, ed. James D. Faubion (New Press, 1994); Friedrich W. Nietzsche, *On the Genealogy of Morals: A Polemic: By Way of Clarification and Supplement to My Last Book, Beyond Good and Evil* (Oxford University Press, 1996).

33. Dorothy E. Smith, *Writing the Social: Critique, Theory, and Investigations* (University of Toronto Press, 1999). See the appendix for my positionality as a researcher.

34. Dorothy E. Smith, *Institutional Ethnography: A Sociology for People* (Altamira Press, 2005), 10.

35. Smith, *Writing the Social*, 49.

Chapter 1

1. Bertolt Brecht, *Refugees' Conversations* (亡命者の対話　ブレヒト・コレク
ション4), trans. Osamu Nomura (Shō bunsha, 1981): 10; Bertolt Brecht, "Conversations in Exile," adapted by Howard Brenton, trans. David Dollenmayer,
Theater 17, no. 2 (1986): 10, https://doi.org/10.1215/01610775-17-2-8. Brecht
wrote the script of *Flüchtlingsgespräche* seemingly in 1940-41, when he was
exiled in Finland. Big Man, whose name turned out to be Ziffel in the later
text, is a chemistry professor, and Small Man, Kalle, is a plant worker. I translated this text from a Japanese translation of the German original (1981) into
English. There is apparently no English published translation from the
German original. But there is an English version of the adapted play by
Howard Brenton, of which I used some part. *Conversations in Exile* is less recognized among Brecht's extensive work, like *Mother Courage and Her Children*
or *The Threepenny Opera*, but it becomes an important text in light of current
wars and refugee waves. It is to be hoped that a full English translation will be
published soon.

2. Klaus Völker, *Brecht: A Biography*, trans. John Nowell (Seabury Press,
1978).

3. Valentin Groebner, *Who Are You? Identification, Deception, and Surveillance in Early Modern Europe*, trans. Mark Kyburz and John Peck (Zone Books,
2007), 25.

4. Richard Jenkins, *Social Identity*, Second ed. (Routledge, 2004) 4-5.

5. Brecht, "Conversations in Exile," 10.

6. Brecht, "Conversations in Exile," 10.

7. Michael Foucault, *The History of Sexuality, Vol. 1: An Introduction* (Vintage Books, 1978).

8. Richard Jenkins, "Categorization: Identity, Social Process and Epistemology," *Current Sociology* 48, no. 3 (2000): 7-25.

9. Jane Caplan and John Torpey, introduction to *Documenting Individual
Identity: The Development of State Practices in the Modern World*, ed. Jane Caplan
and John Torpey (Princeton University Press, 2001), 3.

10. David Lyon, *Surveillance Studies: An Overview* (Polity, 2007), 102-5.

11. Oscar H. Gandy, Jr., "Engaging Rational Discrimination: Exploring Reasons for Placing Regulatory Constraints on Decision Support Systems," *Ethics
and Information Technology* 12, no. 1 (1993): 29-42.

12. Lyon, *Identifying Citizens: ID Cards as Surveillance* (Polity, 2009), 4.

13. Lyon, *Surveillance Studies*, 14.

14. Lyon, *Surveillance Studies*, 26-27.

15. Eli Pariser, *The Filter Bubble: How the New Personalized Web Is Changing
What We Read and How We Think* (Penguin, 2011).

16. Scott Thompson, "Separating the Sheep from the Goats: The United
Kingdom's National Registration Programme and Social Sorting in the Pre-electronic Era," in *Playing the Identity Card: Surveillance, Security and Identification
in Global Perspective*, ed. Colin J. Bennett and David Lyon (Routledge, 2008),

145-162; Simone Browne, *Dark Matters: On the Surveillance of Blackness* (Duke University Press, 2015); Emily van der Meulen and Rob Heynen, "Unpacking State Surveillance: Histories, Theories, and Global Contexts," in *Making Surveillance States: Transnational Histories*, ed. Rob Heynen and Emily van der Meulen (University of Toronto Press, 2019), 3-30.

17. Judith Butler, *Gender Trouble: Feminism and the Subversion of Identity* (Routledge, 1990).

18. Peter L. Berger and Thomas Luckmann, *The Social Construction of Reality: A Treatise in the Sociology of Knowledge* (Anchor Books 1967); Ian Hacking, "Making Up People," in *Reconstructing Individualism: Autonomy, Individuality, and the Self in Western Thought*, ed. Thomas C. Heller, Morton Sosna, and David E. Wellbery (Stanford University, 1986); Ian Hacking, *The Taming of Chance* (Cambridge University Press,1990); Richard Jenkins, "Categorization: Identity, Social Process and Epistemology," *Current Sociology* 48, no. 3 (2000): 7-25.

19. Berger and Luckmann, *The Social Construction of Reality*.

20. Anthony Giddens, *The Constitution of Society: Outline of the Theory of Structuration* (University of California Press, 1984), 19.

21. Giddens, *The Constitution of Society*, 25.

22. Hacking, "Making Up People."

23. Hacking, *The Taming of Chance*, 3.

24. Betty Friedan, *The Feminine Mystique* (Norton, 1963).

25. Carol Hanisch, "The Personal Is Political" in *Notes from the Second Year: Women's Liberation Major Writings of the Radical Feminists*, ed. Shulamith Firestone and Anne Koedt (Radical Feminism, 1970).

26. Butler, *Gender Trouble*.

27. Simone de Beauvoir, *The Second Sex*, trans. and ed. H. M. Parshley (Vintage, 1989).

28. Butler, *Gender Trouble*, Shoshana A. Magnet *When Biometrics Fail: Gender, Race and Technology of Identity* (Duke University Press, 2011).

29. Butler, *Gender Trouble*, 45.

30. Foucault, *Discipline and Punish: The Birth of the Prison* (Vintage Books, 1977).

31. Foucault, *Discipline and Punish*, 201.

32. Foucault, *The History of Sexuality, Vol. 1*.

33. Foucault, *The History of Sexuality, Vol. 1*, 136-38.

34. Foucault, *The History of Sexuality, Vol. 1*, 136-138.

35. Foucault, *Discipline and Punish*, 135.

36. Foucault, *Discipline and Punish*, 155.

37. Foucault, *The History of Sexuality, Vol. 1*, 140.

38. Foucault, *The History of Sexuality, Vol. 1*, 141.

39. Foucault, "Governmentality," in *The Foucault Effect: Studies in Governmentality, with Two Lectures by and an Interview with Michel Foucault*, ed. Graham Burchell, Colin Gordon, and Peter Miller (University of Chicago Press, 1991), 87-104.

40. Kevin Haggerty and Richard V. Ericson, "The Surveillant Assemblage," *British Journal of Sociology* 15, no. 4 (2000): 605-22.

41. Gilles Deleuze and Félix Guattari, *A Thousand Plateaus: Capitalism and Schizophrenia* (University of Minnesota Press, 1987).

42. Deleuze and Guattari, *A Thousand Plateaus*, 9.

43. Gilles Deleuze, *Negotiations, 1972-1990* (Columbia University Press, 1995), 179-80.

44. Zygmunt Bauman and David Lyon, *Liquid Surveillance: A Conversation* (Polity, 2013).

45. Kirstie Ball and Laureen Snider, Introduction to *The Surveillance-Industrial Complex: A Political Economy of Surveillance*, eds. Kirstie Ball and Laureen Snider (Routledge, 2013); Shoshana Zuboff, *The Age of Surveillance Capitalism: The Fight for a Human Future at the New Frontier of Power* (Public Affairs, 2019).

46. Glenn Greenwald, *No Place to Hide: Edward Snowden, the NSA, and the U.S. Surveillance State* (Signal/McClelland & Stewart, 2014).

47. Lyon, *Identifying Citizens*, 107, emphasis original.

48. Groebner, *Who Are You?*, 200-202.

49. Jean Bodin, 1576, cited in Groebner, *Who Are You?*, 201.

50. Anthony Giddens, *The Nation-State and Violence*, vol. 2 of *A Contemporary Critique of Historical Materialism* (Polity, 1987), 1.

51. Edward Higgs, "The Rise of the Information State: The Development of Central State Surveillance of the Citizen in England, 1500-2000," *Journal of Historical Sociology* 14, no. 2 (2001): 176-97, 179.

52. Higgs, "The Rise of the Information State," 183.

53. Anthony Giddens, *The Nation-State and Violence*.

54. Higgs, "The Rise of the Information State," 185.

55. John Torpey, *The Invention of the Passport: Surveillance, Citizenship and the State* (Cambridge University Press, 2000), 93-121.

56. Torpey, *The Invention of the Passport*, 6-7.

57. Hannah Arendt, *The Origins of Totalitarianism* (Harcourt, 1968), 267-302. Regarding nationality, Arendt posed a hard question about citizenship in the final chapter, "Decline of Nation-state: End of Rights of Man," of *Imperialism*, the second part of *The Origin of Totalitarianism*. She noted that if one does not have the citizenship of a state, one's rights cannot be guaranteed anywhere, because rights come into being only as citizenship. The concept of universal human rights does not provide any real protection to refugees or diasporas during wartime. Refugees are barred not only from their places of origin but also from the entire globe, in a state of having no rights. This raises two questions in the contemporary context. Is citizenship still a precondition of human rights today? And is the state really protecting citizens' rights or threatening them?

58. Torpey, *The Invention of the Passport*, 4.

59. Allan Sekula, "The Body and the Archive," *October* 39 (1986): 3-64.

60. Christian Parenti, *The Soft Cage: Surveillance in America from Slavery to the War on Terror* (Basic Books, 2003), 38.

61. Simon A. Cole, *Suspect Identities: A History of Fingerprinting and Criminal Identification* (Harvard University Press, 2001).

62. Cole, *Suspect Identities*, 37.

63. Cole, *Suspect Identities*, 45.

64. Cole, *Suspect Identities*, 136, 164-67.

65. Francis Galton, 1889, cited in Cole, *Suspect Identities*, 77.

66. Sekula, "The Body and the Archive," 37.

67. Keith Breckenridge, *Biometric State: The Global Politics of Identification and Surveillance in South Africa, 1850 to the Present* (Cambridge University Press, 2014), 66.

68. Cole, *Suspect Identities*, 87.

69. Breckenridge, *Biometric State*, 39.

70. Cited in Breckenridge, *Biometric State*, 41.

71. Breckenridge, *Biometric State*, 37.

72. Cited in Breckenridge, *Biometric State*, 22.

73. Breckenridge, *Biometric State*, 23.

74. Breckenridge, *Biometric State*, 75-76.

75. Breckenridge, *Biometric State*, 80.

76. Breckenridge, Biometric State, 82.

77. Breckenridge, *Biometric State*, 81.

78. Breckenridge, *Biometric State*, 84.

79. Breckenridge, *Biometric State*, 88.

80. John Dower, *Empire and Aftermath: Yoshida Shigeru and the Japanese Experience, 1878-1954* (Harvard University Asia Center, 1979).

81. Cole, *Suspect Identities*.

82. Cole, *Suspect Identities*, 67-68.

83. Browne, *Dark Matters*.

84. Browne, *Dark Matters*, 48.

85. Parenti, *The Soft Cage*.

86. Graham Russell Gao Hodges and Alan Edward Brown, *"Pretends to Be Free": Runaway Slave Advertisements from Colonial to Revolutionary New York and New Jersey* (Garland, 1994), cited in Browne, *Dark Matters*, 53.

87. Browne, *Dark Matters*.

88. Browne, *Dark Matters*, 16.

89. Browne, *Dark Matters*, 17.

90. Browne, *Dark Matters*, 17.

91. Butler, *Gender Trouble*.

92. Browne, *Dark Matters*, 21.

93. Cole, *Suspect Identities*, 136.

94. Parenti, *The Soft Cage*, 76.

95. Cole, *Suspect Identities*, 166.

96. Fong, Denise, John Endo Greenaway, Fran Morrison, John Price, Carmen Rodriguez de France, Sharanjit Kaur Sandhra, and Timothy J. Stanley, *1923 Challenging Racism Past and Present* (China-Canada Focus, 2023), 46. https://www.challengingracism.ca/#downloads.

97. Keith Smith, *Liberalism, Surveillance and Resistance: Indigenous Communities in Western Canada, 1877-1927* (Athabasca University Press, 2009), 60-77.

98. Dan Kennedy (Ochankugahe), *Recollections of an Assiniboine Chief*, ed. James R. Stevens (McClelland and Stewart, 1972), 87.

99. Derek G. Smith, "The Emergence of 'Eskimo Status': An Examination of The Eskimo Disk List System and Its Social Consequences, 1925-1970," in *Anthropology, Public Policy and Native Peoples in Canada*, ed. Noel Dyck and James B. Waldram (McGill-Queen's University Press, 1993), 41-74.

100. Ann Meekitjuk Hanson, "What's in a Name?" (2016), https://leapintothevoidwithme.wordpress.com/2016/05/02/whats-in-a-name/.

101. Irma Van der Ploeg, "The Illegal Body: 'Eurodac' and the Politics of Biometric Identification," *Ethics and Information Technology* 1, no. 4 (1999): 295-302.

102. Cole, *Suspect Identities*; Breckenridge, *Biometric State*.

103. Magnet, *When Biometrics Fail*, 16.

104. Magnet, *When Biometrics Fail*, 15.

105. Achille Mbembe, "Necropolitics," *Public Culture* 15, no. 1 (2003): 11-40; Elia Zureik, *Israel's Colonial Project in Palestine: Brutal Pursuit* (Routledge, 2016).

106. Giorgio Agamben, *Homo Sacer: Sovereign Power and Bare Life* (Stanford University Press, 1998).

107. Agamben, *Homo Sacer*, 28.

108. Agamben, *Homo Sacer*, 107.

109. Agamben, *State of Exception* (University of Chicago Press, 2005), 3-4.

110. Maureen Webb, *Illusions of Security: Global Surveillance and Democracy in the Post-9/11 World* (City Lights, 2007), 166.

111. See the preface.

112. Agamben, *Homo Sacer*, 180: "Today's democratico-capitalist project of eliminating the poor classes through development not only reproduces within itself the people that is excluded but also transforms the entire population of the Third World into bare life."

113. Agamben, *Homo Sacer*, 6.

114. Agamben, *Homo Sacer*, 29, emphasis original.

115. Mbembe, "Necropolitics," 11.

116. Mbembe, "Necropolitics," 22-23.

117. Mbembe, "Necropolitics," 24.

118. Hannah Arendt, *The Origins of Totalitarianism* (Harcourt, 1968), 185-221.

119. Mbembe, "Necropolitics," 23.

120. Cole, *Suspect Identities*; Timothy Longman, "Identity Card, Ethnic Self-Perception, and Genocide in Rwanda," in *Documenting Individual Identity*, ed. Jane Caplan and John Torpey (Princeton University Press, 2001); Alfred W. McCoy, *Policing America's Empire: The United States, the Philippines, and the Rise of the Surveillance State* (University of Wisconsin Press, 2009); Elia Zureik, "Colonialism, Surveillance, and Population Control: Israel/Palestine," in *Surveillance and Control in Israel/Palestine: Population, Territory, and Power*, ed. Elia Zureik, David Lyon, and Yasmeen Abu-Laban (Routledge, 2011).

121. Zureik, "Colonialism, Surveillance, and Population Control," 10.

122. McCoy, *Policing America's Empire*, 4, 8.

123. McCoy, *Policing America's Empire*, 14.

124. Breckenridge, *Biometric State*, 24–25.

125. Arendt, *The Origins of Totalitarianism*, 188.

126. Arendt, *The Origins of Totalitarianism*, 204.

127. Arendt, *The Origins of Totalitarianism*, 206.

128. To be fair, Foucault refers to both productive and repressive effects of biopower. Despite a positive connotation of productivity, biopower has generated wars and massacres, structural killings by the state on a massive scale, because "wars are no longer waged in the name of a sovereign who must be defended; they are waged on behalf of the existence of everyone; entire populations are mobilized for the purpose of wholesale slaughter in the name of life necessity." Foucault, *The History of Sexuality, Vol. 1*, 137. Foucault, Agamben, and Mbembe are compatible to this extent of paradoxical complexity of biopolitical mechanisms. However, Foucault's conceptualization is based on Western experiences of modernity and cannot address fundamentally asymmetrical power relations between the colonizing and colonized within an empire-nation-state.

129. Arendt, *The Origins of Totalitarianism*, 206; McCoy, *Policing America's Empire*, 8; Stephen Graham, "The New Military Urbanism," in *The Surveillance-Industrial Complex*, ed. Kirstie Ball and Laureen Snider (Routledge, 2013), 11–26.

130. Ian Duncan, "New Details Released About High-tech Gear FBI Used on Planes to Monitor Freddie Gray Unrest," *Baltimore Sun*, October 30, 2015, https://www.chicagotribune.com/2015/10/30/new-details-released-about-high-tech-gear-fbi-used-on-planes-to-monitor-freddie-gray-unrest/.

131. Arendt, *The Origins of Totalitarianism*; Louise Young, *Japan's Total Empire: Manchuria and the Culture of Wartime Imperialism* (University of California Press, 1998), 14–15.

132. Benedict Anderson, *Imagined Communities: Reflections on the Origin and Spread of Nationalism*, rev. and expanded ed. (Verso, 1991).

133. Breckenridge, *Biometric State*, 17.

134. National Identification Agency of the Republic of Rwanda (NIDA), "ID4Africa: The Annual Forum and Expo on Electronic Identity in Africa," https://id4africa.com.

135. Zeyi Yang, "The World's Biggest Surveillance Company You've Never Heard Of," *MIT Technology Review*, June 22, 2022. https://www.technologyreview .com/2022/06/22/1054586/hikvision-worlds-biggest-surveillance-company/; Shruti Trikanad and Vrinda Bhandari, *Surveillance Enabling Identity Systems in Africa: Tracing the Fingerprints of Aadhaar* (Centre for Internet and Society, 2022), https://cis-india.org/internet-governance/surveillance-enabling-identity -systems-in-africa.

136. Benjamin, "Theses on the Philosophy of History," 258–59: "There is no document of civilization which is not at the same time a document of barbarism. And just as such a document is not free of barbarism, barbarism taints also the manner, in which it was transmitted from one owner to another. A historical materialist therefore dissociates himself from it as far as possible. He regards it as his task to brush history against the grain."

Chapter 2

1. Inoue Testujirō, *The Interpretation of The Imperial Rescript on Education*, rev. and expanded ed. (Japan: Keigyōsha, 1899), 2:165, cited in Eiji Oguma, *The Myth of the Homogeneous Nation* (単一民族神話の起源：〈日本人〉の自画像 の系譜) (Shinyōsha, 1995), 52.

2. Eiji Oguma, *The Boundaries of the Japanese* (〈日本人〉の境界：沖縄・アイ ヌ・台湾・朝鮮 植民地支配から復帰運動まで) (Shinyōsha, 1998), 50.

3. Benedict Anderson, *Imagined Communities: Reflections on the Origin and Spread of Nationalism*, rev. and expanded ed. (Verso, 1991), 6–7.

4. Oguma, *The Myth of the Homogeneous Nation*, 50.

5. Bunmei Satō, *The Alternative History of Koseki* (戸籍うらがえ史考) (Akashi Shoten, 1988), 18, 79.

6. Satō, *The Alternative History of Koseki*, 18, 82–83.

7. Satō, *The Alternative History of Koseki*, 86.

8. Karl Marx, *Capital: A Critique of Political Economy*, vol. 1 (Penguin Books, 1976).

9. Masataka Endō, *Nationality and Koseki in Modern Japanese Colonial Governance: Manchuria, Korea, and Taiwan* (近代日本の植民地統治における国籍と 戸籍 満洲・朝鮮・台湾) (Akashi Shoten, 2010), 116–17, emphasis by Endō.

10. Satō, *The Alternative History of Koseki*, 33, 37.

11. The *koseki* system I discuss in this chapter is mainly about the institution until 1945, the end of the Japanese empire. When Japan was defeated in the World War II and lost all colonies, the Koseki Act and Civil Law were reformed under the Allied Forces' occupation. For details on the reform, see the conclusion. Because the *koseki* system has kept the basic patriarchal framework in the postwar democratization, it is difficult to discuss *koseki* before and after 1945 in a completely separate way, as there is a continuation of the system.

12. Shūhei Ninomiya, *Koseki and Human Rights* (戸籍と人権) (Kaihō Shup-pan, 2006).

13. Today, one can apply to find someone's *koseki* at the municipal office. But many municipalities have set restrictions on disclosing the *koseki* in the past few decades because of growing concerns about privacy. In many cases, a person must prove that he or she belongs to a *koseki* or is a representative of the Koseki members or has any legal reason to access to someone's *koseki*. Nonetheless, the open-to-public principle remains in the Koseki Act.

14. Bunmei Satō, *The Life That Koseki Watches Over* (戸籍が見張る暮らし) (Gendai Shokan, 1991).

15. I personally experienced this process when I gave a birth to my child, because I did not register myself with the Japanese institution of marriage and Koseki, which I don't support. All the troubles I had registering my child as a Japanese citizen are not by accident; they are a social problem long publicly denounced by feminists as discrimination against women and children outside wedlock. The discrimination stems from the restricted right of illegitimate children to inheritance as compared to legitimate children, according to the Civil Law. But in September 2013 the Supreme Court decided that the restricted inheritance is unconstitutional. The Civil Law was finally revised for equal rights in December 2013. Nonetheless, the check box of legitimate or illegitimate child remains on the birth registration form.

16. Satō, *The Alternative History of Koseki*, 95–97.

17. Satō, *The Life That Koseki Watches Over*.

18. Bunmei Satō, *The Reader of Foreigners in Japan: The Basic Knowledge for Borderless Society*, expanded ed. (在日「外国人」読本 ボーダーレス社会の基礎知識) (Ryokufū Shuppan, 1996), 36.

19. Ruth Benedict, *The Chrysanthemum and the Sword: Patterns of Japanese Culture* (菊と刀) (Kōdansha, 1967); Satō, *The Alternative History of Koseki*.

20. Benedict, *The Chrysanthemum and the Sword*, 28.

21. Nohara 1936, cited in Benedict, *The Chrysanthemum and the Sword*, 145.

22. Anderson, *Imagined Communities*, 160.

23. John Dower, *Empire and Aftermath: Yoshida Shigeru and the Japanese Experience, 1878–1954* (Harvard University Asia Center, 1979), 85.

24. Satō, *The Reader of Foreigners in Japan*, 14.

25. Endō, *Nationality and Koseki in Modern Japanese Colonial Governance*, 20–21.

26. This part of the Nationality Act was revised in 1984, because it was against the Convention on the Elimination of All Forms of Discrimination Against Women, which Japan signed in 1980 and ratified in 1985 (Ryōko Akamatsu, "About 'Convention on the Elimination of All Forms of Discrimination against Woman' and 'Princess Sunflower,'" in *Princess Sunflower* (世界中のひまわり姫へ), by Midori Ogasawara (Poplar-sha, 2000). Japanese nationality is now given to children born from a Japanese mother, not only from a Japanese father.

27. Satō, *The Alternative History of Koseki*, 97–98, 152–54; Oguma, *The Boundaries of the Japanese*, 54.

28. Satō, *The Reader of Foreigners in Japan*.

29. Oguma, *The Boundaries of the Japanese*, 71, 111.

30. Oguma, *The Boundaries of the Japanese*, 111-12.

31. Oguma, *The Boundaries of the Japanese*, 132, 148.

32. Satō, *The Alternative History of Koseki*, 154-58; Endō, *Nationality and Koseki in Modern Japanese colonial governance*, 130-33.

33. Oguma, *The Boundaries of the Japanese*, 160-61.

34. Endō, *Nationality and Koseki in Modern Japanese Colonial Governance*, 140.

35. Endō, *Nationality and Koseki in Modern Japanese Colonial Governance*, 151-53.

36. Endō, *Nationality and Koseki in Modern Japanese Colonial Governance*, 162.

37. Endō, *Nationality and Koseki in Modern Japanese Colonial Governance*, 169. This passage is emphasized in the original.

38. Cited in Endō, *Nationality and Koseki in Modern Japanese Colonial Governance*, 169.

39. Endō, *Nationality and Koseki in Modern Japanese Colonial Governance*, 130-31.

40. Giorgio Agamben, *Homo Sacer: Sovereign Power and Bare Life* (Stanford University Press, 1998).

41. Endō, *Nationality and Koseki in Modern Japanese Colonial Governance*, 171, 180.

42. Endō, *Nationality and Koseki in Modern Japanese Colonial Governance*, 185-86.

43. Satō, *The Alternative History of Koseki*.

44. Endō, *Nationality and Koseki in Modern Japanese Colonial Governance*, 191.

45. Endō, *Nationality and Koseki in Modern Japanese Colonial Governance*, 191.

46. Michel Foucault, *The History of Sexuality, Vol. 1: An Introduction* (Vintage Books, 1978).

47. Ian Hacking, "Making Up People"; Judith Butler, *Gender Trouble: Feminism and the Subversion of Identity* (Routledge, 1990).

48. In practice, many municipalities have given the public increasingly limited access to Koseki. People who have no family relations to the subject registered in the Koseki need to justify the access by giving the reasons and relation to the subject.

49. Goeffrey Gorer, "Japanese Character Structure," *The Institute for International Studies* (1943), cited in Benedict, *The Chrysanthemum and the Sword*, 317.

50. Benedict. *The Chrysanthemum and the Sword*, 286.

51. Anderson, *Imagined Communities*.

52. Foucault, *Discipline and Punish*.

53. Foucault, *Discipline and Punish*, 135.

54. Foucault, *Discipline and Punish*, 214.

55. Foucault, *The History of Sexuality, Vol. 1*.

56. Foucault, *The History of Sexuality, Vol. 1*, 141.

57. Foucault, *The History of Sexuality, Vol. 1*, 139.

58. Endō, *Nationality and Koseki in Modern Japanese Colonial Governance*, 122.

59. Endō, *Nationality and Koseki in Modern Japanese Colonial Governance*, 82.

60. Endō, *Nationality and Koseki in Modern Japanese Colonial Governance*, 55-58. The Nationality Act was applied to Taiwan in 1899, and Sakhalin in 1923, but not in Korea. The government officials were afraid that Koreans would obtain the right to secede from Japanese nationality.

61. Agamben, *Homo Sacer*.

62. Leo T. S. Ching, *Becoming "Japanese": Colonial Taiwan and the Politics of Identity Formation* (University of California Press, 2001).

63. Ching, *Becoming "Japanese,"* 174-210.

64. Yasunori Fukuoka, *Koreans in Japan: The Youth Identities* (在日韓国・朝鮮人　若い世代のアイデンティティ) (Chūkō Shinsho, 1993). See also the Japanese author Megumu Sagisawa's novel *Do You Like This Country?* (2000), about her journey to her Korean origin. The author committed suicide in 2004.

65. Anderson, *Imagined Communities*.

66. Hacking, "Making Up People"; Hacking, *The Taming of Chance*.

67. Bunmei Satō, *Discrimination Koseki Makes* (戸籍がつくる差別) (Gendai Shoten, 1984).

68. John Torpey, *The Invention of the Passport: Surveillance, Citizenship and the State* (Cambridge University Press, 2000); Edward Higgs, "The Rise of the Information State: The Development of Central State Surveillance of the Citizen in England, 1500-2000," *Journal of Historical Sociology* 14, no. 2 (2001): 175-97.

Chapter 3

1. Louise Young, *Japan's Total Empire: Manchuria and the Culture of Wartime Imperialism* (University of California Press, 1998), 11-12.

2. Kevin D. Haggerty and Richard V. Ericson, "The Surveillant Assemblage," *British Journal of Sociology* 15, no. 4 (2000): 605-22, 613. Haggerty and Ericson points to the inevitable fragmentation of personal data through online systems: "[W]e are witnessing the formation and coalescence of a new type of body, a form of becoming which transcends human corporeality and reduces flesh to pure information. Culled from the tentacles of the surveillant assemblage, this new body is our 'data double', a double which involves 'the multiplication of the individual, the constitution of an additional self'. Data doubles circulate in a host of different centres of calculation and serve as markers for access to resources, services and power in ways which are often unknown to its referent" (citations omitted). This fragmentation of personhood occurs in colonial surveillance technology, too, without computer.

3. Young, *Japan's Total Empire*, 14.

4. Patrick Wolfe, "Settler Colonialism and the Elimination of the Native," *Journal of Genocide Research* 8, no. 4 (2006): 387-409.

5. Young, *Japan's Total Empire*, 89-90.

6. Pacific War Research Group, ed., *Picture Book: Manshu* (写説 満州), by Kōhei Moriyama (Business Sha, 2005), 28-31, 37-38.

7. Minato Kawamura, *Manchukuo, The Ambition for a Castle in the Air* (満洲国−砂上の楼閣「満洲国」に抱いた野望) (Gendai Shokan, 2011), 17-18.

8. See Young, *Japan's Total Empire*, 270-271, 270n65. The research section of Mantetsu kept changing the name from 1907 to 1945: the Research Department (1907-8), Research Section (1908-32), Economic Research Association (1932-36), Research Department (1938-43), and Research Bureau (1943-45).

9. Yoshihiro Ishikawa, *Revolution and Nationalism 1925-1945: Series China Modern and Contemporary History III* (革命とナショナリズム シリーズ中国近現代史3) (Iwanami Shoten, 2010), 48-51.

10. Ishikawa, *Revolution and Nationalism 1925-1945*, 73. This is referred to as the Liutiaogou Incident (柳条湖事件), based on the location, or 9/18 Incident in China, based on the date of Japan's invasion. Zhang Xueliang decided not to respond to Japan's provocation, which ironically helped Japan's speedy occupation. Zhang Xueliang's father Zhang Zuolin (張作霖) was assassinated in 1928, in a very similar plot by the Kwantung Army, when he was about to arrive in Shenyang by train.

11. Ishikawa, *Revolution and Nationalism 1925-1945*, 78.

12. Shin'ichi Yamamuro, *Chimera: A Portrait of Manchukuo, Expanded ed.* (キメラ 満洲国の肖像 増補版) (Chūōkōron Shinsha, 2004), 125; Rana Mitter, *Forgotten Ally: China's World War II, 1937-1945* (Houghton Mifflin Harcourt, 2013), 56.

13. As such, Japan's war against China began without the declaration, and the battlefield kept expanding through some "incidents." The Japanese government announced the 1931 attack as the Manchurian Incident, framing another watershed in 1937, the clash between the Japanese and Chinese armies in Lugouqiao near Beijing, as the Japanese-Sino Incident. While the Manchurian Incident broke out a fifteen-year war against China, the event in Lugouqiao escalated it to full-scale war between Japan and China. Then, I call the battle after 1937 the Chinese-Japanese War.

14. Yamamuro, *Chimera*, 54-60.

15. "Kingly way" (王道) is the antonym of coercive way (覇道) in Chinese, which uses military and violence to govern. With it, people spontaneously support the power when the king graciously acts for the people. The term was used to mask the coercive realities of Manchukuo. See also Yamamuro, *Chimera*, 10; Young, *Japan's Total Empire*, 130-32.

16. Ishikawa, *Revolution and Nationalism 1925-1945*, 139-40.

17. Ishikawa, *Revolution and Nationalism 1925-1945*, 140.

18. Hideko Itō, *Father's Will: War Makes the Human Beings "Insane"* (父の遺言 戦争は人間を「狂気」にする) (Kadensha, 2016), 157. Chinese ministers had been predominantly Puyi's subordinates and supporters since the Qing dynasty. The Department of State had several departments, such as finance, transportation, and foreign affairs, whose heads were also Chinese. But the second in command was always Japanese, and more powerful than the top.

19. Ishikawa, *Revolution and Nationalism 1925-1945*, 140-141.

20. Yōko Katō, *From the Manchurian Incident to Japanese-Chinese War: Series Japanese Modern History V* (満州事変から日中戦争へ シリーズ日本近現代史5), (Iwanami Shinsho, 2007), 137-40; Ishikawa, *Revolution and Nationalism 1925-1945*, 78-79.

21. Young, *Japan's Total Empire*, 88.

22. The modern development of media and technology is deeply involved with wars, as Friedrich Kittler suggests in *Gramophone, Film, Typewriter* (Stanford University Press, 1999). The major Japanese newspapers, such as *Asahi* and *Mainichi*, increased their circulations with every war, and grew as "national" papers while creating "nationals," culturally, through language (Anderson 1991). War was the best-selling topic for magazines too. However, new communication technologies can be invented from colossal military budgets and are prioritized during war, like in the early stages of the internet.

23. Young, *Japan's Total Empire*, 88.

24. Ishikawa, *Revolution and Nationalism 1925-1945*, 77.

25. Young, *Japan's Total Empire*, 92.

26. Matsuoka originally opposed the Manchurian Incident as an unauthorized military action but consigned himself to the victorious outcome of the occupation, just as his government did. The same tendency is observable among other Japanese diplomats. John Dower elaborates the case of Yoshida Shigeru in *Empire and Aftermath: Yoshida Shigeru and the Japanese Experience, 1878-1954* (Harvard University Asia Center, 1979). Yoshida, the postwar prime minister, was also involved in "managing Manchuria" in 1922-30; he competed with the military elites but defended the Japanese occupation in Northeast China. As an admirer of British imperialism, he tried to obtain British and American approval in dividing Asia under Japan's "go-fast" imperialism and showed his frustration when the two did not accept it.

27. Young, *Japan's Total Empire*, 93.

28. Young, *Japan's Total Empire*, 94-95.

29. Young, *Japan's Total Empire*, 4.

30. Young, *Japan's Total Empire*, 4.

31. Patrick Wolfe, "Settler Colonialism and the Elimination of the Native," *Journal of Genocide Research* 8, no. 4 (2006): 387-409; Sherene H. Razack, *Dying from Improvement: Inquests and Inquiries into Indigenous Deaths in Custody* (University of Toronto Press, 2015); Elia Zureik, *Israel's Colonial Project in Palestine: Brutal Pursuit* (Routledge, 2016); Vicki Chartrand, "Unsettled Times: Indigenous Incarceration and the Links Between Colonialism and the Penitentiary in Canada," *Canadian Journal of Criminology and Criminal Justice* 61, no. 3 (2019): 67-89.

32. Wolfe, "Settler Colonialism and the Elimination of the Native," 388.

33. Prasenjit Duara, *Sovereignty and Authenticity: Manchukuo and the East Asian Modern* (Rowman and Littlefield, 2003), 1.

34. Giorgio Agamben, *Homo Sacer: Sovereign Power and Bare Life* (Stanford University Press, 1998), 8.

35. Agamben, *Homo Sacer*, 28.

36. Asako Takano, *Fingerprints and Modernity* (指紋と近代) (Misuzu Shobō, 2016), 78-79.

37. Takano, *Fingerprints and Modernity*, 80.

38. Masataka Endō, *Nationality and Koseki in Modern Japanese Colonial Governance: Manchuria, Korea, and Taiwan* (近代日本の植民地統治における国籍と戸籍 満洲・朝鮮・台湾) (Akashi Shoten, 2010), 303-13.

39. Agamben, *Homo Sacer*, 18.

40. Fujio Ogino, "The Security and Judicial System of 'Manchukuo': The Background of 'Resistance and Repression,'" in *Resistance and Repression in "Manchukuo"* (「満洲国」における抵抗と弾圧), ed. Fujio Ogino, Toshio Kojima, Kenji Eda, and Takao Matsumura (Nihon Keizai Hyōronsha, 2017), 12.

41. Simon A. Cole, *Suspect Identities* (Harvard University Press, 2001).

42. Fujio Ogino, "The History of Kwantung Gendarmerie: The Repression over Hanman Kōnichi Movement," in *Resistance and Repression in "Manchukuo,"* ed. Fujio Ogino, Toshio Kojima, Kenji Eda, and Takao Matsumura (Nihon Keizai Hyōronsha 2017), 65-167.

43. Ogino, "The History of Kwantung Gendarmerie," 69.

44. This is another example of the Japanese elites having no democratic principles and keeping conforming to the landsliding war situations they opposed in the first place. Although they shared a bitter feeling about the Kwantung Army's unapproved warfare, and were concerned about civilian control over the military, they were imperialist, after all. The elites, including the emperor, were satisfied with the new territory the Kwantung Army brought, and the army took the political initiative to repeat this pattern into the Pacific War. Despite heated internal competition among the elites, they could not stop the irrational expansion of the war, because of their deeply shared belief in imperialism, and sense of superiority over other Asian nations. Dower (1979) reveals how this imperial sentiment was passed on to postwar Japanese politics through Yoshida's career as a diplomat to the postwar prime minister.

45. Ogino, "The History of Kwantung Gendarmerie," 77.

46. Ōsugi's nephew Tachibana Munekazu was born in Portland, Oregon, and had American citizenship. Some sources suggest that Tachibana's parents reported his missing to the U.S. embassy, so the Japanese government needed to investigate his whereabouts and disclose the murders of Tachibana, Ōsugi, and Itō. See also Yamamuro, *Chimera*, 275.

47. Group Saying "No" to Fingerprinting (GSNF), *Resistance to Japan, My Pride: The Report of Visiting China* (抗日こそ誇り——訪中報告書——) (Research Group on Fingerprinting in Northeast China, 1988), 87-88; Kawamura, *Manchukuo: The Ambition for A Castle in the Air*, 56. Amakasu played many roles in both the front and back stages of crafting Manchukuo: escorting Puyi to the national foundation ceremony, reigning over the police organization, leading the fascistic Concordia Association to pacify Chinese anger and conform to the Japanese order, and running the Manchuria Motion Picture Association as president.

He was also involved with the opium business and raised funds for political stratagems. The former gendarmerie captain's active involvements corroborate the character of Manchukuo maintained by surveillance and covert operations.

48. Fujio Ogino, *Tokkō Police* (特高警察) (Iwanami Shinsho, 2012), 158.

49. Ogino, "The History of Kwantung Gendarmerie," 164.

50. Ogino, "The Security and Judicial System of 'Manchukuo,'" 11.

51. Ishikawa, *Revolution and Nationalism 1925-1945*, 141.

52. Ishikawa, *Revolution and Nationalism 1925-1945*, 142.

53. Ishikawa, *Revolution and Nationalism 1925-1945*, 142.

54. Manchukuo News Service, *Manchukuo Annual Report* (満洲国現勢), *the 1932-1933 Edition* (Manshūkoku Tsūshinsha), 39-40.

55. Manchukuo News Service, *Manchukuo Annual Report, the 1932-1933 Edition*, 39-40, my translation.

56. Manchukuo News Service, *Manchukuo Annual Report, the 1932-1933 Edition*, 40, my translation.

57. Manchukuo News Service, *Manchukuo Annual Report, the 1932-1933 Edition*, 40, my translation.

58. Ogino, *Tokkō Police*, 13.

59. Ogino, *Tokkō Police*, 13-17.

60. Ogino, *Tokkō Police*, 25.

61. Ogino, *Tokkō Police*, 29.

62. Naoki Mizuno, "Japan's Occupation of Korea and the Peace Preservation Act" (朝鮮の近代史と日本), in *The Korean Modern History and Japan*, ed. Takashi Hatada (Yamato Shobō, 1987) cited in Yūichi Kaido, "How to Make the Legislation and Society for War: A Comparison Between Pre-WWII Security Legislation and the Abe Administration Circumstances" (paper presented at the public meeting of Kazuo Hizumi Foundation for Promoting Information Circulation, Tokyo, December 16, 2016).

63. Ogino, "The History of Kwantung Gendarmerie," 88. As prime minister, Tōjō later led Japan to the Pacific War. Ogino points out that the position of Kwantung Gendarmerie Commander changed his career, and vice versa. Tōjō established the strict and thorough lines of command to all gendarmerie branches and given the nickname of "Razor Tōjō." Many Japanese elites, including Tōjō, Ishiwara, Itagaki, Matsuoka, Yoshida Shigeru, and Kishi Nobusuke tested out their political techniques of imperialism in Manchuria, brought them back to Japan, and futher applied those totalitarian techniques toward the Japanese population to establish the total war system.

64. Ogino, "The History of Kwantung Gendarmerie," 89.

65. Ogino, "The History of Kwantung Gendarmerie," 92-93.

66. Ogino, "The History of Kwantung Gendarmerie," 83.

67. Ogino, "The History of Kwantung Gendarmerie," 101.

68. Ogino, "The History of Kwantung Gendarmerie," 154.

69. Ogino, "The History of Kwantung Gendarmerie," 8-9; Takao Matsumura, "The Special Transfer by the Kwantung Gendarmerie: To Reveal the

Whole History of Biowarfare Unit 731," in *Resistance and Repression in "Manchukuo*," ed. Fujio Ogino, Toshio Kojima, Kenji Eda, and Takao Matsumura (Nihon Keizai Hyōronsha, 2017), 287-348.

70. Ogino "The History of Kwantung Gendarmerie," 96.

71. Ogino, *Tokkō Police*, 191.

72. Achille Mbembe, "Necropolitics," *Public Culture* 15, no. 1 (2003): 11-40.

73. Endō, *Nationality and Koseki in Modern Japanese Colonial Governance*, 249-303.

74. Endō, *Nationality and Koseki in Modern Japanese Colonial Governance*, 253.

75. Endō, *Nationality and Koseki in Modern Japanese Colonial Governance*, 288.

76. Endō, *Nationality and Koseki in Modern Japanese Colonial Governance*, 289.

77. Takano, *Fingerprints and Modernity*, 73.

78. Endō, *Nationality and Koseki in Modern Japanese Colonial Governance*, 288.

79. Endō, *Nationality and Koseki in Modern Japanese Colonial Governance*, 308.

80. Endō, *Nationality and Koseki in Modern Japanese Colonial Governance*, 309.

81. Ishikawa, *Revolution and Nationalism 1925-1945*, 141.

82. Prasenjit Duara, *Sovereignty and Authenticity: Manchukuo and the East Asian Modern* (Rowman and Littlefield, 2003), 74.

83. Endō, *Nationality and Koseki in Modern Japanese Colonial Governance*, 139-140, 258-261.

84. Endō, *Nationality and Koseki in Modern Japanese Colonial Governance*, 265.

85. Jung-Mi Kim, *An Introduction to the Korean and Chinese People's Anti-Japanese History in Northeast China* (中国東北部における抗日朝鮮・中国民衆史序説) (Gendaikikakushitsu, 1992), 334.

86. GSNF, *Resistance to Japan, My Pride*, 63.

87. GSNF, *Resistance to Japan, My Pride*, 61-62.

88. Kim, *An Introduction to the Korean and Chinese People's Anti-Japanese History in Northeast China*, 349-371; GSNF, *Resistance to Japan, My Pride*, 56-81; Museum of the Imperial Palace of Pseudo-Manchukuo (MIPPM), *Let's Not Forget September 18, 1931: The Historical Facts of the Japanese Invasion in Northeast China* (勿忘"九・一八") (Jilin Fine Arts Press, 2006), 180-86.

89. GSNF, *Resistance to Japan, My Pride*, 66.

90. GSNF, *Resistance to Japan, My Pride*, 67.

91. MIPPM, *Let's Not Forget September 18, 1931*, 180-86.

92. MIPPM, *Let's Not Forget September 18, 1931*, 186.

93. Hiraku Suzuki, "Non-Residential District," in *The Invasion: The Confessions of Japanese War Criminals in China* (侵略―中国における日本戦犯の告白), ed. Association of Returnees from China and Shindokushosha (Shindokushosha, 1982), 49-65.

94. MIPPM, *Let's Not Forget September 18, 1931*, 186.

95. Kim, *An Introduction to the Korean and Chinese People's Anti-Japanese History in Northeast China*, 314.

96. GSNF, *Resistance to Japan, My Pride*, 81, my emphasis.

97. Yulin Yang, Peilin Xin and Naili Diao, *The Investigation of Japanese Kwantung Gendarmerie "Special Transfer"* (日本関東憲兵隊"特別輸送"追跡) (Social Science Resource Publishing, 2004), 82–83; Jingyan Liu, *The Heroes' Spirits on the Black Soil: An Investigation on the Anti-Japanese Soldiers in Jixi Area, Who Were Sent in the Special Transfer and Used for the Biochemical Experiment at the Unit 731* (黒土英魂 鶏西地区抗日志士被"特別移送"第７３１部队做活体细菌実験調査追踪) (Jixi City Archives, Jixi City Local Journal Office, Jixi City Culture and Public Relation Bureau, Jixi City Lion Association, 2015), 78–80.

98. Heilongjiang Provincial Archive, Heilongjiang People Foreign Friendship Association and ABC Project Committee. *The Iron-Clad Evidence of "Unit 731" Criminal Activities—The Kwantung Gendarmerie Special Transfer Documents* (Heilongjiang People Publishing, 2001), 53–68.

99. Heilongjiang Provincial Archive, Heilongjiang People Foreign Friendship Association and ABC Project Committee, ed. *The Iron-Clad Evidence of "Unit 731" Criminal Activities*, 38–52.

100. Yang, Xin, and Diao, *The Investigation of Japanese Kwantung Gendarmerie "Special Transfer,"* 116.

101. Heilongjiang Provincial Archive, Heilongjiang People Foreign Friendship Association, and ABC Project Committee, eds. *The Iron-Clad Evidence of "Unit 731" Criminal Activities*, 64–65.

102. Heilongjiang Provincial Archive, Heilongjiang People Foreign Friendship Association, and ABC Project Committee, eds. *The Iron-Clad Evidence of "Unit 731" Criminal Activities*, 47–48.

103. Yang, Xin, and Diao, *The Investigation of Japanese Kwantung Gendarmerie "Special Transfer,"* 76–77.

Chapter 4

1. Brochure issued by the Jilin City Labor Memorial Museum (2016).

2. Group Saying "No" to Fingerprinting (GSNF), *Resistance to Japan, My Pride: The Report of Visiting China* (抗日こそ誇り――訪中報告書――) (Research Group on Fingerprinting in Northeast China, 1988), 32.

3. The Alien Registration Act was enacted in 1952, when Japan regained independence from the occupying allies and unilaterally denied Japanese nationality to the formerly colonized. Fingerprinting became part of registration and renewal later. The Koreans and Taiwanese in Japan started to refuse this quasi-criminal procedure and it turned into a social movement and diplomatic issue after the 1980s. I describe how colonial ID techniques were passed on to the postcolonial registration system in the conclusion.

4. Asako Takano, *Fingerprints and Modernity: The Technique to Control and Govern Mobile Bodies* (指紋と近代: 移動する身体の管理と統治の技法) (Misuzu Shobo, 2016), 52–53.

5. Takano, *Fingerprints and Modernity*, 56–58.

6. Takano, *Fingerprints and Modernity,* 54–55.

7. Takano, *Fingerprints and Modernity*, 59.

8. GSNF, *Resistance to Japan, My Pride*, 32.

9. GSNF, *Resistance to Japan, My Pride*, 32.

10. GSNF, *Resistance to Japan, My Pride*, 33.

11. GSNF, *Resistance to Japan, My Pride*, 33.

12. Takano, *Fingerprints and Modernity*, 61–62.

13. GSNF, *Resistance to Japan, My Pride*, 33–34.

14. Takano, *Fingerprints and Modernity*, 63.

15. GSNF, *Resistance to Japan, My Pride*, 36.

16. Takano, *Fingerprints and Modernity*, 62; GSNF, *Resistance to Japan, My Pride*, 34.

17. GSNF, *Resistance to Japan, My Pride*, 35.

18. Takano, *Fingerprints and Modernity*, 63–64.

19. GSNF, *Resistance to Japan, My Pride*, 35.

20. GSNF, *Resistance to Japan, My Pride*, 43–44.

21. GSNF, *Resistance to Japan, My Pride*, 46.

22. GSNF, *Resistance to Japan, My Pride*, 45.

23. GSNF, *Resistance to Japan, My Pride*, 50.

24. GSNF, *Resistance to Japan, My Pride*, 84.

25. GSNF, *Resistance to Japan, My Pride*, 51.

26. Takano, *Fingerprints and Modernity*, 75.

27. Takano, *Fingerprints and Modernity*, 76–77, 241–242.

28. GSNF, *Resistance to Japan, My Pride*, 90.

29. GSNF, *Resistance to Japan, My Pride*, 92.

30. Takao Matsumura, *A Labor History of Japan's Imperial Colonies* (日本帝国主義下の植民地労働史) (Fuji Shuppan, 2007), 137.

31. Matsumura, *A Labor History of Japan's Imperial Colonies*, 137.

32. Hannah Arendt, *The Origins of Totalitarianism* (Harcourt, 1968), 206.

33. Arendt, *The Origins of Totalitarianism*, 206.

34. Takano, *Fingerprints and Modernity*, 85.

35. Jung-Mi Kim, *An Introduction to the Korean and Chinese People's Anti-Japanese History in Northeast China* (中国東北部における抗日朝鮮・中国民衆史序説) (Gendaikikakushitsu, 1992); Jun Uchida, *Brokers of Empire: Japanese Settler Colonialism in Korea, 1876–1945* (Harvard University Asia Center, 2011).

36. Matsumura, *A Labor History of Japan's Imperial Colonies*, 123.

37. Kim, *An Introduction to the Korean and Chinese People's Anti-Japanese History in Northeast China*; Minato Kawamura, *Manchukuo: The Ambition for a Castle in the Air* (満洲国−砂上の楼閣「満洲国」に抱いた野望) (Gendai Shokan, 2011).

38. Matsumura, *A Labor History of Japan's Imperial Colonies*, 124–25.

39. Matsumura, *A Labor History of Japan's Imperial Colonies*, 146.

40. Matsumura, *A Labor History of Japan's Imperial Colonies*, 138–39; GSNF, *Resistance to Japan, My Pride*.

41. Takano, *Fingerprints and Modernity*, 87.

42. Matsumura, *A Labor History of Japan's Imperial Colonies*, 139.

43. Takano, *Fingerprints and Modernity*, 91-93.

44. Matsumura, *A Labor History of Japan's Imperial Colonies*, 160.

45. Matsumura, *A Labor History of Japan's Imperial Colonies*, 162.

46. Takano, *Fingerprints and Modernity*, 103.

47. Matsumura, *A Labor History of Japan's Imperial Colonies*, 165.

48. Takano, *Fingerprints and Modernity*, 104.

49. Takano, *Fingerprints and Modernity*, 105-106.

50. Arendt, *The Origins of Totalitarianism*, 243.

51. Max Weber, "Bureaucracy," in *From Max Weber*, ed. Hans Heinrich Gerth and C. Wright Mills (Oxford University Press, 1946), 196-244.

52. Takano, *Fingerprints and Modernity*, 111-12.

53. Takano, *Fingerprints and Modernity*, 108.

54. Takano, *Fingerprints and Modernity*, 109.

55. Matsumura, *A Labor History of Japan's Imperial Colonies*, 146.

56. Matsumura, *A Labor History of Japan's Imperial Colonies*, 150.

57. In April 1945, the Soviet Union declared the nonrenewal of the Soviet-Japanese Nonaggression Treaty signed in April 1941. The Soviet Army crossed the Manchuria border on August 9, 1945. Many soldiers in the Kwantung Army had been already relocated to Okinawa, the Philippines, and other Pacific areas in the final stage of World War II. High-ranking officers who remained in China, including Unit 731, rushed to destroy the military facilities and documents and went back to Japan as soon as they learned of the Soviet attack. Japan announced its official surrender on August 15. Puyi resigned as the emperor of Manchukuo. He was captured by the Soviet Army at the Shenyang airport in flight to Japan and later sent to the Fushun War Criminal Control Centre. The Soviet Army sent the Japanese soldiers to Siberia for forced labor for several years, and some were transferred to the Fushun War Criminal Control Center. See also chapter 5.

58. Matsumura, *A Labor History of Japan's Imperial Colonies*, 151. There is a body of Japanese literature on the experiences of flight from Manchuria. Among them, Fujiwara Tei's *The Shooting Stars Are Alive* (流れる星は生きている) (Chūkō Bunko, 2005) described her survival journey with her three young children from Changchun via Korea, crossing the thirty-eighth parallel under military control on foot, while her husband was taken away to Siberia. The women and children were never well protected in the refugees' groups and often internally abused. In her group, a young child and a baby died not only because of starvation but also abuse and neglect by adults. New facts on their abusive experiences have been unfolded recently.

59. GSNF, *Resistance to Japan, My Pride*, 104.

60. GSNF, *Resistance to Japan, My Pride*, 104.

61. GSNF, *Resistence to Japan, My Pride*, 104; GSNF, "Fingerprints in Pseudo-State of Manchukuo," *Institute of Chinese Affairs* 472 (1987): 25.

62. Matsumura, *A Labor History of Japan's Imperial Colonies*, 189-90.

63. Takano, *Fingerprints and Modernity*, 137, my translation.

64. Matsumura, *A Labor History of Japan's Imperial Colonies*, 191.

65. Takano, *Fingerprints and Modernity*, 133.

66. Matsumura, *A Labor History of Japan's Imperial Colonies*, 197.

67. GSNF, *Resistance to Japan, My Pride,108*; Pacific War Research Group, ed., *Picture Book: Manshu* (写説 満州), written by Kōhei Moriyama (Business-sha, 2005), 152-155; Matsumura, *A Labor History of Japan's Imperial Colonies*, 191.

68. Xueshi Xie, "The Forced Labor in the Final Years of Manchukuo," in *The Research on Mantetsu Labor History* (満鉄労働史の研究), ed. Takao Matsumura, Xueshi Xie, and Kenji Eda (Nihon Keizai Hyōronsha, 2002), 76.

69. Matsumura, *A Labor History of Japan's Imperial Colonies*, 193.

70. Matsumura, *A Labor History of Japan's Imperial Colonies*, 196.

71. Matsumura, *A Labor History of Japan's Imperial Colonies*, 196.

72. Takano, *Fingerprints and Modernity*, 147.

73. The National Passbook Act, cited in Matsumura, *A Labor History of Japan's Imperial Colonies*, 196.

74. Matsumura, *A Labor History of Japan's Imperial Colonies*, 197.

75. Takano, *Fingerprints and Modernity*, 144-45.

76. Xie, "The Forced Labor in the Final Years of Manchukuo," 79-80.

77. Xie, "The Forced Labor in the Final Years of Manchukuo," 81.

78. Shigeru Aoki, *Visiting Wanrenkang: Unnamed Mass Grave in Manchukuo and Chinese Forced Labor* (万人坑を訪ねる—満州国の万人坑と中国人強制連行) (Ryokufū Shuppan, 2013), 143-44.

79. Takahashi Masahiro, "The Pits of Ten Thousand Corpses in Fengman Dam," in *The Chinese Soil Never Forget: The Invasion and Untold War* (中国の大地は忘れない—侵略・語られなかった戦争), ed. Masataka Mori (Shakai Hyōronsha, 1986), 47-72.

80. Takahashi, "The Pits of Ten Thousand Corpses in Fengman Dam," 47-48.

81. Kari Marie Norgaard, *Salmons and Acorns Feed Our People: Colonialism, Nature, and Social Action* (Rutgers University Press, 2019).

82. Aaron Stephen Moore, *Constructing East Asia: Technology, Ideology, and Empire in Japan's Wartime Era 1931-1945* (Stanford University Press, 2013).

83. Takahashi, "The Pits of Ten Thousand Corpses in Fengman Dam," 58-68.

84. Aoki, *Visiting Wanrenkeng*, 147.

85. Aoki, *Visiting Wanrenkeng*, 144.

86. Aoki, *Visiting Wanrenkeng*, 35, 38.

87. Aoki, *Visiting Wanrenkeng*, 43-44.

88. Aoki, *Visiting Wanrenkeng*, 46.

89. Seiichi Morimura, *The Devil's Gluttony* (悪魔の飽食) (Kōbun-sha, 1981); Kim, *An Introduction to the Korean and Chinese People's Anti-Japanese History in*

Northeast China; Shinichi Yamamuro, *Chimera: A Portrait of Manchukuo, Expanded Edition* (キメラ 満洲国の肖像 増補版) (Tokyo: Chūōkōron Shinsha, 2004).

90. Xie, "The Forced Labor in the Final Years of Manchukuo," 90.

91. Xie, "The Forced Labor in the Final Years of Manchukuo," 90-91.

92. Xie, "The Forced Labor in the Final Years of Manchukuo," 91.

93. Xie, "The Forced Labor in the Final Years of Manchukuo," 91-92.

94. Xie, "The Forced Labor in the Final Years of Manchukuo," 89.

95. Xie, "The Forced Labor in the Final Years of Manchukuo," 92.

96. Xie, "The Forced Labor in the Final Years of Manchukuo," 93.

97. Xie, "The Forced Labor in the Final Years of Manchukuo," 94-95.

98. GSNF, *Resistance to Japan, My Pride,* 105-106.

99. Xie, "The Forced Labor in the Final Years of Manchukuo," 99.

100. Xie, "The Forced Labor in the Final Years of Manchukuo," 99-100.

101. Xie, "The Forced Labor in the Final Years of Manchukuo," 99-100.

102. Xie, "The Forced Labor in the Final Years of Manchukuo," 106.

103. Xie, "The Forced Labor in the Final Years of Manchukuo," 109.

104. Li Li, "Uprising," in *The Research on Mantetsu Labor History*, ed. Takao Matsumura, Xueshi Xie, and Kenji Eda (Nihon Keizai Hyōronsha, 2002), 470.

105. Xie, "The Forced Labor in the Final Years of Manchukuo," 110-12.

106. John Dower, *Empire and Aftermath: Yoshida Shigeru and the Japanese Experience, 1878-1954* (Harvard University Asia Center, 1979), 85.

107. Timothy Longman, "Identity Card, Ethnic Self-Perception, and Genocide in Rwanda," in *Documenting Individual Identity: The Development of State Practices in the Modern World,* ed. Jane Caplan and John Torpey (Princeton University Press, 2001).

108. Judith Butler, *Gender Trouble: Feminism and the Subversion of Identity* (Routledge, 1990).

109. Butler, *Gender Trouble*; Shoshana A. Magnet, *When Biometrics Fail: Gender, Race and Technology of Identity* (Duke University Press, 2011).

110. Giorgio Agamben, *Homo Sacer: Sovereign Power and Bare Life* (Stanford University Press, 1998), 21.

111. Agamben, *Homo Sacer,* 29, emphasis original.

Chapter 5

1. Seiichi Morimura, *The Devil's Gluttony* (悪魔の飽食) (Kōbunsha,1981), 16.

2. Jin Chengmin first discovered the Kwantung Gendarmerie's top-secret documents on the Special Transfer in the Heilongjiang Archives in 1997. The documents were originally dug up from the ground of the Kwantung Army's sites, burned or buried. The documents recorded the victims' names, and led to the hearings of the families and communities to investigate. The Jilin Archives also announced the Gendarmerie documents on the Special Transfer in 2001. Many family members learned in this process that their fathers or relatives were killed in Unit 731.

3. Peilin Xin, "The Analysis of 'Special Transfer,'" in *The Iron-Clad Evidence of "Unit 731" Criminal Activities—The Kwantung Gendarmerie Special Transfer Documents* (「七三一部隊」罪行鉄証: 関東憲兵隊「特移扱」文書), ed. Heilongjiang Provincial Archive, Heilongjiang People Foreign Friendship Association, and ABC Project Committee (Heilongjiang People Publishing, 2001), 291-300.

4. Fenglou Liu, "On the Publication of the Iron-Clad Evidence of Criminal Acts by 'Unit 731,'" in *The Iron-Clad Evidence of Criminal Acts by "Unit 731": Special Transfer and Epidemic Prevention* (「七三一部隊」罪行鉄証 特移扱・防疫文書編集), ed. Jilin Provincial Archive, Japan-China Modern History Study Group, and ABC Project Committee (Jilin People Publishing Company, 2003); Zhiqiang Zhang and Yujie Zhao, "The Discovery and Investigation on the Kwantung Army 'Special Transfer' Files," in *The Iron-Clad Evidence of Criminal Acts by "Unit 731": Special Transfer and Epidemic Prevention,* ed. Jilin Provincial Archive, Japan-China Modern History Study Group, and ABC Project Committee (Jilin People Publishing Company, 2003), 469-81.

5. Morimura, *The Devil's Gluttony*; John W. Powell, "Japan's Biological Weapons: 1931-1945: A Hidden Chapter in History," *Bulletin of the Atomic Scientists* 37, no.8 (1981), 44-52.

6. Powell, "Japan's Biological Weapons: 1931-1945"; R. John Pritchard, "Introduction by Dr R. John Pritchard," in *Unit 731: The Japanese Army's Secret of Secrets,* by Peter Williams and David Wallace (Hodder & Stoughton, 1989), ix-xxvii.

7. Powell, "Japan's Biological Weapons: 1931-1945," 47-48.

8. Powell, "Japan's Biological Weapons: 1931-1945"; Peter Williams and David Wallace, *Unit 731: The Japanese Army's Secret of Secrets* (Hodder & Stoughton, 1989), 89-232; Sheldon H. Harris, *Factories of Death: Japanese Biological Warfare 1932-45 and the American Cover-Up* (Routledge, 1994), 149-223; Fuyuko Nishisato, *The Biowarfare Unit 731: The Japanese War Crime Acquitted by the United States* (生物戦部隊７３１-アメリカが免罪した日本軍の戦争犯罪) (Kusanone Shuppankai, 2002), 62-106.

9. Morimura, *The Devil's Gluttony*, 20-22; Yanjun Yang, *Japan's Biological Warfare in China: Recording the Unforgettable History, Revealing the Truth about Biological Warfare* (Foreign Languages Press, 2016), 56-57; Takao Matsumura, "The Special Transfer by the Kwantung Gendarmerie: To Reveal the Whole History of Biowarfare Unit 731," in *Resistance and Repression in "Manchukuo"* (「満洲国」における抵抗と弾圧), ed. Fujio Ogino, Toshio Kojima, Kenji Eda, and Takao Matsumura (Nihon Keizai Hyōronsha, 2017), 287-348.

10. Toshio Arai, "How the Testimonies Were Written," in *Testimonies of the Invasion: The Written Statements of the Japanese War Criminals in China* (侵略の証言：中国における日本人戦犯自筆供述書), ed. Toshio Arai and Akira Fujiwara (Iwanami Shoten, 1999), 267, 272-275.

11. Arai, "How the Testimonies Were Written," 276.

12. Haruo Kanki, ed., *The Three Sweepings* (三光) (Kōbunsha, 1957); Association of Returnees from China and Sinkokudosha, ed. *The Invasion: The Confessions of Japanese War Criminals in China* (侵略: 中国における日本戦犯の告白) (Shinkokudosha, 1982).

13. Morimura, *The Devil's Gluttony*; Powell, "Japan's Biological Weapons: 1931-1945"; Williams and Wallace, *Unit 731: The Japanese Army's Secret of Secrets*; Harris, *Factories of Death: Japanese Biological Warfare 1932-45 and the American Cover-Up*; Keiichi Tsuneishi, *Organized Crimes by Medical Researchers: Unit 731 of the Kwantung Army* (医学者たちの組織犯罪: 関東軍第七三一部隊) (Asahi Shimbunsha, 1994); Nishisato, *The Biowarfare Unit 731*; Daniel Barenblatt, *A Plague upon Humanity: The Secret Genocide of Axis Japan's Germ Warfare Operation* (HarperCollins, 2004).

14. Powell, "Japan's Biological Weapons: 1931-1945," 48.

15. Harris, *Factories of Death,* 116.

16. Yang, *Japan's Biological Warfare in China*, 51-52. See also the Unit 731 Biological War Research Center's website: http://www.anti731saikinsen.net/.

17. Nishisato, *The Biowarfare Unit 731*, 16; Yang, *Japan's Biological Warfare in China*, 3.

18. Yang, *Japan's Biological Warfare in China*, 10-13.

19. Yang, *Japan's Biological Warfare in China*, 20.

20. Yang, *Japan's Biological Warfare in China*, 21.

21. Yang, *Japan's Biological Warfare in China*, 168-82; Nippon Hōsō Kyōkai (NHK), *The Truth of Unit 731: The Medical Elites and Human Experiments* (documentary), August 13, 2017; Group for Investigating "War and Medical Ethics" ed. War and Medical Ethics: The Collusion and Responsibility of Japanese Medical Researchers and Physicians for the "15-year War" (戦争と医の倫理: 日本の医学者・医師の「15年戦争」への加担と責任), Sankeisha, 2012.

22. Yang, *Japan's Biological Warfare in China*, 59-60.

23. Yang, *Japan's Biological Warfare in China*, 60.

24. Yang, *Japan's Biological Warfare in China,* 39-42; Xueshi Xie, "The Forced Labor in the Final Years of Manchukuo," in *The Research on Mantetsu Labor History* (満鉄労働史の研究), ed. Takao Matsumura, Xueshi Xie, and Kenji Eda (Nihon Keizai Hyōronsha, 2002), 98-106.

25. Hideko Itō, *Father's Will: War Makes the Human Beings "Insane"* (父の遺言 戦争は人間を「狂気」にする) (Kadensha, 2016), 96-97, 113-14. According to Shimamura Saburo's statement, the Peace Preservation Bureau (Hoankyoku) was the most hidden police and intelligence section that had branches in each province of Manchukuo. The branch had a secret prison, which was given a fake name, like Mishima Science Research Center or Man-gou Resource Development Company. Shimamura, the branch captain, tortured underground members of the Nationalist Party, with "all kinds of cruel means that human beings can think of." Even when they misidentified some they captured, they killed them all within the prison to keep the bureau secret. During detainment in the

Fushun War Criminal Control Center, Shimamura admitted using many Chinese he had captured as "reverse use," letting them go to the Soviets, and collecting data upon their return. But he arbitrarily killed them when the reverse use caused risk for him, or became useless. He also sent three people to Unit 731. In the aftermath of Japan's defeat, Shimamura fatally poisoned more than ten prisoners, in Mishima Science Research Centre, and burned the building. These are the most hidden parts of Japan's war and colonization in China, and different types of murders were systematically conducted under the shadow of secrecy given to security intelligence.

26. Morimura, *The Devil's Gluttony*, 43; Yang, *Japan's Biological Warfare in China,*56-57; Matsumura, *"The Special Transfer by the Kwantung Gendarmerie,"* 287-348.

27. Morimura, *The Devil's Gluttony*, 43.

28. Torao Yoshifusa, "The Special Transfer—Bacterial Experiment," in *The Three Sweepings*, ed. Haruo Kanki (Kōbunsha, 1957), 33.

29. Peilin Xin, "The Analysis of 'Special Transfer'" in *The Iron-Clad Evidence of "Unit 731" Criminal Activities—the Kwantung Gendarmerie Special Transfer Documents* (「七三一部隊」罪行鉄証：関東憲兵隊「特移扱」文書), ed. Heilongjiang Provincial Archive, Heilongjiang People Foreign Friendship Association and ABC Project Committee (Heilongjiang People Publishing, 2001), 294.

30. Yang, Xin, and Diao, *The Investigation of Japanese Kwantung Gendarmerie "Special Transfer,"* 7.

31. Torao Yoshifusa, "The Special Transfer—Bacterial Experiment," in *The Three Sweepings*, ed. Haruo Kanki (Kōbunsha, 1957), 29-30. Yoshifusa is one of 969 Japanese soldiers transferred from the Soviet Union to China to be detained in the Fushun War Criminal Control Center in July 1950. Soldiers were educated to look back on their cruel deeds against the Chinese, admit responsibility, and confess to the war crimes they committed. Unlike other POW detention centers, there was no forced labor or maltreatment. They were provided warm clothes and Japanese-style food. Chinese prosecutors began the war crime investigation in 1954, and the Japanese soldiers documented their actions. The Shenyang War Criminal Tribunal (the official name is the Special Military Tribunal of China's Supreme People's Court), held in June and July 1956, sentenced twenty-eight high-ranking officials (no death penalty), and released most of the low-ranking soldiers. Yoshifusa's writing is a chapter of the book *The Three Sweepings* written by those soldiers and published in 1957. The Japanese right wing attacked the publishing house Kōbunsha, and *The Three Sweepings* went out of print, but it was reprinted from Shindokushosha as *The Invasion*. This chapter draws on those soldiers' writings and the statements for the trial that unveil the activities of the Kwantung Army, Kwantung Gendarmerie and Unit 731, such as Yoshifusa, Suzuki, and Kamitsubo.

32. Yoshifusa, "The Special Transfer—Bacterial Experiment," 30.

33. Yoshifusa, "The Special Transfer—Bacterial Experiment," 30-33.

34. Morimura, *The Devil's Gluttony*, 89.

35. Yang, *Japan's Biological Warfare in China,* 39.

36. Yang, *Japan's Biological Warfare in China,* 35-39.

37. Yanjun Yang and Qiu Mingxuan, ed. *The List of the Victims by Japanese Biological War in China* (侵华日军细菌战受害者名录) (China Peace Publishing, 2015), 50.

38. Heilongjiang Provincial Archive, Heilongjiang People Foreign Friendship Association, and ABC Project Committee, eds., *The Iron-Clad Evidence of "Unit 731" Criminal Activities—The Kwantung Gendarmerie Special Transfer Documents,* 201-10.

39. Heilongjiang Provincial Archive, Heilongjiang People Foreign Friendship Association, and ABC Project Committee, eds., *The Iron-Clad Evidence of "Unit 731" Criminal Activities—The Kwantung Gendarmerie Special Transfer Documents,* 209.

40. See also Jingyan Liu, *The Heroes' Spirits on the Black Soil: An Investigation on the Anti-Japanese Soldiers in Jixi Area, Who Were Sent in the Special Transfer and Used for the Biochemical Experiment at the Unit 731* (黑土英魂 鶏西地区抗日志士被"特别移送"第７３１部队做活体细菌実験調査追踪 (Jixi City Archives, Jixi City Local Journal Office, Jixi City Culture and Public Relation Bureau, Jixi City Lion Association, 2015), 17-32.

41. Heilongjiang Provincial Archive, Heilongjiang People Foreign Friendship Association, and ABC Project Committee, eds., *The Iron-Clad Evidence of "Unit 731" Criminal Activities—The Kwantung Gendarmerie Special Transfer,* 234-43.

42. Heilongjiang Provincial Archive, Heilongjiang People Foreign Friendship Association, and ABC Project Committee, eds., *The Iron-Clad Evidence of "Unit 731" Criminal Activities—The Kwantung Gendarmerie Special Transfer,* 238-39.

43. Heilongjiang Provincial Archive, Heilongjiang People Foreign Friendship Association, and ABC Project Committee, eds., *The Iron-Clad Evidence of "Unit 731" Criminal Activities—The Kwantung Gendarmerie Special Transfer Documents,* 240-41.

44. Heilongjiang Provincial Archive, Heilongjiang People Foreign Friendship Association, and ABC Project Committee, eds., *The Iron-Clad Evidence of "Unit 731" Criminal Activities—The Kwantung Gendarmerie Special Transfer Documents,* 243.

45. Yang, Xin, and Diao, *The Investigation of Japanese Kwantung Gendarmerie "Special Transfer,"* 298-312; Liu, *The Heroes' Spirits on the Black Soil,* 1-16.

46. Heilongjiang Provincial Archive, Heilongjiang People Foreign Friendship Association, and ABC Project Committee, eds., *The Iron-Clad Evidence of "Unit 731" Criminal Activities—The Kwantung Gendarmerie Special Transfer,* 242.

47. Yang, Xin, and Diao, *The Investigation of Japanese Kwantung Gendarmerie "Special Transfer,"* 152-75; Liu, *The Heroes' Spirits on the Black Soil,* 33-70.

48. Liu, *The Heroes' Spirits on the Black Soil,* 33-70.

49. Itō, *Father's Will,* 45. After her father's death, Hideko Itō, former Diet member and lawyer, learned that her father, Kamitsubo Tetsuichi had put

forty-four victims in the Special Transfer to Unit 731. She wrote the book *Father's Will: War Makes the Human Being "Insane"* (2016), based on statements by the Japanese soldiers who came back from the Fushun War Criminal Control Center.

50. Itō, *Father's Will*, 227-28.

51. Yang, Xin and Diao, *The Investigation of Japanese Kwantung Gendarmerie "Special Transfer,"* 152-53; Liu, *The Heroes' Spirits on the Black Soil*, 61-69.

52. Itō, *Father's Will*, 229.

53. Itō, *Father's Will*, 227-228; Yoshifusa, "The Special Transfer—Bacterial Experiment," 31-33.

54. Matsumura, "The Special Transfer by the Kwantung Gendarmerie," 287-301.

55. Jilin Provincial Archives, Japan-China Modern and Contemporary History Research Group, and ABC Project Committee, eds., *The Iron-Clad Evidence of "Unit 731" Criminal Activities—The Special Transfer and Epidemic Prevention Documents*, 5.

56. Yang, *Japan's Biological Warfare in China*, 41.

57. Yoshifusa, "The Special Transfer—Bacterial Experiment," 27-37.

58. Matsumura, "The Special Transfer by the Kwantung Gendarmerie," 320.

59. Matsumura, "The Special Transfer by the Kwantung Gendarmerie," 320.

60. Matsumura, "The Special Transfer by the Kwantung Gendarmerie," 296, my translation.

61. Yang, *Japan's Biological Warfare in China*, 168-71; Group for Investigating "War and Medical Ethics" ed. *War and Medical Ethics*, 95-99.

62. Hannah Arendt, *Eichmann in Jerusalem: A Report on the Banality of Evil* (Viking Press, 1963).

63. John Dower, *Embracing Defeat: Japan in the Wake of World War II* (W. W. Norton, 1999), 22.

64. Achille Mbembe, "Necropolitics," *Public Culture* 15, no. 1 (2003): 11-40.

65. Giorgio Agamben, *Homo Sacer* (Stanford University Press, 1998), 6.

66. Zygmunt Bauman, *Modernity and the Holocaust* (Cornell University Press, 1989), vii-xiv, 159-61.

Conclusion

1. Michel Foucault, *Discipline and Punish: The Birth of the Prison* (Vintage Books, 1977).

2. Michel Foucault, *The History of Sexuality, Vol. 1: An Introduction* (Vintage Books, 1978).

3. Foucault, *The History of Sexuality*.

4. Giorgio Agamben, *Homo Sacer: Sovereign Power and Bare Life* (Stanford University Press, 1998).

5. Achille Mbembe, "Necropolitics," *Public Culture* 15, no. 1 (2003):11-40.

6. Agamben, *Homo Sacer*, 18.

7. David Lyon, *Identifying Citizens: ID Cards as Surveillance* (Polity, 2009), 4.

8. Edwin Black, *IBM and the Holocaust: The Strategic Alliance Between Nazi Germany and America's Most Powerful Corporation* (Crown Books, 2001).

9. Keith Breckenridge, *Biometric State: The Global Politics of Identification and Surveillance in South Africa, 1850 to the Present* (Cambridge University Press, 2014).

10. Ahmad H. Sa'di, *Thorough Surveillance: The Genesis of Israeli Policies of Population Management, Surveillance and Political Control Towards the Palestinian Minority* (Manchester University Press, 2014); Elia Zureik, *Israel's Colonial Project in Palestine: Brutal Pursuit* (Routledge, 2016).

11. Tokiko Kashiwabara, "Same-Sex Marriage Lawsuit, Unconstitutional in Tokyo High Court, Second following Sapporo High Court," *Femin*, December 15, 2024, 2.

12. *Femin*, "CEDAW Recommendations in Hand," January 25, 2025, 2-3.

13. Hirohi Tanaka, *The Foreigners in Japan: Legal Barriers and Mental Gaps* (在日外国人 法の壁、心の溝) (Iwanami Shinsho, 1995), 46.

14. Yeong-hae Jung, *Sing People's Song* (〈民が世〉斉唱) (Iwanami Shoten, 2003).

15. Tanaka, *The Foreigners in Japan*; John Dower, *Empire and Aftermath: Yoshida Shigeru and the Japanese Experience, 1878-1954* (Harvard University Asia Center, 1979).

16. Tanaka, *The Foreigners in Japan*, 82, 90.

17. Sun-Ae Choi, *Inquiring "My Country"* (「自分の国」を問いつづけて) (Iwanami Booklet, 2000), 42.

18. Midori Ogasawara, "A Tale of Colonial Age, or the Banner of New Tyranny? National Identification Systems in Japan," in *Playing the Identity Card*, ed. Colin J. Bennett and David Lyon (Routledge, 2008), 94.

19. Midori Ogasawara, "Identify and Classify the Entire Population: The Politics of Surveillance in the Common Number System, New Alien Card System, and Secrecy Act," *Buraku Kaiho* 666 (2012): 64-73.

20. Group Saying "No" to Fingerprinting (GSNF), "Fingerprints in Pseudo-State of Manchukuo," *Institute of Chinese Affairs* 472 (1987): 16-27; Asako Takano, *Fingerprints and Modernity: The Technique to Control and Govern Mobile Bodies* (指紋と近代 移動する身体の管理と統治の技法) (Misuzu Shobo, 2016), 155-56.

21. Ogasawara, "A Tale of Colonial Age, or the Banner of New Tyranny?," 104.

22. Midori Ogasawara and Takashi Shiraishi, *We Don't Need the "My Number" System: To Counter the Surveillance Society and Protect Our Personal Information* (共通番号制なんていらない！監視社会への対抗と個人情報保護のために) (Kōshisha, 2012), 78-113.

23. Ministry of Internal Affairs and Communications, *The Information and Communication White Paper* (2022), https://www.soumu.go.jp/johotsusintokei/whitepaper/ja/r04/html/nd238320.html.

24. Ministry of Internal Affairs and Communications, "Mai'na Points Programs," https://www.soumu.go.jp/denshijiti/myna-point/index.html.

25. Midori Ogasawara, "Surveillance at the Roots of Everyday Interactions: Japan's Conspiracy Bill and Its Totalitarian Effects," *Surveillance & Society* 15, nos. 3-4 (2017): 477-85, https://ojs.library.queensu.ca/index.php/surveillance-and-society/article/view/6626.

26. Midori Ogasawara, *Snowden Talks About the Horrors of the Surveillance Society: The Complete Record of An Exclusive Interview* (スノーデン、監視社会の恐怖を語る 独占インタビュー全記録) (Mainichi Newspaper Publishing, 2016).

27. Primo Levi, *If This Is a Man*, trans. Stuart Woolf (Orion Press, 1959); Primo Levi, *The Drowned and the Saved*, trans. Raymond Rosenthal (Michael Joseph, 1988).

28. Aleida Assmann, *Cultural Memory and Western Civilization: Functions, Media, Archives* (Cambridge University Press, 2011), 6.

29. Midori Ogasawara, "The Daily Us (vs. Them) from Online to Offline: Japan's Media Manipulation and Cultural Transcoding of Collective Memories," *Journal of Contemporary Eastern Asia* 18, no. 2 (2019): 49-67, https://doi.org/10.17477/jcea.2019.18.2.049.

30. John Price and Midori Ogasawara, "Racialized Communities Caught in a Maelstrom," *rabble.ca*, July 5, 2024, https://rabble.ca/politics/canadian-politics/racialized-communities-caught-in-a-maelstrom/.

31. Hannah Arendt, *The Origins of Totalitarianism* (Harcourt, 1968), 269.

Appendix

1. On the investigations by Unit 731 Biological War Research Center and their support for the litigation, see the website http://www.anti731saikinsen.net/index.html.

2. *Beijing Review*, "Yukiko Yamabe, the Former People's Liberation Army Soldier: China and Japan," December 2010, http://japanese.beijingreview.com.cn/ztjl/txt/2010-12/09/content_318158.htm. Yamabe's life story is eye-opening in many ways for learning about modern Chinese-Japanese relations and the diverse actors of the Chinese Revolution in 1949. A number of Japanese soldiers and settlers remained in China after Japan's defeat, joined the People's Liberation Army, and witnessed the establishment of the People's Republic of China. It is a hidden side of history that shows how individuals made different choices in the chaotic aftermath of the Japan's defeat. Yamabe remarked on the good relationships of the People's Liberation Army with the farmers, compared to the Nationalist Army, or, needless to say, the Japanese Imperial Army, which motivated her to join it. But due to her brave and unique contribution to the new China, she experienced social discrimination after returning to Japan.

3. Walter Benjamin, "Theses on the Philosophy of History," in *Illuminations: Essays and Reflections*, ed. Hannah Arendt (Harcourt, Brace & World, 1968), 264-65.

4. Benjamin, "Theses on the Philosophy of History," 265.

5. Dorothy E. Smith, *Institutional Ethnography: A Sociology for People* (Altamira Press, 2005).

BIBLIOGRAPHY

English

Agamben, Giorgio. *Homo Sacer: Sovereign Power and Bare Life*. Stanford University Press, 1998.

Agamben, Giorgio. *State of Exception*. University of Chicago Press, 2005.

Anderson, Benedict. *Imagined Communities: Reflections on the Origin and Spread of Nationalism*. Revised and Expanded Edition. Verso, 1991.

Angwin, Julia, Jeff Larson, Charlie Savage, James Risen, Henrik Moltke, and Laura Poitras. "NSA Spying Relies on AT&T's 'Extreme Willingness to Help.'" *ProPublica*, August 15, 2015. https://www.propublica.org/article/nsa -spying-relies-on-atts-extreme-willingness-to-help.

Assmann, Aleida. *Cultural Memory and Western Civilization: Functions, Media, Archives*. Cambridge University Press, 2011.

Arendt, Hannah. *The Origins of Totalitarianism*. Harcourt, 1968.

Arendt, Hannah. *Eichmann in Jerusalem: A Report on the Banality of Evil*. Viking Press, 1963.

Ball, Kirstie, and Laureen Snider. Introduction to *The Surveillance-Industrial Complex: A political economy of surveillance,* edited by Kirstie Ball and Laureen Snider. Routledge, 2013.

Bamford, James. *The Puzzle Palace: A Report on America's Most Secret Agency*. Houghton Mifflin, 1982.

Barenblatt, Daniel. *A Plague upon Humanity: The Secret Genocide of Axis Japan's Germ Warfare Operation*. HarperCollins, 2004.

Bauman, Zygmunt. *Modernity and the Holocaust*. Cornell University Press, 1989.

Bauman, Zygmunt, and David Lyon. *Liquid Surveillance: A Conversation*. Polity, 2013.

Beauvoir, Simone de. *The Second Sex*. Translated and edited by H. M. Parshley. Vintage, 1989.

Benjamin, Walter. "Theses on the Philosophy of History." In *Illuminations: Essays and Reflections*, edited by Hannah Arendt. Harcourt, Brace & World, 1968.

Berger, Peter L., and Thomas Luckmann. *The Social Construction of Reality: A Treatise in the Sociology of Knowledge*. Anchor Books, 1967.

Black, Edwin. *IBM and the Holocaust: The Strategic Alliance Between Nazi Germany and America's Most Powerful Corporation*. Crown Books, 2001.

Bourdieu, Pierre. *In Other Words: Essays Towards a Reflexive Sociology*. Stanford University Press, 1990.

Brecht, Bertolt. "Conversations in Exile." Adapted by Howard Brenton, translated by David Dollenmayer. *Theater* 17, no. 2 (1986): 8–18.

Breckenridge, Keith. "The Elusive Panopticon: The HANIS Project and the Politics of Standards in South Africa." In *Playing the Identity Card: Surveillance, Security and Identification in Global Perspective*, edited by Colin J. Bennett and David Lyon. Routledge, 2008.

Breckenridge, Keith. *Biometric State: The Global Politics of Identification and Surveillance in South Africa, 1850 to the Present*. Cambridge University Press, 2014.

Browne, Simone. *Dark Matters: On the Surveillance of Blackness*. Duke University Press, 2015.

Butler, Judith. *Gender Trouble: Feminism and the Subversion of Identity*. Routledge, 1990.

Caplan, Jane, and John Torpey. Introduction to *Documenting Individual Identity: The Development of State Practices in the Modern World*, edited by Jane Caplan and John Torpey. Princeton University Press, 2001.

Chartrand, Vicki. "Unsettled Times: Indigenous Incarceration and the Links Between Colonialism and the Penitentiary in Canada." *Canadian Journal of Criminology and Criminal Justice* 61, no. 3 (2019): 67–89.

Ching, Leo T. S. *Becoming "Japanese": Colonial Taiwan and the Politics of Identity Formation*. University of California Press, 2001.

Clarke, Simon. "The Neoliberal Theory of Society." In *Neoliberalism: A Critical Reader*, edited by Alfredo Saad-Filho and Deborah Johnston. Pluto Press, 2005.

Cochrane, David. "Whitewash: Hassan Diab Attacks Report Concluding Government Acted Properly in His Extradition Case." *CBC*, July 26, 2019, https://www.cbc.ca/news/politics/hassan-diab-extradition-france-1.5226033.

Cole, Simon A. *Suspect Identities: A History of Fingerprinting and Criminal Identification*. Harvard University Press, 2001.

Commissions of Inquiry into the Actions of Canadian Officials in Relation to Maher Arar. "Report of the Events Relating to Maher Arar: Analysis and Recommendations." 2006. http://www.sirc-csars.gc.ca/pdfs/cm_arar_rec-eng.pdf.

Crenshaw, Kimberlé. "Mapping the Margins: Intersectionality, Identity Politics, and the Violence Against Women of Color." *Stanford Law Review* 43, no. 6 (1991): 1241–99.

Deleuze, Gilles. *Negotiations, 1972–1990*. Columbia University Press, 1995.

Deleuze, Gilles, and Felix Guattari. *A Thousand Plateaus*. University of Minnesota Press, 1987.

Dower, John. *Empire and Aftermath: Yoshida Shigeru and the Japanese Experience, 1878–1954*. Harvard University Asia Center, 1979.

Dower, John. *Embracing Defeat: Japan in the wake of World War II*. W. W. Norton, 1999.

Duara, Prasenjit. *Sovereignty and Authenticity: Manchukuo and the East Asian Modern*. Rowman and Littlefield, 2003.

Duncan, Ian. "New Details Released About High-tech Gear FBI Used on Planes to Monitor Freddie Gray Unrest." *Baltimore Sun*, October 30, 2015, https://www.chicagotribune.com/2015/10/30/new-details-released-about-high-tech-gear-fbi-used-on-planes-to-monitor-freddie-gray-unrest/.

Durkheim, Emile. *Suicide: A Study in Sociology*. Simon & Schuster, 1951.

Fong, Denise, John Endo Greenaway, Fran Morrison, John Price, Carmen Rodriguez de France, Sharanjit Kaur Sandhra, and Timothy J. Stanley. *1923 Challenging Racism Past and Present*. China-Canada Focus, 2023.

Foucault, Michel. *Discipline and Punish: The Birth of the Prison*. Vintage Books, 1977.

Foucault, Michel. *The History of Sexuality, Volume 1: An Introduction*. Vintage Books, 1978.

Foucault, Michel. "Governmentality." In *The Foucault Effect: Studies in Governmentality, with Two Lectures by and an Interview with Michel Foucault*, edited by Graham Burchell, Colin Gordon, and Peter Miller. University of Chicago Press, 1991.

Foucault, Michel. "Questions of Method." In *Michel Foucault: Power, Volume 3*, edited by James D. Faubion. New Press, 1994.

Foucault, Michel. *The Birth of Biopolitics: Lectures at the Collège de France 1978–1979*. Picador, 2008.

Friedan, Betty. *The Feminine Mystique*: A Political Economy of Personal Information. Norton, 1963.

Fromm, Erich. *Escape from Freedom*. Henry Holt, 1994.

Fuchs, Christian. "Political Economy and Surveillance Theory." *Critical Sociology* 39, no. 5 (2012): 671–87.

Galtung, Johan. "Cultural Violence." *Journal of Peace Research* 27, no. 3 (1990): 291–305.

Gandy, Oscar H., Jr. *The Panoptic Sort: A Political Economy of Personal Information*. Westview Press, 1993.

Gandy, Oscar H., Jr. "Engaging Rational Discrimination: Exploring Reasons for Placing Regulatory Constraints on Decision Support Systems." *Ethics and Information Technology* 12, no. 1 (2010): 29–42.

Giddens, Anthony. *The Constitution of Society: Outline of the Theory of Structuration*. University of California Press, 1984.

Giddens, Anthony. *The Nation-State and Violence*. Vol. 2 of *A Contemporary Critique of Historical Materialism*. Polity, 1987.

Glusac, Elaine. "What You Need to Know About Facial Recognition at Airports." *New York Times*, February 26, 2022, https://www.nytimes.com/2022/02/26/travel/facial-recognition-airports-customs.html.

Gorer, Geoffrey. "Japanese Character Structure." Institute for International Studies, 1943.

Graham, Stephen. "The New Military Urbanism." In *The Surveillance-Industrial Complex*, edited by Kirstie Ball and Laureen Snider. Routledge, 2013.

Greenwald, Glenn. *No Place to Hide: Edward Snowden, the NSA, and the U.S. Surveillance State*. Signal/McClelland & Stewart, 2014.

Groebner, Valentin. *Who Are You? Identification, Deception, and Surveillance in Early Modern Europe*. Translated by M. Kyburz and J. Peck. Zone Books, 2007.

Hacking, Ian. "Biopower and the Avalanche of Printed Numbers." *Humanities in Society* 5 (1982): 279-95.

Hacking, Ian. "Making Up People." In *Reconstructing Individualism*, edited by Thomas C. Heller, Morton Sosna, and David E. Wellbery. Stanford University Press, 1986.

Hacking, Ian. *The Taming of Chance*. Cambridge University Press, 1990.

Haggerty, Kevin D., and Richard V. Ericson. "The Surveillant Assemblage." *British Journal of Sociology* 15, no. 4 (2000): 605-22.

Hanisch, Carol. "The Personal Is Political." In *Notes from the Second Year; Women's Liberation Major Writings of the Radical Feminists*, edited by Shulamith Firestone and Anne Koedt. Radical Feminism, 1970.

Harris, Sheldon H. *Factories of Death: Japanese Biological Warfare 1932-45 and the American Cover-Up*. Routledge, 1994.

Harvey, David. *The New Imperialism*. Oxford University Press, 2003.

Harvey, David. *A Brief History of Neoliberalism*. Oxford University Press, 2005.

Hayes, Ben. "The Surveillance-Industrial Complex." In *Routledge Handbook of Surveillance Studies*, edited by Kirstie Ball, Kevin D. Haggerty, and David Lyon. Routledge, 2012.

Higgs, Edward. "The Rise of the Information State: The Development of Central State Surveillance of the Citizen in England, 1500-2000." *Journal of Historical Sociology* 14, no. 2 (2001): 175-97.

Hobson, John A. *Imperialism: A Study*. 1902. 3rd ed., with an introduction by J. Townshend. Unwin Hyman, 1988.

Iacovetta, Franca, and Wendy Mitchinson. *On the Case: Exploration in Social History*. University of Toronto Press, 1998.

Information and Privacy Commissioner of Ontario. "Biometrics." https://www.ipc.on.ca/en/privacy-organizations/data-and-technology-management/biometrics.

International Civil Liberties Monitoring Group. "Canada's No Fly List." https://iclmg.ca/issues/canadas-no-fly-list/.

International Labour Organization (ILO). "Unemployment on the Rise Over Next Five Years as Inequality Persists." In *World Employment and Social Outlook—Trends 2015*, 2015. http://www.ilo.org/global/about-the-ilo/newsroom/news/WCMS_336884/lang—en/index.htm.

Itō, Makoto. "Assessing Neoliberalism in Japan." In *Neoliberalism: A Critical Reader*, edited by Alfredo Saad-Filho and Deborah Johnston. Pluto Press, 2005.

Japanese Constitution. Ministry of Justice. http://www.japaneselawtranslation.go.jp/law/detail/?id=174.

Jenkins, Richard. "Categorization: Identity, Social Process and Epistemology." *Current Sociology* 48, no. 3 (2000): 7-25.

Jenkins, Richard. *Social Identity*, Second Edition. Routledge, 2004.

Kennedy, Dan. *Recollections of an Assiniboine Chief*, edited by James R. Stevens. McClelland and Stewart, 1972.

Kittler, Friedrich A. *Gramophone, Film, Typewriter*. Stanford University Press, 1999.

Klein, Naomi. *The Shock Doctrine: The Rise of Disaster Capitalism*. Alfred A. Knopf Canada, 2007.

LaFleur, William R, Gernot Bohme, and Susumu Shimazono, eds. *Dark Medicine: Rationalizing Unethical Medical Research*. Indiana University Press, 2007.

Lenin, Vladimir Il'ich. *Imperialism the Highest Stage of Capitalism*. International Publishers, 1939.

Levi, Primo. *If This Is a Man*. Translated by Stuart Woolf. Orion Press, 1959.

Levi, Primo. *The Drowned and the Saved*. Translated by Raymond Rosenthal. Michael Joseph, 1988.

Longman, Timothy. "Identity Card, Ethnic Self-Perception, and Genocide in Rwanda." In *Documenting Individual Identity: The Development of State Practices in the Modern World*, edited by Jane Caplan and John Torpey. Princeton University Press, 2001.

Luxemburg, Rosa. *The Accumulation of Capital*. 1951; Routledge, 2003.

Lyon, David. *Surveillance Society: Monitoring Everyday Life*. Polity, 2001.

Lyon, David. "Surveillance as Social Sorting: Computer Codes and Mobile Bodies." In *Surveillance as Social Sorting: Privacy, Risk, and Digital Discrimination*, edited by David Lyon. Routledge, 2003.

Lyon, David. *Surveillance Studies: An Overview*. Polity, 2007.

Lyon, David. *Identifying Citizens: ID Cards as Surveillance*. Polity, 2009.

Lyon, David. *Surveillance After Snowden*. Polity, 2015.

Lyon, David, and Colin J. Bennett. Introduction to *Playing the Identity Card: Surveillance, Security and Identification in Global Perspective*, edited by Colin J. Bennett and David Lyon. Routledge, 2008.

Magnet, Shoshana A. *When Biometrics Fail: Gender, Race and Technology of Identity*. Duke University Press, 2011.

Marx, Karl. *Capital, Vol. 1: A Critique of Political Economy*. 1867; Penguin Books, 1976.

Materials on the Trial of Former Servicemen of the Japanese Army Charged with Manufacturing and Employing Bacteriological Weapons. Foreign Languages Publishing House, 1950.

Mauss, Marcel. *Sociologie et anthropologie*. Presses Universitaires de France, 1968.

Mbembe, Achille. "Necropolitics." *Public Culture* 15, no. 1 (2003): 11–40.

McCoy, Alfred W. *Policing America's Empire: The United States, the Philippines, and the Rise of the Surveillance State*. University of Wisconsin Press, 2009.

Meekitjuk Hanson, Ann. "What's in a Name?" May 2, 2016. https://leapintothevoidwithme.wordpress.com/2016/05/02/whats-in-a-name/.

Mills, C. Wright. *The Sociological Imagination*. Oxford University Press, 2000.

Mitter, Rana. *The Manchurian Myth: Nationalism, Resistance and Collaboration in Modern China*. University of California Press, 2000.

Mitter, Rana. *Forgotten Ally: China's World War II, 1937–1945*. Houghton Mifflin Harcourt, 2013.

Mohanty, Chandra Talpade. "Under Western Eyes: Feminist Scholarship and Colonial Discourses." *boundary2* 12, no. 3 (1984): 333–58.

Moore, Aaron Stephen. *Constructing East Asia: Technology, Ideology, and Empire in Japan's Wartime Era 1931–1945*. Stanford University Press, 2013.

Mosco, Vincent. "Political Economy Theory and Research: Conceptual Foundations and Current Trends." In *The Handbook of Media and Mass Communication Theory*, edited by Robert S. Fortner and P. Mark Fackler. John Wiley and Sons, 2014.

Murakami Wood, David. "What Is Global Surveillance? Towards a Relational Political Economy of the Global Surveillant Assemblage." *Geoforum* 49 (2013): 317–26.

National Identification Agency of the Republic of Rwanda (NIDA). "ID4Africa: The Annual Forum and Expo on Electronic Identity in Africa" (2016). https://id4africa.com.

"Oxfam Study Finds Richest 1% Is Likely to Control Half of Global Wealth by 2016." *New York Times*, January 19, 2015, http://www.nytimes.com/2015/01/19/business/richest-1-percent-likely-to-control-half-of-global-wealth-by-2016-study-finds.html.

Newman, Barclay. *Japan's Secret Weapon*. Current Publishing, 1944.

Nietzsche, Friedrich W. *On the Genealogy of Morals: A Polemic: By Way of Clarification and Supplement to My Last Book, Beyond Good and Evil*. Oxford University Press, 1996.

Norgaard, Kari Marie. *Salmons and Acorns Feed Our People: Colonialism, Nature, and Social Action*. Rutgers University Press, 2019.

Ogasawara, Midori. "ID Troubles: The National Identification Systems in Japan and the (Mis)Construction of the Subject." MA thesis, Department of Sociology, Queen's University, 2008.

Ogasawara, Midori. "A Tale of Colonial Age, or the Banner of New Tyranny? National Identification Systems in Japan." In *Playing the Identity Card*, edited by Colin J. Bennett and David Lyon, 3-20. Routledge, 2008.

Ogasawara, Midori. "Surveillance at the Roots of Everyday Interactions: Japan's Conspiracy Bill and Its Totalitarian Effects." *Surveillance & Society* 15, nos. 3-4 (2017): 477-85.

Ogasawara, Midori. "The Daily Us (vs. Them) from Online to Offline: Japan's Media Manipulation and Cultural Transcoding of Collective Memories." *Journal of Contemporary Eastern Asia* 18, no. 2 (2019): 49-67.

Ogasawara, Midori. "Collaborative Surveillance with Big Data Corporations: Interviews with Edward Snowden and Mark Klein." In *Big Data Surveillance and Security Intelligence: The Canadian Case*, edited by David Lyon and David Murakami Wood. University of British Columbia Press, 2021.

Parenti, Christian. *The Soft Cage: Surveillance in America from Slavery to the War on Terror*. Basic Books, 2003.

Pariser, Eli. *The Filter Bubble: How the New Personalized Web Is Changing What We Read and How We Think*. Penguin, 2011.

Peace Preservation Act of 1941. Nakano Library. http://www.geocities.jp/nakanolib/hou/ht14-46.htm.

Piazza, Pierre, and Laurent Laniel. "The INES Biometric Card and the Politics of National Identity Assignment in France." In *Playing the Identity Card*, edited by Colin J. Bennett and David Lyon. Routledge, 2008.

Piketty, Thomas. *Capital in the Twenty-First Century*. Belknap Press of Harvard University Press, 2014.

Poster, Mark. *The Mode of Information: Poststructuralism and Social Context*. University of Chicago Press, 1990.

Powell, John W. "Japan's Biological Weapons: 1931-1945: A Hidden Chapter in History." *Bulletin of the Atomic Scientists* 37, no. 8 (1981): 44-52.

Price, John, and Midori Ogasawara. "Racialized Communities Caught in a Maelstrom." *rabble.ca*, July 5, 2024. https://rabble.ca/politics/canadian-politics/racialized-communities-caught-in-a-maelstrom/.

Prime Minister of Japan and Cabinet. "Statement by Prime Minister Shinzo Abe." August 14, 2015. http://japan.kantei.go.jp/97_abe/statement/201508/0814statement.html.

Pritchard, R. John. "Introduction by Dr R. John Pritchard." In Peter Williams and David Wallace, *Unit 731: The Japanese Army's Secret of Secrets*. Hodder & Stoughton, 1989.

Razack, Sherene H. *Dying from Improvement: Inquests and Inquiries into Indigenous Deaths in Custody*. University of Toronto Press, 2015.

"Richest 1 Percent to Own More Than Half of The World's Wealth By 2016, Oxfam Finds." *Huffington Post,* January 19, 2015. http://www.huffingtonpost .com/2015/01/19/world-wealth-oxfam_n_6499798.html.

Rubenstein, Richard L. *The Cunning of History: Mass Death and the American Future.* Harper & Row, 1975.

Saad-Filho, Alfredo, and Deborah Johnston. Introduction to *Neoliberalism: A Critical Reader,* edited by Alfredo Saad-Filho and Deborah Johnston. Pluto Press, 2005.

Sa'di, Ahmad H. *Thorough Surveillance: The Genesis of Israeli Policies of Population Management, Surveillance and Political Control Towards the Palestinian Minority.* Manchester University Press, 2014.

Said, Edward W. *Orientalism.* Pantheon Books, 1978.

Su, Sa. *Evidences of Crimes: Archives Left Over by Japanese Army Invading China.* China Intercontinental Press, 2014.

Scahill, Jeremy. *Dirty Wars: The World Is a Battlefield.* Nation Books, 2013.

Secrecy Act of 2013 (Act on the Protection of Specially Designated Secrets). Ministry of Justice. http://www.japaneselawtranslation.go.jp/law/detail/ ?id=2543&vm=04&re=01.

Sekula, Allan. "The Body and the Archive." *October* 39 (1986): 3–64.

Smith, Derek G. "The Emergence of 'Eskimo Status': An Examination of the Eskimo Disk List System and Its Social Consequences, 1925–1970." In *Anthropology, Public Policy and Native Peoples in Canada,* edited by Noel Dyck and James B. Waldram. McGill-Queen's University Press, 1993.

Smith, Dorothy E. *Writing the Social: Critique, Theory, and Investigations.* University of Toronto Press, 1999.

Smith, Dorothy E. *Institutional Ethnography: A Sociology for People.* Altamira Press, 2005.

Smith, Keith. *Liberalism, Surveillance and Resistance: Indigenous Communities in Western Canada, 1877–1927.* Athabasca University Press, 2009.

Thompson, Scott. "Separating the Sheep from the Goats: The United Kingdom's National Registration Programme and Social Sorting in the Pre-electronic Era." In *Playing the Identity Card: Surveillance, Security and Identification in Global Perspective,* edited by Colin J. Bennett and David Lyon. Routledge, 2008.

Torpey, John. *The Invention of the Passport: Surveillance, Citizenship and the State.* Cambridge University Press, 2000.

Trikanad, Shruti, and Vrinda Bhandari. *Surveillance Enabling Identity Systems in Africa: Tracing the Fingerprints of Aadhaar.* Centre for Internet & Society, 2022. https://cis-india.org/internet-governance/surveillance-enabling -identity-systems-in-africa.

Uchida, Jun. *Brokers of Empire: Japanese Settler Colonialism in Korea, 1876–1945.* Harvard University Asia Center, 2011.

Van der Meulen, Emily and Rob Heynen. "Unpacking State Surveillance: Histories, Theories, and Global Contexts." In *Making Surveillance States:*

Transnational Histories, edited by Rob Heynen and Emily van der Meulen. University of Toronto Press, 2019.

Van der Ploeg, Irma. "The Illegal Body: 'Eurodac' and the Politics of Biometric Identification." *Ethics and Information Technology* 1, no. 4 (1999): 295-302.

Völker, Klaus. *Brecht: A Biography.* Translated by John Nowell. Seabury Press, 1978.

Webb, Maureen. *Illusions of Security: Global Surveillance and Democracy in the Post-9/11 World.* City Lights Books, 2007.

Weber, Max. "Bureaucracy." In *From Max Weber: Essays in Sociology,* edited by Hans Heinrich Gerth and C. Wright Mills. Oxford University Press, 1946.

Williams, Peter, and David Wallace. *Unit 731: The Japanese Army's Secret of Secrets.* Hodder & Stoughton, 1989.

Wiretapping Act of 1999. Ministry of Internal Affairs and Communications. http://law.e-gov.go.jp/htmldata/H11/H11HO137.html.

Wiretapping Act of 2016. Ministry of Justice. http://www.moj.go.jp/keiji1/keiji14_00103.html.

Wolfe, Patrick. "Settler Colonialism and the Elimination of the Native." *Journal of Genocide Research* 8, no. 4 (2006): 387-409.

Wood, Ellen M. *Empire of Capital.* Verso, 2003.

Wu, Zhuoliu. *Orphan of Asia.* Columbia University Press, 2008.

Yang, Yanjun. *Japan's Biological Warfare in China: Recording the Unforgettable History, Revealing the Truth About Biological Warfare.* Foreign Languages Press, 2016.

Yang, Zeyi. "The World's Biggest Surveillance Company You've Never Heard Of." *MIT Technology Review,* June 22, 2022. https://www.technologyreview.com/2022/06/22/1054586/hikvision-worlds-biggest-surveillance-company/.

Young, Louise. *Japan's Total Empire: Manchuria and the Culture of Wartime Imperialism.* University of California Press, 1998.

Zuboff, Shoshana. "Big Other: Surveillance Capitalism and the Prospects of an Information Civilization." *Journal of Information Technology* 30 (2015): 75-89.

Zuboff, Shoshana. "The Secrets of Surveillance Capitalism: Google as a Fortune Teller." *Frankfurter Allgemeine,* March 5, 2016. http://www.faz.net/aktuell/feuilleton/debatten/the-digital- debate/shoshana-zuboff-secrets-of-surveillance-capitalism-14103616.html.

Zuboff, Shoshana. *The Age of Surveillance Capitalism: The Fight for a Human Future at the New Frontier of Power.* Public Affairs, 2019.

Zureik, Elia. "Constructing Palestine Through Surveillance Practices." *British Journal of Middle Eastern Studies* 28, no.2 (2001): 205-27.

Zureik, Elia. "Colonialism, Surveillance, and Population Control: Israel/Palestine." In *Surveillance and Control in Israel/Palestine: Population, Territory, and Power,* edited by Elia Zureik, David Lyon, and Yasmeen Abu-Laban. Routledge, 2011.

Zureik, Elia. *Israel's Colonial Project in Palestine: Brutal Pursuit*. Routledge, 2016.

Zureik, Elia, David Lyon, and Yasmeen Abu-Laban. Preface to *Surveillance and Control in Israel/Palestine: Population, Territory, and Power*, edited by Elia Zureik, David Lyon, and Yasmeen Abu-Laban. Routledge, 2011.

Japanese

Akamatsu, Ryōko. "About 'Convention on the Elimination of All Forms of Discrimination Against Woman' and 'Princess Sunflower.'" In Midori Ogasawara, *Princess Sunflower* (世界中のひまわり姫へ). Poplar-sha, 2000.

Aoki, Shigeru. *Visiting Wanrenkeng: Unnamed Mass Grave in Manchukuo and Chinese Forced Labor* (万人坑を訪ねる―満州国の万人坑と中国人強制連行). Ryokufū Shuppan, 2013.

Arai, Toshio. "How the Testimonies Were Written." In *Testimonies of the Invasion: The Written Statements of the Japanese War Criminals in China* (侵略の証言：中国における日本人戦犯自筆供述書), edited by Toshio Arai and Akira Fujiwara. Iwanami Shoten, 1999.

Arai, Toshio, and Akira Fujiwara, ed. *Testimonies of the Invasion: The Written Statements of the Japanese War Criminals in China* (侵略の証言：中国における日本人戦犯自筆供述書). Iwanami Shoten, 1999.

Association of Returnees from China and Shindokushosha, ed. *The Invasion: The Confessions of Japanese War Criminals in China* (侵略―中国における日本戦犯の告白). Shindokushosha, 1982.

Beijing Review. "Yukiko Yamabe, the Former People's Liberation Army Soldier: China and Japan." December 2010. http://japanese.beijingreview.com.cn/ztjl/txt/2010-12/09/content_318158.htm.

Benedict, Ruth. *The Chrysanthemum and the Sword: Patterns of Japanese Culture* (菊と刀). 1946; Kōdansha, 1967.

Brecht, Bertolt. *Refugees' Conversations* (亡命者の対話 ブレヒト・コレクション４). Translated by Osamu Nomura. Shōbunsha, 1981.

Choi, Sun-Ae. *Inquiring "My Country"* (「自分の国」を問いつづけて). Iwanami Booklet, 2000.

Conspiracy Bill of 2017. http://www.moj.go.jp/content/001221006.pdf.

Dugain, Marc, and Christophe Labbé. 2017. *L'homme Nu: La dictature invisible du numérique* (ビッグデータという独裁者). Translated by Kinuko Tottori. Chikuma Shobō, 2017.

Endō, Masataka. *Nationality and Koseki in Modern Japanese Colonial Governance: Manchuria, Korea, and Taiwan* (近代日本の植民地統治における国籍と戸籍 満洲・朝鮮・台湾). Akashi Shoten, 2010.

Femin. "CEDAW Recommendations in Hand." January 25, 2025, 2–3.

Fujiwara, Akira. "The Location of the Japanese-Chinese War History and the Written Statements." In *Testimonies of the Invasion: The Written Statements of the Japanese War Criminals in China* (侵略の証言：中国における日本人戦犯自筆供述書), edited by Toshio Arai and Akira Fujiwara. Iwanami Shoten, 1999.

Fujiwara, Tei. *The Shooting Stars Are Alive* (流れる星は生きている). Chūkō Bunko, 2005.

Fukuoka, Yasunori. *Koreans in Japan: The Youth Identities* (在日韓国・朝鮮人 若い世代のアイデンティティ). Chūkō Shinsho, 1993.

Group for Investigating "War and Medical Ethics" ed. *War and Medical Ethics: The Collusion and Responsibility of Japanese Medical Researchers and Physicians for the "15-year War"* (戦争と医の倫理：日本の医学者・医師の「１５年戦争」への加担と責任), (Sankeisha, 2012).

Group Saying "No" to Fingerprinting (GSNF). "Fingerprints in Pseudo-State of Manchukuo." *Institute of Chinese Affairs* 472 (1987): 16-27.

Group Saying "No" to Fingerprinting (GSNF). *Resistance to Japan, My Pride: The Report of Visiting China* (抗日こそ誇り──訪中報告書──). Research Group on Fingerprinting in Northeast China, 1988.

Heilongjiang Provincial Archive, Heilongjiang People Foreign Friendship Association, and ABC Project Committee, eds. *The Iron-Clad Evidence of "Unit 731" Criminal Activities—The Kwantung Gendarmerie Special Transfer Documents* (「七三一部隊」罪行鉄証: 関東憲兵隊「特移扱」文書). Heilongjiang People Publishing, 2001.

Higuchi, Yūichi. *Kyōwakai* (協和会). Shakai Hyōronsha, 1986.

Hosomi, Kazuyuki. *The Frankfurt School: From Horkheimer and Adorno to the Critical Theories in the Twenty-First Century* (フランクフルト学派). Chūkō Shinsho, 2014.

Imamura, Hitoshi. *Homo Communicans* (交易する人間). Kōdansha, 2000.

Imamura, Hitoshi. *Reading Benjamin's "Theses on the Philosophy of History"* (ベンヤミン「歴史哲学テーゼ」精読). Iwanami Shoten, 2000.

Imamura, Hitoshi. "Postscript." In *Capital, Volume 1 (II)* (資本論 第１巻下), translated by Hitoshi Imamura, Kenichi Mishima, and Tadashi Suzuki. Chikuma Shobō, 2005.

Imamura, Hitoshi. *The Key Words of Contemporary Thoughts* (増補 現代思想のキーワード). Chikuma Bunko, 2006.

Inoue, Testujirō. *The Interpretation of The Imperial Rescript on Education.* Vol. 2 (増訂 勅語衍義). Keigyōsha, 1899.

Ishikawa, Yoshihiro. *Revolution and Nationalism 1925-1945: Series China Modern and Contemporary History III* (革命とナショナリズム シリーズ中国近現代史3). Iwanami Shoten, 2010.

Itō, Hideko. *Father's Will: War Makes the Human Beings "Insane"* (父の遺言 戦争は人間を「狂気」にする). Kadensha, 2016.

Jilin Provincial Archives, Japan-China Modern and Contemporary History Research Group, and ABC Project Committee, eds. *The Iron-Clad Evidence of "Unit 731" Criminal Activities—The Special Transfer and Epidemic Prevention Documents* (「七三一部隊」罪行鉄証: 特移扱・防疫文書編集). Jilin People Publishing, 2003.

Jin, Chengmin, and Masaru Nakano. *The Confession of Old Soldiers.* Vol. 2, *To Children Who Do Not Know the War* (続・老兵の告白 戦争を知らない子供たちへ). Heilongjiang People's Publishing, 2009.

Jung, Yeong-hae. *Sing People's Song* (〈民が世〉斉唱). Iwanami Shoten, 2003.

Kaido, Yūichi. "How to Make the Legislation and Society for War: A Comparison Between Pre-WWII Security Legislation and the Abe Administration Circumstances." Paper presented at the public meeting of Kazuo Hizumi Foundation for Promoting Information Circulation, December 16, 2016.

Kanki, Haruo, ed. *The Three Sweepings* (三光). Kōbunsha, 1957.

Karatani, Kōjin. *The Structure of World History* (世界史の構造). Iwanami Shoten, 2010.

Kashiwabara, Tokiko. "Same-Sex Marriage Lawsuit, Unconstitutional in Tokyo High Court, Second following Sapporo High Court." *Femin*, December 15, 2024.

Katō, Yōko. *From the Manchurian Incident to Japanese-Chinese War* (満州事変から日中戦争へ シリーズ日本近現代史5). Japanese Modern History Series 5. Iwanami Shinsho, 2007.

Kawamura, Minato. *Manchukuo: The Ambition for a Castle in the Air* (満洲国–砂上の楼閣「満洲国」に抱いた野望). Gendai Shokan, 2011.

Kim, Jung-Mi. *An Introduction to the Korean and Chinese People's Anti-Japanese History in Northeast China* (中国東北部における抗日朝鮮・中国民衆史序説). Gendaikikakushitsu, 1992.

Kobayashi, Hideo. *The History of "Manchukuo"* (<満洲>の歴史). Kōdansha, 2008.

Kondō, Shōji, and Takao Matsumura. "Commentary on the Kwantung Army 'Special Transfer' Files." In *The Iron-Clad Evidence of "Unit 731" Criminal Activities—The Kwantung Gendarmerie Special Transfer Documents* (「七三一部隊」罪行鉄証: 関東憲兵隊「特移扱」文書), edited by Heilongjiang Provincial Archive, Heilongjiang People Foreign Friendship Association, and ABC Project Committee. Heilongjiang People Publishing, 2001.

Li, Li. "Uprising." In *The Research on Mantetsu Labor History* (満鉄労働史の研究) edited by Takao Matsumura, Xueshi Xie, and Kenji Eda. Nihon Keizai Hyōronsha, 2002.

Liu, Fenglou. "On the Publication of the Iron-Clad Evidence of Criminal Acts by 'Unit 731.'" In *The Iron-Clad Evidence of Criminal Acts by "Unit 731": Special Transfer and Epidemic Prevention* (「七三一部隊」罪行鉄証 特移扱・防疫文書編集), edited by Jilin Provincial Archive, Japan-China Modern History Study Group, and ABC Project Committee. Jilin People Publishing Company, 2003.

Manchukuo News Service. *Manshukuo Annual Report* (満洲国現勢), 1932–1933 ed. Manshūkoku Tsūshinsha.

Matsumura, Takao. "The Labor Control Policy in Manchukuo." In *The Research on Mantetsu Labor History* (満鉄労働史の研究), edited by Xueshi Xie and Kenji Eda. Nihon Keizai Hyōronsha, 2002.

Matsumura, Takao. *A Labor History of Japan's Imperial Colonies* (日本帝国主義下の植民地労働史). Fuji Shuppan, 2007.

Matsumura, Takao. "The Special Transfer by the Kwantung Gendarmerie: To Reveal the Whole History of Biowarfare Unit 731." In *Resistance and Repression in "Manchukuo"* (「満洲国」における抵抗と弾圧) edited by Fujio Ogino, Toshio Kojima, Kenji Eda, and Takao Matsumura. Nihon Keizai Hyōronsha, 2017.

Ministry of Internal Affairs and Communications. 2022. *The Information and Communication White Paper.* https://www.soumu.go.jp/johotsusintokei/ whitepaper/ja/r04/html/nd238320.html.

Ministry of Internal Affairs and Communications. "Mai'na Points Programs." https://www.soumu.go.jp/denshijiti/myna-point/index.html.

Mizuno Naoki. "Japan's Occupation of Korea and the Peace Preservation Act." In *The Korean Modern History and Japan* (朝鮮の近代史と日本), edited by Takashi Hatada. Yamato Shobō, 1987.

Morimura, Seiichi. *The Devil's Gluttony* (悪魔の飽食). Kōbunsha, 1981.

National Gendarmerie Friendship Group. *The Unofficial History of Japanese Gendarmerie* (日本憲兵外史). National Gendarmerie Friendship Group Association Headquarter, 1983.

Nippon Hōsō Kyōkai (NHK). *The Truth of Unit 731: The Medical Elites and Human Experiments* (documentary), August 13, 2017.

Ninomiya, Shūhei. *Koseki and Human Rights* (戸籍と人権). Kaihō Shuppan, 2006.

Nishisato, Fuyuko. *The Biowarfare Unit 731: The Japanese War Crime Acquitted by the United States* (生物戦部隊７３１−アメリカが免罪した日本軍の戦争犯罪). Kusanone Shuppankai, 2002.

Ogasawara, Midori. *Snowden Talks About the Horrors of the Surveillance Society: The Complete Record of An Exclusive Interview* (スノーデン、監視社会の恐怖を語る 独占インタビュー全記録). Mainichi Newspaper Publishing, 2016.

Ogasawara, Midori. 2019. *Snowden Japan File: How Japan Has Been Involved with America's Global Surveillance Systems* (スノーデン・ファイル徹底検証 日本はアメリカの世界監視システムにどう加担してきたか). Mainichi Newspaper Publishing, 2019.

Ogasawara, Midori. "Identify and Classify the Entire Population: The Politics of Surveillance in the Common Number System, New Alien Card System and Secrecy Act." *Buraku Kaihō* 666 (2012): 64–73.

Ogasawara, Midori, and Takashi Shiraishi. *We Don't Need the "My Number" System: To Counter the Surveillance Society and Protect Our Personal Information* (共通番号制なんていらない！監視社会への対抗と個人情報保護のために). Kōshisha, 2012.

Ogino, Fujio. *Tokkō Police* (特高警察). Iwanami Shinsho, 2012.

Ogino, Fujio. "The Security and Judicial System of 'Manchukuo': The Background of 'Resistance and Repression.'" In *Resistance and Repression in "Manchukuo"* (「満洲国」における抵抗と弾圧), edited by Fujio Ogino, Toshio Kojima, Kenji Eda, and Takao Matsumura. Nihon Keizai Hyōronsha, 2017.

Ogino, Fujio. "The History of Kwantung Gendarmerie: The Repression over Hanman Kōnichi Movement." In *Resistance and Repression in "Manchukuo,"* edited by Fujio Ogino, Toshio Kojima, Kenji Eda, and Takao Matsumura. Nihon Keizai Hyōronsha, 2017.

Oguma, Eiji. *The Myth of the Homogeneous Nation* (単一民族神話の起源：〈日本人〉の自画像の系譜). Shinyōsha, 1995.

Oguma, Eiji.The Boundaries of the Japanese (〈日本人〉の境界：沖縄・アイヌ・台湾・朝鮮 植民地支配から復帰運動まで). Shinyōsha, 1998.

Ogura, Toshimaru. *The Resistance to Globalization and Police Surveillance State: The Critique of Wartime Electronic Government* (グローバル化と監視警察国家への抵抗—戦時電子政府の検証と批判). Kihanasha, 2005.

Ogura, Toshimaru. *The Utopia of Despair* (絶望のユートピア). Katsura Shobō, 2016.

Ōtani, Keijirō. *Gendarmeries—An Autobiographical Memoir of Former East Gendarmerie Captain* (憲兵一元・東部憲兵隊司令官の自伝的回想). Shin Jinbutsu Ōraisha, 1973.

Pacific War Research Group, ed. *Picture Book: Manshu* (写説 満州), written by Kōhei Moriyama. Business Sha, 2005.

Sagisawa, Megumu. *Do You Like This Country?* (君はこの国を好きか) Shinchō Bunko, 2000.

Satō, Bunmei. *Discrimination Koseki Makes* (戸籍がつくる差別). Gendai Shokan, 1984.

Satō, Bunmei. *The Alternative History of Koseki* (戸籍うらがえ史考). Akashi Shoten, 1988.

Satō, Bunmei. *The Life That Koseki Watches Over* (戸籍が見張る暮らし). Gendai Shokan, 1991.

Satō, Bunmei. *The Reader of Foreigners in Japan: The Basic Knowledge for Borderless Society*, Expanded Edition (在日「外国人」読本 ボーダーレス社会の基礎知識). Ryokufū Shuppan, 1996.

Suzuki, Hiraku. "Non-Residential District." In *The Invasion: The Confessions of Japanese War Criminals in China* (侵略—中国における日本戦犯の告白), edited by Association of Returnees from China and Shindokushosha. Shindokushosha, 1982.

Takahashi, Masahiro. "The Pits of Ten Thousand Corpses in Fengman Dam." In *The Chinese Soil Never Forget: The Invasion and Untold War* (中国の大地は忘れない—侵略・語られなかった戦争), edited by Masataka Mori. Shakai Hyōronsha, 1986.

Takano, Asako. *Fingerprints and Modernity The Technique to Control and Govern Mobile Bodies* (指紋と近代: 移動する身体の管理と統治の技法). Misuzu Shobō, 2016.

Takatsu, Hironori. "People Are Threatened All Over the World. Does Japan Have the Culture of Resistance? The Nobel Prize Author Alexievich." *Asahi Shimbun*, December 16, 2016.

Takeuchi, Kazuharu. "Ceremony to Honor Tachibana Munekazu, Who Were Killed with Ōsugi Sakae in Amakasu Incident, Took Place in Nagoya." *Shūkan Kin'yōbi*, October 6, 2017.

Tanaka, Hiroshi. "The Origin of Fingerprinting." *Asahi Journal*, October 9, 1987, 21–23.

Tanaka, Hiroshi. *The Foreigners in Japan: Legal Barriers and Mental Gaps* (在日外国人 法の壁、心の溝). Iwanami Shinsho, 1995.

The Truth of Unit 731: The Medical Elites and Human Experiments (731部隊の真実 エリート医学者と人体実験) (documentary). Nippon Hōsō Kyōkai (NHK), August 13, 2017.

Tsuneishi, Keiichi. *Organized Crimes by Medical Researchers: Unit 731 of the Kwantung Army* (医学者たちの組織犯罪：関東軍第七三一部隊). Asahi Shimbunsha, 1994.

Xie, Xueshi. "The Forced Labor in the Final Years of Manchukuo." In *The Research on Mantetsu Labor History* (満鉄労働史の研究), edited by Takao Matsumura, Xueshi Xie, and Kenji Eda. Nihon Keizai Hyōronsha, 2002.

Xin, Peilin. "The Analysis of 'Special Transfer.'" In *The Iron-Clad Evidence of "Unit 731" Criminal Activities—The Kwantung Gendarmerie Special Transfer Documents* (「七三一部隊」罪行鉄証: 関東憲兵隊「特移扱」文書), edited by Heilongjiang Provincial Archive, Heilongjiang People Foreign Friendship Association and ABC Project Committee. Heilongjiang People Publishing, 2001.

Yamamuro, Shin'ichi. *Chimera: A Portrait of Manchukuo*, Expanded Edition (キメラ 満洲国の肖像 増補版). Chūōkōron Shinsha, 2004.

Yasuda, Kōichi. *The Net and Patriotism: Searching the Shade of Zaitokukai* (ネットと愛国) Kodansha, 2012.

Yoshifusa, Torao. "The Special Transfer—Bacterial Experiment." Edited by Haruo Kanki. *The Three Sweepings* (三光). Kōbunsha, 1957.

"Youth Unemployment Rate Increases. 'More Serious Situation,' ILO Prospects in 2015." *Nihon Keizai Shimbun*, January 20, 2015. http://www.nikkei.com/article/DGXLASGM20H05_Q5A120C1EAF000/.

Zhang, Zhiqiang, and Yujie Zhao. "The Discovery and Investigation on the Kwantung Army 'Special Transfer' Files." In *The Iron-Clad Evidence of Criminal Acts by "Unit 731": Special Transfer and Epidemic Prevention* (「七三一部隊」罪行鉄証 特移扱・防疫文書編集), edited by Jilin Provincial Archive, Japan-China Modern History Study Group, and ABC Project Committee. Jilin People Publishing Company, 2003.

Chinese

Jin, Chengmin. *Collection of Pictures on Japanese Military Germ Warfare* (日本軍細菌战图集). Inner Mongolia Culture Press, 2010.

Jixi City the 11th Committee of Chinese People's Political Consultative Conference, ed. *Jixi Anti-Japanese War Historical Materials: Jixi Political Consultive Historical Materials*. Vol. 10 (鶏西抗日戦争文史資料). 11th Committee of Chinese People's Political Consultative Conference, 2015.

Liu, Jingyan. *The Heroes' Spirits on the Black Soil: An Investigation on the Anti-Japanese Soldiers in Jixi Area, Who Were Sent in the Special Transfer and*

Used for the Biochemical Experiment at the Unit 731 (黒土英魂 鶏西地区抗日志士被"特別移送"第７３１部队做活体细菌実験調查追踪). Jixi City Archives, Jixi City Local Journal Office, Jixi City Culture and Public Relation Bureau, Jixi City Lion Association, 2015.

Museum of the Imperial Palace of Pseudo Manchukuo (MIPPM). *Let's Not Forget September 18, 1931: The Historical Facts of the Japanese Invasion in Northeast China* (勿忘"九·一八"). Jilin Fine Arts Press, 2006.

Yang, Yanjun and Qiu Mingxuan, ed. *The List of the Victims by the Japanese Biological War in China* (侵华日军细菌战受害者名录) (China Peace Publishing, 2015).

Yang, Yulin, Peilin Xin, and Naili Diao. *The Investigation of Japanese Kwantung Gendarmerie "Special Transfer"* (日本関東憲兵隊"特別輸送"追踪). Social Science Resource Publishing, 2004.

INDEX

academia, role of, 214
Act of Respecting Chinese Immigration, 43
Agamben, Giorgio, 19-20, 46-47, 48-49, 87, 159-60, 203-4, 241n128
Ainu people, 65, 68, 69, 70, 77
Alien Registration System, 13, 119, 208-9, 210, 251n3
Allied Forces, 163-64, 207, 235n29
Amakasu Masahiko, 91, 248n47
Anderson, Benedict, 54, 64
anthropometry, 36-67
Anti-Japanese Northeast United Army: formation, 93; intelligence, 185; Manchukuo Army, members from, 185; manifesto, 109; members captured/punished, 109-17, 115-16; Soviet Union, support from, 172; support, cut off from, 106, 140
anti-Japanese resistance. *See also* judicial subjugation: armed groups, 77, 84-85, 92-93; Chinese farmers, protests by, 131; expendable resources, use as, 168-69, 178, 185, 186, 189; influence on policy,

130; Korean and Taiwanese, early movements, 66; Mudanjiang Incident, 190; portrayal of, 85; spy networks, 189; Tokkō, oppression by, 97-98
apologies, demand for, 190, 197
Arar, Maher, 47, xiii
archives and museums, 4, 161-62, 172, 185, 218-19, 223-24, 255n2
Arendt, Hannah, 49, 50, 130, 136, 214, 238n57
artificial intelligence technology, xv
assimilation, 20, 67-70, 75, 77, 104-5, 158-59
Assmann, Aleida, 213
Association of Returnees from China. *See* Chūkiren
Auschwitz. *See* concentration camps and Nazis

bandits, categorization of: collective punishment, 105-6; colonial ID cards, 11; difficulties identifying, 94-96; expendable resources, 185; familial impacts, 109-17; judicial subjugation, 92-93; resistance

bandits (*Cont.*)
members, 85, 92; seven categories and depiction, 93-96; special workers, 154-56; supporters and concentration villages, 106-9; surveillance tactics, 20; thought crime as framework, 96-101; threat of, 113

Baojia. *See hokō* system

bare life, 46-48, 87

Bauman, Zygmunt, 197

Benedict, Ruth, 63, 72

Benjamin, Walter, 228, 233n7, 242n136, xv

Bentham, Jeremy, 30

Berger, Peter, 28

Bertillonage, 36-37, 39, 45

Big man/Small man, 22-24, 236n1

biometric classification and population control: address registration, 144-45; anti-resistance efforts, 140; controlled body as secure body, 156-60; cross-industry use, 125-28, 135; enemies, search for, 139-41; forced labor, experiences of, 146-53; ID cards and fingerprints, establishment, 133-37; introduction and use, 118-21; migrant workers and migration, 122-25, 128-33, 137-39; national identification system, 141-46; racism and disciplinary power, 130-31; settler colonialism, support of, 131-32; thought crimes, vagrants and forced labor, 153-54; war considerations, 133-34, 136-39; Western influence, 121-22; wider applications, 140-41

biometrics. *See also* fingerprinting; ID cards: bodies as surveillance sites, 205-6; colonialism, role in, 10-11, 18; definition, markers, and overview, 9; development and implementation, 41-45; imperialism and neoliberalism, 19; maximum surveillant assemblage and, 117; modern technologies and use, 10, 45, 51, 208-10; power demonstration through, 129; proof against technological neutrality, 52; Western use and influence, 121-22, 202

biopower/biopolitical mechanisms: academic approach and limitations, 31, 203-4; bare life, 47-48, 87; criticism and necropolitics, 48-52; economic pressures and, 73; failure to reflect colonial experience, 45-46; *koseki* and Japanese identity, 201; prosperity and labor control, 159-60; rationalization and power, 194-95; Western *versus* colonial perspectives of, 241n128

Black Lives Matter, 50

body as risky resource, 52, 126, 137, 139, 156-60, 203. *See also* expendable resource identification

body/identity separation, 9, 10, 22-24, 36-40, 245n2, ix-xv

borders, 23, 24. *See also* foreigners, registration and surveillance

Bose, Chandra, 38

Bourdieu, Pierre, 11

Brecht, Bertolt, 22-24, 52, 236n1

Breckenridge, Keith, 38, 39-40, 50, 51

Browne, Simone, 7, 27, 41-43

Butler, Judith, 29-30, 43, 158

Canada, surveillance efforts and policies, 8-9, 43-44, 51, 214, x, xiii

capital punishment, 96, 97, 99-100, 173, 174-75, 176, 192

capitalism, 31-32, 51, 72-73, 201

census, 34, 67, 74, 101, 102, 103

Changchun/Xinjing, 81, 83, 166, 220-223

character of crime, 173

China under Japanese colonialism. *See* Manchukuo (pseudo-state of Manchuria)

Chinese Communist Party, 93, 94, 98, 100, 225

Chinese Exclusion Act, 43

Chinese laborers, treatment of, 39-40, 118, 149, 151-53, 155-56, 160, 202. *See also* biometric classification and population control; body as risky resource; Labor Cards

Chinese nationalism, 87, 120

Chinese Nationalist Army, 83, 84

Chinese People's Liberation Army, 224

Chinese resistance, 84-85, 133, 168-69, 171-72

Chinese Revolution, 83, 262n2

Chinese-Japanese sentiments and relations, modern, 3-4, 17, 83, 219, 220, 225-27, 262n2

Chinese-Japanese War, 133, 137-38, 162

Ching, Leo T. S., 75

Chūkiren, 165

citizenship: Arendt on, 238n7; bare life and the removal of rights, 47; definitions and exclusions, 12, 243n15; international pressures of/protections of, 248n46; Japanese, birthright, 64-65, 243n26; *koseki* system, legacy of, 209; privileges and limitations, 35-36; revocation of, 22

civil and scholarly networks, 1, 3, 165, 224-25, 227

civil registries, 68, 101-5, 142, 144

clothing and physical markings, 44, 149, 150, 155, 156

Cole, Simon A., 43

collective identities: Chinese, prevention of, 88-89, 104-5, 108-9; individual identity, distinguished from, 23-24; state creation of, 30, 70-71, 77-78; suspect, 90

collective memory. *See also* cultural memory: cultural divide, 3-4, 13-14; internet, 6, 17, 213, 218, 231n5, xi, xii; manipulation through, 85-86, 214, 225-26; nostalgia, 149-50, 152, 226, 228

collective punishment, 105-6, 108-9, 111

collective surveillance, 113, 179-80

colonial divide, 225-28

colonial experiences. *See also koseki* system, colonial: artistic expressions of, 108-9, 118; biopower, failure to address, 45-46; everyday lives, approach to, 15-16; fingerprinting, 119, 126, 127-28; forced labor, 146-53, 160; identity struggles, 75-76; maximum surveillant assemblage, 81, 109-17; necropolitics, theory of, 48-52; Special Transfers, lived experiences, 178-90; underrepresented in academic studies, 19, 51-52, 194; Unit 731, family impacts, 197-98; violence and surveillance, 17-18

colonial myth-making, 13, 14, 48

colonial Other: Benjamin, civilization and barbarism, 242n136; biometrics, use for identification, 11; body as risky resource, 156-60; criminalization, 41, 45; dehumanization, 161, 169, 190-93; encounters with, 228, 229; expendable resources, 170-78; identity and hierarchy, 30; *koseki* and creation of, 64-69, 74-75, 77; legalized

colonial Other (*Cont.*)
killing of, 195-98; loyalty, suspi-
cions of, 68; segregation and
classification, 20; state discrimination, 27-28; visibility, creation
of, 149, 150, 156
colonial threshold: biometrics, use of,
202-4; civil registry, 101-5;
creation of, 86-89; defiance of,
159; definition and overview, 20,
81, 113; fingerprinting and mass
identification, 119, 122, 139-41;
fingerprinting and migration
control, 128-33; necropolitical
experience of, 159-60, 196-98;
policing powers, experience of,
92-93, 97-99, 101; population
control, 163; response to missing
colonial experiences, 52; thought
crime and violence, 191-93, 205
colonialism, Japanese. *See also* ID
cards; *koseki* system, colonial:
accounts of, 14; attempts to
maintain population purity, 105;
censorship or ignorance of, 1, 3,
13-15; colony as resource, 77-78,
85 (*See also* body as risky resource;
expendable resource identification); denialism and secrecy,
13-15; dependence on identity
systems, 18; displays of power
through technology, 128-29; early
ambitions, 40; echoes of, 212-16;
goals, 152; governmental systems,
Korea and Taiwan, 65-66;
Indigenous populations, 65;
industry and labor, 122-28,
133-37; internal guidance, 84;
Manchukuo and kingly rule,
81-82, 83-84, 88, 246n18; map of
territories, 2; national identification systems, creation of, 9-12;
process and surveillance, 20;

settler colonialism, use of, 86-89,
113
colonialism, Western, 10, 38-40, 41,
44-45, 119, 121-22, 130. *See also*
colonialism, Japanese
Comfort Women (sexual slavery),
213, 226. *See also* sexual assaults
Common Number System, 211-12
communists/communism. *See also*
thought crimes: Communist
Army, 170; communist bandits,
93, 94; Communist Party,
influence of, 197; mass arrests, 97;
policing of, 98; resistance by, 84;
threat of, 11, 96; Western push
against, 207
community surveillance,
101-9, 111
concentration camps and Nazis, 24,
47, 49, 143, 194
concentration villages, 106-9, 111-12,
139
conscription, 21, 35, 68, 68, 69-70,
120-21, 142, 143-144
continental brides, 105
co-responsibility. *See* lateral
surveillance
corona virus pandemic, 212, 217-18,
232-33n12, xiv, xx
corporate colonialism, 82
corporate surveillance and data
collection, 8-9, 32, 231n2, 231n5
correction centers, 154
Council of Department of State
(Manchukuo), 84
covert surveillance, 197
Criminal Tribes Act, 41
criminals, classification and biometrics, 36-37, 41, 45, 121-22. *See also*
colonial Other
crises and surveillance technology,
46, 212, 233n12. *See also* War on
Terror

cultural biases, 225–26. *See also* anti-Japanese sentiments, modern

cultural memory, 3–4, 152, 213, 225–26, 228–29, 253n58, 259–60n47. *See also* collective memory; media, role and influence:national papers and war

Cultural Revolution, 184

Daitō Company, 132, 133–35, 151

Daomuguo Police Branch, 179, 180

dark sousveillance, 43

Darwin, Charles, 37

data collection, colonial purpose, 6

data collection, historic, 7

data collection and analytics, modern, 6, 8, 32–33

data doubles, 245n2

de Beauvoir, Simone, 29

dehumanization, 161, 169, 190–93, 194–95, 198, 205

Deleuze, Gilles, 32

Democratic People's Republic of Korea, 93. *See also* Korea, under Japanese rule

denialism, 14, 108–9, 151–52, 213

Department of Defense (United States), 231n5

Department of Indian Affairs/Indian Agents (Canada), 44

The Devil's Gluttony, 177

Diab, Hassan, 232n11, xiv

Didao Coal Mine, 154, 218

Diet, 66, 83, 97, 190, 259–60n47

Digital Agency, 212

digital neocolonialism, 213–16

digitization, 210–13

disciplinary power, 30–31, 34, 70–78, 102, 129, 201

dividuals, 32

Dower, John, 247n26, 248n44

drones, 50

dual nationalities, 103

economic pressures, 85–86, 127, 130, 141–45, 152

Edo regime. *See* Tokugawa regime

Emergency Act (War Measures Act), 233n12

Emergency Labor Regulation, 143

emperor, loyalty to, 61–63, 68, 96, 207. *See also* Hirohito (emperor); Puyi (emperor)

Empire of Manchukuo. *See* Manchukuo

Endō, Masataka, 70

Ericson, Richard V., 32, 80

escapes and escape attempts, 147–48, 149, 153, 155–56, 166

Eskimo Disk List System, 44

eugenics, 37, 38, 88–89

evidence, destruction of, 16–17, 137, 163, 253n57, 257–58n25

expendable resource identification: classification through surveillant assemblage, 171–78; criteria, lose and intentional interpretation, 190–93; evidence and cover-ups, 163–65, *181–83*; legalized killing of colonial Other, 195–98; long term surveillance and rationality, 162–63; process development, 169–71; rationalization, 173, 176–77; research and need for bodies, 166–69; resources, use of, 194–95

Facebook-Cambridge Analytica scandal, 6

farmers, 1, 93–95, 120–21, 146–49, 262n2

Faulds, Henry, 37

Federal Bureau of Investigation (FBI), 22, 850

feminist theory, 29–30, 42–43

Fengman Dam, 118, 147, 149–51, *150*, 160

fieldwork, 15, 16-17, 217-29

Fingerprint Act, 128

Fingerprint Management Bureau, 120, 135, 139-41, 145, 156, 210

fingerprinting: alien registration, 119, 251n3; civil registry, proposed for, 104; colonial surveillance, 42-43, 79-81; compulsory, 21; criminals and use in prisons, 121-22, 129, 135, 210; experience of, *148*; Hamburg method, 121; ID cards and, 107-8, 117, 133-37, 157-60; invention and colonial development, 37-40, 119; investigation of use, 119; Japanese settlers, 139; labor management, 118-20, 123-24, 125-28; military associations, 139; national identification systems, 5, 141-46; positive depictions of, 128; postcolonial use, 11, 208-10; resistance to, 126

First Nations, 44

forced labor: Fengman Dam, *150*; Jixi Coal Mine, 233n3; legacy and secrecy, 3; lived experiences, 118, 147-53, 160, 219; POWs and special workers, 154-56, 253n57; vagrants, classification and detention, 153-54

Foreign Workers Policing Rules, 132

foreigners, registration and surveillance, 35, 43-44, 65, 119, 209-10. *See also* migrant workers

Foucault, Michel: biopower, 24, 46, 157, 201, 241n128; disciplinary power, 34, 72-73; genealogy, 15; panoptic model and disciplinary power, 30-31, 158; population management, 49; racism as biological label, 48; sovereign power, biopolitical shift in, 205; theoretical use, 19

Freedom Convoy, 233n12

freedom of speech and the press, 97

Fudan University, 220

Fujie Keisuke, 98

Fushun Coal Mine, 1, 118-20, 122-25, 127-28, 149, 154-57, 160, 218

Fushun tribunal. *See* war crime tribunals

Fushun War Criminal Control Center, 164, 165, 189, 218, 253n57, 257n25, 258n31, 259-60n47

Galton, Francis, 37-38, 40

gender equality, 12-13, 29-30, 42-43, 55, 60-61, 207-8, 243n15, 243n26

Geneva Protocol, 163, 166

Giddens, Anthony, 28, 33-34

Gilyak people, 68

Good People Certificates. *See* ID cards; resident cards

Google, xii

Great Depression, 85

Greater East Asia Co-Prosperity Sphere, 13, 202

Group Saying "No" to Fingerprinting (GSNF), 119, 126, 127-28, 248n47

Guantanamo Bay, 47. *See also* War on Terror

Guattari, Félix, 32

Hacking, Ian, 28

Haggerty, Kevin D., 32, 80

half-farmers/half-bandits, 93-95

Hanman Kōnichi movement, 99

Haque, Azizul, 38

health data collection, 6, 233n12

Heilongjiang Provincial Archives, 161-62, 172, 185, 255n2

Henry System (Edward Henry), 37-39, 121

Hideko Itō, 257n25, 259-60n47

hierarchy and identity, 60-64

Higgs, Edward, 34-35

Hirohito (emperor), 90, 207, 208

hisabetsu-buraku, 207

Hokkaido, 65, 69

hokō system, 105–6, 111, 113

Holocaust survivors, 213

honseki, 59, 62, 66–67, 68, 69–70, 73–74

Hooper, Tom, 215–16

Hoshino Naoki, 149–50, 152–53

human experimentation, 161–63, 166–70, 194–95, 205

human rights, protection of, 128–29, 208, 238n57

ID cards. *See also* passports; visas and permits: archived and surviving, *4,* 5, 219; biometrics and, 20–21; colonial experiences of, 17; compulsory use and carrying, 5, 11, 153; concentration villages and, *107,* 107–9, 111–12, 139; employment cards, 123–24, 125–28; fingerprint identification and data, 1, 80, 117, 118–21, 133–37, 157–60; Foreign Resident Cards, 210; Labor Cards, *134,* 134–35, 138–39, 141, 145–46, 149, 156, 202; *Les Misérables,* 200–1; migration and immigration, 43–44, 132–33, 209; postcolonial use and resistance, 5, 10, 208–10, 211–12; power of, 200–1; resident cards, 107, 139–40, 166, 202; surveillant assemblage and, 79–81; tracked movements, 101

identification documents, historical use, 22–25, 35, 38, 41–42, 44, 74

identification systems, postcolonial, 21, 199–201, 215–16

identity, vulnerability of, 9, 23, 33, 199–201, 215–16

identity systems and state power: bare life, 46–48; biopower, theory and criticisms, 31, 45–46;

categorization and control, 25–30; control societies, 32–33; disciplinary power, 30–33, 34; nation state, use of surveillance, 33–36; necropolitics, 48–52; racialized surveillance, 41–45; scientific approaches, rise of, 36–40

immigration and biometrics, 43–44, 209–10

impacts, inter-generational, 3–4, 109–13, 184, 190, 198, 213, 224, 255n2. *See also* colonial experiences

Imperial Constitution, 58–59, 66

Imperial Rescript on Education, 55, 63

inclusive exclusion, 87, 159–60

Indigenous populations, 44, 86

Industrial Development Five-Year Plan, 120, 133, 149

industrialization, 34, 57, 64, 73, 86

The Infinite Dream, 149–50, 152

informants, 98–99

information and communication technologies (ICTs), 6, 8, 41–42

information state, 19

internal Others. *See* colonial Others

internalized surveillance, 74–76, 77, 84

International Military Tribunal for the Far East, 164

internet, 6, 17, 213, 218, 231n5, xi, xii

The Invasion, 165

Ishii Shirō, 163, 164, 165–67, 207

Ishiwara Kanji, 83, 90, 91, 249n63

isolationism, 53–54, 57, 217

Israel: government, 206; occupation of Palestine, 48–50

Itagaki Seishirō, 83, 88, 90, 91, 249n63

Itō Noe, 91, 248n46

Japan, postcolonial period, 11, 76, 224, 251n3, 262n2
Japan, surveillance efforts and policies, 210-12
Japanese Army: Chinese Nationalist Army, conflict with, 83, 133; Comfort Women, system of sexual slavery, 213, 226; confessions by, 165, 169, 188-89, 258n31, 259-60n47; destruction of evidence, 16, 163, 167; labor shortage, response to, 142 (See also Unit 731); prisoners of war and forced labor, 154; surrender, 253n57; violence against civilians, 13
Japanese Consulate, 169
Japanese identity: emperor, loyalty to, 20, 61-63, 68, 99, 207; eugenics and, 89; Japanese Nationality Act, 74-75; koseki system and creation of, 201; postcolonial presence, 207-8; threats to, 96
Japanese settlers, 86-87, 262n2
Japanese Socialist League, 96
Japanese-Chinese War, 246n13
Japanese-Manchuria Labor issue Meeting, 130-31
Jehol Province, 98-99
Jilin Province, 83: Jilin Archives, 255n2; Jilin City Labor/Workers Memorial Museum, 150, 151, 152-53, 218; Jilin University, 218, 219, 220, 221
Jin Chengmin, 255n2
Jixi City, 1, 3: Jixi City Museum, 4, 218; Jixi Coal Mine, 233n3
judicial subjugation, 92-93, 99, 100
Juki-Net, 211-12

Kamitsubo Tetsuichi, 164, 187, 188, 258n31, 259-60n47
Kamo Unit, 166
Kawashima Kiyoshi, 164, 169

Khabarovsk War Criminal Trial, 164, 169
Kim Il-song, 93
Kingdom of Ryūkyū, 65
kingly rule, 88-89, 95, 104-5, 246n15
Kittler, Friedrich, 247n22
Klein, Mark, 231n2
Korea under Japanese colonialism: annexation of, 82; categorization, effects of, 77; concentration villages, 106-9; conscription, 69-70; fingerprinting, 21, 251n3; government and koseki, 66-67, 68; honseki, 73-74; Japanese national-ity, 65, 74-75, 245n60; Korean migrants, control of, 131; postcolo-nial impacts, 75; racial classifica-tions and hierarchy, 20, 30, 101; resistance and bandits, 93-94, 97; state of exception, 74-75; travel, limitations on, 74
Korean governor-general, 129
Koseki Act, 58, 128, 202, 208
koseki system: author's experience with, 221; colonial surveillance, comparison to, 158-59; colonial threshold, inapplicable to, 10, 101-2; development and use, 10, 20, 56-57, 58-60; disciplinary power, 70-73, 76; fingerprinting, consider-ation of, 122; honseki, 59, 70, 73-74; Japanese nationality and identity, 64-65, 76-78, 201; nation building and system development, 53-56; normalization of, 12-13, 14-15; patriarchal structure and gender discrimination, 60-64, 243n15; postcolonial presence, 207-8, 242n11; private sector use, 10; record access and public nature, 59, 71, 243n13, 244n48; social identity and hierarchy, 28-29, 30; soul training, 103

koseki system, colonial: Alien Registration System and, 209; disciplinary power, 73-76; fingerprinting, 128; identity creation, lack of success, 56; Japanese identity and, 64-68; Korean Koseki Order, 68; postcolonial influence, 209; racial order, creation of, 202; role and impact, 20; segregation and impact, 68-70

Kōtoku Shūsui, 96

Kwantung Army: colonial management, role in, 82-86, 88; colonial threshold, irritation with, 88; evidence destruction, 162-63; POWs and special workers, forced labor, 154; resistance, conflict and surveillance, 106-7, *107*, 111; soldiers, confessions of, 258n31, 259-60n47; Special Exercise, 143-144, 171; surveillance, role in, 79-80; sweeping operations, 139-140

Kwantung Gendarmerie: creation of, 89-90; expendable resource identification, 168-69, 170-71; forced labor, enforced by, 147; population treated as potential bandits, 95; role shift post 1931, 90-93; severe punishment, intentional use, 100-1; soldiers, confessions of, 258n31; Special Transfer files, 11-12, *114-16*, 219; Special Transfers, categorization of, 172-78, 190-93; surveillance, role in, 81; Unit 731, victims sent by, 112

Kwantung Government/Government-General, 82

Labor Card system: cards, surviving, *134*, 138-39; compulsory carry, 153; Daitō Company, use of, 150; establishment of, 120, 133-39; lived experience, 149; passbook system, root of, 144, 145-46, 156

labor control: biometric classification and surveillance, 118-20, 133-37, 202-3; cross-industry participation, 125-28, 135; disciplinary action, reasons for, 124; Japanese settlers, fingerprinting of, 139; labor service teams, 146; migration, limitation of, 128-31; military demands, 142-46; private work as public duty, 141-42, 143; registration, classification and restriction, 122-24; separation of worker groups, 155; strikes and resistance, 124-25, 126

Labor Control Act, 134, 136, 141-42

Labor Control Committee, 129-30, 132

labor disputes, 96, 124-26

Labor Service, 146

Labor Vitalization State Association, 141-42

Laborer Fingerprint Control Act, 133

lateral surveillance, 71, 76-77, 105-6

League of Nations (Lytton Report), 84

Les Misérables, 200-1, 215-16

Levi, Primo, 213

Li Fengqin, 189-90

Li Gang, 178-80, *179*, 184, 197

Li Houbin, 178, 179, 180-84, 188

Li Manchu, 185

Li Pengge, 189-90

Liaoning, 83

Liu Rixuan, 178, 180

Liutiaogou Incident. *See* Manchurian Incident

logs. *See maruta* (logs)

Lü Guiwen, 146-49, *148*, 154

Luckmann, Thomas, 28

Lyon, David, 9, 26, 33

MacArthur, Douglas, 207

Magnet, Shoshana, 45

Manchukuo (pseudo-state of Manchuria): author, use of term "Manchukuo", 14; threshold, position as, 20; depiction as harmonious nation, 83-84, 88; establishment and governance, 3, 11, 81-86, 135-36, 246n18, 248n47; historical context and under-standing, 80-81; Japanese nostal-gia for, 149-50, 152, 228; map, 2; modern provinces, 218; national-ity, invention of, 104; political duality of, 87; settler colonialism and, 131-32; surveillance methods, 21; systematic murders, 257-58n25

The Manchukuo Annual Report, 93-95

Manchuria Migration Association, 105

Manchuria, pseudo-state of, 14

Manchuria Reclamation Company, 131-32

Manchuria Workers/Labor Associa-tion, 133-35, 139, 141

Manchuria Youth Reclamation Volunteer Army, 138

Manchurian Communist Party, 100

Manchurian Incident, 83-85, 90-93, 130, 170, 246n13, 247n26, 248n44

Manchurian Police, 169, 170. *See also* Li Houbin

Manmō Keori, 126, 154, 159

Manshū Nippō, 128, 129

Mansoor, Ahmed, 232n7

Mantetsu: armed immigrants, recruitment program, 131, 132; Economic Research Association/Department, 88, 129; fingerprint-ing and data collection, 126-27; founding of, 82; Matsuoka and, 85; miners, recruitment and

management/tracking, 122-24; South Manchuria Industrial Society and, 125

marketing, 6, 8, 9

marriage, control of: continental brides, 105; *koseki* systems, 12-13, 60-64, 67-68; *koseki* system, postcolonial, 207-8, 243n15; lateral surveillance, 71; racial categorization and, 49; state permission for, 57

maruta (logs), 169, 191, 205

mass graves. *See wanrenkeng*

Matsuoka Yōsuke, 84, 85, 247n26, 249n63

maximum surveillant assemblage: bandits, judicial suspension and violence, 96-101; bodies as surveillance sights, 205-6; civil registry, 101-5; concentration villages, 106-9; definition and theoretical framework, 32-33, 79-81, 113-17; enhanced efforts, 98; expendable resource evalua-tion, 162-63, 190-93; *hokō* system, 105-6; ID cards and biometrics, 117; intelligence and policing networks, creation of, 89-93; lived experiences, 109-13, 114-16; Special Transfers, hunt for, 169-71, 195-98; targets of, 93-96; thought crime, 90-91

Mazigh, Monia, xiii

Mbembe, Achille, 19-20, 48-49, 204, 241n128

McCarthyism, 22

McCoy, Alfred, 49-50

media, role and influence: bandit portrayal, 85-86; criticism of policing powers, 97; Face-book-Cambridge Analytica scandal, impact of, 6; fingerprint-ing, positive depiction, 128;

freedom of the press, 97, 214;
internet, 6, 17, 213, 218, 231n5, xi,
xii; opposition, 97; Manchukuo as
utopia, 89; national papers and
war, 247n22; stereotypes, use of,
225; surveillance and public
perceptions, 214; terror/terror-
ism, use of, 234n17
Meiji Restoration and Regime, 54, 57,
62, 65, 72-73, 201
migrant workers: biometric regulation and classification of, 122-25;
exclusion from nationalities, 88;
ID card requirements, 132-33;
national identification system,
144-46; pay and treatment,
127-28, 130; recruitment from
North China, 142; South Africa,
39-40; strikes and resistance,
124-25; travel restrictions, 104
migration control, 86-89, 120,
128-33, 137-39
military violence against civilians,
13, 155, 165
Mishan Mine, 153
misinformation, 213-14
Mitter, Rana, 235n29
Miyashita Takichi, 96
Mobile Fingerprint Unit, 140
Mobilization Act, 69
model villages. *See* concentration
villages
Mori Sango, 192
Morimura, Seiichi, 165, 171, 177
Mudanjiang Incident, 190
museums. *See* archives and museums
Muslim communities, surveillance
of, xiii-xiv
My Number System, 211-12

Naganuma Setsuji, 193
Nagasaki, 53
Nagashima Tsuneo, 180-82, 184, 185

names, 39, 44, 60-62, 65
national identification systems,
general, 7-8, 9-12, 16, 95, 104. *See
also koseki* system
national identification systems as
surveillance: colonial Other and
Japanese nationality, 64-68;
colonial use, 56; disciplinary
power, 70-76; early national
registration systems, 56-57;
enforcement of segregation and
assimilation, 68-70; hierarchy and
identity, 58-64; Manchukuo,
development of, 120-21; national
identity, creation of, 76-78;
National Passbook System, 141-46;
postcolonial use and digitization,
210-12; private sector use, 10;
worker restrictions, 156
national identity/nationalism:
creation of, 20, 58-60; dual
nationalities, 88, 103; hierarchy,
loyalty and bloodlines, 60-64;
honorable service and, 141-42,
143; *koseki*, role of, 76-78; Manchukuo, creation of, 104; nationalism, threat of, 83; nationality and
territories, 35-36; Other, creation
of, 64-68; place in state, 59-60;
self-discipline and surveillance,
72; slogans, 59, 68, 85; sovereignty
and, 54-55; struggles with,
75-76
National Labor Service Act, 143
National Passbook System, 5, 5-6,
120-21, 141-46, *144, 145,* 156,
202-3
National Security Agency (NSA), 6,
32-33, 231n2, xi-xii, xiii
National Soldier Act, 142
National Total Mobilization Act, 134
Nationality Act, 64-65, 101, 102,
103-4, 128, 243n26, 245n60

nation-states and nation building, 33–36, 51, 53–55, 56–57, 59–60, 72–73, 78

Nazis. *See* concentration camps and Nazis

necropolitics, 48–52, 159–60, 196–98

New Foreign Resident Control System, 210, 212

New Labor Structure, 141–46

Nichiman Shōji, 151

Nietzsche, Friedrich, 15

ninbetsu-chō, 57

Nomonhan Incident, 191

North China Workers Association, 142

Northeast Colonial History museum, 218

NSO Group, 232n7

Ōba Shigema, 121, 122

occupational surveillance, 106–9

Ochankuga'he (Kennedy), Chief, 44

Ogino, Fujio, 98, 100

Okinawa Prefecture/Okinawans, 65, 69, 70, 77

One Hundred Million Total Uniform Number System, 211

Original Japanese, 64, 65

The Orphan of Asia, 75

Ōsugi Sakae, 91, 248n46

Palestine, occupation of, 48–50, 206

pandemic. *See* corona virus pandemic

panoptic surveillance, 32, 71, 76–77, 106–9, 158–59

panopticon (prison), 30–31

parallel surveillance, 28–29, 58–59

Parenti, Christian, 41–42

Pass Law, 38–39

Pass System (Canada), 44, 51

Passbook System. *See* National Passbook System

passports, 9, 22–24, 35, 74. *See also* identification documents

patriarchy and hierarchy, 12–13, 20, 28–29, 58–64, 207–8

Peace Preservation Act (various), 96–97, 99, 100, 192

Peace Preservation Bureau, 169, 257n25

Pegasus spyware, 232n7

Peilin, Xin, 169–70

People's Liberation Army, 262n2

People's Republic of China, 4, 17, 161, 219–23, 258n31, 262n2

Pingdingshan Massacre Memorial Hall, 218

police/policing: bandit surveillance, 154–55; colonial data collection, 67; colonial population control, 73–74; fingerprinting and resources, 129–30; *hokō* system, 105–6; household investigation and registration, 102–3; increased powers, 97–98, 213; military, 89–93; South Africa, 38–40; Taigyaku Incident, impact, 96–97; Tokkō police, 81

Policing Control Committee, 97–98, 100

population control, 18, 20–21, 48–52, 57, 73, 101–5, 106–9

postcolonial era, 197–98, 199–201, 206–12

Powell, John W., Jr., 165

preventive detention, 153–54

PRISM, xii

prisoners of war, 154–56, 165, 170, 171, 253n57, 258n31

privacy concerns, 9, 211, 243n13, 244n48

Professional Technique Registration Order, 139

Pseudo-Manchukuo Imperial Palace Museum, 218

pseudo-state and use of "Manchu-kuo", 14
public perceptions: manipulation of, 85-86; privacy invasion, 211; secrecy and shaping of, 204-5; state surveillance, normalization of, 12-13, 14-15; surveillance as inert force, 200; technology and surveillance, 6; Unit 731 revelations and uproar, 165
Puyi (Emperor), 83-84, 91, 246n18, 248n47, 253n57

racial categorization. *See also* social categorization: bodily surveillance, 41, 43; colonial use, 20, 48-49; dehumanization of, 48; hierarchy, creation of, 70; ID documents and, 43-44; inferiority and categorization, 45; *koseki* system and racial order, 20, 70; South Africa and passbooks, 38-39; surveillance and biometric identification, 202; suspect identity of, 113
racialized surveillance, 37-38, 41-45
racism, 37-38, 43, 45, 48, 50, 119, 130-31
railways, 82-83
refugees, 238n7, 253n58
religious surveillance, 57, 69, xiii-xiv
Republic of China, 5, 83, 85, 132
research challenges, methods and approach, 15-17, 217, 222, 223-27
Resident Basic Registration Act, 210-11
resident cards, 107, 139-40, 166, 202
Resisting Japan, Our Pride, 119, 122
resource dependence, 85-86
revisionism, 13-15
rhizomatic structures of surveillance, 8, 32, 80, 215
rice riots, 85

Royal Canadian Mounted Police (RCMP), 44, xiii
Russo-Japanese War, 81-82, 85, 90, 191, 202

sabotage, 155-56
safety farms. *See* concentration villages
Sakhalin, 68, 101
San Francisco Peace Treaty (1952), 208
Sang Guifang, 186-89, *187*
Sang Yuanqing, 186-89
Satō, Bunmei, 12, 62-63
scholarly networks. *See* civil and scholarly networks
secrecy. *See also* Unit 731: attempts at, 255n2; censorship or ignorance of colonial past, 1, 3, 13-15; evidence destruction, 257-58n25; forced labor, 151-52; murder of prisoners for, 257-58n25; Peace Preservation Bureau, 257n25; Special Transfers under, 194-95; surveillance, protection of, 204-5
security concerns, 11, 34-35, 58, 129-31
Security Correction Act, 153
Security Court/Special Security Court, 92, 100
segregation, 69-70
self-discipline, 72
self-surveillance, 30-31, 43, 102
settler colonialism, 86-89, 113, 131-32, 137-39, 159-60
severe punishment, 99-101, 113, 170, 195. *See also* Special Transfers
sexual assaults, 13, 155, 165
sexual slavery system, 213, 226
Shenyang War Criminal Tribunal, 164-65, *187, 188*
Shenyang/Fengtian, 83
Shigeru Aoki, 152

Shimamura Saburo, 257-58n25
Shinzō Abe, 212
Shōwa Steel, 151, 154, 155
shūmon ninbetsu-chō, 57
slavery, 7, 38, 41-43, 48-49. *See also*
    forced labor; sexual slavery
    system
slogans, use of, 59, 68, 85, 141
Smith, Dorothy, 15-16
Snowden, Edward, 6, 32-33, xi-xiii
social categorization. *See also* colonial
    classification; *koseki* system,
    colonial; racial categorization:
    categories and identity, 23;
    character of crime, 173; criminals,
    labeling of, 36-37; definition and
    overview, 9, 26; function of, 27;
    gender performance and surveil-
    lance, 29-30, 42-43; identity
    systems and state surveillance,
    25-29; justification of violent
    actions, 153-54; legitimacy, 60-61;
    migrant control, justification of,
    129; occupation as social class, 57,
    137; soldier/laborer dichotomy,
    142; surveillance tactics, 20;
    technology and assumptions, 45
social Darwinism, 38
socialists, 96-97, 98
soul training, 31, 71, 102-3, 143,
    153-54, 208
sousveillance, 43
South Africa, surveillance and
    influence, 38-40, 48-49, 50, 122,
    202, 206
South Manchuria Industrial Society,
    125, 126
South Manchuria Railway Company.
    See Mantetsu
sovereign power, 27-28, 30-33,
    46-52, 58, 196
sovereign violence. *See also* severe
    punishment; Special Transfers;

Unit 731: concentration villages,
    106-9; dichotomy with colonial
    discourse, 89; informants, use and
    torture, 98-99; legalized killing,
    91, 96, 195-98; lived experiences,
    17-18; mass arrests, 97; modern
    iterations, 199-206; nationality
    and security laws, 20; overview,
    19; policing the colonial threshold,
    97-98; prosperity and labor
    control, 159-60; severe punish-
    ment, 99-101, 113
Soviet Union: Chinese resistance,
    support of, 92, 93; invasion of
    Manchuria, 253n57; Japanese
    prisoners of war, 258n31; Kwan-
    tung Army and, 143, 191; Soviet
    Army, 138, 143, 253n57; spies and
    resistance, 171-72, 185, 189; war
    crime trials by, 164
Special High Police. *See* Tokkō police
Special Permanent Residency, 209-10
Special Source Operations, xi-xii
Special Transfers: classification and
    requirements, 11-12; criteria,
    172-78, 190-93; development of,
    169-71; documentation, discovery
    of, 255n2; files, *114-16, 181-83*;
    lived experiences, 178-90; Notice
    Regarding Special Transfers, *172*
special workers, 154-56. *See also*
    prisoners of war
spies and intelligence networks. *See
    also* Kwantung Gendarmerie:
    colonial identification system, use
    of, 12; data, distribution and
    manipulation, 214; double agents,
    171, 185; informants, use and
    torture, 98-99; labels, challenges
    of, 190-93; military intelligence,
    169, 171-72, 178, 185, 189; Peace
    Preservation Bureau, 257-58n25;
    recruitment, 131, 178, 185; Special

Transfer criteria, 172–77; spy as security threat, 11, 155–56; spy as Special Transfer criteria, 172, 173, 174; Unit 731, sent to, 171; US and Filipino resistance, 49–50

spyware, 232n7

starvation, 108, 112, 140

state of exception, 68–69, 74–75, 87–89, 159–60, 195. See bare life

state surveillance, 8–9, 12–15, 30–31, 33–36, 74–76, 89–93, 194–95, 233n12

Status Registration Act, 128–29

Student Labor Service Act (1942), 143

students, 146

Subjugation Cards, 155

Sun Futing, 186, 188

surveillance, modern, 6–7, 45, 214–15

surveillance as colonial tool, 20, 26, 33–34, 199–206, 214–15

surveillance capitalism, 9

surveillance studies, overview, 6–7, 51

surveillance technology, predatory nature of, xiii

suzerainty, 54, 65

Suzuki, Hiraku, 91, 258n31

synoptic surveillance, 71–72, 76–77

Tachibana Munekazu, 91, 248n46

Taigyaku Incident, 96

Taiwan under Japanese colonialism: assimilation attempts, 69; honseki, 73–74; identity and hierarchy, 20, 30, 75–76, 245n60; intellectuals and identity crisis, 75; koseki system, 65–68, 70, 77, 101, 102; postcolonial period, 21, 75, 251n3; travel, limitations on, 74

Takano, Asako, 122, 145

Tanaka, Hiroshi, 13

technological advancements. See also biometric classification and

population control: dangers of, 52; data collection and sharing, 231n5; data doubles, rise of, 245n2; display of, 149; historical overview, 19; human experimentation, 166–69, 194–95; media and, 128, 247n22; necropolitics and, 51; postcolonial surveillance, 210–16; surveillance studies, 6–9

technological determinism and positivism, 215

technological neutrality, 52

Temporary Bandits Punishment Act, 99

Temporary Civil Registry Act, 103

Temporary Hokō Act, 105

Temporary Rebel Punishment Act, 99

Temporary Residence File, 74

Temporary Residence Registry Act, 144

terminology, use of: conflicts and wars, 246n13; Japanese names for concentration villages, 108–9; koseki system, 242n11; Manchukuo and Manchuria, 14; private work as public duty, 141–42; terror/terrorism/terrorist, 234n17

Thompson, Scott, 27

Thought Correction Act, 153–54

thought crimes: bandits, identification and persecution, 96–101; criteria, Special Transfers, 172, 173, 175; investigations, 81; mass arrests, 97; policing and intelligence, scrutiny by, 90–93; special courts and judicial subjugation, 92–93; Special Transfer criteria, 172–78, 191–93; vagrants, classification and hunting, 153–54

Three Sweeping Tactics, 109

The Three Sweepings, 165, 258n31

Tōjō Hideki, 97–98, 249n63

Tokkō police, 81, 96, 97

Tokubetsu Kōtō Keisatsu. *See* Tokkō police

Tokugawa regime/shogunate, 53-55, 57, 62

Tom (enslaved person), 42

Torao Yoshifusa, 258n31

Torpey, John, 35

torture, use of, 13, 97, 98-99, 171, 192, 257n25

Toyotomi Hideyoshi, 56-57

travel restrictions, 21, 44, 74, 104, 107, 108, 111-12, 140. *See also* migrant workers

Treaty of Portsmouth, 81-82

Trudeau government, 232n11, 233n12

Tsuchiya Yoshio, 192

Ueda Yatarō, 167, 169

Unit 731: boiler tower, *167*; confessions, 258n31, 259-60n47; controversy and secrecy, 13; establishment of, 166-69; evidence and cover-ups, 16, 112-13, 161-65, 167, *181-83*, 219, 253n57, 255n2; families of victims, lived experiences, 178-90; International Center for Unit 731 Research, 218; officials of, 259n47; overview, 11-12; special prisons, *168*; Special Transfers, 112, *114, 115, 116, 172*; victim categorization, 171-78; victims of, 169-71, 257n25

Unit 731 Biological War Research Center, 224

Unit 731 War Crime Exhibition Hall, 218, 224

United Nations, Elimination of Discrimination Against Women, 208

United States, surveillance efforts and policies, 8, 22, 36-37, 41-43, 49-50, 214, x-xi, xiii

United States Army, 164, 165

vaccine passports, 232-33n12

vagrants, 153-54

villages, destruction of, 166

visas and permits, 4, 17, 132-33, 218, 219-23

voting rights, 70, 83

Wage Control Regulation, 143

Wang Mingshen (Wang Zhenda), 110, 111, 112, 114, *115*, 116, 117

Wang Xuancai, 81, 109-13, *110*, 197

wanrenkeng, 3, 151-53, *152*, 160, 223

war crime exhibits, 150-53, *152, 168*, 184, 190, 218

war crime tribunals, 163-65, 192, 207, 258n31

War on Terror, 8, 21, 47-48, 50, 209-10, 234n17, x-xi, xiii-xiv

Weber, Max, 34, 136

western influence, 159-60

Westernization, 20, 53-54

white gaze, 37, 43

Wolfe, Patrick, 86

Workers Association. *See* Manchuria Workers/Labor Association

workplace surveillance, 34, 122-25

World War I, 35, 82, 122

World War II, 13, 68, 119, 143, 206-7, 226, 235n29, 253n57

Xie, Xueshi, 154, 156

Yang Jingyu, 140

Yang Yanjun, 171, 177

Yoshida Shigeru, 40, 209, 247n26, 248n44, 249n63

Yoshifusa Torao, 99, 164, 169, 170-71, 192

Young, Louise, 80–81, 85–86, 92, 196
Yuan Meizhen, 184–86, 188
Yuan Wenqing, 184–86
Yukiko Yamabe, 224, 262n2

Zhang Xueliang, 83, 94, 246n10
Zhang Zuolin, 246n10
Zhu Yuntong, 112, 117
Zhu Yunxiu, 112, *116*, 117
Zureik, Ellia, 49

The authorized representative in the EU for product safety and compliance is:
Mare Nostrum Group
B.V Doelen 72
4831 GR Breda
The Netherlands